Fighting Emperors of Byzantium

Fighting Emperors of Byzantium

John C. Carr

Pen & Sword
MILITARY

First published in Great Britain in 2015 by
Pen & Sword Military
an imprint of
Pen & Sword Books Ltd
47 Church Street
Barnsley
South Yorkshire
S70 2AS

ISBN 978 1 78383 116 6

A CIP catalogue record for this book is available from the British Library

Typeset in Ehrhardt by
Mac Style Ltd, Bridlington, East Yorkshire
Printed and bound in the UK by CPI Group (UK) Ltd, Croydon, CRO 4YY

Pen & Sword Books Ltd incorporates the imprints of Pen & Sword Archaeology, Atlas, Aviation, Battleground, Discovery, Family History, History, Maritime, Military, Naval, Politics, Railways, Select, Transport, True Crime, and Fiction, Frontline Books, Leo Cooper, Praetorian Press, Seaforth Publishing and Wharncliffe.

For a complete list of Pen & Sword titles please contact
PEN & SWORD BOOKS LIMITED
47 Church Street, Barnsley, South Yorkshire, S70 2AS, England
E-mail: enquiries@pen-and-sword.co.uk
Website: www.pen-and-sword.co.uk

Contents

Prologue		vi
List of Plates		ix
Chapter 1	From Rome to Byzantium: Constantine the Great and his Successors	1
Chapter 2	Goths, Huns and Theodosius	36
Chapter 3	Justinian I, The War Manager	65
Chapter 4	Heraclius, Christian Soldier	82
Chapter 5	Leo the Isaurian Saves Europe	107
Chapter 6	Blood on the Floor: A Cacophony of Emperors	120
Chapter 7	The Macedonians	138
Chapter 8	The Bulgar-Slayer and Lesser Figures	165
Chapter 9	Rear-Guard Heroism: Romanos Diogenes	185
Chapter 10	The Komnene Revival and The Crusades	196
Chapter 11	Angeli and Latins	216
Chapter 12	Constantine Goes Down Fighting	228
Epilogue		258
Notes and References		260
Sources and Further Reading		267
Byzantine Emperors 313–1453		268
Index		270

Prologue

Ninety-eight men and four women occupied the Byzantine throne from the inauguration of the empire on Monday morning, 11 May 330, to its elimination in a welter of blood and fire in the early hours of Tuesday, 29 May 1453. These include the seven Latins who reigned during the fifty-seven-year occupation of Constantinople by the Fourth Crusaders and their descendants in the thirteenth century, plus those Byzantines who did not submit to the Crusader occupation and remained legitimate in exile. The story starts conventionally from Constantine I; but to him the term 'Byzantine emperor' would have been a curious one, as he was, and considered himself, a lineal Roman emperor in the Augustan tradition. Of the ninety-eight male emperors (a few of whom were momentary or mere infants), forty-eight – roughly half – can be considered fighting emperors in that they personally took the field against Byzantium's enemies at some point during their reign.

'The human heart,' wrote Maréchal de Saxe, an eighteenth century French strategic theorist, 'is the starting point of all matters pertaining to war.'[1] Such a view has not been popular among military historians since about the middle of the twentieth century, when social and economic theory began to cast their dreary mists over the discipline. Now the great determinisms – economic, geographical and neo-Freudian – have given way to a kind of technological super-determinism. Modern warfare, with its unmanned drones and algorithmic combat simulation and analysis models, would seem to depend less on de Saxe's 'human heart' than on dropping and dragging icons on a computer screen.

If there is any broader narrative to note, it is the very dramatic one of a Christian empire which spent a thousand years preserving civilization in an eternally troublesome corner of the world, and which ultimately went down fighting with supreme heroism in defence of Christendom and the preserved treasures of Greek and Roman culture on which the intellectual and spiritual structure of the West has been built. These treasures are always under threat, not least from within the western world itself. The fighting emperors of Byzantium personally battled to safeguard their world, their people and Christianity. Some won, some lost.

Of course, the role of a monarch now is vastly different from what it used to be. It is hard for us today to envision a fighting monarch. For the past few centuries being a king or queen has meant leading a comfortable, privileged and highly protected life as 'head of state', a ceremonial figurehead. The full resources of state security are employed to ensure that such people and their families do not run the slightest risk of personal harm and are protected on every side for their entire lives. Such coddling would have been incomprehensible in past ages when a monarch's prime duty was to protect state and people by riding at the head of the army and putting himself (and sometimes herself) actively in harm's way. If a king or emperor was not up to the job, either by age or character, either his princes filled in for him or he was none-too-delicately removed and replaced by someone tougher.

In the seventeenth century Edward Gibbon noted acidly that 'the generality of princes, if they were stripped of their purple and cast naked into the world, would immediately sink to the lowest rank of society, without a hope of emerging from their obscurity.' But the term 'generality' does allow for exceptions. If there is any royal figure in our own age, for example, who has shown signs of having the stuff of a fighting king, it is Britain's Prince Harry. Having served as a combat helicopter pilot in Afghanistan, he has not flinched from risking his life for his country. Third in line to Britain's throne until July 2013 (when the birth of his elder brother Prince William's heir George Alexander Louis put him back several slots), Harry will not become king unless extraordinary circumstances intervene. But it may be sobering to note that in earlier times such 'extraordinary circumstances' were common – murder, enemy action, court intrigue, disease or that distressingly frequent phenomenon in royal annals, the 'hunting accident'.

Until about a hundred years ago it was normal, in the Anglo-Saxon world at least, to dismiss the 1,123-year saga of the Byzantine Empire in the words of W.E.H. Lecky, as: 'a monotonous story of the intrigues of priests, eunuchs and women, of poisonings, of conspiracies … of perpetual fratricides'.[2] There were plenty of those, to be sure, but more positive attitudes saw the light in the twentieth century thanks to outstanding scholars such as Will Durant in America and Sir Steven Runciman and later John Julius Norwich in Britain.

The material on Byzantium is, of course, vast, and anyone wanting a rounded picture of the empire cannot do better than read Lord Norwich's riveting three-volume *Byzantium*, the despair of anyone else trying to write about the subject. I realized early in my own project that to compress eleven tumultuous centuries of imperial history into a single moderate-sized volume, even limited to the military aspects, would be a considerable task. So I have concentrated the chapters around the main fighting emperors, leaving regrettably little room for the others. Much of interest has had to be left out. I describe every Byzantine emperor who ever went into combat primarily in human terms and only secondarily as part of a 'process' or supposed wider political phenomenon. 'Men are everything,' said George Canning, a nineteenth century British prime minister, 'measures comparatively nothing.' I make no pretence at academic rigour or precision; what follows are stories of flesh-and-blood people and the military and political challenges they were called upon to meet.

I can only hope that what remains is not too sketchy a pageant, and so let the curtain open on the royal protagonists of a grandiloquent, jewel-encrusted period of military history that has not yet had the full recognition it deserves in Western historiography, but richly rewards those who delve into it.

John C. Carr
Athens, June 2014

List of Plates

1. Constantine I (the Great) [Palazzo dei Conservatori, Rome]
2. Artist's reconstruction of the Theodosian Wall [Ekdotiki Athinon]
3. Heraclius attacks Khusrau II; twelfth-century enamel [Louvre; *Der Spiegel*]
4. The Golden Gate today [C. Schug-Wille: *Art of the Byzantine World*]
5. Contemporary illustration of Greek Fire [*Der Spiegel*]
6. Krum captures Nikephoros I [Vatican Library, Rome]
7. Leo V is proclaimed emperor; Skylitzes miniature [National Library, Madrid]
8. Leo VI the Wise [National School Book Organization, Athens]
9. Basileios II the Bulgar-slayer [National School Book Organization, Athens]
10. Michael IV [Athens Numismatic Museum]
11. Mosaic depicting the Empress Zoe [Sancta Sophia]
12. The Varangian Guard; Skylitzes miniature [National Library, Madrid]
13. Emperor, possibly Romanos IV Diogenes, receiving reports from agents; Skylitzes miniature [National Library, Madrid]
14. Alexios I Komnenos (left) with Christ; twelfth-century miniature [Vatican Library, Rome]
15. Michael VIII Paleologos [*Der Spiegel*]
16. Manuel II Paleologos [National School Book Organization, Athens]
17. View of the Bosporus today [Author]
18. The interior of Sancta Sophia today [Author]
19. A Greek comic book depiction (c. 1965) of Constantine XI being struck down [Author]
20. Statue of Constantine XI Paleologos at Mitropoleos Square, Athens [Author]

Chapter One

From Rome to Byzantium: Constantine the Great and his Successors

Late in October 312 Flavius Valerius Constantinus, commanding a Roman army composed mainly of Gauls and Britons, scanned the wooded hills north of Rome. After weeks of hard marching across Europe, over the snowy Alps and down through the plains of Italy, fighting most of the way, he was finally within sight of his goal. One more battle and Rome, the seat of the greatest empire the world had ever seen, soon to celebrate a thousand years since its founding, would be his.

If ever a conqueror fervently believed he deserved such a prize, that man was Constantinus – better known to subsequent history as Constantine. To his 90,000 infantry and 8,000 cavalry, the great bulk of them Gauls, Teutons and Britons who would gladly follow him into hell, he was the man most fitted to assume the mantle of Roman emperor in the face of a half dozen lesser men who also were after the imperial throne. The general himself, just under 40 yet well aware of the perils of overweening pride – a host of recent unfortunate emperors had been assassinated for their arrogance – tried not to let the adulation go to his head. His motive for seeking the supreme post was no mere crude lust for power. Something had recently happened to him which utterly altered his thinking on the nature of human governance.

Lording it in Rome was Maxentius, a high-liver of questionable morals at best, a bestially cruel occultist at worst. For six years he had ruled propped up by the spears of the Praetorian Guard which he knew could eliminate him at any time if he stopped doing their favours. Having lost three battles to his advancing rival already, Maxentius had set up his forces for a stout defence at Saxa Rubra, or the Red Rocks, on the Via Flaminia a few miles north of Rome. Constantine was not unduly worried; his army's morale was high, and not just because it was unbeaten in the field. For Constantine was under a growing conviction that his successes so far were the result of something mysteriously greater than good generalship or even the fortunes of war.

As Constantine himself much later told his biographer Eusebius of Caesarea, in the early afternoon of 28 October, when battle was imminent, his attention was caught by a flaming cross appearing in the sky together with the words IN THIS CONQUER. 'At this sight,' writes Eusebius, 'he himself was struck with amazement, and his whole army also.' Though Constantine was a Roman, he claimed to see the words written in Greek (*en touto nika*). That same night, he said, he dreamed that a voice directed him to adopt the symbol of Christ – the letters X and P (known as the chi-rho, or the first two letters of Christos, the Greek name for Christ) and put it on his soldiers' shields. The X was bisected vertically by the P, whose loop became a symbolic halo. Constantine ordered every shield emblazoned in that way, and it was thus arrayed that his men advanced to confront the forces of the pagan Maxentius.

Modern scholars, of course, have tried to pick this legend apart. In fact, just where and when Constantine experienced his life-changing vision is not clear. Early chroniclers such as Lactantius and Eusebius assumed that it was at Saxa Rubra on the eve of the assault on Rome; Constantine himself appears not to have been too precise when describing the events. Most historians guardedly accept Eusebius' version, though some suggest that the famous vision could have appeared rather earlier in the campaign, and that it might not necessarily have even been a Christian one.[1]

In our supposedly rational post-Enlightenment era, commentary on this event has ranged from polite scepticism to outright disbelief. Serious academic historians, it is assumed, are like modern journalists, having little truck with signs and heavenly portents. The mystic experience has been variously explained away as either a solar atmospheric phenomenon or a blatant lie manufactured to boost the spirits of the many Christians in Constantine's army as well as the contingents of Mithras-worshippers whose own emblem was a cross of light. Even Eusebius confesses that he found the story hard to believe, relenting only when Constantine 'with an oath' affirmed the truth of what he saw.

Our concern here is not with the spiritual significance of the flaming cross in the sky – one either believes it or not according to the presence or absence of faith on the reader's part – but with its military effect, which was enormous. First, Constantine was never known for any kind of mental instability – in fact, throughout his career as soldier and emperor he was a paragon of clear-headed resolve and coolness. Such a personality carries great weight with the ordinary soldier of the line, who in the end is the best judge of his commander. Any falsity or cynical propagandizing in

Constantine would have been detected by his men, who adored him precisely because of his honest and forthright reputation. The influence of Helena, his devoutly Christian mother, helped mould his character, though we don't know whether he was a Christian believer himself at the time; very likely he was masking his true beliefs to avoid alienating the dominant pagan element in the empire. But if he swore that he saw the cross in the sky, his men were overwhelmingly prepared to believe him. Knowing the nature of soldiers, he could not have got away with a lie, even the most persuasively uttered one.

Second, the cross gave Constantine's army an ideal to fight for that was much more powerful than a mere desire for adventure or conquest or booty. God Himself, it seemed, was issuing the marching orders to overthrow the corrupt pagan regime in Rome. If men are to fight, they fight best for something they consider above and greater than themselves, something that will blunt the natural fear of death. If there was one moment in time when the pagan establishment of antiquity received its death-blow from newly-emerging Christian military power, this was it. Whether the vision was dreamed up by court and scribe as a propaganda narrative, or whether it was real, just as Constantine insisted it was, it tore up the narrative of European history and changed the script.

But should Christians have taken up arms in the first place? The question depends on Jesus Christ's view of war and military affairs as recorded in the Gospels. The simple answer is that, as military affairs are a symptom of a fallen world, they were not the concern of Christ, whose true concern was not with symptoms but with the underlying spiritual disease. Individual soldiers, however, were a different matter. He sympathized with them as having to do a sometimes unpleasant and dangerous job under orders. He also seems to have approved of the idea of discipline as encouraging a faithful life. Then what are we to make of Jesus' stern reaction in the Garden of Gethsemane, when the apostle Peter drew his sword and sliced off the ear of a hapless synagogue employee in a vain attempt to avert his master's arrest?[2] 'All they that take the sword shall perish with the sword,' Jesus pronounced, and healed the victim's ear for good measure. We can view this as a key moral distinction between those who initiate aggressive violence out of evil and egoistic impulses and those who are compelled by defence or the orders of superior officers to do violence to their fellows; by implication, the latter can be excused.

Peter's rash act (if indeed it was he) can be considered the first recorded instance of someone taking up the sword in defence of Christianity. Yet violence, holy or otherwise, was very far from the minds of those who made up the early Christian communities in the latter centuries of the Roman Empire. The tenor of the new creed at first was intensely pacifist. But along with this pacifism came a profound rejection of the Roman emperors' claim to divinity. Consequently, to the Roman authorities the Christian rejection of the state's claims upon one's soul was nothing short of treason. It was Nero who first violently persecuted the Christians, burning them 'to light up [his] games'.[3] The persecutions were to continue on and off for the next 300 years.

Roman society in the early Christian era suffered a protracted and gradual decay. The upper classes had become enervated by the accumulation of wealth and idle luxury, while the poverty level among the rest of the population was rising. Farming, trade and industry progressively declined, with the result that all classes had less incentive to work and create. The only organization retaining any vigour was the army which, in order to guard the vast outreaches of the empire, had to be manned mainly by mercenaries. These were men from many ethnic groups whose profession eroded any sense of allegiance to a cause or particular society. They were ready to follow anyone who could secure enough booty to keep them paid and satisfied. Any mercenary commander who could deliver this gained the power to usurp the imperial throne. Between 192 and 284 no fewer than thirty-three soldier-emperors seized power this way; most were assassinated when the soldiery's preference fixed on someone else as a better source of handouts.

It took Diocletian (284–305) to restore some order and tenure to the imperial office. His attempt to hold the empire's administration together took the form of a rigid socialist dictatorship with himself – the earthly representative of Jupiter, no less – as sole dictator. Diocletian, a hard man who had risen through the military ranks from humble farm slavery, was the first to realize that the empire had become too large and unwieldy to be governed from a single centre. Boldly in the circumstances, he decided that the empire should be formally split into eastern and western halves, each under an Augustus who would have a Caesar, something like a vice president, under him to be groomed for the eventual succession. Perhaps Diocletian's most radical reform was to fix a twenty-year term limit to each Augustus' reign; but during those twenty years an Augustus would exercise near-absolute power in order to safeguard the realm from external and internal foes. To everyone's surprise, Diocletian stuck to his own rule, stepping down in 305.

Diocletian established his palace and seat of government at Nicomedia (modern Izmit) in what is now Northwest Turkey on the Asian coast of the Sea of Marmara. Within a few years this city had attained, in Edward Gibbon's words, 'a degree of magnificence which ... became inferior only to Rome, Alexandria and Antioch in extent or populousness'. In 286 he hand-picked a trusted general named Maximian to share the office of Augustus in the West. More momentously, he moved the seat of western imperial power from Rome to Milan. Diocletian picked Gaius Galerius to be his Caesar in the East, while Constantius Chlorus became Caesar in the West. This tetrarchy (meaning four sources of authority) of two Augusti and two Caesars under them appeared to work fairly well at first, but simmering religious issues helped undermine it.

Diocletian is an intriguing figure. He began life as a slave in the province of Dalmatia (present-day Croatia) but managed by sheer ability to rise in the ranks of the army and become a general. Uneducated, he nevertheless proved a genius in the science of governing. The sole surviving marble bust of Diocletian shows a wide Balkan head framing the habitual grimace of one who has experienced much of the world and of human nature, little of it good. To him, the new doctrine of Christianity simply pandered to human weakness, hence it was a political disease to be fought. Partly because of his hard-knocks life, he took a dim view of humanity in general, believing that the people, officialdom and the 'barbarians' needed to be cowed into absolute submission if the Roman state was to operate at all. 'Byzantinism,' writes one authority, 'began with Diocletian.'[4]

Though a complete despot, Diocletian was a conscientious and hard worker. By the time he voluntarily stepped down in 305, in the twenty-first year of his reign, he was also ill, which may have made the decision easier. Utter confusion followed Diocletian's departure. The two points of apparent stability were Rome, where Maximian's son Maxentius ruled, and York, the seat of Constantius Chlorus whose son Constantine was already highly popular with the garrisons in Britain and Gaul. When Chlorus died at York in 306 the western army acclaimed Constantine as his successor. The scene was set for a clash.

The Roman army, however, had long ceased to be a 'national' one in today's commonly accepted sense of the term. There were far too few genuine Roman – not to mention Italian – men available to give the army a unified make-up. Inevitably, the great bulk of Rome's far-flung legions had to be made up of mercenaries from the ethnic groups that Rome had conquered, and even from outside the frontiers. Of these, the Germans proved the most efficient at the business of fighting. It was Germans who were best able to rise through the ranks to the ultimate office of *magister militum*, the formal title of the commander-in-chief. The army was kept separate from the civil authorities but completely under the emperor's authority.

Mercenaries, by nature or necessity, tend to be rootless men. Having cut most of their ties to family and community, some take up arms out of a wish for adventure, of economic need or to run from the law. They, too, search for inner solace and by the end of the third century a great many had found it in Christianity. After all, had not Christ been humble, despised and spurned and ultimately crucified by supposed 'social superiors'? In some such manner the teachings of Jesus became the religion of legions of soldiers and sergeants and probably a good number of junior and field officers as well; senior commanders, on the contrary, were largely the products of, and addicted to, wealth and the perks of pagan power.

This is not the place to go into the complex causes of the decline of the Roman Empire, which even now are not completely understood. Gibbon was probably on the right track when he theorized that a long period of peace and prosperity under the Antonine emperors 'introduced a slow and secret poison' into the state, as such periods regrettably seem to do in any age. Social and personal ties were loosening. Thoughtful commentators were aware, somehow, that 'the world has grown old'.[5]

A sense of imminent cataclysm was at hand. This left the military, manned by vigorous men from the provinces, as the only truly energetic element in Roman society. It was this structure that attracted growing numbers of dispossessed to the legions, from ex-slaves and criminals to unemployed farmers and artisans.

Christianity has been blamed for being a factor in the decline. But this begs the question of what is meant by 'decline'. The old Roman order had long been decaying from within, a result of the inexorable infections of economic inequality, cultural and spiritual bankruptcy and corruption at the top; Christianity merely gave it the coup de grâce. And it was Constantine's soldiers with the symbol of Christ on their shields who physically delivered that coup at the Milvian Bridge on the Tiber.

Constantine I (313–337)

The great nine-ton marble head that gazes out portentously from its incongruous position on the wall of the Palazzo dei Conservatori in Rome impresses us with its air of strength and purpose. The firm-set lips suggest a no-nonsense resolve, though the large, staring eyes betray thoughtfulness behind the tough exterior. The head has been described as intimidating and contemptuous, but of course it is extremely risky to try to read the inner man into a sculpture, however brilliantly done. Flavius Valerius Constantinus did not enter the world with the best of advantages. Born around 274 at Naissus (present-day Niş in Serbia), he was the eldest son of Constantius Chlorus, the Caesar of the western empire after Diocletian. He may well have been illegitimate, as his mother Helena, described by some as a 'barmaid,' was Chlorus' legal concubine, a sort of half-way house between having a wife and a mistress.[6]

Constantius Chlorus had earned his spurs as a competent officer who had been assigned to hold the fort in the north, as it were, while Maximian was busy trying to consolidate his own position. As Chlorus was suppressing the German tribes as far as the Danube, Maximian was not doing so well, and so in 288 Diocletian took over operations in the north-west for two years before urgent business in the Middle East two years later drew him back. Around 290 Diocletian, to keep an eye on both wings of his sprawling domain, transferred his headquarters to Sirmium on the Danube, not far from present-day Belgrade. He obviously didn't think much of Maximian's ability to hold down the West. At Milan in 291 Chlorus was appointed Caesar to Maximian. Until then Chlorus maintained his liaison with Helena. But with his promotion, officialdom decreed that for appearances' sake he must be formally married, but not to just anybody. As for strategic reasons he needed to cement his relationship to his boss Maximian, as a means of holding the ruling caste together, he could have no objection to the order to marry Maximian's stepdaughter Theodora. Though Helena and her young son were necessarily sidelined, and Chlorus sired no fewer than six children with his new bride, there is no sign that any resentment clouded the arrangement or that mother and son were disadvantaged at court, as later developments were to show. Within a couple of years, Constantius Chlorus had pacified the troublesome Rhine region and had returned to Britain in triumph, sailing grandly up the Thames and praised as 'restorer of the Eternal Light'. Later Chlorus moved his headquarters to York as a buffer against the aggressive northern British tribes.

Constantine was not in Britain to share these successes, having been seconded to Diocletian and his Caesar Galerius in the East. Of Constantine's early character we have few indications; all our sources agree that he was a sober and clever youth, but with a character more suited to soldiering than education and officialdom. His second-string official status at court could well have helped him develop a core of steel that he would later put to effective use against the imperial establishment. Relations with his father appear to have been good despite the latter's required second marriage, a fact which also impressed itself upon the soldiery. With the tetrarchy solidly established in 293 as a new structure for the empire, Constantine started his military career in the hot and dusty climes of what are now Turkey, Palestine and Egypt.

As the 20-year-old son of Constantius Chlorus, Constantine was given the rank of military tribune. He acquitted himself well in combat on several fronts, with the Persians in the East and the Sarmatians along the Danube. He may well have been present at the discomfiture at Carrhae (now Harran in Turkey) in 296, a sad echo of the massacre of 25,000 Romans at the hands of the Parthians at the same spot 243 years before. The following year Constantine was transferred to the Danube front to fight the Sarmatians by the side of Galerius. A much later report has him personally seizing a Sarmatian 'savage' by the hair and throwing him at Galerius' feet, and then riding through a swamp to clear a way for a decisive attack on the enemy. By such or other means, Galerius could not have failed to appreciate that here was a man of no mean ability. A frisson of anxiety must also have gone through him, as officers of ability were too prone to becoming rivals for the throne and hence deadly foes overnight. Galerius couldn't afford to let Constantine out of his sight, and kept him, in effect, as a hostage in his court.

By the time he turned 30, Constantine had much to be proud of. As a battle-seasoned senior officer, he rode at Diocletian's side on the emperor's inspection tours of the garrisons. His conquests were also of a sexual nature; we know that he had a son Crispus by a young girlfriend (or wife) named Minervina of whom nothing more is heard; Crispus seems to have been placed under the care of his grandmother Helena. But in 303 Constantine was concerned with bigger things, as that was the year Diocletian planned to celebrate twenty years in power, the vicennalia. The occasion, to be held in Rome, would also mark the tenth anniversary (decennalia) of Constantius Chlorus' elevation to the post of Caesar in the West. Constantine had never been to Rome, and he surely looked forward to seeing his father again after many years of absence. But there were other anticipations in his mind as, shortly before the Rome festivities were to begin, Diocletian called the tetrarchs together at Milan and told the others he intended to abdicate the throne, as promised, after twenty years in power.

To minimize the expected cut-throat rivalry for power his announcement would trigger, the canny Diocletian insisted that Maximian step down at the same time, to clear the decks for both Caesars. Maximian reluctantly agreed to comply, the abdication date for both being set for two years hence, in 305.

The arena was thus cleared for the two Caesars-in-waiting, Constantine and Maximian's son Maxentius.

But Diocletian didn't count on the prejudices of the Roman populace, to whom he was a remote figure. During the festivities a circus structure collapsed, killing hundreds and perhaps thousands of spectators. Diocletian was jeered in the streets and left Rome in disgust.

On 1 May 305 the abdication ceremony was held in Nicomedia. As described by the historian Lactantius, the entire officer corps of the eastern legions stood at attention as Diocletian took off his imperial purple cloak to confer it on his successor. The soldiers expected it to be draped over Constantine's shoulders, but instead it was placed on an obscure little-known nephew of Galerius named Maximinus Daia. We cannot know how Constantine reacted to that unexpected snub; most likely he hid his consternation and humiliation under a rigid mask of politeness. Moreover, he certainly knew that, whatever the power plays and intrigues of the East, his real prospects lay in the West with his father's forces. Constantius Chlorus, in fact, had just become Augustus of the West in place of Maximian who stepped down along with Diocletian. The chess pieces were lining up.

Galerius may have won this move. But at the same time he was compelled to accede to Chlorus' request to have Constantine by his side as the Caesar-in-waiting. The record here is obscure. Galerius may have let Constantine go by securing a deal by which the latter recognized Galerius as senior Augustus. But Constantine himself claimed that he took advantage of a party when the wine was flowing freely and Galerius was drunk and slipped out, mounting his horse for an epic ride across Europe to meet his father at Boulogne. From there, father and son sailed across the channel, defeating the Picts and ending up at York. It is there that Constantius Chlorus died in the early summer of 306, with Constantine, his second wife Theodora and her children by his bedside.

In the eyes of the Roman army of Gaul and Britain, Constantine was the man of the hour, having proved his worth and courage many times over. The army promptly acclaimed him as Augustus. In doing so it was following a well-established, if not always peaceful, tradition. This was long before the age of fast communications, and even the most urgent official messages from, say, Nicomedia or Milan to York would take many weeks, during which anything could happen. When emergency issues of state arose, as in the unexpected death of an Augustus or Caesar, key decisions had to be made on the spot. The army was the only organization capable of underpinning the authority of a new leader and providing the necessary power to enforce it. Constantine may not quite have expected the honour which the troops gave him. He certainly did not let it go to his head; Galerius, he knew, would be instantly on his guard when the news arrived in the East. The last thing Constantine wanted was to be regarded as another power-hungry general, and so while graciously accepting his army's accolade as Augustus, he also accepted Galerius's confirmation of his lesser post of Caesar.

Maxentius, meanwhile, had not been idle. In October 306 he got the Praetorian Guard to acclaim him emperor. The Guard had seen its once-mighty power reduced to ten cohorts which seethed with discontent over rumours that their pay would be cut. Maxentius' coup was popular at first, as one of his first acts was to halt the persecution of Christians. But Galerius could not countenance what amounted to treason, and with Galerius and Maxentius now squaring off, Constantine had to decide where his advantage lay. Galerius appointed Flavius Licinius as Augustus of the West; Constantine responded by marrying Maxentius' sister Fausta, on the basis of which he declared himself Augustus to challenge Licinius. Later commentators would imply that some sentiment had been brewing between Constantine and Fausta, who had purportedly handed him the glittering insignia of tribune – 'a helmet gleaming with gold and jewels' – before he began his campaigns in the East. But as Fausta was only about fifteen in 307 when she was married to Constantine, that story is questionable at best.

By 308 chaos was threatening, with no fewer than six ambitious self-styled augusti angling for supreme power. In Rome Maxentius and his father Maximian shared power uneasily until Maximian thought of grabbing the crown for himself. In 310 Constantine marched with lightning speed across France and holed up Maximian in Marseilles. According to Lactantius, the faithful Fausta told Constantine of her father's plot to assassinate him in their bedroom. Duly warned, Constantine seized the old man and gave him his choice of demise. Maximian opted for 'the noose for an unseemly death from a lofty beam'. Galerius further opened the playing field by dying in his turn the following year.

Maxentius lorded it in Rome as *princeps invictus*, or unbeatable prince, propped up by a rubber-stamp Senate and the swords of the Praetorian Guard. He is portrayed as living a life of dissolute and insecure luxury on the Via Appia, prone to guzzling wine and lamenting the brevity of human life (though blissfully unaware that his own days were numbered) while enforcing a cruel regime; his early toleration of the Christians appears to have been reversed. He had a consuming fear of his brother-in-law Constantine and ordered the destruction of all busts and statues of him. That only made

Constantine more then ever determined to get him out of the way, and by 312, aided by the general Probus who had joined his cause, he had trounced Maxentius' forces in successive battles at Susa and Turin in the shadow of the Alps, and at Verona. By October Constantine was at Saxa Rubra where the history-changing visions occurred to him.[7]

Maxentius in his cups seems not to have been very security-conscious. His engineers had built an emergency pontoon bridge next to the Milvian Bridge, equipped with a self-destruct mechanism in the form of a central bolt that could be pulled to collapse the bridge if any enemy began thundering over it. Word of the mechanism would surely have got out among the secret Christians in Maxentius' army. Maxentius himself was highly anxious. His enemies report that he sacrificed a human infant for some divine sign of what was in store for him – an act, if true, not calculated to restore any of the popularity he might once have had. The portents seem to have told him that he should go outside the walls to confront Constantine, which he decided to do.

Meanwhile, Constantine's sympathizers within the walls had not been idle. One tradition has it that Constantine's secret faction had managed to snare no fewer than 300 owls, to release them all at once as a signal for Constantine to attack. The story, admittedly, strains credulity. On the other hand, it's not unreasonable to suppose that some signalling involving birds may well have been attempted. The owl was the emblem of Athene, the Greek goddess of wisdom (the Roman Minerva). We are told that at the sight of the flock of owls soaring into the sky and settling onto the walls of Rome, Constantine – resplendent in a new suit of armour – ordered the trumpets to sound the advance.

Not many details are known about the Battle of the Milvian Bridge, except that it did not last very long, as Constantine had the advantage from the start. The first rank of Maxentius' infantry and cavalry broke under Constantine's initial onslaught, leaving the tougher Praetorian Guard holding the northern head of the Milvian Bridge. Constantine may well have taken a page out of the military manual of the fifth century BC Athenian General Miltiades, who famously defeated a large Persian force at Marathon by retreating in the centre while pressing flank attacks in order to wrap up the advancing enemy. When Maxentius and his commanders north of the river realized they were in danger of being cut off, they made for the bridge post-haste. As with the story of the owls, legend intervenes again with an account of a patrician named Poplius whose eyes were put out on Maxentius' orders because he protested when his daughter was taken as a palace concubine. According to this story, Poplius and a band of trusted men were at the southern head of the bridge when the retreating cavalry came thundering across it. When they were at the mid-point, Poplius ordered the emergency pin pulled and the bridge collapsed, toppling men and horses into the water. A more accepted story is that the engineers panicked and pulled the bolts too soon. Maxentius and many of his men were still on the far bank, and turned to the adjacent stone Milvian Bridge that turned out to be too narrow for the fleeing hundreds. Many, including Maxentius himself, were pushed over the side by the crush and drowned, pulled under by the weight of their armour; Maxentius may be given a scrap of posthumous credit by the fact that he was one of the last to retreat.[8]

Constantine enjoyed an obsequious welcome into Rome by the shell of a Senate and the relieved people. Maxentius' body was lifted from the Tiber and ceremoniously chopped to pieces. The head was paraded through the city on the tip of the spear and then shipped to Carthage as proof for the African provinces that Constantine was now in charge. Work at once began on a triumphal arch to stand between the Colosseum and the Forum, sumptuously decorated with battle reliefs in the tradition of the old Roman emperors; the project took some three years to complete and remains a major Roman landmark.[9]

Constantine now paused to consolidate his position. Licinius seemed to be firmly in control of the East, and therefore a semblance of cooperation was necessary. In February 313 both Augusti met in Milan to issue one of the weightiest decisions in the history of mankind. This was the Edict of Milan which granted full religious liberty to all Christians in the Roman Empire, east as well as west. There was nothing new about the content; it merely confirmed an earlier edict of toleration by Galerius. But Constantine was the first ruler in a solid position to enforce it, albeit with Licinius' help. The properties of Christians seized during the recent persecutions were restored. A Christian priest named Miltiades was officially recognized as bishop of Rome (i.e. the first pope) and given a handsome dwelling belonging to Empress Fausta on the Lateran Hill.

Licinius, however, had his hands full with his bitterest foe, his own Caesar Maximinus Daia. This man was accused of insisting on the right to give virgins their first sex experience (the infamous *droit de cuissage*) and of beheading Christian bishops. Licinius is credited with dreaming of an angel who adjured him to 'pray to Supreme God with all your army' and thus secure victory. Lactantius writes that Licinius on waking remembered the words and ordered his soldiers to recite them three times on their knees.

In the ensuing battle at Adrianople (313) Maximinus Daia fled, ultimately poisoning himself in Tarsus; according to Lactantius, the poison took four excruciating days to work, during which Maximinus became insane with the agony. Licinius cleansed his realm fairly thoroughly of any remnants of Maximinus' family by putting them to death. But as Licinius was Constantine's brother-in-law, there wasn't much Constantine could do about it. That situation changed in 315 when Licinius' wife Constantia (Constantine's sister) bore him a son – an immediate rival to Constantine's own eldest son Crispus.

By this time Constantine had moved his own base to Trier in Germany, to keep the restive North European territories under control. Around 317 he moved his headquarters farther east to Sardica (modern Sofia in Bulgaria), leaving his son Crispus, just thirteen, in charge of Trier as Caesar. The move east had an obvious significance: Constantine was asserting control over Licinius' territory. Moreover, Licinius thoroughly resented Constantine's huge popularity in Rome. Then Constantine himself had a second son, whom he named Constantine after himself – a sign that he might be preparing a dynasty. An attempt by Licinius to recruit a Roman senator into a plot against Constantine backfired badly. War between the two was declared in October 316.

The forces of both stalked each other through the valleys of what is now Serbia, Constantine with 20,000 foot and horse, Licinius with about 35,000. Licinius had the worse of the first encounter at Cibalae, losing an immense number of men and fleeing under cover of darkness. Establishing himself at Philippopolis (modern Plovdiv), he sent a peace mission to Constantine which was rebuffed. Three months later, in January 317, Licinius confronted Constantine on more or less equal terms in the plain of Arda, just south of modern-day Sofia. The battle was long and vicious; when night fell Licinius' forces had to fall back. Constantine, figuring that Licinius would seek refuge in Byzantium, hastened in that direction but Licinius in fact had gone south towards Greece and doubled back to be in Constantine's rear. At this point both Augusti had lost a considerable number of men, and there was probably much battle-weariness in the ranks on both sides. Constantine accepted Licinius' second plea for peace, sealed at Sardica in March, which gave Constantine all of the Balkans and Greece as well as the post of senior Augustus. Licinius withdrew to rule his truncated domain from Nicomedia, while Constantine's son Crispus established his authority at Trier.

The agreement was a mere breathing-space between rounds. As Licinius revived the persecutions of Christian believers, in 323 Constantine set out from the Greek port of Thessalonica with 130,000 men into Thrace in search of his rival. In two battles Licinius and his 160,000 men were vanquished and the whole empire fell into Constantine's lap. Licinius promised to behave himself, but he apparently was tempted to intrigue, for the following year he was executed. If Licinius was indeed plotting against Constantine, he had imitators in the closest folds of the new emperor's family. Given Constantine's noble history so far, it is with a sense of shock that we read of the executions of none other than his second wife Fausta and son Crispus in 326. We can only speculate on the motives for this double deal of death. Contemporary writers such as Zosimus hint that both might have been having an affair. Crispus was the fruit of Constantine's first marriage, brave and capable in the field, hence the probable object of jealousy on the part of his stepmother Fausta, who wished to promote her own three sons and three daughters. It's not too far-fetched to imagine Fausta scheming to dispose of Crispus, even to the point of engineering a sex scandal. Whatever the details, the affair must have been serious enough to temporarily derange Constantine's mind, as at the same time he ordered the death of Licinius' son Licinianus whose mother was Constantine's sister Constantia. To make matters yet worse, Constantine soon repented of doing away with his son and blamed Fausta who, say some, was either boiled to death in her bath or left naked on a mountain to be eaten by wild beasts; other evidence suggests that she in fact survived to outlive her husband.

In light of this sordid episode, would it be right to call Constantine a Christian? The question is a valid one, yet we just don't know enough about the affair to be able to judge. Being a Christian is not the same as being a saint. A Christian soldier remains a soldier, sometimes being called upon to kill in the line of duty. Harshness may be necessary even in the devoutest leader. One popular school of thought, originating perhaps with Gibbon, claims that Constantine's toleration and later personal acceptance of Christianity was political rather than spiritual, a recognition that the new creed was now unstoppable and hence the only vehicle by which he could attain supreme power. Given the historical record, however, that would be overstating the case for cynicism. The faith of Constantine's mother Helena, strong and never in doubt, must have left a mark on her son. Moreover, Constantine himself was hugely impressed by the fact that since he had adopted the standard of the cross he had never lost a battle. His own personal philosophy was that greater forces outside himself were pushing him onwards to supreme power, a view fully in step with Christian doctrine.

Of theology Constantine knew little and cared less. Though he gave his bishops every respect and facility he looked on them as holy civil servants assigned to develop the spiritual side of the empire while he took care of the power side. That does not mean to say he was indifferent to the forms of ritual; but he saw Christianity essentially in military terms, as a vital ingredient in cultivating those qualities of discipline, obedience, inner calm and courage that are the attributes of an effective soldier. Christians, he found, were more reliable than others in the moral sphere and hence made better soldiers; they tended to shun the squabbles and ego games of politics and class warfare and to uphold family values.

For the first few years of his sole rule Constantine had his share of theological headaches. This is not the place to analyse the serious heresies that almost at once broke out to threaten the unity of the young Christian church. But the emperor, alarmed at how corrupt human nature managed to seep through the sacerdotal robes of some clergy, felt he had to temporarily rescind the Edict of Milan. Priestly squabbles irritated his soldierly mind. He wrote to the instigator of one major heresy, a gaunt ascetic priest from Egypt named Arius:

> You, Arius ... should have kept silence. [These] are problems that idleness alone raises, and whose only use is to sharpen men's wits ... these are silly actions worthy of inexperienced children, and not of priests or reasonable men.[10]

He cracked down by calling the first ecumenical council, which met in Nicaea near Nicomedia in 325, to set holy doctrine in stone once and for all. When all the speeches were made and issues hammered out, the result of the council was what Constantine wanted – a firm statement of the Christian faith that has endured, in the form of the Creed, in Christian churches to this day.

By the end of the second decade of the fourth century Constantine felt secure enough to realize a long-standing ambition to finally abandon Rome as an impractical capital for the empire and set up a new one within easy reach of Greece, Egypt, Mesopotamia and Palestine as well as providing a buffer against the threatening pagan tribes to the north and the ever-hostile Persians. Rome was an awkward place from which to manage a Mediterranean empire; its only port was Ostia at the mouth of the Tiber, poorly situated for eastward voyages. The Romans, as descendants of a stolid agrarian people, had never taken to the sea in a big way, and the capital was declining as a result. Rome, moreover, was heavily tainted with the old paganism.

New trends in trade and religion were emanating from the Eastern Mediterranean, and so that's where Constantine decided his 'new Rome' would have to be. Nicomedia was too reminiscent of Diocletian and Galerius. For some time Constantine had been eyeing a town a short distance up the coast which sat right on the easternmost tip of the European continent – a town which, like Rome, rested on seven hills. This was the old Greek trading town of Byzantion. The strategic sea passage separating Europe from Asia, which assumes its narrowest point at the Bosporus, had been known and prized by the east Mediterranean peoples since very ancient times. The long and bloody Trojan War, or its equivalent, which ended around 1180 BC was simply one of the mighty struggles for control of the Dardanelles Strait through which Greek and Roman merchants could tap the fertile farms of the Black Sea coasts and the markets of the hinterlands. The power of classical Athens, for example, was built on the grain shipped south through the straits. According to legend a Greek named Byzas, a native of Megara, set up a colony at that point and named it after himself: Byzantion (later Latinized into Byzantium, as will henceforth be used here). Twenty-two centuries later a French traveller was struck by the city's strategic location:

> One might say that the straits of the Dardanelles and the Black Sea were made to carry riches from the four corners of the earth. From the Black Sea comes the wealth of the Mongols, India, the far north, China and Japan. From the [Mediterranean] come the wares of Egypt, Ethiopia, the African coasts, the West Indies and the best that Europe has to offer.[11]

Much influenced by ancient history, Constantine had first considered building his Nova Roma on the site of ancient Troy at the mouth of the Dardanelles, and work on buildings was actually begun. But the superior qualities of Byzantium eventually impressed him more. Accounts of the time give supernatural explanations for his change of mind. Constantine himself said God came to him in a dream. Others said that eagles flew down from the mountains of Asia Minor and picked up the tools, carrying them across the Bosporus to where they would be of better use. The English chronicler William of Malmesbury elaborates further, writing that a wrinkled old woman appeared to the emperor in a dream and was transformed into an attractive young girl; shortly afterwards Sylvester, the bishop of Rome (Pope

Sylvester I), appeared to him in another dream saying that the young girl represented Byzantium which he would similarly make young again.

These are legends that accumulate around any momentous undertaking. Many stories are told of Pope Sylvester, made a saint by the Roman Catholic Church. One is that when Constantine contracted leprosy the pagan priests advised him to bathe in the warm blood of newly-butchered babies; not surprisingly, he rejected that madly criminal solution. The apostles Peter and Paul appeared to him in a dream and advised him to send for Sylvester, who baptized him with holy water, curing the disease. The story was cherished by the Romans for many centuries afterwards, and offered a convenient explanation of why the emperor eventually converted to Christianity a few days before his death.

We cannot dismiss out of hand the story that Constantine personally traced out the line of western land walls of the new city with the point of his lance, a distance of some ten miles. When his attendants got tired of walking, he chided them by saying he would stop 'only when He, the invisible guide before me, thinks fit to stop'. Gibbon sarcastically wonders who that 'extraordinary conductor' could have been, but as in the vision of the cross in the sky, Constantine himself sincerely believed he was being divinely guided in all he did. Founding a new capital city and relocating the centre of gravity of a vast empire would have been a colossal undertaking requiring an appropriate degree of resolve. Could even such a vigorous man as Constantine have managed it without a rock-solid religious faith and sense of superhuman purpose?

In November 324, in the fabled footsteps of Byzas, Constantine set out to reinvent the centre of the empire on the foundations of the city that had already stood for a thousand years. From every point of view the location had advantages. The inlet known as the Golden Horn which separated the two European portions of the city provided a number of safe harbours for vessels approaching from either the Bosporus or Sea of Marmara. Every vessel passing in either direction between the Aegean and Black Seas had to sail close enough to shore to be subject to a passage toll. The sea itself was, and still is, rich in fish; even today on warm evenings scores of anglers jostle one another for space on the quays and bridges of the Bosporus for their evening meal. Farm produce from the fertile European and Asian hinterlands, especially wheat and wine, found its way easily to markets on all four points of the compass. Strategically, the city was an ideal headquarters for an army that could be sent in any direction by land or sea; Gaul and Britain, the lands around the Euphrates River, Russia and the Mediterranean and Italy, all lay on radii like the spokes of a wheel.

The construction of Constantinople – the city of Constantine – took six years, and no expense or effort was spared. To risk a more recent historical analogy, it was as if sometime in the nineteenth century Queen Victoria had decided to abandon old and tired Britain as the centre of the British Empire and move the seat of government lock, stock and barrel across the Atlantic to New York, building it from scratch, skyscrapers and all, to unify the English-speaking world from a new position of commercial and military power, and taking hundreds of monuments from Britain to adorn the new wide streets. And as in such a case the British Empire would soon have been renamed the American Empire, the Roman became the Byzantine.[12]

Rarely can nations or empires claim a specific moment in time as their beginning. Yet with the Byzantine Empire we are reliably informed that it officially opened for business on Monday morning, 11 May 330, with the elaborate ceremonies for the dedication of Constantinople as the new Roman capital (the official name continued to be Nova Roma, but no one ever called it that). The city at that point contained some 50,000 inhabitants, many of whom were relocated imperial functionaries and their families. As the sun rose on that portentous Monday, Constantine emerged from his new palace to proudly gaze on the gleaming new Hippodrome adjoining it, thronged with what one cynical observer called an 'intoxicated multitude [of] men so drunk they could not hold their liquor'. The emperor was not unduly put out. He soaked up public adulation, however it might be fuelled. The same commentator scoffed that Constantine 'desired to be praised by the unstable masses' who could 'barely pronounce' his name.[13]

Such critics, however, were a minority. Constantine, like Dicoletian before him, was a firm believer in the power of pomp and circumstance to keep the social and political structure in place. *L'état*, to play with Louis XIV's phrase, was unmistakably *lui*. And the more it was dinned into the masses, the better off everyone would be. Constantine was emperor by divine right – appointed, according to Eusebius, 'by God's own will'. This basic tenet was not open to dispute. Eusebius theorized that the emperor 'frames his earthly government according to the divine original, feeling strength in its conformity with the monarchy of God'. Eusebius, and certainly Constantine, had no faith in democracy which they equated with 'anarchy and disorder'.[14] Whatever his private feelings about being elevated to superhuman status by his subjects, he certainly did not object to the erection in the new forum of a hundred-foot pillar of Egyptian porphyry topped by a sculpted likeness of himself with golden rays radiating from his halo. To underline the divine message, a number of Biblical relics were deposited inside the twenty-foot marble base, such as the axe that Noah used to build the Ark, some loaves left over from Christ's miraculous feeding of the crowds, and the jar of ointment from which Mary Magdalene anointed Christ's head.

The celebrations and games for the inauguration of Constantinople, we are assured, lasted forty days. They began with a procession that may or may not (the evidence here is vague) have featured a gilded wooden statue of the emperor, an emblem of the city in his right hand, being trundled around the Hippodrome flanked by a formation of richly-clad guards holding white candles. We do know that this statue was thus paraded on the city's birthday of 11 May for many years afterwards, with the emperor of the time rising from his special seat, the kathisma, to salute the memory of the founder.

It is a measure of the vigour of Constantine, who was over 50 when he settled into his new palace, that he did not neglect the troublesome northern frontiers of the empire where he had first earned his spurs. In the 320s the Goths, a Teutonic people who had been displaced from their Northeast European and Scandinavian homes by invaders from the East (of whom more later), were aggressively trying to carve out securer abodes in Central and Southern Europe. This brought them into conflict with the Roman forces along the Danube, where Constantine personally subdued them in the summer of 328 and bridged the Danube to secure its left (northern) bank. This was familiar territory to him, and he spent the next year or so tirelessly ranging through what is now Germany and down into his Balkan birthplace. Little is known about these campaigns, except that only once was he seriously discomfited, when somewhere in Eastern Europe a Gothic formation of 500 cavalry attacked the imperial camp and slaughtered great numbers of Romans; Constantine himself fled for his life, just in time to return to his new capital to inaugurate it.

In the spring of 332 a Gothic group, presumably under pressure from the North and East, tried to seize territory belonging to the Sarmatians in what is now Hungary. The Sarmatians appealed to Constantinople for aid, and so the emperor led a force to what is now Bulgaria while summoning his eldest son, Constantine Caesar, from Gaul to help. A battle or battles were fought somewhere near the Black Sea coast, and we next hear of the Goths being decisively trounced, thousands of them being left to perish of hunger and cold. As Constantine took on the honorific title of Gothicus Maximus II (to mark his second victory over the Goths), he fortified the now-secure Danube border with a series of *quadriburgia*, or four-towered forts, that appear on coins of the time. But if the Goths had been satisfactorily dealt with, the Sarmatians now became restive. Pressures from the north were pushing them, too, into others' lands. In the summer of 334 Constantine (one imagines rather wearily, at 60) rode north again. This time there seem to have been no overt hostilities; about 300,000 Sarmatians were peaceably resettled inside the empire's frontiers to cultivate available land and provide soldiers for the Roman-Byzantine army. New coins were minted with a grand *Victor Omnium Gentium* (Victor of All Peoples) added to Constantine's already extensive laurels. It was a fitting sequel to what turned out to be Constantine's last campaign.

He had expended a great deal of energy on building up the civil and military administration. To cement it all together he had no compunction about using his full official title, that reads like a literary shelf of trophies: Imperator Caesar Flavius Constantinus Pius Felix Victor ac Triumfator Pontifex Maximus Germanicus Maximus IIII Sarmaticus Maximus II Gothicus Maximus II Dacius Maximus Tribunicia Potestate XXXIII Consul VIII Imperator XXXII Pater Patriae Proconsul.[15] This dazzling string was intended not only to intimidate potential foes: it also served to remind his own people of his awesome majesty. Yet the immense task of administration was too much even for a leader of Constantine's considerable propensities; as he got older he picked four men to share the high-level administrative burden as praetorian prefects while he retained supreme command of his adoring army. In the civil sphere the *magister officiorum*, or palace chief of staff, something between a prime minister and private secretary, occupied the highest non-royal rung, aided by the *quaestor*, who drafted the laws. These two officials kept a wary eye on the praetorian prefects to ensure that they did not abuse their powers while administering an empire-wide army of civil servants from clerical scribes to police detectives and postmasters.

The military command was divided between the commander of the foot soldiers, the *magister peditum*, and commander of the cavalry, the *magister equitum*, both of whom held honorary cabinet rank. The Byzantine-Roman army itself at this time probably numbered around 150,000 men. The great majority of serving soldiers were non-Roman, from the provinces of both the East and the West – Germans and Anatolians, Greeks and Britons, Gauls and Celts. Greeks and Romans, especially if they were wealthy landowners, were still preferred for the higher ranks, though as we have seen, the Germans had displayed their talents in high command. As for the faith of the army, Constantine was canny enough not to arm-twist Christianity on his men; he knew that many, especially from the East, were Mithriasts and pagans. But by the 330s Christianity was the prevailing faith in the army and undoubtedly its psychological driving force.

Constantine himself ordered prayers on the Constantinople parade grounds every Sunday (a day which he first set aside as an official day of prayer and rest). The 22nd Primigenia Legion stationed near what is now Cologne in Germany and named after the pagan goddess of fortune changed its name to Constantinia Victrix that has Christian connotations. Chapels for baptism began appearing at camps such as that of the 2nd Augusta Legion at Richborough in Kent as well as at forts along the Rhine. God and Christ proved to be more than enough of a moral substitute for the now-attenuated abstract notion of an *Imperium Romanum* for which few were prepared now to give their lives. 'The Roman army,' noted one fifth century writer, 'took in barbarians and sent home Christians.'[16]

In foreign policy, Constantine's last years were taken up with concern over the Holy Places, especially Jerusalem. In 326 his mother Helena Augusta, possibly to seek spiritual solace following the killing of Crispus and Fausta, travelled to Palestine and distinguished herself through acts of charity, including building churches at the sites of Christ's birth and crucifixion. Constantine supervised the process in detail from Constantinople. Our sources agree that Helena discovered the True Cross, sending parts of it plus some of the nails that had pierced Christ's hands and feet to Constantinople. Constantine placed the nails in his horse's bridle.

This concern of Constantine for the Holy Places indicates how faith informed his major decisions. Palestine could not be considered an area of vital economic importance to the empire; in fact, more often than not, it had given successive headaches to generations of Roman emperors. But given the importance of Jerusalem to Christian belief, Byzantium had to administer the place to ensure that its priceless spiritual heritage remained intact and that it remained accessible to pilgrims. Constantine, in fact, was the first crusader, seven centuries before crusading became fashionable in the West. For a serious threat had emerged on the eastern horizon – the revived Persian kingdom under the Sasanid dynasty, which again, like the empire of Darius and Xerxes of old, was looming over the East Mediterranean seaboard. Constantine was considering what to do about this when in the spring of 337 he became ill while travelling to Nicomedia on a religious mission.

We don't know the precise nature of his illness, but at 64 he was quite definitely overworking himself. There is also a possibility that he was being progressively poisoned by rivals seeking the throne. Warm baths proved to no avail, so he moved across the gulf to the baths of Helenopolis, a town he had built to honour his mother, and prayed there. To return to Constantinople he had to pass through Nicomedia, but when he reached the outskirts he felt he could no longer go on. So he took a step which doubtless he had been planning for many years, but now judged could no longer be delayed. He called the local ecclesiastics together and told them what was on his mind.

> The long-awaited time has finally come, when I have hoped and prayed to obtain the salvation of God … I had thought to receive it in the waters of the Jordan … but it pleases God, who knows what is best for us, that I should receive it here … I shall prescribe henceforth a way of life that befits His service.

There and then Bishop Eusebius of Nicomedia baptized Constantine into the Christian faith.[17] Then the emperor doffed the purple – vowing never to wear it again – and put on a vestment 'white and radiant as light' and lay down on a white couch, purified inwardly as well as symbolically.

Much has been made of Constantine's 'deathbed conversion' and the implication that he opportunely became a Christian only when death was staring him in the face and he realized what the Winning Side was. That is too cynical a view to take, and even Gibbon does not stoop to it. Constantine was well aware of having been all too human during his life, with perhaps more than the usual share of sin burdening him. A leader, however idealistic, often had to act harshly in the interests of the people and society whom he led and had an obligation to protect. Government, affairs of state and sin were coterminous. As long as he was emperor, Constantine would have been compelled to sin on a daily basis. Now, suspecting that his life was drawing to its close, he judged it to be the right time to finally commit his soul to Christ. Constantine's words to his baptizers, as relayed by Eusebius, are revealing in another point. As his remark about the Jordan River reveals, he was planning to take arms against those who threatened the Holy Land – namely, the Sasanid Persians – and find fulfilment by being baptized, like Christ, in that river. He hoped he could recover from his illness and live on to do more of God's military work, such as protecting the Holy Places.

God did not so choose. Shortly after donning his white robe, on 22 May 337, a Sunday, Constantine died. His body was placed in a coffin of gold which was carried to Constantinople draped in the imperial purple. He had reigned twenty-four years – or thirty-one if we include the period from his acclamation in Britain. For some fifteen weeks the golden coffin lay in a ring of candles in the main hall of the palace. Then, in a funeral ceremony which he himself had planned long before, Constantine was led out in solemn procession, headed by his eldest son Constantius and formations of soldiers in full combat gear; spearmen and heavy-armed infantry flanked the coffin itself. The cortege, followed by a great crowd, left the palace and entered the Mese, the main street of Constantinople. Just short of the walls that the emperor had marked out with the aid of his heavenly guide, the procession turned right to the newly-completed Church of the Holy Apostles. There the emperor was laid to rest alongside replicas of twelve sarcophagi which he had intended to represent the twelve disciples of Christ, with himself as a self-styled thirteenth.[18]

Does Constantine I deserve his widely-used sobriquet 'the Great'? Judgements on him vary widely. One recent one is that he was 'a political showman who slashed his way to power'.[19] Stephenson, one of his more recent biographers, concedes that Constantine had 'many public images', yet paints a composite portrait of 'a charismatic and effective commander', though 'stubborn, vain and narcissistic ... a lofty sovereign on a high throne, decked out in silk and gold'. That hardly sounds a qualification for the title 'Great'. More fulsome is the urbane Lord Norwich, who frankly places Constantine on the highest of historical pedestals, up there with Alexander the Great and Alfred the Great of England, the most influential man in history outside Jesus Christ, Buddha and the Prophet Muhammad. Among the Greeks he stands high in the pantheon of heroes; the Greek Orthodox Church reveres Constantine I (alongside his mother Saint Helena) as *isapostolos*, equivalent to an apostle on the level of Saints Peter and Paul, to this day.

Constantine II (337–340), Constantius II (337–361), Constans I (337–350)

As happens so often with larger-than-life leaders, Constantine I was as unfortunate in his offspring as he was endowed with nobility and ability during his reign. Within weeks of his elaborate obsequies, his three sons by Fausta – Constantine II, Constantius and Constans – proved to be as unlike their father as anyone could be. Constantine, for all his nation-building, had left no hard-and-fast succession rule, and the army soon made clear that it would like to see all three sons rule jointly, carrying on their revered father's tradition. But almost at the outset, mistrust and naked ambition soured the brothers' relations. The tussle for the throne of Constantinople quickly became ugly.

The eldest son who assumed the title Constantine II on his father's death was in his mid-twenties. As a swaddling infant he had been named Caesar of the western part of the empire and on maturity appeared to be a competent enough administrator. But it was Constantius, the middle brother and Caesar of the East, who was nearest to Constantinople and presided over his father's funeral, making sure to stay in the public and military limelight.[20] Constans, barely into his teens, was given the Italian peninsula and Roman heartland.

On 9 September 337 Constantine II, Constantius and Constans were named joint Augusti, three emperors reigning simultaneously, as the army desired. At this point Constantius appears to have taken matters into his own hands to eliminate a host of lesser potential rivals. Using an unlikely rumour – but widely believed by the army – that his father had been slowly poisoned, he engineered a massacre of anyone except his own brothers who might have been suspect. His half-uncle (Constantine's brother), Julius Constantius, was cut down in his palace along with his eldest son; another half-uncle, Delmatius, met the same fate with his two Caesar sons. Two of Constantine's brothers-in-law, both consuls, were also knocked off in underworld style, without a trial. Constantius, still only 20, was proving a harder man than anyone expected. With the domestic playing field now cleaned by a bloodbath, the three brother-emperors met at Viminacium on the Danube to decide who would ultimately rule what. Constantine II appeared content with his western domains, basing himself at Trier. In 338 he continued his interrupted campaigns against unconquered Germans. Constans was given a vast domain to rule, from Italy through to the Balkans, to the very gate of Constantinople; he set up his headquarters at Naissus, where his father had been born. This left Constantius free to face the growing Persian menace in the East, eager to prove himself in battle and 'stain his right hand with blood'. But it was already winter and the Persian army had pulled back.

Constantius stained his right hand instead with more domestic blood. A notable victim was Flavius Ablabius, a former praetorian prefect with a history of nasty intrigue. Eunapius relates that one day an official party appeared at Ablabius' door bearing a letter from the emperor. We are not told what the letter said, but Ablabius was extremely suspicious and confronted the messengers arrogantly – why should he kowtow to a young stripling Augustus of 20? The messengers' reply was to reveal their true mission, draw swords and hack Ablabius to pieces 'like some animal cut up at a public feast'.

Constantine II, the eldest son, could not rest easy in Trier. The intrigues of the imperial court, of course, extended their tentacles to all parts of the empire. Constans, with perhaps the impetuosity of youth, suspected his eldest brother of trying to snatch Italy and North Africa from him. As Constantine marched east to help Constantius in 340, passing through North Italy, Constans sent a force to ambush him at Aquileia. Constantine perished in the encounter and his brother, consumed by hate, had his body thrown into the Alsa River and Constantine's name erased from all official inscriptions.

And Constantius approved of the deed. His mind was now free to concentrate on the Persians, which he did for the next ten years. The palace at Constantinople saw his face only a few times, as he spent his summers campaigning and his winters at Antioch. His adversary was the Persian Sasanid King Shapur II (of whom more later), who was persecuting the Christians of Armenia. The hard core of the Roman-Byzantine army was the corps of heavy-armoured Gothic cavalry set up on the example of the Persians and employing the effective tactics of the Parthians, a warlike west Asian tribe. The horsemen were known as the Cataphracts (= armoured, in Greek). Some of them and their mounts were sheathed in flexible scaled or chain-mail breastplates (*lorica squamata*), while other units did away with armour, relying instead on speedy hit-and-run attacks with the spear and lance; some of these latter carried shields. A section of the Cataphracts had the job of long-range sniping with the javelin or bow. Their ordnance also included a broadsword hanging from the shoulder, an iron helmet, a chain-mail breastplate and greaves, and a small battle-axe for close-order combat.

The Roman-Byzantine infantry, as in classical Greece, was divided into heavy-armed and light-armed, plus a highly-mobile body of peltasts who carried very little in the way of weaponry except short javelins and the small pelte shields which gave the specialization its name. A heavy-armed legionary wore body armour and a close-fitting round helmet plus cheekpieces, and carried a long shield of about two-thirds his height, plus a javelin or a long Macedonian lance, or *sarissa*, which sometimes was over 6ft long. The light-armed troops' weapons were arrows, javelins and slingstones. With such forces Constantius kept the Persians at bay for ten years while keeping his army combat-experienced. The main bone of contention was Armenia, where Shapur had begun persecuting the resident Christians. In 350 the Persians attacked the key town of Nisibis (in modern North Iraq). Constantius was in the middle of trying to stem the assault when news arrived that all was not well with his little brother in the West.

Constans turned out to be capable enough in the field, crossing into Britain in 343 to put down an outburst of unrest. But he quickly gained a reputation for greed, arrogance, cruelty and loose living, qualities not calculated to endear him to the soldiery. He was accused of failing to pay the army on time and spending hours with homosexual lovers. But these flaws paled beside those of the man who emerged as his deadliest foe. Magnentius was a pagan Gaul who had fought well under Constantine I, rising in the ranks from common soldier to general. The western army's dissatisfaction with Constans crystallized into open revolt in 350 when Marcellinus, the commander of the imperial bodyguard, acclaimed Magnentius as Augustus. Constans fled towards Spain, but his pursuers caught up with him in the Pyrenees and murdered him. Vetranio, Constans' infantry commander, proclaimed himself Augustus in Central Europe, though Magnentius' men managed to seize Rome.

Constantius, tied down at Nisibis, pondered his alternatives. He was inclined to support Vetranio against the barbarian Gaul usurper. But when he was able to detach himself and travel west in December 350, he gave Vetranio a generous retirement package and placed Gallus, Constantius' young cousin, as Caesar in his place. Gallus had been one of the lucky few in Constantius' circle to survive the massacre of 338, probably because of his youth. Constantius was then free to tackle Magnentius, whose reputation for savagery had spread far and wide.

Constantius and Magnentius clashed at Mursa (in what is now Croatia) on 28 September 351. The battle was recorded by Zosimus, who writes that Magnentius began the fight by setting fire to the wooden gates of the town, hoping to clear the way for an assault. While the defenders poured water on the fires, Constantius' forces approached. Magnentius hid four companies of Gauls in a derelict stadium overgrown with trees, but the intended ambush failed, so that the mass of both armies slugged it out on the plain outside Mursa. By dark the Roman force had gained the upper hand, though with estimated losses of 40 per cent, while Magnentius' army suffered at least 60 per cent losses. Among them was Magnentius himself, possibly during the abortive stadium ambush.

Constantius saw his victory not only as revenge for his murdered younger brother but also a vindication of faith-based military policy. Four months earlier, Cyril, the Bishop of Jerusalem, claimed to have seen 'an immense cross formed from light, in the sky, which stretched above the holy Golgotha as far as the holy Mount of Olives', and visible to the entire population of Jerusalem, Christian and otherwise. Though the modern consensus is that the phenomenon was probably a natural event called a 'solar halo', Cyril had no doubt that its purpose was to divinely inspire Constantius in his battles.[21]

But was Constantius a true Christian? There were plenty of people in Constantinople prepared to doubt it, for he himself was a declared follower of Arius, a priest who alleged that Christ was not fully divine, in contrast to the established creed. Arianism, as the trend became known, gained a large following in the western and eastern provinces alike, and was seen by the established church as a dire threat to the political unity of the empire. The people of Rome, on the other hand, appeared to have few such doubts when he rode into the city in triumph. They noticed he was rather shorter than they had imagined, and marvelled that as he rode along and the adulatory roars of the crowd echoed off the surrounding hills, he stood steady as a rock in his chariot, looking neither to the left nor right, not even moving when the chariot wheels bumped over a rut. The true heir of Constantine the Great could not afford to do anything less. It was all part of the demigod image that an Augustus had to cultivate to keep his power intact.

There was still the awkward presence of Gallus in Central Europe as Caesar. But this hapless man had long since outlived his brief usefulness, and in 354 Constantius had no compunction about doing away with him by poisoning at Pola – the same town where Crispus, Constantine's eldest son, had met his end. Gallus' half-brother Julian was elevated as Caesar in his place, but proved to be no pushover; he was popular (as will be seen below) and had the support of the entire western army who wanted him as Augustus. Constantius was preoccupied with his defences against the Persians, and when he heard of Julian's move in 360 he flew into a towering but helpless rage. For the short term he sent messages to the Germanic tribes to keep Julian occupied along the Danube, and when winter came prepared to move against Julian himself.

The chroniclers tell us that just as Constantius set out from North Syria to Constantinople he came across a headless corpse by the roadside. This was taken to be a bad omen, and duly at Tarsus on the Mediterranean he was attacked by a fever that quickly became severe enough to halt him completely. In the nearby village of Mopsucrenae he died, on 3 November 361. This last of the heirs of the great Constantine was just 44, and, it was said, had never suffered a day of illness in his life.[22]

Julian (the Apostate) (361–363)

Julian found himself emperor in Constantinople with a major enemy ready-made for him: the Persians, 'that secret empire which for a thousand years had stood off expanding Europe and Asiatic hordes, never forgetting its [ancient] glory'.[23]

The Persian Sasanid dynasty had originated with one Sasan, a priest of Persepolis whose son intrigued his way up to become governor of a key province. Ardashir, this son's son, seized the throne in 224 to begin the dynasty. It was Ardashir who fired the Persian nobles and people into a new nationalism, a task inherited and enhanced by his son Shapur I, who instituted a brief Persian golden age. Shapur's first encounters with Roman forces, though, were not generally successful until 260, when he sacked Antioch and captured (West) Roman Augustus Valerian in the field.

This Persian triumph was short-lived, as neighbouring Palmyra, allied to Rome, pushed the Persians back across the Euphrates. As is usual in noble families, a few generations of great ability were followed by an ebb tide of mediocrity and incompetence. After Shapur I's death in 272 a series of nonentities assumed what by now had become the official title 'King of Kings, King of the Aryans and the Non-Aryans, Sovereign of the Universe, Descendant of the Gods'. When the peace-loving King Hormizd II died in 309, the nobles passed over his son and handed the crown to a half-brother who had not yet emerged from his mother's womb.[24] Shapur II is probably the only monarch in history who began to reign before he was born. This was four years before the battle of the Milvian Bridge. When he was about 20, already battle-hardened and displaying a notable streak of cruelty, he would have heard of the building of Constantinople. By then he had added the words 'Brother of the Sun and Moon' and 'Companion of the Stars' to his pedigree (as if the original lineup had not been enough) and determined to live up to them as best as he could.

As early as 324 Constantine I had sent a veiled warning to the teenaged Sasanid king advising him to treat his Christian subjects well or face military action. Shapur was too young to openly defy the warning, so he bided his time until 334 when he invaded Armenia and deposed its Christian king. Constantius, still a prince, restored the Armenian monarch but Constantine, in his final years, knew that a showdown with the uppity Shapur would have to come.

Shapur's campaign to seize Armenia foundered on the resistance of Constantius. He also had chronic troubles in the East, and so it was not until 353 that Shapur was free to advance on the Byzantine outposts in Mesopotamia with the support of a hitherto mysterious people called the White Huns. The campaign was a stalemate, but Shapur kept whatever small gains he made. When Constantius died in 361, the Persian ruler of the universe, from what he must have been told, no doubt believed his successor would be a pushover.

Few Byzantine emperors have received the degree of fascinated attention than the scholarly, somewhat eccentric young man who succeeded Constantius on the throne in Constantinople in relation to the paltry two years he was on it. He is known mainly for the ideological and religious coup which he staged, wresting Byzantium momentarily away from Christendom and dragging it uneasily back into the era of the Olympian gods. The experiment backfired badly, but that has not prevented generations of secularist historians and novelists, from Gibbon onwards, from paying him a flattering attention that would probably have astounded him.

Flavius Claudius Iulianus, better known to history as Julian, was born in 332 and just 5 when Constantius began the bloody purge of his family; his tender age most probably spared him along with his sickly but scarcely older half-brother Gallus. Nonetheless, both boys lived under Constantius' deep suspicion, and when Julian was 9 they were both sent to the remote castle of Macellum in Cappadocia, probably so they would not become focal points for anti-palace intrigues. His sole companions were books, and for six years Julian imbibed an impressive corpus of classical learning, including Greek philosophy. His personality developed alongside his erudition, and at 15 he was invited back to the capital. But his personal popularity worried the emperor, who politely banished him again, this time to Nicomedia, where he willingly deepened his philosophic studies.

Classical philosophy and Christianity, however, were in uneasy alliance in the minds of rulers and many thinking men. Julian absorbed both, and came out unashamedly in favour of the former. One major reason was that the Christian world at the time was riven by the Arian doctrinal controversy that had come to the point of igniting bloody riots in the cities. If that was official Christianity, he wanted no part of it. Yet however much he might wish to spend his life in the groves of academe in the quiet company of Plato and Aristotle, Julian could not completely ignore politics. They pressed in on him menacingly in 351, when the emperor appointed Gallus as Caesar of the eastern provinces with his headquarters at Antioch. Gallus ruled with an untoward harshness which cost him his head. Julian was confined with his books for a few months in Italy, until Constantius became convinced he wasn't any danger and sent him to live in Athens, the empire's most famous university town, in 355.

Julian spent six happy months in Athens in the company of some of the brainiest scholars of the day. One of them was his friend Gregory Nazianzen, who later recalled the appearance of his geeky fellow-student: 'hunched and twitching shoulders, a wild and darting eye … ridiculous facial expressions … ever-nodding head and halting speech.' The picture reveals someone who lives too much in his head and is subject to nervous tics. His nervousness increased when, without warning, he was called to Milan. Trembling inwardly, he wondered what he had done. But to his surprise Constantius offered him the hand of his sister Helena – a development believed to have been engineered by the empress Eusebia, who viewed the young philosopher with sympathy. He also found himself Caesar of Gaul. Thus at 23, Julian had to doff his philosopher's simple cloak and put on the regalia of a Roman general. His task, Constantius told him, was to push back the German tribes that had surged into the Rhine area, sacked Cologne and taken scores of other towns and were penetrating into Gaul. He was given a guard of 360 men and sent westward over the Alps to turn himself from a thinker into a soldier.

Perhaps the long years of bookish introversion had masked a smouldering subliminal aggressiveness that required a military environment to bring it out. In the winter of 356 the young Caesar-general plunged wholeheartedly into military training, studying the art of war as zealously as he had studied the classics. The chance to prove himself in the field came that spring, when he attacked the Germans at Reims and drove them back, retaking Cologne in the process. A German tribe called the Alemanni (hence the French word for Germany: Allemagne) surrounded Julian at Sens, where he conducted a steady defence for a month, making sure at the same time that the local people and army were well-provisioned – conduct that showed he was a good quartermaster as well as campaigner.

Shortly afterwards Julian collided with a much bigger Alemanni force near Strasbourg, trouncing it by forming his own men into a wedge-shaped crescent that smashed the enemy's front, with himself in the front line. Gaul, however, was still not safe. From Strasbourg Julian marched east against the Franks who were ravaging the Meuse Valley and sent them packing over the Rhine. He entered Paris as the army's hero; many soldiers hoped the 26-year-old bookworm turned warrior would be the next emperor. Of course, the adulation got back to Constantius, who would have been less than human if he had not decided to keep a keen eye on his suddenly capable cousin. After five years administering Gaul, during which Julian established a reputation for just and humane government, Constantius made abortive attempts to undermine him. The empress Eusebia played a nefarious part here; childless, she reportedly bribed Julian's staff to give abortifacients to his wife Helena, who appears to have miscarried several times, and when Helena finally gave birth to a boy, the midwife cut the umbilical cord too near the body and the infant bled to death. Finally, in 360, Julian received orders to send 300 of his best men from each Gallic regiment to the Persian front to boost the counteroffensive against Shapur II.

The previous year, the King of Kings and Brother of the Sun and Moon had written haughtily to Constantius demanding that Armenia and Mesopotamia, 'fraudulently extorted' by the Romans, be returned; otherwise he, Shapur, would shortly move against Constantius with all his forces. The order to Julian may have been justified, but at the same time he must have known by now that a serious attempt to weaken him was underway. The emperor's order would gut the core of his army. It also ran counter to what Julian had promised his men, who had enlisted on condition that they not be transferred beyond the Alps. Nonetheless, not wishing to display overt opposition to Constantius at this stage, he asked his men to obey the imperial order. As he may have expected, they refused point-blank, even when he promised to transport their families east with them at his own expense.

It was evening when, in his Paris palace, Julian retired to his bedchamber to rest. The noise of the soldierly mob beneath his window was growing ever more ominous. As he admitted later, he wondered whether his last hours had come, whether he was about to meet the grisly fate of so many past Roman emperors who had got on the wrong side of the army. Looking through a window, he prayed to Zeus as the noise in the night grew louder. He claimed that Zeus duly gave him 'a sign' that he should obey the army's will. This will soon became apparent; far from wanting to harm him, the army wanted to proclaim him Augustus. But that, too, presented a problem for him.

> [I] resisted as long as I could [Julian wrote], refusing to accept either the acclamation or the [royal] diadem. But since I alone could not control so many … somewhere about the third hour [about 9 a.m.] some soldier or other gave me the collar.

The 'collar' was a gold chain worn by one of the army's standard-bearers who, since there was nothing more suitably regal around, took off the ornament and put it on Julian's head. Whether he liked it or not, Julian was in the running for emperor.

He knew enough history to know that claiming the imperial throne on a forest of spears was a risky business and could well be lethal. Again he pleaded with the soldiers to obey the call to march east, but they would not listen. In fact, there was only one way they would march east – to Constantinople, to place their beloved general on the imperial throne. Julian caved in to their wish, and in 361 he set out with 23,000 men who could be persuaded to leave their homes in Gaul. The army was split into three, with the first section of 10,000 men crossing over the Alps and through North Italy into what is now Croatia. The second, also numbering 10,000, was to take a more northerly route through what is now Switzerland, leaving Julian himself with 3,000 picked troops to head north-east to the headwaters of the Danube and sail down the mighty river on boats. All three formations were to meet up at Sirmium, just west of present-day Belgrade. Julian probably decided on this elaborate and time-consuming scheme to make his force appear much larger than it was, and perhaps play for time as well. But coordination was poor, with the result that Julian got to Sirmium ahead of everyone else. It was at Sirmium that Julian at last revealed to the world something he had been keeping more or less a secret for years: in a proclamation he professed to 'publicly adore' the Olympian gods, adding rather dubiously that the army shared the same beliefs. At Naissus the news reached him that Constantius was dead. He was convinced it was Zeus' doing.

Towards the end of 361 Julian, 31, rode into Constantinople and took the throne. He proved to be rather unlike the usual run of late Roman emperors. The admiring Ammianus, a close friend, described him thus:

> His hair lay smooth as if it had been combed; and his beard was shaggy and trained to a point; his eyes were bright and full of fire … His eyebrows fine, his nose perfectly straight, his mouth a bit large, with full lower lip; his neck thick and bent, his shoulders large and broad. From his head to his fingertips he was well-proportioned.

The ever-modest Julian did not consider himself particularly good-looking. He let lice have the free run of his scraggly beard which he likened to 'a thicket for wild beasts', rarely cut his hair or nails and kept his fingers 'black with ink'.[25] To take an analogy from a future age, Julian was the nearest thing to a hippie that ever sat on the Byzantine throne, where he reverted to his studious, ragged-philosopher ways. As his inky fingers attested, he wrote incessant anti-Christian tracts. In June 262 he banned Christians from the teaching profession. His own belief was an odd conflation of numinous systems long on mysticism but short on logic. In personal conduct, ironically, he could be considered more of a Christian than most who officially adhered to the faith. He surrounded himself with the empty pomp of the old gods, styling himself *pontifex maximus* in the old Roman manner and dedicating a palace chapel to the sun. He outdid even his most zealous priests in the daily mass sacrifice of animals, deeming it his vital business, in the words of the inimitable Gibbon, 'to bring the wood, to blow the fire, to handle the knife, to slaughter the victim, and, thrusting his bloody hands into the bowels of the expiring animal, to draw forth the heart or liver, and to read, with the consummate skill of an *haruspex*, the imaginary signs of future events.'[26]

A devout Christian population could not be expected to put up with this sort of thing for long. To them he quickly became The Apostate, or abandoner of the faith.[27]

The army also was not as pagan as he fondly believed. Perhaps he mistook the high regard for his soldierly qualities for approval of his beliefs. Partly it was to keep the army's trust that in 362 he decided, like another Alexander, to take the field and deal with the Persian threat once and for all. His first stop was Antioch, where he mustered his army. Here the implacable forces of market economics took a hand when food merchants in the city took advantage of the influx of soldiery to raise prices. Julian, the philosopher-ruler, tried to reason with the merchants to keep their prices reasonable; when they refused to listen he fixed the prices of wheat and other staples by decree, importing large quantities of wheat from Egypt to keep the price down. The merchants howled that they could not make a profit this way, bought up the imported wheat and took their trade elsewhere, leaving the Antiocheans hungry and hugely distrustful of the bearded intellectual who tampered with their bread. A suspicious fire destroyed a shrine to Apollo; Julian retaliated by closing the cathedral at Antioch and executing a priest. This was not the best of auspices to begin a major campaign. Not surprisingly, a great many Antiochenes breathed sighs of huge relief when on 5 March 363 the emperor set off with 90,000 men to smite the Persians.

His spirits were high; he was certainly conscious of following in Alexander the Great's footsteps to bring the lights of classical Greece to the benighted hordes of the East. His army marched through northern Syria, past what is now Aleppo, then veered north-east into modern-day Iraq to where the Tigris and Euphrates rivers nearly converge. The way was not easy. The Persians were conducting a strategic withdrawal along scorched-earth lines, with the result that the provisioning of the Roman-Byzantine army was a constant problem. Julian proved himself the ideal general, sharing his men's hardships and scant rations, and marching with them on foot through the implacable wastes. To round out his good example, he absolutely refused to take sexual advantage of the flood of captured Persian women offered to him. Resistance was sparse and easily overcome, but when Julian arrived at Ctesiphon, the Persian capital, he found Shapur's large Persian army drawn up between the walls of the city and the west bank of the Tigris. The army included elephants which, everyone knew, struck terror into horses.

Julian's men were tired and hungry, and the elephants across the Tigris were trumpeting defiantly, but nonetheless he ordered an assault across the river. The first wave was driven back, but a second, stronger attack succeeded beyond even Julian's hopes. We are not sure of the details of the battle, but the Persian army, elephants and all, was routed in short order. If we are to credit Ammianus Marcellinus, the chronicler of Julian's campaign, some 2,500 Persians fell to a mere 70 Romans. At this point, Shapur employed his legendary cunning. He reportedly had the noses chopped off two Persian noble volunteers who, thus mutilated, crossed to Julian's camp offering to desert on the pretext that their king was a cruel monster, and they had the faces to prove it. Julian believed these two men, who somehow led his army into the trackless desert away from Ctesiphon. Julian was also talked into burning his river fleet, which admittedly would not have been much use for the march back upstream. We may assume that at some point Julian became aware of Shapur's ruse, and moreover, learned that a much bigger Persian army was close at hand. Morale in the army was low. The heat was scorching, with flies so thick, according to Ammianus, that they hid the sun. Flooding rivers turned the sand into quagmires. Food was short, as ever. Julian wished to press on, but his generals, seconded by the great bulk of the soldiery, flatly refused.

On 16 June Julian bowed to the inevitable and ordered a retreat along the left bank of the Tigris. Ten days later, near Samarra, the Persians struck with devastating force. Shapur's elephants sent Julian's cavalry flying. The emperor himself didn't even pause to don his armour, but sped straight into the heart of the action, shouting encouragement to his men. The gesture appeared to work; the Persian attack faltered, and then began to fall back. At this point a spear slammed into Julian's right side below the ribs. He tried to yank it out but slashed his right hand on the spear's razor edge. The spear had penetrated his liver, and the camp doctors held out no hope.

According to Ammianus, Julian died bravely, telling those huddled around him in his tent that he was happy to be about to rejoin 'heaven and the stars'. Lying in pain, he nonetheless found the strength for a debate about the nobility of the human soul. 'Suddenly,' writes the chronicler, 'the wound in his side opened wide, the pressure of the blood checked his breath, and after a draught of cold water for which he asked, he passed quietly away, in the thirty-second year of his age.'

A legend immediately arose around Julian's death that as he lay mortally wounded on the ground he cupped some of his blood in his hand and gasped, 'Vicisti, Galilaee!' ('Thou hast conquered, Galilean!') Most modern writers dismiss the story as a Christian fabrication intended to show that the pagan Julian in his last moments acknowledged Christ. Yet there is nothing intrinsically unbelievable in the story, and so we leave the reader to judge. Indeed, it was widely believed in subsequent years that the fatal spear had been hurled not by a Persian but by the ghost of Saint Mercurius, a Christian officer whom Julian had ordered executed for his faith. Which at once raises the question of whether Julian was slain by one of his own men. Many Byzantines openly believed so, including the historian Sozomen, who went so far as to praise the unknown assailant for performing 'for the sake of God and religion ... so bold a deed'. The theory is reinforced by the fact that no Persian came forward to claim the reward that Shapur had offered for whoever should kill Julian. On the other hand, Julian had always displayed extraordinary valour in combat, and that is what a soldier respects most of all. Was he so hated, even among his own men, for his paganism? The verdict, like so many in history, must remain open.

Chapter Two

Goths, Huns and Theodosius

Jovian (361–363), Valentinian I (364–375), Valens (364–378), Gratian (375–383) and Valentinian II (383–392)

With Julian unexpectedly dead in Iraq, the army leadership had to come up with his successor fast. One might imagine there would be no lack of eager candidates, but no-one seemed to want to take the political risk against the Flavian family which since Constantine I had had a monopoly of the throne. The morning after Julian's death the army assembled at Samarra to settle on a new emperor. Their first choice was a senior general, Sallustius Secundus, but he flatly declined on the grounds that he was too old and not in the best of health. Ammianus Marcellinus, who was present at the meeting, reports that someone shouted out the name of Jovian, the Imperial Guard commander. Jovian was popular, and young at 32, and a Christian. He liked to drink and womanize – though soldiers in any age wouldn't necessarily consider that a minus – and he lacked that indefinable quality known as 'class'. Ammianus professed himself at a loss to explain why Jovian was picked. He thought that during the meeting a false rumour spread that Julian had recovered, and that the resulting exultant cries of 'Julianus! Julianus!' were mistaken by many for 'Jovianus! Jovianus!' Whatever the truth, the lanky and awkward figure of Jovian was acclaimed emperor.

Jovian had no choice but to continue the withdrawal, if only to get to Constantinople to be crowned. The Persians, who had learned of Julian's death, constantly sniped at the retreating column. After the army, carrying Julian's embalmed body, crossed to the west bank of the Tigris and relative safety, Shapur II offered a victor's terms which Jovian at once accepted; these were for a thirty-year peace between Persia and Byzantium in exchange for five Roman frontier provinces – including eighteen key fortresses – to go to Shapur as well as a Byzantine pledge not to aid Christian Armenia.

The army was furious. Despite its fatigue and shock at the loss of Julian, there was plenty of fighting spirit left in it. Ammianus spoke for the majority of the army when he wrote that it would far rather 'fight ten battles' than give up a single fortress to the enemy. But Jovian, intent on cutting his losses, grimly led the army for seventy desolate miles westward to Nisibis; all the camels and pack-mules had to be slaughtered and the men barely made it. As he had signed Nisibis over to the Persians, he could not encamp within its limits without provoking Shapur, but he ordered all the Nisibians to evacuate their city before the Persians could seize it. Ammianus described heart-rending scenes of 'the mother who had lost her children, or the wife her husband … clinging to their doorposts, embracing their thresholds and pouring forth floods of tears'.[1]

That unpleasant task done, Jovian ordered Julian's body to be taken on to Tarsus on the coast for burial while he with the bulk of the army proceeded to Antioch. The army trudged wearily through the vicious heat of a Middle East summer, bearing before it the holy labaron first hoisted by Constantine I. In the early autumn the army straggled thankfully into Antioch, and after a well-earned rest, in mid-October it set out for Constantinople at an easy pace. All along the route Jovian was acclaimed as the restorer of the official Christian faith. At Ankyra (modern Ankara) on the first day of 364 he and his infant son Varronianus were acclaimed consuls in a special ceremony, though the child's deafening howls worried some of the superstitious people present. Their premonition turned out to be accurate. Jovian never got to Constantinople. Six weeks later he halted for the night at Dadastana, about half-way to Constantinople. He must have been extraordinarily hungry and thirsty, for he wolfed a large quantity of mushrooms, washing them down with generous draughts of wine. The next morning he was found dead in bed. Some said a severe attack of indigestion had killed him; others claimed that it was fumes from a charcoal heater – what we would recognize today as carbon monoxide poisoning. He had reigned for eight months.

It took ten days for the army to nominate a successor from among a choice of ambitious but illiterate soldiers. The one who was eventually acclaimed was Valentinian, an uncouth 42-year-old who had risen through the ranks from humble origins in what is now Hungary. Contemporaries described him as possessing a massive physique and commanding presence. He also had an unpredictable and violent temper and – what was distressingly frequent among such people – a streak of extreme cruelty. On 28 March he was crowned Valentinian I, with his younger brother Valens as co-Augustus. Valentinian set up his palace at Milan and administered the West, leaving Valens to rule the eastern part of the empire from Constantinople.

Valens, short, fat, bent-legged and cross-eyed, shared the brutal tendencies of his elder brother but none of his physical attributes or courage in the field. As a weak character he could be relied on to faithfully carry out his brother's wishes and much of the dirty work. To complete his unpopularity, Valens adhered to the Arian heresy. Yet time gave him no breathing-space, for in 365 the Persians again began troubling the eastern frontier, breaking the truce they had agreed with Jovian. Shapur II probably had no intention of sticking to the thirty-year peace treaty he had wrung out of Jovian, and with the death of the latter he sensed weakness in the Byzantine leadership. Valens set out to deal with the situation, but hardly had he ridden a few days than an incipient revolt at home called him back. One Procopius, a distant cousin of Julian (not to be confused with the better-known historian Procopius of a later time) who had been the one deputed to accompany Julian's body for burial in Tarsus, set himself up as the sole remaining survivor of the Flavian family to challenge Valens. The army rushed to Procopius' support; Valens fled to Ankyra, from where he sent a panicky message to his brother in the West to help. But Valentinian was already hard-pressed holding back barbarian pressures in Gaul and along the Rhine, and could do nothing.

Procopius' challenge was astonishingly short-lived. Somehow he managed to antagonize several influential supporters who, in the feverish political atmosphere of the capital, switched their allegiance back to Valens. Within a mere few weeks Procopius was hunted down and beheaded at Philippopolis (now Plovdiv), his head being sent to Valentinian as a present. Valens gave vent to his murderous revenge by massacring anyone of importance who could even have been suspected of favouring Procopius. That done, he spent the next few years pushing back troublesome Goths along the Danube, while his brother was similarly occupied in Gaul. In 367 the Picts and Scots invaded Britain, threatening major instability on the island. Valentinian sent in an able Spanish-born general named Theodosius, who within three years left Britain secure and relatively peaceful. Barely had Valentinian dealt with that sector than a sharp new threat emerged from what is now Hungary, where an aggressive local tribe accused the Romans of murdering their king and setting up forts in its territory. The tribe's protest letter to Valentinian may not have been a model of diplomacy, as when it was read to the emperor on 17 November 375, his blood pressure turned his face 'an alarming shade of purple' and he pitched forward, felled by a lethal stroke. Few were sorry to see him go.

Valentinian probably had not been in the best of health anyway. In 367 he had fallen seriously ill; worried that he might not survive, he nominated his son Gratian as Augustus to succeed him. After his stroke, in his final hours of consciousness, he called for his son by his second marriage, a boy of four also named Valentinian, and had him proclaimed co-Augustus with Gratian, who was away in Trier. Gratian, just 16, was thus placed in direct rivalry with the younger Valentinian. This left Valens as the senior Augustus for East and West. By the end of the 370s he had to face new enemies from the north – the Goths. Great numbers of this people had been displaced from their original homes in Scandinavia and sought sanctuary and a warmer climate in Eastern Europe and the Balkans. These were mostly Ostrogoths, or eastern Goths, who sought the emperor's permission to settle in safe lands in Thrace. Valens agreed, but hadn't counted on a venal local governor named Lupicinus who fleeced the newcomers mercilessly. Faced with starvation, the Goths rose up against Lupicinus, who was trounced in battle near the modern port of Varna in Bulgaria. This was the signal for the enraged Goths to move on the centre of the empire itself.

Through the winter of 378 it was touch and go, as the Roman-Byzantines only just held the Gothic waves surging towards Constantinople. In the spring Valens himself took the field, while Gratian agreed to bring another force from the west. Valens defeated a large Goth force at the Maritsa River but had to retire to Adrianople (modern Edirne) to deal with a Goth attempt to get around the rear. At Adrianople he received a message from Gratian suggesting that he wait for the promised reinforcements from the west. But Sebastian, Valens' general, talked Valens into at once attacking the 10,000 Goths besieging Adrianople. The outcome was a disaster for the Romans. Valens, according to one tradition, burned to death inside his blazing tent after being hit by an arrow. Sebastian and two-thirds of the Roman-Byzantine army also perished.

Gratian, still a year short of 20, had his own hands full in the west, so he sent a messenger to Spanish Galicia where he knew a capable officer was living quietly on his estate. This was Theodosius, the son of the Theodosius who had pacified Britain and had been executed by Valens for some obscure intrigue. Theodosius junior donned his armour, and put his military talents to use against the Goths in Thrace. Such was his success that in 379 a grateful Gratian elevated him to co-Augustus with his headquarters at Thessalonica. On 24 November of that year Theodosius rode in triumph into Constantinople, taking his place as the sixth effective emperor of Byzantium.[2]

Theodosius I (379–395)

The young Gratian's career went swiftly downhill, which was peculiarly tragic as he was intelligent and athletic, a good Christian and an unassuming character, a prodigious sportsman and a passable poet. He gave every promise of a long and accomplished reign in the Western Empire. Yet there were flaws in this golden image; while still in his early twenties he spent a little too much time on entertainments and – a fatal mistake for any military commander-in-chief – favoured some units of the army at the expense of others. Among the favoured was his personal corps of tall, blond Alani. Before he knew it, a Britain-based general named Magnus Clemens Maximus had proclaimed himself Augustus and was heading south across the English Channel.

Gratian's forces met Maximus north of Paris. The encounter was evenly matched until Gratian's Moorish cavalry corps switched sides and gave Maximus the decisive advantage. The reasons for the defection are not known; perhaps bribery was involved, or the dark-skinned Moors felt racially slighted by Gratian's preference for the Nordics. The fleeing Gratian was overtaken by Maximus' forces at Lugdunum (Lyon). He was promised a safe-conduct, but while having dinner with his captors he was murdered.

Theodosius, who had been four years on the Constantinople throne when Gratian was killed, was shocked at the news. But he could do little about it. As the Huns were pressing in from the north and the Persians from the east, the usurper Maximus had to be tolerated for the time being. While Maximus was in Trier, Gratian's 12-year-old half-brother Valentinian II held nominal power in Milan. The hapless boy was pulled in separate directions by his ambitious mother Justina and Bishop Ambrose, the leading clergyman of the Western Empire. Justina was an Arian, which triggered fears that a mature Valentinian would rule as a heretic. With a ready-made excuse to hand, Maximus invaded Italy. Valentinian and his mother fled east to Thessalonica, where Theodosius gave them refuge and planned his counterstroke.

Throughout history we meet leaders who, the chroniclers assure us, were prominent in every virtue – handsome, intelligent, brave in battle, devoutly religious and wise as administrators. Yet too often such paragons have a single yet major flaw – such is their overwhelming self-assurance and sense of rightness, combined with the Herculean task of keeping order in a far-flung domain, that their temper is hard to keep under control. Occasionally their patience snaps and they prove to be capable of appalling acts of cruelty. Such a man was Theodosius I. In June 388 he had disentangled himself from eastern concerns enough to move quickly up through what are now Serbia and Bosnia, taking Valentinian with him, to confront Maximus' forces on the Sava River. Morale in the army was high, as the troops forded the river – we are told, fully-armed – and sent Maximus reeling as far as North Italy, where the rebel surrendered. Theodosius and Valentinian moved on to Rome, where Theodosius received a warm welcome despite (or perhaps because of) his efforts to stamp out the last vestiges of paganism and establish Rome as a Christian city. Theodosius then retired to Milan and Valentinian took up his post in Gaul.

It was while Theodosius was in Milan that an incident occurred that was to try his patience beyond the breaking point and mar his otherwise bright reign with its only really black mark. For some time the people of Thessalonica had been chafing under a number of grievances, chief among them being the delinquency of billeted barbarian troops. The grievances erupted in violence in 390 when Botheric, the captain of the Thessalonica Imperial Guard, arrested a popular charioteer for an undefined 'gross immorality'. A modern analogy would be if, say, today a star footballer were jailed for not paying a traffic fine and the football club's more violent fans set fire to the police station. But the analogy is admittedly weak, and cannot adequately convey the seething social passions of the times. Botheric, an alien Goth, was unpopular at the best of times, so to no one's surprise rioters broke into his headquarters and slew him on the spot, tearing the body to bits and carrying those bloody bits around the streets in triumph.

It was probably this act of mob brutality, rather than the grievance itself, which aroused Theodosius to murderous fury. He was also influenced by a wealthy and unscrupulous Gallic lawyer named Rufinus, whose aim was ultimately to seize the throne. Without apparently thinking through his decision, he sent secret orders to punish the entire population of Thessalonica. In an act paralleled in modern times only by the Nazi reprisal massacres on occupied populations, the people were invited to the city hippodrome under the impression that they would enjoy some games; instead, the soldiers butchered some 7,000 men, women and children. By tragic irony, Theodosius had almost at once regretted his initial order and had sent a countermanding instruction, but it had arrived too late. Outrage rippled through the Roman world. Bishop Ambrose banned the emperor from attending Mass until he should publicly repent. In fact, when Theodosius tried to enter the cathedral at Milan, Ambrose personally barred the way. After some weeks of a standoff, the bishop won; Theodosius doffed his magnificent robes, put on a sackcloth, and humbly bare-headed, entered the church as a poor penitent and confessed his heinous sin, begging God to forgive him.

Was Theodosius truly repentant? The answer is probably yes, as most authorities agree that his massacre order was quite out of character. Was he influenced by his generals? Again, probably yes. We must also not discount his hot-blooded Spanish origins and impatience with any kind of insubordination or interference with well-ordered government. The emperor, duly forgiven and with a feeling of intense relief, returned to Constantinople, but his western troubles were not over, for Valentinian was proving to be not quite up to his task.

Valentinian II was still just 20 when the business of ruling from Gaul landed heavily on his shaky shoulders. During his absence in Constantinople and Milan, the Frankish chief of his militia, a boastful and arrogant man named Arbogast, had assumed de facto power. When in 392 Valentinian wrote to Arbogast to assert his own power, the Frank tore up the letter with haughty relish. A few days later Valentinian was found dead in his quarters. Foul play was at once suspected, but never proved; in fact, great pains were taken to show that the young Augustus had taken his own life. Whatever the truth, Arbogast's hand was strengthened, and he placed a pliable scholar named Eugenius on the Western throne. As Eugenius was strongly suspected of having pagan sympathies, in 394 Theodosius took the field against Arbogast and his puppet, to restore religious orthodoxy as well as political order.

At 49 the emperor was still relatively in his prime, but ill-health may have been plaguing him (and it's not unreasonable to suppose that it could have affected his judgement in the decision to massacre the Thessalonians). Moreover, his second wife Galla, whom he loved intensely, had just died in childbirth. Steeling his heart, with an able Vandal officer named Stilicho as his second-in-command plus 20,000 Goths in his army of about twice that number, Theodosius headed up through the Balkans to bring Arbogast and Eugenius to heel. Among the Goth officers was a brilliant young commander named Alaric. The Frankish strongman Arbogast duly moved out of Milan to meet him with an approximately equal force. Theodosius became suspicious when he found the eastern Alpine passes undefended and feared entrapment; but Arbogast apparently didn't want to risk mountain combat. On 5 September 394 the emperor came upon the enemy camp at a stream called the Frigidus (now the Vipacco), north of Trieste in what is now Slovenia.

Eugenius was in Arbogast's camp, a virtual puppet of the Frank, who now openly proclaimed his paganism by erecting a statue of Jupiter by the camp and emblazoning his men's shields with images of Herakles. Theodosius launched an attack at once, sending the Goths in first. They broke against Arbogast's sturdy Gallo-Roman defence, suffering heavy casualties. That evening Arbogast had the idea of sending a detachment to close off the mountain pass in the imperial rear, while Theodosius fretted through the night about what to do. The next morning the emperor reportedly received news that some of Arbogast's men intended to desert. This is difficult to understand, as soldiers generally don't abandon a winner. Theodosius himself prayed for divine aid, and the prayer seems to have been answered, as on the second day a violent easterly gale blew along the Frigidus Valley, hurling clouds of dust into the faces of Arbogast's troops and – if we are to credit some sources – whipping the troops' arrows back at them. At the height of the windstorm Theodosius charged, this time successfully. Eugenius was the first to be captured and brought cringing into Theodosius' presence. Eugenius' pleas for mercy were silenced by his head being lopped off. Arbogast wandered in the mountains for several days, but with the emperor's agents hot on his heels, took his own life.

In Milan, Theodosius wisely pardoned Eugenius' supporters. But by now he was becoming seriously ill. Barely 50, he bestowed the succession on his two sons, Arcadius and Honorius. The latter, just 10, made the arduous winter trip from Constantinople, arriving in Milan in mid-January 395. Theodosius revived enough to give the boy a joyous welcome and drag himself to watch the games in his son's honour. In the middle of the festivities Theodosius collapsed, and a few hours later he was dead. His body lay in state for forty days in the palace, then Bishop Ambrose delivered a funeral oration and sent off his old foe's body under heavy escort for burial in Constantinople.

Soon after his death, Theodosius I acquired the title 'The Great', which persists today. One could question that grand sobriquet, as his military exploits, though respectable, were no better or worse than a host of other leaders and generals. The justification, if there is any, lies rather in his peacetime record. In the sixteen years of his reign Theodosius consolidated the Byzantine state, fortified the capital and the borders, strengthened the army, reorganized the administration and the judiciary and above all enforced a uniform state Christianity that became the bedrock of the imperial ideology and the moral basis for Byzantine foreign policy for as long as the empire would last.

Arcadius (395–408) and Theodosius II (408–450)

During his reign Theodosius had not been unaware of a new threat that had recently washed over Asia and was by now ensconced in parts of Eastern Europe to the north-west of the empire. It was a branch of the western Mongols called the Hsiung-nu, which Europeans, shocked and awed by the fury of their irruption, shortened into a single terrifying syllable – Huns. Like a human tsunami this incredibly hardy tribe had begun its colossal westward surge from its origins somewhere to the north of the Aral Sea and Lake Balkash in central Asia. The reasons are still vague; perhaps unusual drought conditions forced the Hsiung-nu out of their pastoral homes, toughened them, and steered them towards the places where settled peoples were convenient targets.

The Huns first erupted into the Byzantine consciousness about 370, probably in the reign of Valens, when they had been in Russia for about twenty years and had displaced the Ostrogoths in Ukraine. Traders and travellers had brought back unflattering descriptions of an alien people of 'fearful swarthy aspect'. The Hun, they reported, had a 'shapeless lump instead of a head, and pinholes rather than eyes'.[3] Yet he was grudgingly admired at the same time for his horsemanship and prowess in war; young Hun boys were brought up with a Spartan grimness so that 'before they receive the nourishment of milk, they must learn to endure wounds'. They were taught to eat, sleep and fight in the saddle. The Romans and other Europeans marvelled that such short and thick-set types – almost a misshape of a human being – could turn out to be the most formidable warriors the world had yet seen.

Unlike the Goths and other 'barbarian' intruders on the fringes of the empire, the Huns were not in the business of mass ethnic migration. Their object was plunder, pure and simple. Gradual infiltration and long-term military occupation were not for them. The Hunnish army placed a premium on speed and physical endurance to deliver lightning knockout blows. The Hun soldiers were organized into clans, with each clan leader acting as the equivalent of a divisional commander. Each cavalryman was equipped with a javelin, composite bow and small wooden shield clad in leather. Some wore a metal or leather helmet. Higher ranks had a breastplate of chain mail and carried a sword in addition to their regular weaponry. Wealthier men could afford armoured horses, though these were not numerous.

Battle tactics were based on speed and surprise. A typical encounter might begin with a pelting charge on the enemy and simultaneous rain of arrows at short range. This would often be enough to send the enemy line reeling, but if the enemy fought back, the Huns would wheel for a disciplined withdrawal, firing their arrows all the way. At some point they would halt and harass the advancing enemy until he became disorganized, at which point the Huns would rally and charge again, this time successfully. When the Huns began to recruit large numbers of Germans in their ranks, tactics changed. German habits of wearing armour and carrying heavier shields and battleaxes, not to mention their heavily armoured horses, eventually resulted in the Huns trading speed for strength – a trade-off that would gradually weaken the Huns as a fearsome force.

The initial hammer-blows of the Huns had displaced the Goths from Northeast Europe. These Goths split into two main groups: the Ostrogoths (Eastern Goths) who moved into south Russia and Eastern Europe, and the Visigoths (Western Goths) who surged into Central Europe and eventually made Spain their stronghold. These Goths in turn bumped up against other barbarian European peoples such as the Germans, Franks, Lombards, Alani and Vandals (to name just the largest) who in turn were pushed to seek refuge in the hospitable Southern European lands of the Romans and Byzantines. The pressures and tensions caused by this long, drawn-out process, and the resulting fluidity of ethnic and cultural boundaries in Eastern and Southern Europe, were the cause of Byzantium's wars for at least two centuries.

Valens had initially allowed the hunted Goths to settle in what are now Romania, Bulgaria and north-east Greece, but he had done nothing to alleviate their sufferings at the hands of corrupt and rapacious Byzantine tax collectors. As we have seen, he paid for this neglect by his sticky end at Adrianople. Theodosius was smarter; recognizing that the Goths could be a formidable fighting force, he redressed their grievances and organized them into what became known as the *foederati*, meaning roughly an allied corps which, however, was under the emperor's direct command. The Goths, who appear to have wanted little more than to live in peace, free from both the Hun threat and venal Roman officials, appreciated the gesture. A mere two years after Adrianople, they were flourishing in their new homes, eager servicemen in the Byzantine cause.

Several very capable men emerged from the ranks of the Gothic *foederati*. One of them, Alaric, had risen in the ranks from a young age and acquitted himself well in the battle of the Frigidus. Another veteran of the Frigidus was Stilicho, a Vandal whose commanding presence and long military experience were supplemented by diplomatic experience as a Byzantine envoy to Persia. By marrying strategically into the imperial family Stilicho positioned himself to be named *magister militum*, or commander-in-chief, in Italy where he could run the show in Milan behind the façade of the weak Augustus Honorius.

Arcadius, who inherited the eastern throne in Constantinople, was far from being emperor material. All of 18 at the time of his accession, he was slow-witted and apparently characterless – yet another instance, in a history that's filled with them, of a son conspicuously devoid of his father's talents. The usual explanation can be offered, such as his and his brother's upbringing in a sheltered and affluent environment. But in Arcadius' case the incapacity seems to have been congenital. To those who dealt with him he had a disconcerting habit of often closing his heavy-lidded eyes as if about to go to sleep. Of course, there was no lack of powerful men at court who tried to dominate both emperor and state. One was Rufinus, suspected of involvement in the Thessalonica massacre and himself angling for the throne. Another was Eutropius, an old eunuch with 'an egg-bald head and wrinkled yellow face,' who was the Superintendent of the Sacred Bedchamber (a sort of high chamberlain) and quite as corrupt and unscrupulous as Rufinus.[4]

The two men's deadly rivalry focused on who would provide a bride for the emperor. Rufinus wanted his own daughter as empress, while Eutropius' candidate was Eudoxia, the pretty daughter of a German general, who had grown up in Constantinople. As Eutropius was in the habit, writes the historian Zosimus, of 'leading Arcadius like a sheep,' he had little trouble in getting Eudoxia into the emperor's presence first. Arcadius appears to have been smitten. On 27 April 395, three months after Theodosius' death, they were married in full view of the adoring populace of Constantinople. But at this point Arcadius' nuptial concerns were distracted by a new and unexpected military threat.

The immediate cause was the ambition of Alaric, who deeply resented the elevation of Stilicho to *magister militum* of the Western empire, wanting the post for himself. As such he schemed to take Constantinople, as the city's defences were weakened by the absence of the bulk of the imperial army in Milan. Alaric's missed promotion provided the excuse he needed, and before long his forces were almost within sight of Constantinople's walls; Rufinus, disguised as a Goth, paid a few clandestine visits to Alaric and could well have bribed him to withdraw. At the same time Arcadius, who might not have been as stupid as he looked, messaged Stilicho to send the imperial forces back from Milan post-haste. Stilicho complied, but when he got to Northern Greece, instead of proceeding to Constantinople he veered south to confront Alaric. A second imperial message ordered him back to Italy.

This left Alaric free to ravage Greece, which he did with a thoroughness intensified by the fanaticism of Arian Christian monks in his entourage who wanted to eradicate all traces of Greece's glorious but pagan past. Alaric's Goths surged through the famous pass at Thermopylai, where Spartan King Leonidas I had fought to the death nearly 900 years before. Athens was spared destruction only because Alaric was wined and dined (and perhaps heavily bribed) by the local imperial garrison and not, as some chroniclers fancied, because Alaric quailed at the vision of the scowling goddess Athene and the ghost of Achilleus defending the Acropolis. Stilicho returned to Greece with a fresh imperial force and in spring 396 he laid a trap for Alaric at the Pholoe heights near ancient Olympia. But just as the trap was about to be sprung, Stilicho let Alaric go. The reason remains a mystery. It was rumoured that the order came from Arcadius, who wanted Alaric as *magister militum* of the Balkans. Whatever actually happened, Alaric slipped back into Italy to fight another day.

On 27 November the imperial force under the Goth Gainas marched home through the Golden Gate, to be ceremoniously welcomed by Arcadius in person. Joining the emperor was the strutting Rufinus, basking in his achievement of having bribed Alaric away on his first approach to the city. We are told that Rufinus mingled cordially with the officers and men, apparently cultivating support for an attempt at the throne. If that was the case, it was a tragic miscalculation. What Rufinus mistook for sociability was in fact a deadly snare. As he was chatting with some soldiers, swords were drawn and in a moment he was dead. Rufinus' right wrist was hacked off and paraded around the city; Zosimus reports that those who carried the hand pulled playfully at the exposed tendons so that the fingers opened and closed – a grisly reference to Rufinus' well-known rapaciousness.

No one knows who, if anyone, ordered the murder of Rufinus, but the main beneficiary was undoubtedly his bitter rival Eutropius, who could now rule the sheepy emperor unhindered while presiding over a regime of untrammelled corruption. In 399 he got himself appointed consul, an exalted office surviving from the Roman republic and second only to the emperor himself. The Byzantines themselves resented Eutropius as a jumped-up ex-slave and eunuch at that, but Arcadius was in his thrall. Not so Eudoxia, who had a personality rather stronger than her husband's and was determined to break Eutropius' hold over him. This was not out of any love for Arcadius; she in fact despised him as unmanly and sought satisfaction in ill-concealed sexual adventures elsewhere. By 400 the marriage had broken down completely. Eutropius was eventually arrested and exiled to Cyprus, then brought back, tried and executed. The general Gainas toyed with the idea of seizing the throne, but gave up the idea when he saw the state of public opinion. It was when his Gothic troops were on the point of leaving Constantinople one evening that the people thought they were assembling in the streets for a coup. Some hotheads in the crowd barred the gates, and a hostile demonstration soon turned into an all-night massacre; by morning thousands of Goths lay dead, many burned alive in a church where they had sought sanctuary. The fleeing Gainas ended up a captive of the Hun king Uldin, who sent the general's head to Arcadius.

Arcadius died in 408, at the age of 31. The cause is not known, though foul play has never been suggested; he may have had a weak constitution that succumbed quickly to illness. In his last years he was fortunate enough to have a wise and competent politician named Athemius as praetorian prefect who calmed the crisis atmosphere that had gripped the empire. Anthemius' foreign policy priority was to improve relations with both the alienated Western empire and the Persians. He sent expeditions to hold back the Huns and Germans from the Danube and set up naval patrols along the river. Yet competent though he was, he had to reckon with Alaric, who at a mere 30 had already accumulated an ordinary soldier's lifetime of military experience. He accepted the imperial appointment of *magister militum* as a stepping-stone to hoped-for rule of the Western Empire. Honorius, the Augustus there, was proving to be as useless as his younger brother in Constantinople. In early 402 Alaric's formidable Visigothic force, including the soldiers' families, rolled down the Isonzo River Valley into North Italy. While settling his people on secure land in a warm climate, Alaric made plans to bring the West Roman empire under his heel. Honorius panicked. It was anxiously whispered that while he was reviewing his cavalry a couple of wolves darted beneath his horse; when the wolves were killed, human hands were found in their stomachs. As Alaric approached Milan, Honorius fled west to Asti but Stilicho drew up his defending force to meet Alaric at Pollentia. The battle was long and bloody, ending in Alaric's retreat. He was worsted again by Stilicho a few days later at Verona, but yet again allowed to escape.

The empress Eudoxia, meanwhile, had not been making herself very popular in Byzantium. The saintly patriarch of Constantinople, John Chrysostom, condemned her dissolute ways and was deposed and exiled for his pains. But in 404 she died while miscarrying her child. Arcadius followed her to the grave four years later, giving Stilicho a gateway to supreme power in the East and West. But a Vandal wearing the imperial purple was unthinkable to many of the empire's subjects. Stilicho was respected, but not popular. He may have given voice to his ultimate ambition incautiously, as in August 408 Honorius had him tried for treason and executed. What followed was a savage purge of the Gothic and Hunnish units in the Roman army; those who escaped fled to Alaric who gathered up about 30,000 of them, all burning with revenge against the Romans. In November Alaric appeared at the walls of Rome and besieged the city. As the Roman populace starved, Honorius remained unmoved in his new palace at Ravenna in the north. Relief came when the Romans bought off Alaric with a massive ransom that absorbed almost all the city's moveable wealth. When the Roman nobles complained of being thus fleeced, Alaric told them they were lucky to escape with their lives.

Honorius foolishly rejected Alaric's overtures of peace, to be unceremoniously deposed and replaced by a provisional Augustus, a Greek named Priscus Attalus. Honorius and his court were about to sail to Constantinople when six legions of Byzantine troops, totalling about 40,000 men, landed to support him. They had been sent by his young nephew Theodosius II (of whom more below) and revived Honorius' spirits considerably. Alaric in revenge sacked Rome brutally in the summer of 410 – the first time the Caput Mundi had fallen to an external foe in 800 years. Weeks later, Alaric sickened and died. Slaves were sent to divert the Busento River near Cosenza, bury him beneath the riverbed and set the river back on its course. After the burial the slaves were put to death so that no one would know Alaric's last resting-place, a mystery that has endured to this day. Alaric was succeeded by his brother-in-law Ataulf, who agreed to withdraw the Gothic army on condition that he marry Honorius' half-sister Galla Placidia. She, a daughter of Theodosius I and hence of royal lineage, was eager enough to make the match. In 414 she and her beloved Ataulf set up court in Gaul, though their married bliss was brief as he was assassinated the following year. But the empire had not heard the last of Galla Placidia.

Theodosius II was 7 when he succeeded his father Arcadius in 408. But any hopes that the boy would have some of the stern stuff of his grandfather and namesake were quickly dashed when it became apparent that, though he was highly intelligent and personable, his talents lay in fields far removed from leadership and statecraft. Until he was 13 he was under the tutelage of the praetorian prefect Anthemius; during that time, by one of the ironies of history, Theodosius' name was given to a new and powerful defensive wall for Constantinople for which Anthemius was actually responsible. The Theodosian Wall is still visible, running from the Golden Gate (now

Yedikule) to about midway up the Golden Horn (approximately where the Çevre Yolu motorway crosses it), battered and ravaged by time and war, its reddish battlements and buttresses separating inner Istanbul from the western suburbs.

While Theodosius was being brought up in the security of the palace, indulging his interests in sport, literature and penmanship – he was known affectionately, if a little condescendingly, as Kalligraphos, the Calligrapher – Anthemius took firm hold of the reins of diplomacy and military strategy.[5] In 413, as work began on the wall, he renewed a peace treaty with Persia and reinforced the Danube fleet. Uldin, the Hun king, had recently attacked the frontier and had been beaten off, but only just. But Anthemius hadn't reckoned on a particularly ambitious member of the royal family who decided a year later that the family needed to reassert its right to take charge. This was Theodosius' younger sister Pulcheria, who at a mere 15 years of age but with a resolve of someone at least twice as old, sidelined Anthemius and got herself proclaimed Augusta, leaving her mild-mannered teenaged brother to enjoy his nature walks and calligraphy.

Pulcheria had little trouble ruling the emperor and her two younger sisters, and for a few years the palace resembled a cloister as she insisted on strict chastity for all, and a strict regimen of prayers and devotions. Theodosius was exempt from the no-sex rule, as he was, after all, the emperor and had to procreate sooner rather than later. In 420 he began to feel the desire for a wife, and asked his powerful Augusta sister to find him one. She had not far to look, as an Athenian woman of exceptional appearance and attainments had recently arrived in Constantinople. This was Athenais, the daughter of a philosopher named Leontios; she seems to have been swindled out of her inheritance by her two brothers and had come to the seat of the empire to seek redress. Athenais combined looks and brains to an exquisite degree, and Pulcheria made sure she was presented at court. Theodosius had already considered and rejected several candidates for his hand and bed, but when he saw Athenais and had a chance to converse with her in pure classical Greek, his heart was won over. After Athenais was baptized a Christian (and given the official name Eudocia as Athenais was considered too pagan-flavoured), she and Theodosius were married in June 421.

A year later Athenais had a daughter whom she named Eudoxia. Athenais adapted to Christianity exceptionally well – perhaps her philosophical background helped here – and was to remain devout for the rest of her life. In 423 she was elevated to the rank of Augusta, on the same plane as Pulcheria, who about this time began to wonder if her protégé had not become her rival. Theodosius and his court idolized Athenais, and so few were surprised when Pulcheria began to scheme to bring the glamorous Athenian lady down a peg or two.

Theodosius was not totally oblivious to the demands of the state. In 410 Anthemius had sent 40,000 troops to relieve his uncle Honorius at Ravenna, enabling the western emperor to resist Alaric. Theodosius was just nine at the time, but surely will have been told of what was happening in his name. Galla Placidia, after losing her husband Ataulf, had been remarried to a rather obtuse soldier only to be widowed a second time. Honorius declined into violent semi-madness, forcing her and her two children to seek refuge in Constantinople.

Pulcheria almost certainly pushed Theodosius into acting swiftly to save what could be saved of the Western Empire. First he appointed Galla Placidia Augusta of the west, with her 4-year-old son Valentinian as Caesar, then prepared an army and personally led it as far as Thessalonica – perhaps the only time the tender Theodosius ever actually went on campaign. In 425 the Byzantine army took Ravenna with minimal casualties thanks to an audacious assault across a defensive lagoon. Galla Placidia's son, now 6, was taken to Rome to be crowned as Valentinian III. But by now the attention of Theodosius and his generals was wrenched away from Italy by a renewed threat from the Huns.

The Hun kingdom had been paralysed by civil strife until about 420, when their King Rua pulled the realm together and unsuccessfully assaulted the empire's northern borders on the grounds that Theodosius had been sheltering opponents of Rua's regime. After Rua's death in 434 the Hun leadership devolved on his two nephews, Bleda and Attila, who renewed the attacks on Byzantium on a much larger scale, driving deep into Thrace and intimidating the unwarlike Theodosius into giving up the dissidents plus an annual tribute of gold that would buy trade benefits. Theodosius reneged on the deal after two years. Perhaps he was aware that plague had broken out in the Hunnish army and that Bleda and Attila were embroiled in wars on other fronts. It was 441 before Bleda and Attila were again ready to measure swords with the Byzantines. They had beefed up their ranks with Germans and East Europeans who supplied the heavy-armed infantry and cavalry contingents. They had also, thanks to past brushes with the Byzantines, polished their knowledge of siege warfare. Regional shifts in power also favoured the Huns. The Vandals had swept over North Africa, sending pirates to harry imperial shipping and forcing the Western Empire to weaken its northern defences. The Persians had never ceased being a potential threat in the east, using any excuse to renew hostilities. Bleda and Attila surged across the Danube, sweeping aside the Byzantine naval patrols and penetrating deep into the Balkans. At Viminacium (near present-day Kastolac in Serbia), Attila wiped out the defenders, levelling the town. Singidum and Sirmium fell in quick succession.

The government in Constantinople was shaken, but placed a great deal of faith in the massive Theodosian Wall. Theodosius himself decided on the sordid but well-tried tactic of bribery. Attila, whose appetite was for battle rather than what might be called regime change, accepted the emperor's peace feelers – sweetened with generous donations of money and gifts – and agreed to a one-year truce. With this Theodosius was able to buy time to recall the reinforcements he had sent to the Western Empire to fight the Vandals. When the truce year was up, Attila demanded to know what would happen. Theodosius – certainly on the advice of others and perhaps Pulcheria who cattily cast asperions on his manhood – refused to hand over what remained of the Hunnish dissidents who sought sanctuary in Constantinople, yet professed himself eager to keep up negotiations. Infuriated by this duplicity, or perhaps glad of a pretext to renew the war, Attila once more set his hordes in motion.

The Hun leader was approaching 50, which at that time, and in his race, was near the end of his useful military life. Some accounts claim that Attila got his first experience of Southern European civilization (and climate) when he was sent to Rome aged twelve as a hostage for good behaviour by his uncle Rua, and stayed there for nearly twenty years until called to rule with his brother Bleda. His expeditions into the Balkans had earned him the oft-quoted sobriquet 'Scourge of God', an image which he cultivated for maximum intimidating effect. He may well have believed that he represented divine vengeance for the many sins of the Romans and Byzantines. Be that as it may, the reputation was enough for Theodosius and his court this time to seriously panic as Sardica (modern Sofia) and Philippopolis (Plovdiv) fell to the Hun. Theodosius considered fleeing across the Bosporus.

But the expected blow on Constantinople didn't come. Siege warfare against powerful walls was not the Huns' strong point. Instead, Attila diverted his army into the Gallipoli peninsula to deal with a Byzantine garrison stationed there. The diversion gave Theodosius time to consider another deal, but a far more humiliating one than any that had gone before: to give up all dissident Huns in the empire plus 6,000 pounds of gold, to be topped up each year by 2,100 pounds in tribute. Some dissidents refused to be handed over, knowing what kind of death would await them at Attila's hands and asking to be put to a swift end by the Byzantines as the lesser evil; several were thus obliged. Pacified by the gold, Attila retired beyond the Danube and began thinking of setting up a stable kingdom in Eastern Europe.

Theodosius foolishly allowed himself to endorse a plot to assassinate the Scourge of God by way of a Byzantine mission to Attila's court. Attila quickly got wind of the plot and did away with the would-be assassins, but received the mission itself with great cordiality. The Greeks watched in wonder as, according to Priscus, Attila insisted on eating off a rough wooden platter while the others used silver.

> Gold and silver goblets were handed to the men at the feast, whereas his cup was of wood. His clothing was plain, and differed not at all from that of the rest, except that it was clean.[6]

No jewels or other ornaments adorned either Attila's sword or his horse. The contrast with the sumptuous Byzantines could not have been better shown up.

Marcian (450–457), Leo I (457–474) and Leo II (474)

Theodosius' long but ineffectual reign was brought to an abrupt close in 450, when he was 49, by that common cause of untimely royal demise, a hunting accident. He had recently experienced a humiliation when his teenage cousin Honoria proposed marriage to none other than Attila, probably out of nothing more than rebellion against Pulcheria's suffocating tutelage; Honoria went so far as to send the Hun her ring, but he brushed away the offer with contempt – he had all the women he wanted, and Greco-Roman maidens may not have been his type. Pulcheria was still influential, but at the cost of alienating the accomplished Athenais, who went to live a life of pious and charitable works in Jerusalem, where she ended her days.

As Theodosius had left no male heir, Pulcheria moved quickly to furnish one by marrying a senator and ex-officer named Marcian who, as the Augusta's husband, by rights became the emperor. The marriage was probably a paper one only, but Marcian's accession was important in that it was the first time a Byzantine emperor received the royal diadem from the Patriarch of Constantinople. This began a precedent that was to vastly increase the power of the church over imperial affairs. At 58, Marcian was experienced in the field, having been captured by the Vandals in 441. Thanks to his noble bearing, the Vandal Chief Gaiseric had let him go. With Pulcheria seconding him, Marcian cleaned up the public administration and lowered taxes on the less well-off. He gradually eased out some of the foreign mercenaries in the Byzantine army, replacing them with his own Greeks and Romans. Taking advantage of Attila's preoccupation with a new attack on the West, Marcian took a calculated risk in cutting off the tribute to the Hun while beefing up the frontier defences including the Danube naval patrols. He wouldn't have needed them, as Attila met his match at a ferocious encounter deep inside France on the Mauritian Plain (Méry-sur-Seine) in 451, whipped back by a force of Franks, Bretons, Burgundians and Visigoths under the Roman general Aëtius. After the battle some 160,000 men, if we are to believe the chroniclers of the time, lay dead on the field.[7]

The year 453 saw two key deaths. Pulcheria ended her days, a single-minded servant of the state till the last, leaving a grieving Marcian to deal with an untimely outbreak of those religious controversies which were to regularly dissipate a great deal of the emperors' energy for many centuries. As for Attila the Hun, after being dissuaded by Pope Leo I from invading Italy anew, he retired to Pannonia to mull over whether he should accept Honoria's proposal of marriage, which presumably still stood. Meanwhile, other young brides were available to satisfy this sexagenarian warlord. He took one of them to bed in his tent one night and was found dead in the morning. The diagnosis was that he choked on his own blood when his erotic exertions, exacerbated by an evening of overeating and heavy drinking, broke a blood vessel.

Marcian himself died in 457. This provided the chance for the German born commander-in-chief in the east, the general Aspar, to seize the imperial throne and perhaps even start a new dynasty. With Attila dead, the Huns had ceased to become a threat. As Aspar sensed that an outright grab for the throne might be unseemly, he hand-picked a Thracian chiliarch named Leo out of the army to be ceremoniously raised on the army's shields as emperor while he, Aspar, ruled behind the scenes.[8] But if Aspar imagined that Leo would be a pushover, he was badly mistaken. Leo I turned out to have a stubborn mind of his own. Short on book-learning but long on hard experience, he was what the empire needed after the bookish Theodosius II and brief interlude of Marcian. He lost no time in sidelining Aspar and his Germans in favour of the tough Isaurians, a battle-happy tribe from what is now Southeast Turkey. Employing all the tricks of palace intrigue and partisan politics, Aspar fought back. His main ally was Leo's brother-in-law Basiliscus, an educated Greco-Roman who thought a great deal of himself.

Aspar's downfall came from an unexpected source which so far had not been a serious player in Byzantine power – the navy. In 468 Leo was talked into launching an attack on the Vandal kingdom in South Italy and North Africa. The Vandal king Gaiseric was persecuting orthodox Christians in North Africa, which was a prime source of wheat and therefore not to be risked. Procopius, our main source for this and later campaigns (and a participant in this one), writes that Basiliscus led up to 100,000 men in 1,000 ships to smite Gaiseric at Carthage. The force was massive for its time – but its commander was nowhere near up to the job of leading it. Basiliscus, landing near what is now Cape Bon, the northeast tip of Tunisia, unaccountably failed to move on Carthage even as Heraclius, a general, was leading another Byzantine force towards the city from the southeast. Basiliscus naively fell for a ruse of Gaiseric, who duped him into believing that the Vandals would submit; instead, the Vandal war fleet loosed a chain of fireships on the Byzantine vessels. The Byzantines had little chance; Basiliscus himself fled early in the encounter. He managed to slink into Constantinople hoping to remain unobserved, but he was soon detected and fled to the altar of Sancta Sophia for dear life. He was saved from execution only through the influence of his sister the empress.

This did not reflect well on Aspar, who tried to mend his relations with Leo. At the same time, however, Aspar's eldest son Ardabur was enmeshed in a plot to lure the Isaurians away from Leo's influence. In late 471 Leo's patience snapped. 'One morning in the imperial palace,' writes Lord Norwich, 'his guards suddenly drew their swords and cut down both Aspar and Ardabur.' The deed earned the emperor the dubious sobriquet of Macelles – butcher – and indeed Leo's harsh methods did not endear him to the more sensitive of his subjects, but all agree that he was firm and fair. When he died in February 474, he left behind an empire strengthened.

Leo may have been ill in his final months; we know that he arranged for his 7-year-old grandson Leo, the child of his daughter Ariadne and son-in-law Zeno, to succeed him. Ariadne persuaded her father to crown the boy co-emperor. After Leo I's death the boy emperor Leo II lived a mere nine months before he, too, went to join his ancestors. For such an untimely death the rumour mill, of course, worked overtime. Suspicion centred on Ariadne who supposedly wanted nothing in the way of her husband Zeno's accession to the throne. It is a reasonable supposition, though on the other hand, child mortality in the fifth century spared no class, high or low, and so the verdict must remain open.

Zeno (474–491, including Basiliscus, 475–6), Anastasius I (491–518) and Justin I (518–527)

Europe in the year 475 was in a state of often violent flux and restructuring. The old Roman Empire as the world had known it for nearly half a millennium was reduced to a faintly flickering flame that needed only a gust of wind to sputter out. The Eastern Empire based on Constantinople was now bearing aloft the Roman torch and the Christian culture that went with it. The rest of Europe seethed with tribes, some Christian, some not; Germans and Goths, Vandals and Franks, Angles and Saxons and a host of others began to coagulate in lands that would later form distinct nations.

The last Roman legions had pulled out of Britain early in the fifth century in order to defend Italy against the Ostrogoth and Hun invaders. The resulting vacuum was soon filled by incursions of Angles, Saxons and Jutes who drove back the Romanized Celts in what one authority has called 'the most thorough and complete conquest made by any barbarian nation'.[9] At the same time the Franks consolidated their ownership of Roman Gaul. While these embryonic national movements were presaging a new ethnic order in Europe, in Italy the Ostrogoths delivered the death blow to what remained of the Western Roman empire, which had been in steep decline for decades.

After a period of uncertainty following the death of Honorius in 423, the army placed 6-year-old Valentinian III, the son of Placidia and her second husband Constantius, on the throne. The effective ruler for the next quarter of a century, however, was Placidia. Yet Rome was tottering under constant assaults by Goths and Huns. Valentinian himself was widely disliked, and one morning as he rode out of Rome for a bit of archery practice a couple of soldiers stabbed him to death. His widow called in Gaiseric from Carthage to rid Italy of its foes. The Vandals obliged, but instead of setting Italy on the right path they methodically looted Rome of all its remaining wealth and shipped it off to Carthage. In the wake of that disaster a German warlord named Ricimer took over the running of the rump Western Empire, appointing eight successive puppet emperors as figureheads in Rome. The last of them was a young boy named Romulus, the son of the army commander Orestes who had toppled the seventh puppet and wielded real power. But the Gothic mercenaries in the Western Roman army were getting impatient. Under a senior officer named Odoacer they demanded nothing less than one-third of all Italy, including the same proportion of all Italian-owned property. Orestes flatly refused and was murdered.

It's hard not to sense the supreme historical irony in perceiving that there have been only two Romuli in history, and that they should have stood like bookends at the birth and death of old Rome. And whereas legend endowed the first Romulus with near-godlike powers, the precise opposite is true of the last. Orestes' son, surrounded by enemies in the palace at Ravenna, was as frightened and helpless a little boy as any could be. There was no lack of ambitious and ruthless men who would have little compunction in putting the lad to death, but Odoacer was not totally devoid of human feeling. Taking Romulus aside, he quietly told him to abdicate and sent him off to live on a generous pension with his relatives outside Rome. The boy needed little prompting. And so on 4 September 476 the last true Roman emperor stood down, leaving an imperial power vacuum in Italy.[10]

When Odoacer sent little Romulus packing, Zeno had been emperor in Constantinople for two years. Despite an eventful seventeen-year reign, our knowledge of him is fragmentary. An Isaurian by origin, his real name was Tarasis of Rusumblada; he had positioned himself for the throne by marrying Leo I's eldest daughter Ariadne. Tarasis had earned Leo's gratitude by supporting him against Aspar and the Germans. Though the Isaurians were valued as good fighters, Tarasis felt that his position in court required him to be somehow more Greek, and so changed his name to Zeno, after a fifth century BC philosopher. A competent Goth-fighter, he was lucky enough not to be a part of Basiliscus' debacle at Carthage. A jealous Aspar tried to do away with him, but he fled to Antioch, where he stayed for two years as commander-in-chief of the east (*magister militum per Orientem*), and dabbled in religious issues as a sideline.

When the 7-year-old Leo II died, his father Zeno, as official co-emperor, became emperor – perhaps the only royal succession in history where the father followed the son and not the other way round. From the outset of his reign Zeno's plate was full, mostly of domestic problems. The main foreign issue was not so much the implosion of the Western Empire – though that, of course, was a real concern – than on what to do about the Vandals who were posing a naval threat in the Mediterranean. Realizing that his options were extremely limited, he sent envoys to make peace, and such were their skills in the diplomatic tactic of bribery that Gaiseric agreed to repatriate his Byzantine prisoners.

At home Zeno was the target of continuous and complex conspiracies. His rivals included a newly-energized Basiliscus and the lover of Leo I's widow, a senior palace official. Zeno became so nervous that one day he jumped up from his seat at the Hippodrome and fled Constantinople that same night for his native Isauria. Basiliscus usurped the throne to inaugurate a period of utter misrule that was mercifully brief. He ordered a slaughter of the crack Isaurian troops in Constantinople, slapped onerous taxes on the people, assassinated those whom he distrusted, and meddled so catastrophically in church affairs that the clergy draped the altar of Sancta Sophia in black. We are told that it took a brave and saintly hermit who had lived on top of a pillar for fifteen years, Daniel the Stylite, to get down from his perch and personally browbeat Basiliscus into revoking his unpopular church policies. (Daniel then climbed back up his pillar, where he remained for eighteen more years.)

The situation was too bad to last. In 476, the same year in which Romulus Augustulus was removed, an unexplained fire destroyed Constantinople's great public library plus a collection of ancient Greek treasures. Basiliscus appointed his nephew, a notorious dandy-about-town named Harmatius, as head of the army (*magister militum*). After mincing about town dressed up as the Homeric hero Achilleus, he led the army against Zeno who was holed up in the hills of Isauria. Zeno easily talked the weak-willed fop into joining him by promising him the job of praetorian prefect. As Zeno re-entered Constantinople in July 477, Basiliscus fled again to Sancta Sophia; again he escaped the sword of punishment, but he was exiled to Cappadocia and died of cold and hunger after being holed up in a cistern.

Back in his palace, Zeno turned his attention to events in Italy. When Odoacer toppled the last Western Roman emperor he ordered the Senate to send Zeno the imperial insignia as a sign that he would recognize only one Roman emperor, the one in Constantinople. Zeno, of course, was perfectly happy to agree, confirming Odoacer as Governor of Italy and restoring the unity of the empire. Zeno also fobbed off at least one pretender to the Roman throne by diplomacy. In 479, however, Zeno's Roman brother-in-law Marcianus, sidelined by Odoacer, launched a bid for the throne of Constantinople. He put together a secret fifth column in the heart of the capital and moved on the palace and on the house of an Isaurian general named Illus, one of the emperor's trusted senior soldiers. They came very close to success. Zeno himself had never been very popular, and the attackers were joined by ordinary citizens who pelted the imperial troops with stones from their housetops. But that night Illus brought in an Isaurian detachment and is believed to have bought off many of the rebels. Zeno escaped capture, while Marcianus fled to the Church of the Holy Apostles. When Marcianus' expected Gothic reinforcements failed to arrive, he was arrested and exiled to a distant monastery.

It would appear that Illus had earned the undying gratitude of the emperor, but instead Zeno became deeply suspicious of him. The dowager empress and widow of Leo I, Verina, seems to have played a murky role here, trying to play both men off against each other. There is evidence that Zeno connived at an unsuccessful plot to kill Illus, who fled eastwards and raised the standard of revolt in 484. An army sent against Illus by Zeno was defeated. A second punitive expedition was rather more successful, but its leader, an Ostrogoth named John the Hunchback, required four years to finally reduce Illus' resistance in the Fort of Papurius near Seleucia. Zeno soon had the grim pleasure of receiving Illus' head as a present.

How far Zeno determined military policy, and whether he ever took part in military operations himself, remains unclear. Zeno's problems with the Goths were more or less concurrent with his domestic woes. When a new leader of the Ostrogoths named Theodoric arose to contest Odoacer's control of Italy, Zeno saw in him an opportunity to get rid of Odoacer who had become too powerful. As a young hostage in Constantinople for ten years, Theodoric had received a thorough Greek and Latin education. Setting up his headquarters in Ravenna, he became renowned for his justice and fairness, his cultivation of arts and letters, and his revival of agriculture. Zeno also needed Theodoric to contain another Theodoric (named the Cross-eyed) who was threatening the Eastern Empire in the Balkans. After a confusing game of diplomatic and military chess, when no one – perhaps not even Zeno – knew who was friend or foe, Theodoric the Cross-eyed ended up advancing on Constantinople. But his army's heart wasn't in it, and the Cross-eyed had to turn back, dying in an accident soon afterwards.

Theodoric's ultimate aim was simple enough: like Alaric before him, he wished to find and keep a secure home for his Ostrogoth people. This explains the kaleidoscopic series of alliances and broken agreements and confusing relations with Byzantium that marked his career. He manoeuvred for advantage at every stage, and by 490 was well on the way to becoming master of Italy while Zeno looked on approvingly from the East. But the strain of years of crisis was telling on the emperor. In addition to the troubles with Basiliscus, Illus and the Goths, he had to go to Palestine to suppress a revolt by the Jewish Samaritans in 484. Jewish sources say Zeno ordered the Samaritans to convert to Christianity and executed many of them when they refused. Samaritan rebels under Justa struck back in 484, to be overcome by Zeno's local commander Asclepiades. Justa's head was the third such prize which Zeno had the privilege of receiving in the mail.

By 491 Zeno was quite ill. He was uncomfortably aware that he had no sons to succeed him; after little Leo II, his other son had died in adolescence of a lifestyle typified by overindulgence in pleasures of the flesh. His nearest kin, his brother Longinus, was not a man to inspire confidence. Zeno himself was universally unpopular; Byzantine public opinion unfairly blamed him for the loss of the Western Empire. His reputation worsened when he had an alleged conspirator strangled on the mere basis of a soothsayer's prophecy. In his few hours of leisure he would play a form of backgammon, in which he was extraordinarily unlucky. On 9 April he died, possibly of an attack of dysentery or epilepsy. One gruesome tradition records that he passed out after a heavy drinking bout and was believed dead; he recovered after being put in his coffin, but his wife Ariadne ignored his cries to be let out and he was thus consigned to the tomb. One can scarcely get less popular than that.[11]

The empress Ariadne, more in touch with popular opinion than her late unlamented husband, knew that the immediate issue would be the succession, as Zeno had left no living sons. There was his brother Longinus, but he seems to have been a lightweight, not to be taken seriously. Ariadne's favour quickly fell upon a senior member of the Corps of Silentiaries, whose job, as the name implies, was to stand guard outside the imperial living quarters and ensure that the imperial couple had a peaceful slumber. There were thirty Silentiaries, men of the highest cultural and moral calibre, who also had important secretarial and recording duties. Ariadne's choice was Flavius Anastasius, born in what is now Albania and already over 60 at the time. Anastasius had the long fair hair of the East European, while one of his eyes was brown and the other blue, a feature that may have added to his charm. More importantly from the people's point of view, his religious orthodoxy was flawless. Moreover, he had a reputation as an upright man on whom no scandal could be pinned. 'Give us a Roman orthodox emperor!' the crowd had shouted at Ariadne when she appeared in the streets. They had never warmed to the Asian heretic Zeno. Six weeks after Anastasius' accession, Ariadne set the seal on the deal by marrying him.

But if the people thought they had a crowd-pleaser in the palace, they were mistaken. The first concern of Anastasius I was to put the state finances in order, which involved savage cost-cutting in all sectors. Public morals were tightened up; gladiatorial contests with wild animals were banned, as well as all-night partying. The mass disappointment fuelled by these measures played into the hands of the spurned Isaurians, led by Zeno's brother Longinus. Anastasius had been on the throne for barely a year when

Isaurian street gangs rampaged through Constantinople, torching some of the capital's finest buildings. Anastasius was forced to arrest Longinus and rid the city of all Isaurians including the family of the late Zeno, whose property was confiscated even to the ornate imperial robes.

But the threat from the Isaurian gangs paled before a worse menace that had grown out of what we might call sports hooliganism. Almost since the foundation of Constantinople, sporting events in the Hippodrome had attracted large and passionate crowds. There had been originally four teams of athletes, the reds, whites, blues and greens. In time the first two had dwindled away, leaving the Blues and Greens as sole rivals. If the tribalism had been limited to athletics, little harm would have been done. But by the close of the fifth century the two sides had morphed into ugly amalgams of violent louts, political party activists and thuggish armed militias. The entire city seemed to be split into fanatical Blues and Greens engaged in constant gang warfare, with the former favoured by the upper classes and Greco-Roman aristocracy and the latter more popular among the working and business classes and civil servants. There was also a religious dimension to the conflict, with the Blues upholding orthodoxy and the Greens leaning towards the Asian heretics.

Anastasius considered himself what we might call today a 'progressive' leader, favouring trade and industry over the old landed nobility. This tended to sway him towards the Greens, though he was careful not to show preference for either side. He was not a military man (though an ivory frieze shows him riding a spirited horse and holding a banner) and preferred conciliation to collision. He was also well past his prime, yet felt he had to do something to suppress the strife, especially as in 501 Anastasius' own illegitimate son lost his life in a gang battle. But the emperor could not in the end hide his partiality to the Greens and attempted unwisely to tamper with the orthodox liturgy, thus earning a rather undeserved reputation as a 'heretic'. An enraged mob marched threateningly on the palace, and Anastasius, now over 80, had them restrained only with difficulty, but a year later the mob's patience snapped again. This time a riot inside Sancta Sophia resulted in considerable casualties. Two days later furious crowds thronged to the Hippodrome threatening death to all heretics. Anastasius let them roar and burn down important buildings for a couple of days, then walked out calmly to face some 20,000 demonstrators baying for his blood.

> He slowly removed his diadem and laid aside the imperial purple. He was ready there and then, he told them, to lay down the burden of the

> Empire; all that was necessary was that they should name his successor … The tall, white-haired figure was still handsome, the voice firm and persuasive. Gradually, the clamour ceased.[12]

Anastasius' one solid contribution to defence policy was to build a thick thirty-mile wall blocking off the land approaches to Constantinople from the west. The wall connected the Sea of Marmara at Selymbria (now Silivri) to Derca on the Black Sea (near present-day Ormanli). The Bulgars, an offshoot of the Huns, had been making a nuisance of themselves in Thrace recently, while the Goths were also still active under a leader named Vitalian, who three times led his forces up to the wall but got no farther. The emperor, meanwhile, carefully considered who would succeed him. His nearest male kin were three nephews, whom he invited to dinner at the palace one evening. He had prepared three couches for their post-prandial relaxation; under one of the pillows he placed a scrap of parchment with the word REGNUM (= realm) on it. The intention was to see which nephew would choose that couch, for the issue to be decided by pure chance. But the old man's plan was upset in an unexpected way, as two of the young men – apparently gay lovers – chose to share the same couch, and as luck would have it, that with the secret message under the pillow remained unoccupied. The nonplussed emperor prayed for another sign that night, and the story goes that it was divinely revealed to him that the man who first entered the royal bedchamber the next morning would be his successor. That person would ordinarily be the royal chamberlain, but when morning dawned the first caller was not the chamberlain but the commander of the Corps of Excubitors, a grizzled old officer named Justin.

Not much is known about the Excubitors of the Byzantine court. Unlike the Silentaries, who were the equivalent of a civilian senior security service, the Excubitors were a military body. They first appeared in the reign of Leo I who sought some insurance against the unreliable allegiance of the Germans in the army, and had assumed increasing importance since. A clue to their duties is given by their name, which derives from Latin for 'out-of-bed'. From this we can surmise that they were an elite palace guard providing round-the-clock protection for the imperial household, if necessary doing without sleep. By Anastasius' time there were 300 Excubitors, including some of the toughest men in the army. When Anastasius saw the unwitting Justin walk in, he lowered his head in respect. Shortly afterwards, on 9 July 518, Anastasius died aged 87, and the usual scramble for power began.

Justin was offered a large bribe by the chief imperial eunuch who was fielding his own candidate. Still concealing his intentions, he kept the money for himself but placed the Excubitors on the alert. The record here is sketchy; while the Senate debated the succession, crowds poured into the Hippodrome to see what would happen and the Blues and Greens found a new excuse to brawl in the streets. The Excubitors called on their commander to restore order by proclaiming himself emperor. Justin at first refused, perhaps playing coy, but the Senate insisted, and so Justin I, no spring chicken at 66, found himself the nineteenth emperor of Byzantium.

It was a dizzying rise for a Macedonian peasant boy who had started out with nothing more than the shirt on his back, a chunk of bread in his pocket and an overabundance of ambition and physical stamina. Around 460 he and two friends had set out to find their fortunes in Constantinople, ending up in Leo I's newly-formed Excubitors. Over the decades Justin rose gradually to senior rank through genuine ability rather than high-placed connections. One report says that when Justin was acclaimed emperor, he was already dressed for the part, suggesting that he had planned it all along. Others claim that he was led through the Hippodrome to the palace to have the imperial robes put on him; this version is backed up by the letter that he wrote to Pope Hormisdas in Rome, claiming he didn't have much choice. Whatever the truth, he showed his gratitude by giving each of his soldiers a pound of silver. And to keep his back secure, he had the chief eunuch and his rival imperial candidate done away with.

Justin was popular with the masses from the outset. He was lavish with his public entertainment subsidies, in sharp contrast with his penny-pinching predecessor. Though illiterate and uneducated, his experience and character made up for the deficiency. He gave the Goth Vitalian a senior position in the government (to have him murdered two years later). Heretics were hounded out of the realm as Justin rigorously enforced orthodoxy and tried to mend broken fences with the popes in Rome. Theodoric, the real master of Italy, noticed this and made overtures to Justin to offset the papal influence, but the rapprochement turned out to be brief as the fact could not be hidden that Theodoric, like all Goths, was an Arian heretic. Theodoric's death in August 526 put paid to that potential problem.

In the east the Persians were showing signs of renewed restiveness under their King Kavadh. The bones of contention, as always, were the regions bordering on both empires, which alternated between Byzantine and Persian administration according to the strength or weakness of either side at any particular time. One such region was Lazica, taking up what is now the south-east coast of the Black Sea in Turkey. The kings of Lazica had usually looked to Persia for protection, but in 522 their new king Tzath had gone to Constantinople for his coronation, receiving a Byzantine wife as a reward. A miffed Kavadh connived with the Sabiric Huns in the north Causacus to attack Byzantium. But the Sabiric Huns squealed to Justin, and for punishment Kavadh had thousands of them massacred.

As Persia was still not strong enough to measure swords with Byzantium again, Kavadh tried a ploy to lull Justin into complacency. Relations between the two rulers, in fact, had been cordial on the surface, so Kavadh suggested that one of his sons, named Khosru, be adopted by Justin; Khosru would live at the Byzantine court until the time came for him to succeed his father. But Justin's advisors saw through the subtle scheme – if Khosru were formally adopted by the imperial family, might he conceivably claim the Byzantine throne at some point? Justin pointed this out to the Persians, who huffily withdrew their proposal.

Ever since Constantine I, the protection of the Holy Places had been a key tenet of Byzantine foreign policy. As long as the Persians were weak and royal ladies such as Helena and Athenais helped build up the Christian presence in Jerusalem, there was little to fear. But in 523 a fanatic Jew named Dhu Nuwas began killing Christians in Southern Arabia. Justin sent a Byzantine fleet to ferry the soldiers of the Christian Ethiopian general Ela Atzheba to the Arabian Peninsula to attack Dhu Nuwas, who was killed.[13] The Christian presence in the Middle East was assured, though it could never be taken for granted.

Justin's last few years were darkened with worsening Blue-Green gang violence, both of whose members sported Hunnish hairstyles (probably similar to the 'Mohican' of a more recent time). Law enforcement was implacable; some of the worst offenders were hanged and burned at the stake, yet few solid citizens dared walk the streets alone at night. The emperor left the management of this social problem to his Macedonian nephew Flavius Petrus Sabbatius, who took over more and more of the imperial duties as Justin declined – and made no secret of his preference for the Blues. By the time Justin died of cancer in August 527, Sabbatius had already de facto assumed supreme power and was now known by his imperial adoptive name – Justinian.

Chapter Three

Justinian I, The War Manager

Justinian I (527–565)

For generations of readers of Byzantine history and viewers of documentaries, one face has been the face of the entire thousand-year empire. It has graced the covers of countless books (Lord Norwich's first volume being merely one of the latest) and still has pride of place in libraries of coffee-table art tomes. Justinian's brash, youthful and clean-cut features jump out at us even through the imperfect medium of the famous sixth century mosaic in the church of San Vitale in Ravenna. It's impossible not to be transfixed by the penetrating hazel eyes and thin yet supremely confident smile. Even the beginning of a double chin – a remarkable touch of honesty by the unknown genius who designed the mosaic – adds to the realistic impression.

The transition from Justin I to Justinian was about as seamless as it gets. Four months before his death, Justin had bowed to the inevitable and crowned Justinian co-emperor. But Justinian already knew the imperial ropes, as it were, as he had been managing them for almost ten years already. At his accession he was 45 and at the peak of his powers. In contrast to his letterless uncle – and thanks to that uncle's care and munificence – he was extraordinarily well-read in law and theology. For the first time since Constantine I, Byzantium had an emperor who was determined to enforce strict religious orthodoxy and the rule of law throughout the realm as a matter of security, and had the clout to do it. He was fortunate enough to require little sleep, earning him the sobriquet *akoimitos*, or sleepless. He kept to a workaholic regimen and disciplined his appetites by sticking to a vegetarian diet.

It might surprise the reader to learn that Justinian was not a fighting emperor by this book's definition. He never measured swords personally with a fighting foe. Yet his contribution to Byzantine warfare was as great as any general's in the field, and perhaps greater, since he knew how to pick his generals. He had served some time as an officer in a palace regiment called the Scholae, but apparently did not consider a lasting military career. His talents lay more in administration than in soldiering; he knew it, and left war to the professionals, with excellent results. Justinian had fallen seriously ill from some unknown malady in 524, and when he recovered he married one of history's most interesting women – the daughter of a bear keeper, a burlesque dancer and actress named Theodora. Justin and his empress were horrified at his choice, considering Theodora a low-life unworthy of membership in the royal family, but Justinian tweaked the laws so as to allow her to marry into higher society, as long as she repented of her sexually riotous past. This she duly did, and thus began the chequered career of one of the most famous royal couples in history.

Justinian's sheer stamina enabled him, in the words of Procopius, to beaver away at state affairs 'from early dawn to midday, and far into the night'. He studied incessantly. On the minus side, he was subject to occasional lapses of courage and, if we are to credit Procopius, had moments when he was 'insincere, crafty and hypocritical'. Perhaps these are necessary attributes for all men of power in all ages who wish to keep that power. Nonetheless, he made himself accessible to even the lowliest of his subjects – as long as they knelt to kiss the hem of his robe or toes of his shoes. For he was conscious of being an interloper in the royal lineage of Byzantium, and to offset that disadvantage he increased the pomp and splendour of his court. The measure seemed to work.

Justinian's periodic lapses of confidence almost spelled his doom five years into his reign. In January 532, during sporting events in the Hippodrome, a delegation of Greens walked up to the imperial box complaining loudly of social discrimination. Justinian's first reaction was to threaten them with dire punishment, while the Blues in the crowd rose threateningly to support the emperor. It was the trigger for another round of street fighting, which the authorities scotched by arresting seven ringleaders from both factions; four were beheaded and a fifth hanged, but when the noose was tightened on the last two – a Blue and a Green – the rope broke. Both escaped and were spirited off to safety in a church, protected by sympathetic monks. At this the Blues and Greens joined forces and stirred up a full-scale people's revolt fuelled by chronic working-class grievances over excessive taxation. Before Justinian quite realized what was happening, rampaging mobs had emptied the jails, murdered police officials and torched the church of Sancta Sophia and even part of the emperor's palace. As the ominous roar of '*nika*!' – 'win!' – rose into the smoke-filled air of Constantinople, the wealthier citizens fled for their lives across the Bosporus. The leaders of the revolt demanded the sacking of two unpopular ministers; Justinian hastily complied. Then they raised a senator named Hypatius, a nephew of the late Anastasius, to be their new emperor, seating him in the place of honour in the Hippodrome.

Justinian, hiding in the palace, was quite unnerved and prepared to flee the city. Not so Theodora, who now showed of what stuff she was made. Procopius, who was certainly no fan of Theodora's and lost no chance to smear her personal character, nevertheless had to admit she had extraordinary courage. 'Every man … must sooner or later die,' Procopius cites Theodora as saying as the mob thundered outside the palace walls, 'so how can an emperor allow himself to be a fugitive?' Of course the royal couple had every means of escaping; the sea was nearby and ships were waiting, and they had plenty of money to live on. But could they live with themselves if they chose that way out? Theodora warned her scared husband that he might well 'regret that [he] did not choose death in preference. As for me … the purple is the noblest winding-sheet.' Whatever happened, she was staying put.[1]

These fighting words bucked up Justinian who turned to Belisarius, one of his generals who had recently returned from service on the Persian front, to see if he could restore order. Belisarius had no doubts that he could. Together with another general named Mundus, he slipped out of the palace and mustered all the troops he could find. Once in formation they marched on the Hippodrome where the insurrectionists were still milling about and shouting. While Narses, the commander of the Imperial Bodyguard, blocked the main gate to prevent anyone from getting out, Belisarius and Mundus gave no quarter; in one of the worst bloodbaths in Byzantine history, in a very short time some 30,000 corpses covered the track and seats of the stadium, and the sand was sodden with blood. Hypatius, quaking in terror, was arrested. Justinian was inclined to pardon him, but here again Theodora imposed her will. The unfortunate pretender was executed and his body cast into the sea.

The story of Theodora and the Nika Riots has often been told. The significance of the riots for military history lies in the harsh lesson they taught Justinian who, we have seen, did not consider himself a natural soldier. The lesson was that an emperor, soldier or not, needed to display strength and wherever necessary, ruthlessness. The appalling butchery in the Hippodrome appears to have stamped out the Blues and Greens (for the time being, at least) and, remarkably, raised Justinian's own image in the eyes of the law-abiding majority. Another lesson was the folly of taxing the people to pay tribute to give to the Persians. Intent on restoring a measure of social peace, he rebuilt Sancta Sophia in more or less the magnificent form it retains today. The construction took five years and when the great church was consecrated on 27 December 537 Justinian was taken to see it. The emperor, according to reports, stood gazing at it for some time and then murmured, as if to himself, 'Solomon, I have beaten you.' Sancta Sophia, the biggest church in Christendom at the time, had far more than architectural or even religious significance. It symbolized two things: first, Justinian's intention of forging a powerful law-enforcing state whose moral underpinning would be provided by the church; and second, his great foreign policy objective of reviving the complete Roman Empire by recovering Rome and all Italy under the emperor's rule.

The military side was assigned to the capable Belisarius, whose brutal efficiency in dealing with the Blues and Greens got him promoted to *strategos autokrator*, or literally general-emperor. It was a rank probably created to give the commanding general the authority of the absent emperor in the field. (It might also encourage thoughts of a coup, though Justinian knew what he was doing, as there was never any evidence that Belisarius harboured any disloyal sentiments.) Much had to be done. North Africa had to be reclaimed from the Vandals, the Ostrogoths driven out of Italy and the Visigoths from Spain, and the Franks and Saxons neutralized in Gaul and Britain. In terms of manpower, the Byzantine army at that time totalled about 200,000 men, though they were almost all non-Greek mercenaries from all over the empire, as universal military service for Byzantine citizens had been abolished a century before. The mercenaries' discipline was often questionable, and all too often they preferred rapine and plunder over good order after a battle. A strong general and regular pay could usually be depended on to keep the ranks in line, but that could not be guaranteed.

Some mercenaries were better fighters than others – for example, the Macedonians, Thracians, Isaurians and Armenians. All were in almost constant training. The senior officers made sure that their religious motivation remained high, as the maintenance of the orthodox Christian state, encircled by real and potential foes, was the chief foreign policy tenet of Byzantium. The heavy-armed infantry and cavalry (the Cataphracts) wore breastplates, helmets and greaves and were armed with shields, swords and short spears. Backing them up, or serving as skirmishers, were the *toxotai*, or archers. Crack units were assigned to guard crucial border points; these men, the *akritai*, or frontier guards, became permanent residents of those regions, settling there with their families on land granted by the emperor. These *akritai* attained great importance in the defence of the state, and gave rise to many chivalrous legends that survive in Greek literature today. The chief cities of the Byzantine domain were all powerfully walled, with rectangular or circular towers, and surrounded by a deep ditch or a moat. The fortifications were paid for by the *kastroktisia*, or special castle-building tax.

The Byzantine navy, though not yet as important as the army, was big enough to dominate the Eastern Mediterranean. The largest warships were the *karaboi*, resembling large and bulky galleys. More numerous and efficient were the *dromones*, based on the ancient trireme, each of which could carry 300 men, of whom 70 were marines. Smaller vessels could carry between 130 and 160 men each. Naval tactics had not changed much since the 480 BC battle of Salamis; the chief objective of a warship was to ram an enemy vessel and if possible send the marines on board to capture it. The navy was also highly useful in blockades, and it was only Basiliscus' incompetence that cost him his fleet to the Vandals off Carthage in 468. The seamen were mostly volunteers from the Aegean islands and the coast of Asia Minor.

In early 533 the shipyards on the Golden Horn were busier than usual with the hammering and sawing of timber. Belisarius was preparing the first stage of Justinian's grand plan – the ejection of the Vandals from North Africa. In the seventy-odd years since the Carthage disaster the Vandal rulers had become indolent and softened by overindulgence in Greco-Roman culture. The time to hit them was now. One morning in June Justinian stood at his palace window to view Belisarius' ninety-two sleek and fast *dromones* escorting 500 troop transports, their colourful pennants rippling in the wind as they sailed off southwards.

Misfortune struck early in the voyage. While the fleet was still in the Dardanelles a couple of drunken Hun soldiers murdered one of their comrades, and Belisarius had them hanged at Abydos. Discipline had to be kept tight. When the fleet reached Methone on the southwest corner of the Peloponnese, hundreds of crewmen fell ill with food poisoning traced to mouldy ships' biscuits. Penny-pinching civil servants in Constantinople were blamed, but the fleet had to delay for days before the men could recover and the ships be resupplied with provisions. At Catania in Sicily Procopius, who was on Belisarius' staff, learned that the Vandals still had no inkling of the Byzantine expedition. In early September Belisarius landed on the coast at Ras Kaboudia. The slow march north to Carthage took more than a week, with the result that Gelimer, the Vandal king, had plenty of advance warning and drew up his forces to confront Belisarius ten miles from Carthage.

Gelimer's army suffered from a lack of coordination, which enabled Belisarius' savage Hun cavalry to decide the issue in the hard-fought Battle of the Tenth Milestone. Two days later Belisarius with 15,000 troops entered Carthage. If we are to believe Procopius, the men were well-behaved, avoiding displays of arrogance and paying for everything they acquired. Though Gelimer himself escaped, Justinian rejoiced at the news of the easy victory. But the emperor displayed faulty military judgement in ordering Belisarius too quickly back to Constantinople for a triumphal parade. Gelimer employed the general's absence to reform the Vandal army and build it up to more than it had been before, and in December he moved to recapture Carthage. Belisarius returned post-haste and marched to stop the Vandals at Tricamarum, about thirty miles west of the city. He took the initiative at once, relying on his Romans and Greeks to charge the enemy before deploying the Huns, whom he suspected might be disloyal. But he need not have worried as, seeing Gelimer fall back, the Huns completed the destruction with their irresistible cavalry charge. Gelimer wandered in the desert for several weeks until captured by a Byzantine detachment. His sufferings had probably affected his mind, as when he was brought before Belisarius all he could do was laugh uncontrollably.

Belisarius led his delayed victory parade through Constantinople in the summer of 534. Not since the days of Augustus had a Roman capital witnessed such a spectacle. In the procession walked Gelimer and what was left of his family, followed by a host of wagons loaded with booty. The procession wound up at the Hippodrome, where Justinian and Theodora waited in the imperial box. Gelimer bowed deeply to the emperor, quoting Ecclesiastes in a low voice: 'Vanity of vanities, all is vanity.' The imperial couple offered to make him a patrician if he would embrace the official faith, but he declined, preferring the second offer of a comfortable retirement. His Vandal prisoners were inducted into the Byzantine army as *Vandali Iustiniani* and sent off to the Persian front – not the best of postings.

Justinian's talents lay more in crafty diplomacy than in military strategy, and he used them to good effect to ease the way for the second stage of his plan, to claw back Italy. Brushing aside the weak objections of Pope Agapitus I, Belisarius seized Sicily and crossed into Italy. His progress up the peninsula was almost unopposed. He took Naples by sending 400 soldiers to crawl through an old aqueduct under the walls. The Roman people and clergy cheered him as he entered the city through the Asinarian Gate (now the Porta San Giovanni) in December 536 – here, finally, after long years of Ostrogoth aliens, was a genuine Christian Roman. The joy was short-lived, however, as the following March the Ostrogoth king Witigis raised 150,000 men and besieged Belisarius' 5,000-strong force in Rome. The siege lasted a year, during which Witigis cut off Rome's food and water supplies. In February 538 the Byzantine general John moved on the Ostrogoth stronghold of Ravenna and captured it, forcing Witigis to withdraw from Rome. It was then that Witigis was captured, just north of the Milvian Bridge. Justinian, worried about a resurgence of Persian power in the east, extended peace feelers to the Goths, but Belisarius dealt with them by taking Ravenna.

In 540 King Khosru I of the Persians, who was fully Justinian's equal in ability and influence, attacked the Byzantine domains in the early spring. Antioch successfully resisted, but at great cost in lives. Khosru, the greatest of the Sasanid dynasty, had built up an impressive standing army among other notable achievements. He trampled over Syria, killing and plundering, forcing tribute money from Justinian whose main preoccupation was Italy. But once Belisarius had seized Ravenna, the general was recalled. Justinian's motives, however, appear not have been purely military. For some time the emperor suspected that Belisarius might invest his success and popularity as *strategos autokrator* in a bid for the throne. (Theodora, we may be sure, played on those fears, if she was not the actual instigator of them.) There certainly was plenty of historical precedent for such a concern. Moreover, Belisarius was a fine-looking man and his troops idolized him. At home in Constantinople, he cut an impressive figure, emerging from his house in the mornings with a dazzlingly grand retinue. His own conduct was unfailingly modest and unassuming. But the façade was misleading.

Since his recall he had not been his usual confident self. He appeared preoccupied and hesitant and had difficulty in making decisions. The fact was that his wife Antonina, to whom he was completely devoted, was having an affair with their godson. He appears not to have known about it until after he left for the Persian front, and when he learned the truth he was devastated.[2] Yet they were soon reconciled, and accordingly by 542 Belisarius had recovered his spirits enough to receive a Persian embassy which reported back to Khosru that it had encountered 'a general who in manliness and wisdom surpassed all other men'. The campaign of that year was derailed by an unexpected and deadly foe – bubonic plague. Arising in Egypt, it swept over the whole Eastern Mediterranean as far as Constantinople, where the death toll in a single day hit 16,000. Forty per cent of the city's population perished and Justinian himself lay critically ill for weeks, leaving Theodora to conduct the imperial business. Theodora plotted, even in those dark days, to prevent Belisarius from succeeding her husband, going as far as to strip the general of his command as well as his wealth and household servants. When Justinian recovered he reinstated Belisarius in his general-in-chief's rank and gave him back most of his money, then sent him to deal with a worsening situation in his old battleground, Italy.

The Goths had a new king, Totila, who took advantage of Belisarius' absence to sweep through Italy from the north, defeating the Byzantines at Faenza and bottling them up in Ravenna, Rome and Naples. The Goth had impressed the Roman people by his magnanimity which stood in sharp contrast to the indiscipline and rowdiness of the imperial barbarian auxiliaries who had been unpaid for months. He promised freedom for slaves, a redistribution of land and an end to the hated Byzantine taxation. In the face of all this Belisarius felt his disadvantages very keenly, demanding more men and money. 'The greatest part of your army,' he warned Justinian in a letter, 'has enlisted and is now serving under the enemy's standards.' But time was also on the Goths' side. By the time the generals John and Isaac arrived with reinforcements including Hun cavalry, Totila was at the gates of Rome.

Belisarius and John agreed that the best way to relieve Rome was from the south, but that's as far as the agreement went. Belisarius urged an immediate naval expedition up the Tiber from Portus (now Ostia) at the river's mouth. John, on the other hand, argued for a land attack from the south. Belisarius suggested a compromise, to sail the fleet up the Tiber as the main army marched up its east bank. Isaac received strict orders to remain at Portus and guard the Tiber mouth, not to move in any circumstances, but he flouted his orders and foolishly attacked a Gothic garrison, getting himself captured. Bessas, the imperial garrison commander in Rome, was helplessly inactive, so on 17 December 546 some disloyal Isaurian troops opened the gates of Rome and let Totila in with 10,000 men. Yet again the Eternal City underwent a sacking. Totila broke off the Rome operation to move against the Byzantines in Ravenna, which enabled Belisarius to re-establish control in Rome for three years before having to abandon it to the Goths again.

When Belisarius was recalled home a second time in 549 he had little to show for five strenuous years of trying to maintain the Byzantine presence in the West. Italy, in religion and in politics, was too far detached from the empire now for any meaningful or lasting reunification to be possible. The mood in Constantinople was grim, as Theodora had just died of cancer and the grief-stricken Justinian was in no shape to make any decisions. Belisarius wanted one more stab at Italy, but the emperor vetoed it. Rome itself had lost at least nine-tenths of its population, the Senate was no more and Milan was almost wiped off the map. With few left to till the soil, thousands starved. Italy became a devastated shell of its former self, to stay that way for hundreds of years.

Justinian survived Theodora by sixteen years. For much of that time he was preoccupied by thorny religious issues that at any moment could upset the stability of the state. But he was not about to give up the Byzantine military presence in Italy. In 551 he sent Narses, now in his seventies but still vigorous, with 35,000 men to join John in Italy. Narses paid the Byzantine soldiers' arrears, which must have improved their morale considerably, and met the forces of Totila on the Via Flaminia, at Gualdo Tadino near Ravenna. Totila tried to trick Narses by attacking unexpectedly, but the Byzantines had the better of the situation from the outset; Totila was mortally wounded. Totila's successor Teia was unable to stem Narses' advance. The Byzantines and Goths clashed again near Mount Vesuvius, where Teia was killed by a lance thrust. That blow effectively ended the Gothic presence in Italy. Narses became the governor of Rome, which the Byzantines administered for sixteen years in conjunction with the compliant papacy.

Justinian is known to history mainly for his far-reaching and dramatic reforms in law and administration. But what, in his long reign of thirty-eight years, had he accomplished in foreign and military policy? Gibbon dismissed Belisarius' victories as 'vanity', and one must agree that the emperor's grand dream of reviving the full Roman Empire turned out to be illusory. When the Gothic war was finally over Justinian was 73, an 'old man, not caring for anything', according to one observer. He sought refuge in theology, leaving the army to shrink to one-third of its former strength and frontier castles from Spain to Iraq to crumble. To ease his mind further he bought a fifty-year peace with Persia. Belisarius was brought out of retirement to repulse a new incursion of the Huns, while the Anastasian Wall at Selymbria was repaired. But the emperor's pathological jealousies returned anew, and soon after his latest military triumph Belisarius found himself charged with high treason. For eight months the general lived in disgrace and poverty, until Justinian repented and gave him back his life, so to speak. Belisarius ended his days in comfortable retirement in 565. One of the great commanders of history, had he been of a different character he may well have achieved the throne and become a fighting emperor as well.[3]

Justinian spent most of 565 working at his theological projects and on the night of 14 November he was at his desk when he suffered a probable heart attack. The only one with him at the time was his chamberlain Callinicus.

What happened in the agonizing moments between Justinian's collapse and his death will never be known. Callinicus claimed that the dying emperor named his nephew Flavius Justinus as his successor, but we have only the chamberlain's word for it. Flavius Justinus was sent for and taken to the palace where the emperor was laid out on a bier. Few realized it at the time, but the old Roman Empire finally died with Justinian. From now on the Latin influence would wane and the Byzantine Empire would be increasingly Greek in language and culture.

Justin II (565–578), Tiberius II Constantine (578–582), Maurikios (582–602) and Phokas (602–610)

Flavius Justinus, the son of Justinian's sister Vigilantia, was living with his wife Sophia in a handsome mansion overlooking the sea, and employed as *kouropalates*, or chief of staff of the palace. On the night of Justinian's death the Excubitors barred the gates to the palace grounds; the following morning the people of Constantinople learned the news in the Hippodrome, while Flavius Justinus was taken to Sancta Sophia to be ceremonially raised on a shield and crowned by the patriarch as Justin II.

He was about 45, roughly the same age as his late uncle when he took the throne. A proud man, he strongly disagreed with Justinian's policy of paying off enemies with tribute to keep them away from the frontiers – indeed, in his inaugural speech he went so far as to publicly criticize the practice. Justin's first act was to arrange for the payment of all outstanding imperial debts, after which he and Sophia solemnly walked behind Justinian's funeral cortège, watching as the body was laid beside that of Theodora in the Church of the Holy Apostles.

Justin's next act was to halt tribute payments to a Hunnish people called the Avars, who flush with money for eight years had kept the peace on the north-west frontiers. The Avars moved west, where they came up against their powerful neighbours the Lombards, a Central European people who had been Christianized under Justinian and had provided contingents for Narses in his subjugation of Italy. Under pressure from the Avars, the Lombards under their King Alboin in 569 moved into Northern Italy, which is still called Lombardy. Within a few years they had overcome weak Byzantine resistance to take over Ravenna, Rome and Naples as well. The popes of Rome, despairing of Byzantine help, turned to the Franks for protection. The Avars, in revenge for Justin's cutting off their allowance, invaded Dalmatia. Justin sent the commander of the Excubitors, Tiberius, to stop them, but after three years of exhausting combat Tiberius had to admit failure, and in the end Justin found he had to pay far more to the Avars than his uncle ever had.

In 571 the Persians' King Khosru reacted similarly when Justin halted tribute payments to him, too. Armenia at the time was divided into Byzantine and Persian spheres of influence. When Armenia's overwhelmingly Christian population rebelled, the Persians invaded and took the strategic Byzantine fortress of Dara on the Euphrates as well as 2,000 maidens who, we are told, rather than face the grim consequences of such capture, deliberately drowned themselves in a river. For a man of rigid thinking like Justin, these were severe blows to his pride. When combined with the intractable and insufferable religious politics of Byzantium, they seriously strained his mind. He was not one to be able to adapt to circumstances, and accordingly his reason cracked under the pressure. He was aware enough of his mental weakness, leaving Sophia to really run the empire. Thanks to her influence he took the precaution of naming Tiberius as his successor in December 574. It was Sophia who in that year authorized a considerable payment to Khosru to keep him away. Justin progressively dealt with his stress through the medium of insanity. Courtiers and family watched appalled as he sat in a toy cart and had himself pulled through the palace like a child, to the strains of loud organ music (to blot out the demons in his head, he said) and sank his teeth into anyone who couldn't get out of his way fast enough. Grim jokes circulated around the city that he would have a couple of attendants for lunch every day. John of Ephesus adds that Justin would have fits of barking like a dog and at least once tried to leap out of a palace window.

The biting and barking emperor nevertheless had his moments of lucidity when he could act to all intents and purposes like a responsible statesman. One of these occurred in September 578 when he called his potentates together and informed them that he had decided to abdicate. Gibbon quotes his words as the very essence of rueful wisdom:

> Delight not in blood; abstain from revenge; avoid those actions by which I have incurred public hatred … As a man, I have sinned; as a sinner, even in this life, I have been severely punished.

Justin went on to point to some of his ministers who 'have abused my confidence and inflamed my passions', and who would assuredly account for their misdeeds in the next world. Defining the essence of statesmanship, he went on:

> I have been dazzled by the splendour of the diadem: be thou wise and modest … You see around us your slaves, and your children … assume the tenderness of a parent … cultivate the affections, maintain the discipline of the army; protect the fortunes of the rich; relieve the necessities of the poor.

There was not a dry eye in the hall as Justin, the upright man driven mad by the evils of the world, placed the imperial diadem on the kneeling Tiberius with the closing words, 'May the God of heaven and earth infuse into your heart whatever I have neglected or forgotten.' A week later he was dead.

Tiberius, the commander of the Excubitors and now emperor, found himself in an odd position.[4] While Justin lived he could not formally take the throne, and moreover had to contend with Sophia, who wielded the real power – not for nothing was she Theodora's niece. Tiberius certainly was respected, having acquitted himself well in action against the Persians on the ill-fated Syrian front. While serving as Caesar and heir-apparent to Justin, he had been kept on a meagre state salary while Sophia controlled the treasury and barred his own wife and daughters from the palace.

When Justin died Tiberius got his revenge by placing Sophia under close arrest; his own wife, the new empress, was finally able to see the inside of the palace. He seems to have been a stolid soldier and realist, just the kind of sovereign the Byzantines needed after the bizarre interlude with Justin. One of his first concerns was to strengthen the army after its recent demoralizing reverses at Persian hands. He now had control of the treasury as well, and amply used its resources to form an elite guard of 15,000 barbarian auxiliaries, known as *foederati* on the model of those set up by Theodosius I nearly two centuries before.

Tiberius spent heavily on the army, paying his soldiers liberally with gold from the treasury. In the civil sphere he permitted the revived Blues and Greens to form official parties again and broadened the powers of the Senate in what the public approved as a move towards democratization of the state. These genuine good intentions earned him great popularity. Yet, as happens so often with popular leaders, the fiscal policies to maintain that popularity proved to be ruinous. On 13 August 582 Tiberius fell violently ill in one of his summer palaces after wolfing down a dish of mulberries. It was widely believed that he had been poisoned, perhaps by a vindictive Sophia. As he lay dying in agony, Tiberius beckoned to his son-in-law, an officer named Maurikios, whom he had designated as his successor the previous week. 'Make your reign your finest epitaph,' were the emperor's last words.

Maurikios was as good as his word.[5] Like his father-in-law, he had seen service on the Persian front and had a practical turn of mind which served him well. Probably of Armenian origin, Maurikios had been appointed *magister militum per Orientem* in 577. He made up for his lack of military experience by a victory over the Persians in 581 and married into the imperial family. His accession to the throne found the empire still at war with Persia and having to contend with the aggressive Avars and Slavs in Eastern Europe.

As the Persians were the greater menace, Maurikios concentrated his initial campaigns in that sector. He also could have detected a creeping weakness in the enemy, as the formidable Khosru I had died in 579, to be succeeded by his son Hormizd IV. Maurikios, the first Byzantine emperor to lead an army since Zeno more than a century before, cleared Byzantine territory to the Tigris and beyond. This was about the time that a people called the Arabs were making themselves felt in the Middle East; Tiberius had actually enrolled some of them in the Byzantine forces. In 589 Hormizd was toppled and murdered by a general, Bahram Chobin, who stood in for the underage Khosru II. When this second Khosru came of age and demanded de facto power, Bahram Chobin refused, so the young king fled to Constantinople. Maurikios, against the cautious advice of the Senate, sent the young Khosru with 35,000 Byzantine and royalist Persian troops to seize the throne at Ctesiphon. Bahram Chobin drew up an army to meet them at Ganzak and was trounced by the competent Byzantine generalship of John Mystakon and Narses (another Narses, apparently unrelated to the victor of the Italian campaign). Now secure on his throne, Khosru II (now dubbed Parvez, or Victorious) rewarded his Byzantine benefactor by ceding him the rich lands and cities of Western Armenia. After nineteen years of intermittent conflict, at one lucky stroke Byzantium was freed from the huge financial burden of buying peace on the Eastern front.

Maurikios was now free to concentrate on the Avars. These had been Byzantium's rather uneasy allies against the Slavs, who by now were pouring into the Balkans. Maurikios was familiar with their methods. In the Strategikon, a comprehensive military manual which he is credited with writing, he notes:

> The Avars are very cunning and very experienced in warfare. As nomads they are accustomed to heat, cold and privations. They hide their thoughts and are perpetually considering how to trap and exhaust their enemy.

The Avars were armed with chain mail body armour, swords, bows and javelins. Their horses were protected by metal plates or thick padding in front, and the riders were adept at shooting arrows on the gallop. The Avars would generally shun close-order fighting with the Byzantines, preferring hit-and-run tactics, feints and encirclement.

> In battle against them [Maurikios wrote], the flanks must be protected by cavalry, and a field of combat must be chosen that has no forests, swamps or depressions.

Taking advantage of the Persian War, the Avars had raided as far as Thessalonica and the outskirts of Constantinople itself. Maurikios, again flouting the advice of the Senate and his family who did not want him in any more danger, led the army into Europe in 591. On the Black Sea coast he was recalled by the news that a Persian diplomatic mission had arrived at the palace. He left the European campaign to his general, Priskos, who commanded the Danube fleet, and his brother Petros, who chased the Avars north of the Danube, accomplishing Maurikios' objective. The Avars' leader, the Khagan Bayan I, broke the terms of a truce in 598, with the result that the Avars and Slavs were brought decisively to heel in 600.[6]

It would have seemed natural for any emperor with Maurikios' luck to try and revive Justinian's old dream of reunifying the Roman Empire. The Byzantines were still in Ravenna, but their relations with the popes in Rome were getting steadily worse. Maurikios, himself not in the best of health, was making plans to have his eldest son Theodosius succeed him in Constantinople and his second son Tiberius rule in Rome. He had four more sons, whom he may have destined for Alexandria and other outlying centres. In preparation he reorganized the military administrations in the east and west into exarchates (from the Greek words for 'outer' and 'authority'). The Exarchate of Ravenna can take some credit for slowing down the Lombard advance in Italy. But that would be the emperor's sole success in that sector, for serious unrest was roiling through the Byzantine army for several reasons.

The lack of money, of course, was high on the list. Past outpourings of tribute, plus the insane overspending of Tiberius II, had depleted the imperial coffers to the point at which Maurikios was forced to cut his soldiers' rations by one-quarter – a move that almost ignited a mass mutiny. Worse was to come. In 599 he decided he hadn't enough funds to ransom some 12,000 Byzantine prisoners in Avar hands, with the result that the prisoners were slaughtered. Three years after that, he ordered the army to spend the winter beyond the Danube instead of coming home. The men needed their winter home break to sell their booty in Constantinople and help provide for their families. For men who had been fighting incessantly for eight months in an implacably hostile environment and had been looking forward to some home leave, this was the last straw. Ignoring the pleas of their commander, the emperor's brother Petros, they refused to cross the Danube. A centurion named Phokas became the focal point of the unrest, focusing it into a demand that Maurikios abdicate in favour of his 17-year-old eldest son Theodosius.

Maurikios' reaction was dramatic and harsh. Theodosius, recalled from a hunting trip, was flogged on his father's orders on suspicion of being in league with the rebels. The emperor's father-in-law Germanos, under a similar suspicion, fled for his life to the altar of Sancta Sophia. To defend the city against Phokas' advance, Maurikios mobilized 2,400 thugs from the Blue and Green street gangs. But the majority were Greens unwilling to oppose the mass of people who were now rioting in the streets hurling imprecations at the emperor. On the stormy evening of 22 November 602 Maurikios, his wife and eight children slipped out of the palace grounds in disguise and boarded a boat intending to cross the Bosporus to the Asian shore. But the wind and rain carried the boat south across the Gulf of Nicomedia. Once ashore Maurikios was immobilized by an attack of gout, and Theodosius set out eastwards (perhaps on his father's instructions) to the court of Khosru Parvez, his father's protégé.

In the city Germanos crept out of his sanctuary and considered assuming the imperial purple for himself, but the Blue and Green leaders refused to back him. Phokas and his rebel army were now at the gates of the city and the factions deemed it safer to cast their lot with him as any other course would trigger a civil war. Phokas, who at first claimed not to have imperial ambitions, called on the patriarch, Senate and delegations of the people to meet him at the church of Saint John the Baptist, where he was crowned emperor. The next day he rode through the city in a chariot pulled by four white horses, scattering handfuls of gold pieces to his cheering subjects.

The joy was brief. According to the historian Theophylact Simocatta, to whom Phokas was nothing more than an 'impudent centaur,' the new emperor showed his true colours when he had Maurikios and his family arrested. During a ceremony in the palace some of the Blues present were heard to caution him loudly that Maurikios alive would remain a threat. When Phokas' hitmen reached Maurikios, he was forced to watch as his four younger sons were slaughtered like sheep, finding the courage to murmur,

'Thy judgements are just, O Lord.' Was he now regretting his past abuse of the army? After uttering those words he was beheaded at one stroke. The five headless bodies were thrown into the sea and the heads taken to Constantinople to be publicly exhibited. The empress Constantina and her two daughters were packed off to a monastery. Away in Ctesiphon, Khosru II vowed revenge against the usurper who had treated his benefactor so dreadfully.

If Maurikios had been considered miserly and unfeeling, he was a veritable angel of light compared to the man who now assumed the helm of the Byzantine Empire. Phokas, by all accounts, had absolutely nothing to redeem him. He was a sadistic and bloodthirsty character, red-haired and beetle-browed, with a large scar across his face. A reign of pure terror followed the executions of Maurikios and his sons; among his subsequent victims were the late emperor's brother Petros and probably Theodosius, though a persistent rumour had it that he remained safe in Ctesiphon. Phokas spared the terrified Germanos on condition that he take holy orders, which he did. Execution techniques were sadistically refined. In addition to beheading with the axe, the victims were despatched by strangling with a bowstring – and they were the lucky ones. Slow torture did for the rest.

Khosru Parvez hurled his forces with all his strength against the monster in Constantinople. Narses, the Byzantine commander in the east and quite as capable as his earlier namesake, saw the chance to turn against his beastly master and joining forces with Khosru seized Edessa (modern Urfa in Syria). Phokas, buying off the Avars with colossal tribute, cunningly invited Narses to Constantinople under a safe-conduct and had him burned alive when he got there. The Byzantine army was now in the hands of Domentziolos, an inexperienced and incompetent nephew of Phokas. In 607 the Persians, having overrun most of West Mesopotamia, Syria and the Asia Minor heartland, arrived at the Bosporus, the very gate of Constantinople, while the Avars continued their raids on the denuded Western Front.

Small wonder that Phokas was in constant danger of his life from plots. His response was to execute thousands of suspects, not even sparing ex-empress Constantina and her daughters. Blues and Greens, Christians and Jews, rioted from Constantinople to Jerusalem, turning Phokas even more paranoid. It was too bad to last, though deliverance came from an unexpected quarter. One of those observing events with dismay was the Exarch of Carthage, a soldier named Heraclius who had been approached for help by dissident circles in Constantinople. Heraclius, an ex-general of Maurikios who had seen service on the Persian front, spent 608 assembling a large army and fleet to topple Phokas. Beforehand, he had taken the precaution of halting grain supplies to the capital to weaken the regime.

Heraclius' army, commanded by Niketas, started off overland, while in 609 Heraclius' son, also named Heraclius, sailed the fleet across the Mediterranean to Thessalonica. The younger Heraclius took his time, swelling his forces at each stop, until he arrived outside the walls of Constantinople on 3 October 610. Phokas, now isolated and universally hated, was captured and taken to see Heraclius on his ship. 'Is this the way you've governed the empire?' Heraclius demanded. Phokas retorted surlily that he doubted Heraclius would run it any better. Heraclius delivered Phokas up to the Blue and Green mob that took great pleasure in tearing him to pieces; John of Antioch writes that he was chopped up for dog food.

Chapter Four

Heraclius, Christian Soldier

Heraclius (610–641)

Phokas' blood and guts had not yet been cleaned from the Hippodrome as Heraclius stood in the Chapel of Saint Stephen in the palace grounds to wed his longtime fiancée Fabia. As soon as that was done he was crowned emperor. About 35, fair-haired, tall and well-built, he elicited wild cheering as he stepped out of the palace, his bride on his arm, on 5 October 610. Yet there were few of his subjects who were not aware that Byzantium was in greater danger than ever before.

The imperial treasury was virtually bankrupt and the army was on the brink of dissolution. Slavs and Avars continued to roam and raid the Balkans at will, even to the walls of Constantinople. The Persians under Khosru Parvez were unstoppable, steamrollering over the Middle East, their insolent banners visible across the Bosporus. Heraclius momentarily wavered; like Justinian before him he thought of leaving Constantinople to its fate and moving the capital of the empire to Carthage, a city he knew better. Such a move might have made strategic sense, but the citizens and clergy would not hear of it. It was Patriarch Sergios, a strong-willed cleric of the kind who often have more backbone than politicians and kings, who bucked him up by pledging the considerable wealth of the church to build up a new army. Sergios got the emperor personally to declare in Sancta Sophia that he would never desert Constantinople. Churches around the realm were stripped of their tonnage of gold, silver and precious stones to save the empire. Some of the money went to paying off the Avars so that Heraclius could concentrate on the overriding military objective that had formed in his mind – to rescue the great and holy city of Jerusalem.

Many writers have called Heraclius the first crusader, though that honour must go to Constantine I three centuries before him. Whereas the long-running conflict with the Persians in Western Asia was primarily about trade routes, Jerusalem, as the cradle of Christianity, was the big, non-negotiable emotional issue. The policy of protecting Jerusalem had remained essentially unchanged since Constantine, though as long as Palestine had been in Roman and Byzantine hands there had been no sense of urgency. In 543 Justinian and Theodora had built the massive church of Saint Mary Mother of God (also known as the Nea, or New Church) near the remains of Solomon's temple, helping boost the city's roaring tourism and pilgrim trade. Yet the evils of the Blue and Green rivalry penetrated even here, 'filling [Jerusalem] with crime and murder,' according to one chronicler. Byzantine troops sometimes had a hard time restoring order.

Jerusalem became a hot-button issue when Khosru II, well on his way to expanding the Sasanid realm as far as he could, besieged the city in 614. The besiegers were led by the general Shahrbaraz, one of history's great commanders, but ferocious to the point of being known as the Royal Boar. As Jerusalem was disorganized by Blue-Green rivalry, Shahrbaraz, aided by 20,000 Jewish troops eager to get in a hit at the Greco-Romans, burst in 'like mad dogs,' according to an eyewitness monk. For three horrifying days, hardly a Christian was left alive. Many more thousands of Christians were led captive to Persia. The few survivors, huddling on the Mount of Olives, saw the burning city as 'a flame, as out of a furnace, [reaching] up to the clouds'.[1]

The Persians carried away relics of Christ's passion, including the True Cross, the lance which had pierced Jesus' side, and the sponge which, filled with vinegar, had been given Him to drink.[2]

Heraclius' immediate retaliation against this supreme provocation resulted in defeat. He therefore bided his time for eight years until embarking on a bold gamble. These eight years are something of a mystery to historians, who have precious little record of them. But almost certainly Heraclius spent them rebuilding his military structure. It is also safe to say that the Byzantine navy, still the mistress of the Mediterranean, was all that stood between the empire and disaster. These were probably the years in which Heraclius reorganized the empire into military districts, or *themes* (from the Greek term thema, or military division). Each *theme* was to be run by a divisional general (*strategos*) whose men would receive land grants in the region so as to bind them more fully to its defence. It was a feudal arrangement that was to prove highly effective in that it ensured a ready supply of well-trained and motivated troops at any time, reducing the risky dependence on alien mercenaries. There were sixteen *themes* in the beginning, from the Aegean Sea Theme in the west to the Chaldias Theme in the far north-east (around present-day Trabzon in Turkey).

Heraclius' career was almost cut short in 619, when the crafty Avars lured him to negotiations at Selymbria. While making a pretence of talking they planned to attack the Theodosian Wall and cut him off when he tried to rush back. The scheme almost worked. Heraclius got wind of the plot at the last minute and jumped on his horse to escape, disguised as a peasant. He just made it through the gates ahead of the pursuing Avars and successfully led the defence from the wall. After this nasty incident, he could resume his plans against the main foe in the East, and in 622, after attending a mass in Sancta Sophia, Heraclius marched. The normal route against the Persians would be into the Black Sea and along the north coast of what is now Turkey. But the Persians were just across the Bosporus and in control of most of the Asia Minor heartland, so he instead led a fleet down the eastern Aegean Sea to Rhodes, continuing north of Cyprus and into the Bay of Issus to attack the Persian domains from there. A court poet contrasted the Persian and Greek camps: in the former, he said, 'naked houris danced for the generals' delectation' to the clash of cymbals, whereas Heraclius 'sought delight in psalms ... which awoke a divine echo in his soul'.[3] The psalms proved more effective and Shahrbaraz, caught by surprise, was defeated. The next year Heraclius penetrated as far as Armenia and Azerbaijan, defeating three Persian armies sent to stop him

These were fine campaigns, but Constantinople was by no means safe. Shahrbaraz was sent to coordinate operations with the Avars in Europe. The King and Master of the Whole Earth, as Khosru liked to style himself, arrogantly messaged the Byzantine emperor that as God seemingly had been unable to deliver Jerusalem out of the hands of Christ's foes, '[c]ould I also not destroy Constantinople? Have I not destroyed you Greeks?' The latter claim was a bit excessive. Heraclius, far from being destroyed, had sent a corps to fight in Iraq and was keeping another back for home defence. Beefing up his army were 40,000 horsemen from a hitherto obscure Turkic tribe, the Khazars.

And Khosru Parvez was not as confident as his letter to Heraclius might indicate. Like all absolute rulers he grew to be pathologically jealous of anyone who might display leadership abilities rivalling his own, and Shahrbaraz fit that bill perfectly. Accordingly, the Great King sent secret orders to Shahrbaraz's second-in-command to do away with his general. The efficient Byzantine intelligence service intercepted the message and sent it on to Heraclius, who invited Shahrbaraz to a meeting and showed him the order. The Royal Boar thus neutralized, Heraclius led a fleet into the Black Sea to land north of the Persian heartland, while sending his Khazar cavalry to attack overland. Khosru and 40,000 men retreated towards Nineveh, the old Assyrian capital.

Heraclius' immediate war aim was to recover the stolen holy relics, and he spared no effort to do so. His army supported him to a man. The emperor would often open his Bible at random and claim to be guided by what he would find. However, winter was approaching, and the army needed to rest. Heraclius chose the western shore of the Caspian Sea where his second wife Martina, who was with him, used the interval to have their baby. In that region he found eager Hun allies, with whom he smashed more Persian armies in the spring. At the start of 625 Heraclius was encamped near Lake Van. By now his old foe Shahrbaraz, having somehow restored his faith in his king, was back in command of a Persian army. When Shahrbaraz ambushed the Byzantines north of the lake, Heraclius annihilated the Persians in a surprise night attack and sent their general fleeing 'naked and shoeless', according to a report of the time. But Shahrbaraz was nothing if not resilient. On 1 March 626 Heraclius' army started on a long and exhausting march in a large square formation, first north past Mount Ararat, and then veering west for 200 miles along what is now the Murat River, before moving south to take Amida (Diyarbakir), and then east again to the Euphrates. Shahrbaraz dogged his steps unseen, and managed to get to the Euphrates in time to cut a vital rope bridge across it. By the time the Byzantines had discovered a ford and crossed, Shahrbaraz had lined up his force and was waiting for Heraclius on the far bank of the Sarus River.

The only way across for the Byzantines was via a small bridge, and they were tired after their long march, yet they threw themselves over the bridge without hesitation. The command decision, whoever made it, was disastrous. The Persians – imitating the tactics of the Athenian general Miltiades at Marathon 1,100 years before – pretended to retreat and thus drew the Greeks into a trap, wiping out their advance guard. But this initial success went to the Persians' heads; instead of preparing to meet a second Byzantine wave they wasted time pursuing the survivors of the first. Heraclius charged across the bridge on his horse, the faithful Dorkon, his rearguard thundering behind him. Theophanes reports that he encountered 'a giant Persian' whom he despatched with a single sword stroke. Shahrbaraz sent archers to block the bridge, but Heraclius rode blithely through them as if they were ninepins. A rain of missiles bounced harmlessly off his armour. Theophanes adds that Shahrbaraz, watching the emperor sweeping all before him, could only exclaim in wonder to one of his staff that arrows and spears had about as much an effect on Heraclius 'as on an anvil'. The

Persians, the fight knocked out of them, had to retreat, but the menace of Khosru Parvez was far from over.

The situation at home, meanwhile, had taken a critical turn. In June 626 the Avars and Slavs took advantage of Heraclius' absence in the East to make a concerted attempt on Constantinople. Against an estimated 80,000 invaders the capital could muster just 12,000 regular troops, but they were boosted by many civilians eager to be in on the fight. Outside the walls the smoke rose from scores of villages and churches the invaders put to the torch while thousands of refugees crowded into the city. The defenders, however, had a stout leader in Patriarch Sergios, who along with a patrician named Bonos fearlessly paraded the clergy along the top of the wall each day, holding high an icon of the Virgin Mary. The Persians on the other side of the Bosporus, probably lacking siege machinery, remained inactive.

Throughout July the Avars' siege engines hammered the Theodosian Wall, but to little effect, so on 2 August the Khagan of the Avars invited Bonos to his camp for a parley. Once there Bonos and his delegates were compelled to remain standing while three high-ranking Persians occupied the seats of honour. If this was an attempt to scare the Greeks with the signs of a Persian alliance, it backfired. Bonos stormed out of the camp, more determined than ever to carry on the fight. The three Persian dignitaries were intercepted as they were sailing back across the Bosporus. One was beheaded on the spot, the second had his hands cut off and was sent back to the Avars, and the third led for execution on a boat in full view of the Persian camp. The hapless man's head was flung ashore with a sarcastic note, 'Here's your third ambassador,' attached to it.

The hardball had its intended effect, as a week later a flotilla of Persian craft appeared in the Bosporus to quietly ferry away the Persian garrison. Before they could get far the Byzantine navy pounced on them, killing most of the crews and towing the ships home as booty. In the Golden Horn, meanwhile, the Avars had been awaiting a fire signal to withdraw their own vessels into the Sea of Marmara. Bonos lit a decoy signal, with the result that the Avar vessels ran into a Byzantine ambush which in the space of an hour reduced them to matchwood. The Avars, thoroughly demoralized, hastily struck camp. Many vowed they had seen the Virgin Mary herself striding along the wall of Constantinople – Sergios' icon had its desired effect. As the enemy hordes vanished over the horizon, the people of the city rushed out to celebrate and give thanks at the unscathed church of the Virgin at Blachernai.[4]

While Sergios was leading the tumultuous defence of Constantinople, the emperor was weighing strategy in the East. The Khazars, not seeing any immediate advantage from their alliance with Byzantium, had melted away into the Asian steppes. Khosru had assembled a new army under the general Razates who had typical orders to defeat the Byzantines or die in the attempt. Razates got his chance to achieve the latter distinction on 12 December 627 when he encountered Heraclius at the ruined city of Nineveh – actually on the plain of Gaugamela, where Alexander the Great had vanquished Darius III in 331 BC. The location was thus auspicious from the start. After both sides had carefully manoeuvred their forces into position, the lines clashed and fought ferociously for eleven hours. As neither side seemed to be gaining an advantage Razates challenged Heraclius to single combat. As George of Pisidia relates it, Heraclius spurred on Dorkon and sliced off the Persian general's head – the second such efficient beheading-at-the-gallop credited to Heraclius in the space of less than two years. Two more Persian commanders were detached from their heads when they rushed to avenge their general. At nightfall the Persians turned and fled, leaving behind massive casualties.

The last lap of the pursuit of Khosru, and the recovery of the Christian holy relics, was played out in early 628. Heraclius was hot on the heels of the Master of the Whole Earth as he fled with his family and a few courtiers to Susiana. Heraclius torched the royal palace at Ctesiphon. But Khosru II's days were drawing to a close. His son Kavadh-Siroes and Shahrbaraz, who had found himself on the king's death list again, toppled him and consigned him to a dungeon where he was allowed only the flimsiest diet of bread and water. Kavadh-Siroes executed all his half-siblings (by the Christian Shirin), and five days later had his father put to death agonizingly slowly by a steady shower of arrows. This house-cleaning duly completed, Kavadh-Siroes sued for peace. When his ambassadors reached Heraclius at Tauris (Tabriz), the emperor treated them with respect, adding (probably truthfully) that he never had intended that Khosru Parvez should perish. The resulting treaty was all that Byzantium wanted; it gave back all the Western Asian territory it had lost, including Armenia. Far more important for Heraclius, the Greeks were promised the return of the True Cross.

The people and clergy of Constantinople prepared a tumultuous welcome for Heraclius. The Persian king, declaimed Patriarch Sergios from the pulpit of Sancta Sophia, had gone 'the same way as Judas Iscariot'. It was late summer when the emperor and the army marched up to the Bosporus to cross into the joyful city whose whole population had gathered on the

European shore, waving olive branches and holding lighted candles. His almost-grown children by his first marriage greeted him first in a tearful reunion; their father had, after all, been gone six years and faced countless mortal dangers. But before the people could have the privilege of seeing their emperor ride triumphantly into the city proper through the Golden Gate, he needed to have the True Cross with him. The wily Shahrbaraz had hidden it, agreeing to hand it over only after receiving an assurance of friendship. A clever bit of diplomacy enabled the Byzantines to finally regain the holy relic, and thus on 14 September Heraclius was able to stage his grand entrance. Besides the True Cross, the people also marvelled at four elephants that the army had brought back – the first time such beasts had been seen. They also wondered at their emperor's haggard appearance. He had visibly aged since anyone had last seen him; he was in his fifties, most of his luxuriant fair hair was gone and he appeared to stoop. Patriarch Sergios was waiting at Sancta Sophia, where in the hushed imperial presence he raised up the True Cross before the altar.

Constantinople was to be only a temporary home for the True Cross, for eighteen months later, on 21 March 630, Heraclius rode up to another Golden Gate – this time Jerusalem's – where the relic truly belonged. This Golden Gate had been specially set into Jerusalem's East Wall to receive the sacred objects carried off by the Persians sixteen years before. Resplendent in his imperial robes, Heraclius dismounted to carry the True Cross personally through the gate and to the Church of the Holy Sepulchre, aromatic plants and rich carpets strewn in the path.[5] When the solemnities were over, and to make sure that Jerusalem remained safely in Byzantine hands, he eliminated its Jews (as allies of the Persians) by massacre, banishment and forced conversion. With the Persians quite neutralized, Heraclius would have been justified in considering himself a second Constantine the Great. He had fought valiantly to save his empire and could look forward to a glorious remainder of his reign. But he wasn't allowed the privilege, for another and much newer enemy had already arisen to measure swords with the Byzantine Empire.

From time immemorial the inhabitants of the Arabian peninsula and its adjacent lands had organized themselves along lines that were the very antithesis of the structured and stratified Roman and Byzantine polities, where grand state edifices were built on the rule of law. The Arabs had evolved a way of life that placed a high premium on the individual and his freedom to wander the deserts as he pleased, calling no man master. The harsh and unforgiving desert was no place in which the ideals of a common social purpose, and a respect for order and discipline, could take root. 'Since the days of Ishmael,' writes a leading authority on Arab history, 'the Arabian's hand has been against every man and every man's hand against him.'[6] The sole institution that did flourish by common Arab consent was the apparently highly destructive practice of the *ghazw*, or raid. What among more settled peoples would be considered mere brigandage became the very bedrock of the early Arab and Bedouin economy and society. A man, to be a man, had to raid and plunder men of other tribes, often with bloody consequences. 'Our business is to raid the enemy,' exulted the Arab poet al-Qutami, 'and on our own brother, in case we find nobody else!'

The other side of the coin of the Arab character was a rigid and unswerving loyalty to family and hospitality to the stranger in need. As in the hallowed ideal of the *ghazw*, there was no room for deviation or compromise. Yet as populations grew in the more fertile south seaboard of Arabia, the trend towards settled civilization picked up momentum. Trade ties with Egypt and India helped the Sabaeans and Himyarites (in what is now Yemen) to build up prosperous states. In the less-stable north the Nabataeans gradually followed suit, their greatest visible achievement being the city of Petra, hewn spectacularly into the red rock of the Jordanian desert. The Ghassanids, an Arab dynasty, ruled this region in the sixth century and by the time of King al-Harith II (c. 529–569) the Ghassanid Kingdom was firmly in the Byzantine camp as a key ally against the Persians.

Al-Harith was as ruthlessly competent as they come. We are assured that the mere mention of his name made the mentally ill Justin II scurry under his bed in terror. When he defeated the rival Lakhmid Kingdom under al-Mundhir III in 529, Justinian rewarded him by appointing him overlord of all the Arab tribes of Syria with the exalted rank of patrician. In 544 al-Mundhir captured one of al-Harith's sons and slaughtered him in a sacrifice to the Arab fertility goddess. After waiting ten patient years al-Harith had his revenge, despatching al-Mundhir at the battle of Qinnasrin. There were probably considerable casualties on the Ghassanid side, as Arab tradition says that al-Harith's daughter Halimah personally anointed a hundred warriors with perfume, and clad them in their shrouds to prepare them for death. When the old king called on Justinian in Constantinople in 563, the emperor was forcibly impressed by his bearing. Al-Harith's son Alamundarus paid an official visit to Constantinople in 580, where he received a crown.[7] Yet something seems to have gone sour in the Ghassanids' relations with Byzantium, for we next hear of Alamundarus being arrested on suspicion of treachery and taken in chains to Constantinople and then to prison in Sicily.

His son al-Numan attacked Byzantine territory but was soon overcome in his turn. Thereafter the Ghassanid Kingdom dissolved.

The revelations of Muhammad the Prophet among the sand dunes of Central Arabia in about 610 proved to be a game-changer of epic proportions. His preaching of Islam, the religion of submission to Allah, flew straight into the face of the traditional ferocious Arab individualism. It was at first mocked and resisted in many quarters. Yet, by some relentless process, within a few years the new religion had replaced the old anarchic and self-serving habits in many an Arab heart. Muhammad personally (human nature permitting) provided his own example of humility. The realization dawned that here, at last, was something greater than mere individual or even clan self-interest. By the standards of historical time, it was as if a switch had been thrown. The absolutist mind-set of the Arab was now recruited into the noblest of collective causes, and just as the Byzantine emperors were ideologically committed to defending and if possible expanding the realm of Christ, so the early Arab Muslims became fanatically intent on spreading the word of Allah as revealed to his *rasul*, or Prophet. The stage was set for a tectonic collision.

Muhammad died in 632 and was succeeded by his elderly father-in-law and early associate Abu-Bakr as the first caliph (*khalifah* = successor). Abu-Bakr's two years as caliph were consumed by quarrels among the undisciplined Arab adherents of Islam, to subdue whom he employed a skilful strategist, Khalid ibn-al-Walid, as his military chief. Within six months Khalid had established the caliphal authority over all the Arabian Peninsula. This unlikely military genius who had sprung out of the wastes of Arabia was now in a position to challenge the pre-eminent power of Byzantium. Heraclius probably had little idea of what would ensue when he decided to halt the lavish payments to some Arab tribes south of the Dead Sea. The resentment this move generated played directly into the hands of the Muslims, who had no difficultly in bringing round their South Syrian kin. Compared with the tired and corrupt Byzantine tax-collectors, the Muslims represented an exciting new power. The Bedouin warriors themselves saw before them new vistas of conquest and plunder. In fact, economic gain outdid religious zeal as the prime motive for Arab raids outside Arabia proper. Thus the poet abu-Tammam, addressing himself to the Bedouins:

> Not for Paradise didst thou the nomad life forsake; Rather, it was thy yearning after bread and dates.[8]

A year before Heraclius restored the True Cross to Jerusalem, one of the Prophet's adopted sons, Zayd ibn-Harithah, led 3,000 men to capture the Byzantine border post of Mutah, where the coveted Mashrafiyah swords were made. Zayd needed the swords to help his men wrest Mecca from the unbelievers. The Byzantines repulsed the raid with little difficulty, though no one in Constantinople at the time would have imagined that the battle was the opening encounter in a relentless struggle between Islam and Christianity that would last for more than 800 years, see the destruction of the imperial city, and never quite finish.

The clashes intensified. In February 634 Yazid ibn-abu-Sufyan met the Byzantines south of the Dead Sea and inflicted a stinging defeat on them. Heraclius intervened, sending his brother Theodoros south with a fresh army. Theodoros was caught in the outskirts of Damascus in March by Khalid ibn-al-Walid, who had led his hardy cameleers on a dramatic eighteen-day forced march through a waterless desert from the frontiers of Iraq. Sidestepping Theodoros, he invested Damascus, whose Byzantine garrison evacuated the city in September 635 – probably thanks to betrayal within the walls. According to Arab chroniclers, the people of the towns that fell to Khalid 'went out to meet him accompanied by players on the tambourines and singers and bowed down before him'.

Heraclius, to halt this new and alarming foe that had welled up from the deserts, beefed up Theodoros with 50,000 soldiers. Khalid moved out of Damascus to meet Theodoros with some 25,000 men at one of the most desolate places he knew – the dusty valley of the Yarmuk River, a tributary of the Jordan. For weeks both sides skirmished at the spot; when Khalid judged that the enemy had been worn down enough, on 20 August 636, as the scalding wind blew stinging sand into the Byzantines' faces and obscured the sky, Khalid attacked with great fury. The soldiers of Theodoros' army, fronted by chanting priests and crosses carried aloft, had no chance. Hundreds of Byzantines and their Armenian and Arab allies were cut down in the first wave; the panic-stricken survivors of that first strike were driven into the riverbed to be butchered there. A few made it to the other side, but they, too, were despatched. Theodoros was killed early in the action. In the space of a few hours Heraclius lost all Syria. 'What an excellent country that is for the enemy,' he is reported to have lamented on hearing the news of Yarmuk.

Two years later Jerusalem, which Heraclius had entered in triumph with the True Cross only eight years before, fell to Khalid's relentless attacks. The caliph at the time was Umar, a massive and imposing but unpretentious man, who visited the city shortly after the conquest. The Greek Orthodox Patriarch Sophronius, who acted as his guide, frowned at the caliph's shabby clothing and crude manners and confided to an aide that here, at last, was 'the abomination of desolation spoken of by Daniel the Prophet as standing in the holy place'.[9] Farther east, the Arabs under Saad ibn-abi-Waqqas trounced the Persians at Qadissiyah by employing similar tactics to those of the victors of Yarmuk, taking advantage of a dust storm. Within a few weeks Saad had entered the Persian capital of Ctesiphon with virtually no casualties, sending the Persian king Yazdagird III fleeing to the north and finishing him at Nihawad in 641. (Yazdagird himself was murdered by his own men in a miller's hut.)

After Umar's death in 644, the elderly Uthman became caliph. By now the conquests of Khalid and Saad had altered the centre of gravity of the newly-minted Islamic world. Al-Kufah (later Baghdad) became the chief administrative centre of Iraq. But Persian power was by no means extinct. It took ten years for the Arabs to subjugate the bulk of Persian lands and Islamize the region. In the meantime, another illustrious Arab general, Amr ibn-al-As, was conquering Egypt and North Africa with amazing ease, after vanquishing a Byzantine army at Ayn Shams (Eye of the Sun) in July 640. The great city of Alexandria fell to the Arabs a year later. The reasons were as much theological as military. Most of what we now call the Middle East had adhered to the Monophysite version of Christian doctrine which, in short, denied the human nature of Christ. The resulting simmering hostility to Byzantine orthodoxy as decreed from Constantinople made it easy for the Muslim Arabs to put over their own new, simplified and vigorous form of religious faith that made the Muslim military conquest easier to digest by the local people.

Heraclius reacted to these disasters with consternation. His best days were far behind him. He and his empire had spent enormous amounts of money and manpower to stem the encroachments of the Persians in the east, and the Avars and Slavs in the west, not to mention in the attempt to claw back Italy. By the time of Yarmuk, Heraclius was ill, his mind tormented by the obsession that God had somehow abandoned him. Yet he got together the stamina for one last feat, riding to Jerusalem just before the Arabs took it, and retrieving the True Cross. On the long journey back to Constantinople, he mind deteriorated. The sight of the Bosporus struck an unaccountable terror into him, so he stayed holed up for weeks in the Hiera palace on the Asian side. So afraid of water was this once steely-nerved warrior that the only way he could be induced to cross was by riding over a bridge of boats with tree branches on either side to hide the sight of the sea.

A visibly dying ruler is a signal for his potential heirs to start jockeying for position. Heraclius had two sons by different mothers; the elder, Constantine, appeared to be the natural successor, but Martina, the mother of the younger Heraklonas, schemed to place her own son on the throne. Martina pressed her claim skilfully, with the result that on 4 June 638 Heraclius tremblingly placed the diadem of promised succession on Heraklonas' head. Standing by was Constantine, who had already been designated co-ruler with his father. Heraclius declined rapidly, the victim of dropsy and a sinister-sounding genital ailment that reportedly made him urinate upwards so that he had to place a wooden board across his abdomen to avoid spattering himself in the face. His last days were consumed in those intractable religious wrangles which were fully capable of making any Byzantine emperor's life miserable. When he died on 11 February 641, it was as a grotesque shadow of a once-great leader. With him perished also the hallowed Roman usage of Augustus and *imperator* Caesar; from now, on the Greek *basileus*, or king, would be the standard title for Byzantium's emperors.

Constantine III and Heraklonas (641), Constans II Pogonatos (641–668), Constantine IV (668–685), Justinian II Rhinotmetos (685–695 and 705–711), Leontios (695–698), Tiberius III (698–705), Philippikos (711–713), Anastasius II (713–715) and Theodosius III (715–717)

Heraclius had welded the Byzantine army into an integral part of the state. The establishment of the *themes* had been a major step in building a loyal and efficient military based on regional defence needs. Heraclius' predecessor-but-one, Maurikios, had laid the theoretical framework with his twelve-part manual Strategikon, which systematized military practice from organization and supply to battle tactics, training and military justice, and described the fighting practices of other nations and tribes. In the middle of the seventh century the Byzantine army numbered about 150,000 men, with a high proportion of professional soldiers among them. State military spending came to about 35 per cent of the national budget, including border fortifications, communications and the maintenance of local militias.[10]

Weaponry had developed through the sixth century, with the cavalry now armed with a 3.6m lance and smaller javelin of about 2.5m. Both cavalry and infantry also used swords about 90cm long, sheathed in leather scabbards slung over the left shoulder. The heavy cavalrymen wore a *clibanium*, or sheet metal breastplate that sometimes had short sleeves to protect the underarm area; these men were known as *clibanarii*. Some added a chain-mail hood. Shields came in various shapes and sizes. The heavy infantry carried oval shields up to 1.2m long, while the cavalrymen's shields were smaller and circular, averaging 75cm in diameter; lighter infantry had smaller round shields.

The soldiers' helmets were of forged iron welded together in four or six parts and about 2mm thick. There were slits between the welded parts to enable the wearer to see and breathe and moderate the temperature inside the helmet in the hot sun and heat of battle. The sole helmet decoration was a reinforcement in the form of an iron strip curving around the forehead. A half-millimetre-thick copper-lined cheekpiece protected the jaw area, and a metal or leather extension covered the back of the neck.

The Strategikon was the first comprehensive all-arms military manual in history and was not to be bettered until the twentieth century. Its pages contain instructions on how to coordinate infantry and cavalry, and heavy-armed and light-armed units. The task of the light infantry, for example, was to support the heavy infantry and harass the enemy at the same time. The heavy infantry was the main striking force, forming a nucleus around which the rest of the army could rally in battle. The lighter cavalry, made up largely of horsemen from the steppes of the Caucasus, would jab at the enemy's flanks and rear. The heavy cavalry was to charge and break the solid enemy line in case the heavy infantry failed to do the job.

A typical battle encounter would open with the three sections, or *meroi*, of the army strung out in a line, each *meros* (division) numbering some 7,000 men. A *meros* was subdivided into *chiliarchies*, roughly equivalent to brigades, of about 1,000 men each, which in turn were made up of *moirai*, or regiments of between 300 and 400 men.[11]

Some two-thirds of a force in the field was concentrated in the centre for maximum effect, with a reserve in the rear. The techniques of feinting and mock retreat were refined (though there seems to have been a mess-up at the battle of the Sarus River, with near-disastrous results for Heraclius.)

Heraclius' successors struggled to contain the first explosive stage of Arab expansion without his abilities. Constantine III, aged 29 at his accession, and Heraklonas, 26, were not even given the chance. As a spirited teenager with every promise of a brilliant reign ahead of him, Constantine had bravely defended Constantinople in the Avar siege of 626. But tuberculosis had wasted him in the years since. Sickly and depressive, he was dead just three months into his reign. There were loud denunciations of Martina as having had a hand in her stepson's death; circumstantial evidence was apparently compelling enough for both her and her natural son Heraklonas to be arrested. She was punished by having her tongue hacked out while Heraklonas was one of the first to suffer a grotesque form of imperial punishment that was now coming into vogue – rhinotomy, or slitting of the nose, that probably originated in the East. Anyone without a nose was thus rendered ineligible for the throne, as only a physically unblemished man could become emperor. (But that rule was not to last for long.)

It thus fell to Heraclius' second son by his first wife, also named Heraclius, to assume the throne as Constans II at the age of 11. While he was still a minor the Senate had the job of administering the empire, which in foreign policy terms meant trying to stem the Arab advance. Alexandria had just fallen, or was about to fall, to the armies of Amr ibn-al-As. Two years later the caliph Umar died, to be replaced by the elderly Uthman, who recalled Amr to the Arabian Peninsula, enabling the Byzantines to recapture Alexandria. But Amr sped back and in 646 sacked the place. A new capital of Egypt was established down the Nile at al-Fustat (which later became al-Qairah, or Cairo). A Byzantine punitive force of 120,000 men under Gregory, the Exarch of Carthage, suffered a heavy defeat at Amr's hands.

So far the Arabs had lacked a navy, and keen minds realized that one was needed urgently. Credit for raising a naval consciousness among the Arabs goes to the governor of Syria, a capable officer named Muawiyah. The forests of Lebanon provided ample timber for a fleet, and by 649 Muawiyah had trained a force of sailors strong and competent enough to hurl against Cyprus, a major Byzantine naval base. Muawiyah personally led the landings, which were successful, adding the first island to the Muslim domains. Constans was now 17, and probably old enough to help shape military policy. He and the Senate negotiated a two-year truce with the Arabs. Muawiyah used the truce to build more ships, which he flung against the island of Rhodes, with devastating results, in 654. To thwart this incursion into Greek seas, Constans personally led the Byzantine fleet of about 500 *dromones* against Muawiyah's ships, encountering them off the coast of Lykia (southwest Turkey). The resulting Battle of the Masts, as it became known, severely mauled the Byzantine navy. The Arabs cannily tied each one of their ships to a Byzantine one, to facilitate boarding and close-order combat. The poet al-Tabari described the sea as 'saturated with blood'. When it became clear that the Greeks were being worsted, Constans escaped with his life by changing clothes with an ordinary seaman who was subsequently killed.

An outbreak of internal dissention among the Arabs gave Constans a reprieve. Uthman, plagued by family intrigues and power plays, was stabbed to death while reading the Koran at home. The killers were followers of Ali, the Prophet's cousin, who was proclaimed the fourth caliph in 656. As a blood relative of Muhammad, Ali claimed a special legitimacy for the office of caliph, but the relatives and supporters of Uthman nursed their revenge. Their ringleader was none other than the conqueror of Cyprus and Rhodes, Muawiyah, but before they could act, Ali was stabbed in the forehead with a poisoned sabre while walking to a mosque. The killer most probably acted on personal rather than political motives, yet the result was that Muawiyah, the favourite of the generals Khalid ibn-al-Walid and Amr ibn-al-As, was proclaimed caliph in Jerusalem in 660.[12]

Constans II, now a mature 48, had grown a luxurious dark beard, conspicuous even for the time, which gave him the cognomen Pogonatos, or Bearded One. While Muawiyah was busy consolidating his own rule, establishing the Umayyad dynasty at Damascus and shunning foreign adventures for a while, Constans had to put up with a bewildering series of religious and ecclesiastical issues involving heretic bishops and suspicious popes in Rome, the details of which need not concern us here. The only military consequence of these issues was that in 653 a Byzantine force landed in Italy and carried off Pope Martin I who was subject to incredible indignities and brutalities in a Constantinople dungeon on charges of conspiring against the emperor.

If Constans, having lost the bulk of his Eastern provinces to the Arabs, wanted to preserve what he could of the Byzantine presence in the West, his treatment of Pope Martin was the worst possible move in the circumstances. It can be explained by his own callous character, which tended towards the paranoid; he had his own brother, a priest, put to death as a potential rival to the throne; historians claim he suffered conscience-stricken nightmares of his blood-spattered brother thereafter. To redeem himself, he personally undertook to salvage what he could of Italy, now dominated by the Lombards and threatened from the south by the Arabs who were already raiding Sicily. In 662 he sailed for Thessalonica, and it wasn't until a year had passed that he crossed the Adriatic, landing at Tarentum (Taranto), overcoming a small Lombard force and advancing up the Italian peninsula to Benevento.

Grimuald, the Lombard king, had plenty of time to send strong reinforcements to the garrison at Benevento. A military courier named

Sesuald, sent on ahead to notify the garrison that relief was on the way, was captured by the Byzantines. Constans offered to spare Sesuald's life if he would disinform the Benevento garrison that they could expect no help. The courier agreed, but as soon as he was led to the town walls he shouted up at defenders that Grimuald's army was close at hand and they should not lose heart. This brave man just had time to add a request that his family be taken care of before a Byzantine sword lopped off his head, which was put in a Byzantine catapult and hurled over the wall. Foiled at Benevento, Constans moved up to Rome, where there was still some support for the imperial cause. After removing a great part of the city's wealth, in July 663 he moved south and set up his court in the Sicilian city of Syracuse.

There he remained for five years, while Constantinople was governed by the Senate. But if any of the Syracusans had entertained hopes of wise Byzantine rule, those hopes were dashed by the rapacity of the imperial tax collectors. The officials' greed and venality split families apart, drove men into peonage, women into prostitution and children into servitude. News of this state of affairs would certainly have got back to Constantinople, which in the meantime was under siege by Arab forces under Muawiyah's son Yazid. So few were surprised when, on 15 September 668, one of Constans' Greek servants crept up on the emperor as he was lounging in his bath and brought a heavy soap-dish down on his head.

It's possible that the murder had been instigated by Constans' eldest son, who inherited his father's hard streak along with his throne as Constantine IV. The new emperor's first challenge came in the first year of his rule, in the form of a curious religious mutiny by some of the army's Asia Minor units demanding that Constantine rule jointly with his two younger brothers on the model of the Holy Trinity. The emperor had little patience with this sort of thing; when the ringleaders came to the palace to argue the case he had them executed and their bodies publicly exhibited. Constantine's suspicion naturally fell on his brothers, who were given the rhinotomy treatment disqualifying them from any kind of rule.

Such bursts of harshness aside – and in the intrigue-filled atmosphere of the time, we cannot be sure that they were totally unjustified – Constantine IV proved to be a competent emperor. Early in the game he had shown himself to be tough when necessary, and that is one of the basic standards by which a fighting emperor should be assessed. Byzantium was fortunate to have him, and not a moment too soon as the caliph Muawiyah, from his new capital in Damascus, plotted a strategy that he hoped would smash the Greco-Roman Christian Empire for good. Cyprus and Rhodes had been just the opening stages in the campaign. As he repudiated the tribute he had agreed to pay Byzantium, the island of Chios and the Asia Minor coast fell into Muawiyah's hands until in 672 the Arab fleet appeared in the Sea of Marmara and Arab troops fortified themselves at Kyzikos, just fifty miles from Constantinople itself.

Muawiyah had acquired his fleet partly by taking over the well-equipped Byzantine shipyards on the Syrian coast along with their technicians and probably many seamen as well.[13] These acquisitions helped the Arabs, traditionally suspicious of the sea, to become familiar with that element in an amazingly short time, as witnessed in the Battle of the Masts. When Constantine assumed the throne Yazid's forces were at the very gates of Constantinople. Yazid himself fought bravely in the successive skirmishes while the Prophet's elderly standard-bearer, al-Ayyub al-Ansari, attained immortality by dying of dysentery and being buried beneath the walls, his tomb later becoming a place of pilgrimage. Yazid eventually had to withdraw, and the Arab fleet now came to take his place. But the Byzantines were ready for it, thanks to a wonderful new secret weapon.

One of the refugees fleeing the Arab conquest of Damascus was a Greek scientist named Kallinikos, who concocted a mixture of sulphur, tartar, Persian gum, pitch, nitre, petroleum and pine resin which could be set alight and sprayed through primitive flame-throwing machines. The exact formula of Greek Fire is still imperfectly known, but of its devastating efficiency there is no doubt. Gibbon has left us a vivid and elegant description of it and its use:

> From this mixture, which produced a thick smoke and loud explosion, proceeded a fierce and obstinate flame … It was either poured from the rampart in large boilers, or launched in red-hot balls of stone or iron, or darted in arrows and javelins … [it] was most commonly blown through long tubes of copper, which were planted on the prow of a galley, and fancifully shaped into the mouths of savage monsters, that seemed to vomit a stream of liquid and consuming fire.

The first to suffer its destructive effects were the Arab seamen whose own formidable siege engines and catapults proved worse than useless. Greek Fire devoured wood and flesh alike; it couldn't be doused by water, but floated blazing on the sea surface, cremating those who jumped overboard trying to save themselves. (The only liquid said to be able to put out Greek Fire was urine, affording Lord Norwich a wry observation that it gave 'a completely new dimension to the technique of fire-fighting').[14] For five successive summers Muawiyah's navy moved on Constantinople, only to be burned up by Greek Fire each time. Only on Muawiyah's death in 680 did the Arabs give up. Their fleet abandoned the Aegean Sea completely, running into a severe storm north of Cyprus which further depleted its strength.

But Constantine IV could hardly rest on his laurels, as yet a new enemy was pressing on his western frontier. These were the Bulgars, a Finno-Ugric people whom the invading Huns had left behind in Eastern Europe. In the reign of Constans Pogonatos they had infiltrated into Slav lands in what is now Romania. Now, under their able King Asparuch, they had crossed the Danube into what is now Bulgaria, directly threatening the empire. Immediately after seeing off the Arab fleet, Constantine acted quickly against the Bulgars, leading a fleet into the Black Sea and up to the mouth of the Danube, with the intention of striking inland to deal with the main Bulgar forces. The imperial troops found themselves stuck in marshland, while Constantine himself was laid low by an attack of gout. Because of this, many men somehow got the impression that the emperor had fled, which in turn triggered a general disorganized withdrawal. The Bulgars pounced at this point, driving the Byzantines back across the Danube and slaughtering their prisoners.

Constantine, recovered but chastened, found it expedient to pay Asparuch an annual bribe to keep him away from the capital. Indeed, the Bulgars were finding the Balkans pleasantly fertile for permanent settlement; Asparuch established the Bulgar capital at Varna and overcame the surrounding Slav peoples, establishing a Bulgarian state that has endured to the present. As for Constantine, his next five years were taken up with internal administration, especially the intractable ecclesiastical issues which were a permanent thorn in the Byzantine side. By the time he was 30, and after having upheld religious orthodoxy in the face of intricate heretical challenges, the church hailed him as 'a new Constantine the Great'. He did not have long to enjoy the honour, as three years later he died of dysentery.

Constantine's son Justinian was just 17 when he succeeded his father as Justinian II in 685. Even then he was notorious as an arrogant and disagreeable youth who seemed to have inherited more than the normal share of the Heraclian line's hard streak, which in his case emerged as extreme paranoia. Historians are unanimous in describing him as a blood-crazed inhuman monster. The first years, though, were promising for him. The Umayyad Arabs were quiescent; since Muawiyah three caliphs had come and gone in short order. But in 685, the year of Justinian II's accession, the great

Abd-al-Malik (Father of Kings) succeeded to the caliphate in Damascus. At first Abd-al-Malik continued his predecessors' cautious policy of paying tribute to Byzantium, even when Justinian – the 'tyrant of the Romans' to the Arabs – ratcheted it up, personally demanding an additional horse and slave every Friday. Byzantium and the Arabs agreed to share Cyprus, while Justinian pulled back a few of the more extended military outposts in Asia for a tighter defence of Asia Minor. To populate the areas south and east of Constantinople, Justinian marched to Thessalonica and into the Balkan hinterland, uprooting thousands of Slav families and relocating them to the Opsikion military *theme* (in present day north-west Turkey). Perhaps a quarter of a million Slavs were resettled in this way. It seemed as if the new emperor was wisely ensuring a supply of military manpower for the defence of the empire, but the project boomeranged badly.

The first test of the Slav soldiers' mettle came at Sebastopolis in 692, during a clash with Arab forces. Large numbers of them, doubtless resentful at being wrenched permanently from their Balkan homes, deserted to the enemy. These desertions cost Byzantium almost the whole of Armenia, and here Justinian revealed his true brutality. Theophanes the historian claims that thousands of Slavs were butchered in revenge, and their bodies thrown into the Sea of Marmara.[15] At about the same time social rules were tightened to absurdity. Women were forbidden to dance, men were not allowed to attend the public baths in the company of a Jew and 'long-haired hermits' were barred from the streets. There was also to be no more playing dice, giving Christmas presents or curling hair 'in a provocative or seductive manner'. Justinian made an abortive attempt to arrest Pope Sergius I, which only made the Byzantine administration in Italy more despised than ever. At home he cultivated a primitive Marxism by raising up a peasant class which he larded with money stolen from the upper classes; the patricians who could not or would not pay up were tortured over blazing fires by Justinian's chief treasurer, an ugly eunuch named Stephanos who was never without a whip; on one notorious occasion he even whipped the emperor's own mother. In 695 the aristocracy had had enough and rose in revolt.

They found a willing leader in a senior officer named Leontios who had recently served a three-year jail term for losing battles against the Arabs but had just been appointed military governor of the Hellas *theme*. Justinian probably didn't know that (as historians of the time claimed) Leontios while behind bars had been told by a visiting monk that he would one day be emperor. If the story is true, the general contempt in which the emperor was held would not have made the prediction a particularly hazardous one. Leontios moved on the guards' barracks, freeing those who had been confined there for their opposition to the emperor and marching them to Sancta Sophia. By now they had been joined by an enthusiastic host of Blues supporters (the factions were still quite alive and kicking). The patriarch received them all with joy, exclaiming that finally what 'the Lord hath ordained' had come to pass.

With the Blues and his own men behind him, Leontios invaded the palace, seized Justinian and took him in chains to the Hippodrome along with his despised ministers. There, as the crowd roared insults at him, his nose was duly slashed in the now time-honoured manner. He got off lightly compared to his ministers (perhaps including the brutish Stephanos), who were dragged by their feet behind wagons into the middle of the city and burned alive. Justinian was exiled to Cherson in the Crimea. But Byzantium had by no means seen the last of him; after all, he was still only 26, and nose or not, he had no intention of resigning himself to his fate.

Leontios reigned for three years, but never managed to become popular. Since the Blues supported him, he automatically earned the enmity of the Greens. Besides, his competence to rule seems to have been in some question. His downfall came in 698 when the Arabs under the energetic Abd-al-Malik, having swarmed across North Africa, overran Carthage, putting an end to the Byzantine presence there. A Byzantine fleet sent to regain the city bungled badly; rather than return to face the consequences of defeat, one of the senior commanders, a German named Apsimar, decided to topple the emperor. Apsimar's men enthusiastically seconded him, acclaiming him as Basileus and sailing with him to Constantinople. By the time he arrived he had changed his name to the more imperial one of Tiberius and had recruited the Greens to his cause. The public, moreover, was eager for a change, and for the second time in the space of three years a reigning emperor was dragged from the palace to suffer the now-standard nasal surgery. The noseless Leontios was packed off to a monastery where he could do no more damage and Tiberius III assumed the diadem.

As an experienced soldier, Tiberius proved competent enough. The start of the eighth century saw him hard-pressed to stem Arab raids in Northern Syria and Cilicia. The Arab armies, influenced by Byzantine practice, had upgraded their organization; in Asia Minor, for example, they had adopted the divisional system whereby five divisions constituted the centre, wings, vanguard and rear guard. There was little outward difference between the Byzantine and Arab soldier, especially in the size and shape of the shields. The Arab standing army numbered about 60,000, while the navy, also built on the Byzantine model, was made up of galleys each crewed by more than a hundred rowers, plus marines stationed on the upper decks. Within seven years the exertions of Tiberius enabled Byzantium to breathe more easily, but he hadn't counted on the paranoid vengefulness of Justinian.

During the tedious years of his exile in Cherson, Justinian had not ceased to plot a bloody comeback. By 703 his intrigues had embarrassed the authorities of Cherson to such an extent that they decided to pack him off back to Constantinople, but he was tipped off in time and escaped to the Ukrainian hinterland to the domain of the Khazar Turks whose *khagan* (king), Ibuzir, offered him the hand of his sister. The girl most likely had no choice but to join herself to this repulsive and facially deformed man who now embarked on a career as a fighting emperor of sorts, but not the kind likely to read well in the history books. Tiberius sent an armed mission to Ibuzir's court to collect Justinian. The squad claimed to be his new bodyguard, but with the intuition of the paranoiac he realized what was afoot; inviting a couple of squad officers to his home, he pounced on them and personally strangled them.

Though Justinian's Khazar wife Theodora was now pregnant, he left her with her brother and escaped in a fishing boat to Cherson where he got some supporters together to continue the journey across the Black Sea. When the ship was caught in a severe storm Justinian brusquely dismissed all suggestions that he placate God by promising to change his murderous ways, growling that he would rather drown on the spot than exercise the slightest clemency to those who had driven him from his throne. The boat safely reached the shore of the Bulgars whose king, Tervel, agreed to help Justinian regain the throne of Byzantium in return for a marriage alliance with yet another royal daughter. In spring 705 Justinian brought his mixed army to the walls of Constantinople. His demand that the gates be opened to him was met with gross insults. Told of a disused water mains running under the north wall, he personally crawled through it, probably accompanied by some soldiers. In a short time the palace guard was neutralized. Tiberius, knowing what was in store for him, fled across the Bay of Nicomedia.

If there had been any doubts about Justinian's savage madness before, there could be none now. His face was as repulsive as his mind; mucus would often flow uncontrollably from his open nasal orifices. In February 706 he had Tiberius and his predecessor Leontios seized and dragged into the Hippodrome, just as he had been ten years earlier. While the mob bayed for their blood, Justinian took a page out of his role model Caligula, planting a purple boot on the bowed neck of each man. As he did so, the crowd roared the verse from Psalm 91 – 'Thou hast trodden on the asp and the basilisk …' Leontios and Tiberius were taken away to be beheaded. But any traces of popular approval soon evaporated when Justinian named Tervel as Caesar, second in power only to himself. The people of Constantinople were stunned at this honour accorded to a barbarian king whose soldiers were itching to loot and rape. But that was nothing compared to the reign of terror that the monstrous emperor now inaugurated.

The bodies of generals and staff officers who had somehow earned the emperor's suspicion graced gibbets along the walls of Constantinople. Other opponents, real or imagined, were stuffed into sacks weighted with stones and thrown into the sea, presaging the later Ottoman practice of getting rid of royal rivals. The precise number of those put to death is not known. The patriarch himself was blinded and exiled to Rome. Such judicial blinding had been elevated to a precise art: a large silver dish was heated until it was red-hot; when vinegar was poured over it, the victim was forced to stare into the resulting acid vapours until they burned away the retinas of his eyes. (A quicker method, preferred in later times, was to simply gouge out the eyes with a rod.) News of these horrors must have reached Ibuzir, who nevertheless valued his alliance-by-marriage to Justinian too much. When the emperor's estranged wife sailed to Constantinople to reunite with her husband,

> [T]he watching crowd gasped again as the truth slowly dawned: this ogre who was their Emperor, this monster of inhumanity who seemed to breathe only bitterness and hatred, was in love.[16]

Justinian's affection for his Theodora (a grotesque travesty of the love of their more famous namesakes nearly two centuries before) may have been genuine in its twisted way. It is quite possible that her influence moderated some of his brutal urges. We find him repatriating 6,000 Arab prisoners and sending workmen to help Caliph al-Walid I build a huge mosque at Medina; in return, al-Walid sent back shiploads of pepper. Yet the people of Constantinople shook their heads in mistrust. The empress, good as she might be, was still an alien Khazar, and of course there was the conspicuous issue of Justinian's lack of a nose – an infliction that had been specially designed to bar people like him from the throne! For this he was popularly dubbed Rhinotmetos, or Slash-Nose, a cognomen that has endured in history. (Some sources say he wore a golden artificial nose to conceal the disfigurement.)

The honeymoon with the Arabs was brief. Hostilities resumed in Central Asia Minor in 709 when the Arabs seized parts of Cappadocia; the Byzantine defeat can be attributed directly to Justinian's elimination of his senior officer corps several years before. But before he could do anything to remedy the situation in that theatre, his attention was switched to Italy, where the Exarchate of Ravenna showed signs of secession from the empire. Justinian's reaction was typical: he sent a punitive expedition which arrested all the local officials and took them in chains to Constantinople. There, seated on his gem-encrusted throne, he sentenced the lot to death except the archbishop of Ravenna, whose eyes were put out.

Theodora's brother, the Khazar *khagan*, made a move against Justinian by occupying Cherson. A strong Byzantine force sailed to Crimea, where seven of the leading citizens of Cherson were roasted alive and many others drowned in weighted sacks, no doubt on Justinian's personal orders. Elemental revenge struck the Byzantine fleet on its way back, when a storm drowned most of its men. When Justinian heard the news he dissolved in insane laughter and planned another expedition, but in the meantime the Khazars had beefed up their defences and overcome the Byzantine garrison in Cherson. In 711 the *khagan* ordered the massacre of a Byzantine diplomatic mission and appealed to an Armenian exile named Bardanes to become the focus of opposition to Justinian.

Out of his mind with rage, the emperor sent a general, Maurus, to Cherson with orders to wipe the city and its people off the face of the earth. After some initial success, Maurus found himself facing a far larger body of Khazars and decided that anything was better than going back to Justinian and admitting failure. Soon he was accompanying Bardanes – now renamed Philippikos – in a fleet to topple the hated Slash-Nose. The time was now, as Justinian was on his way to quell a revolt in Armenia. When he received the news, he turned back in a rage, but Philippikos was too quick for him – on 4 November, twelve miles from Constantinople, Justinian was seized and beheaded on the spot; the head was sent to Philippikos in the palace and the population went wild with joy. The rest of Justinian was not thought fit for a decent burial and was thrown into the Sea of Marmara. Also slain were his 7-year-old son Tiberius and possibly Theodora as well.

Justinian II was a complete ogre, far surpassing even the nastiness of Phokas, yet he did not lack courage, and can be legitimately named among the fighting emperors of Byzantium. It could be argued that his courage was of the mentally deranged kind, untempered by any sense of caution or strategic wisdom. In his own distorted way he improved the empire's defences and secured more manpower by reorganizing the *theme* system and easing the lot of peasants who had been oppressed by wealthy landlords. He also, curiously, built up relations with the popes of Rome to their most cordial level in many years. Yet when the last of the Heraclian line was finally eliminated, the overwhelming sentiment in Byzantium was good riddance.

In Philippikos their new emperor, however, the people would be disappointed. Dissolute and pleasure-loving, his only real interest was to dabble in thorny theological issues. This way he quickly earned the enmity of Pope Constantine I in Rome, followed quickly by the far more active hostility of Bulgarian King Tervel, whose army marched up to the walls of Constantinople to avenge his ally Justinian II. Philippikos, shaken out of his hedonistic torpor, brought in troops from the Opsikian *theme* across from the Sea of Marmara to boost the defence. Far from helping him, however, the reinforcements burst into the palace on 3 June 713, rousted him from an afternoon nap and took him to the Hippodrome where, in a changing-room, he was deprived of his eyes in the now-common punishment. In his two-year reign he had done nothing to inspire confidence.

The Senate, with a keen ear to the ground, acted with alacrity to fill this unexpected power vacuum. The following day they picked a former palace chief secretary named Artemios, crowning him in Sancta Sophia as Anastasius II. He began his reign by putting some order back into the Byzantine administration, repairing the defensive walls, ensuring an adequate food supply in case of a siege and building new ships for the navy. But the Arabs were again on the warpath, and on the principle that offence is the best defence, he used Rhodes as a naval base from which to strike at the Arabs in Syria. It was a good plan, but Anastasius hadn't counted on the bloody-mindedness of the troops from the Opsikion *theme*, who had developed a taste for aggressive independence; deposing Justinian II had made them drunk with their own importance. Despatching their commanding officer by clubbing him on the head, the Opsikion troops turned back to march on Constantinople. On the way they somehow found a mild-mannered tax-collector named Theodosios and persuaded him at the point of a sword to lead the mutiny. Once in the capital they caused enough trouble to have Anastasius deposed after a two-year reign and the reluctant taxman put in his place as Theodosius III.

The new emperor's first and only test came a year after his accession, when Abd-al-Malik's brother Maslamah led 80,000 Arabs and Persians on a determined attempt to take Constantinople. While the Arab land forces crossed into Europe over the Dardanelles, 1,800 Muslim ships appeared off the city 'like a moving forest' of masts. Luckily, the entrance to the Golden Horn was barred by a chain, but Maslamah was nothing if not persistent and didn't let that faze him. Theodosius himself scarcely needed persuading that he was not up to the task of defending an empire and in early 717 he agreed to abdicate, to retire thankfully to a monastery. Waiting in the wings was a real fighter.

Chapter Five

Leo the Isaurian Saves Europe

Leo III (717–740)

The Isaurians, as we have seen, were a tough and warlike tribe from what is now Southeast Turkey and a vital part of Byzantine defence since the early years of the empire. But Leo the Isaurian, despite his appellation, wasn't one of them. Originally named Konon, after an Athenian admiral of the fifth century BC, he was a descendant of a family that had originated in Eastern Asia Minor but had migrated to Thrace in Europe. We first hear of him as an officer in the Imperial Guard who somehow escaped Justinian II's bloody purges and was entrusted with delicate military-diplomatic negotiations with turbulent tribes in Syria and the Caucasus. Justinian's successor Anastasius II confirmed Leo as military governor of the Anatolikon *theme* in Western Asia Minor.

Before the Arabs under Maslamah advanced on Constantinople, Leo had confronted them before the city of Amorion, which was his headquarters. Rather than risk battle, Leo negotiated an Arab withdrawal with Suleyman, the Arab commander on his front. The details of how he did this are obscure.[1] Leo was a fluent Arabic speaker and understood the Arab mind; Suleyman seems to have been duped into thinking that if Leo became emperor in Constantinople, he would become the Arabs' ally. Maslamah's forces were about to resume their assault on Constantinople in the spring, but Leo had not the slightest intention of becoming his helper. Having neutralized Suleyman, he joined Artabasdos, the governor of the Armeniakon military *theme* abutting the Black Sea, and marched on the capital himself, overcoming a small force under Theodosius III's son. When Theodosius abdicated, Leo entered the Golden Gate on 25 March 717 to be crowned Leo III in Sancta Sophia. The crowds lining the roadsides saw a thickset man of medium height in his early thirties, with a dark beard and moustache curling down to his chin. His large hazel eyes were set rather close together in a habitually melancholy expression, as if not quite believing his extraordinary fortune in having attained the highest office of Byzantium from his peasant origins and half-expecting the bubble to burst at any moment. He would need every ounce of luck he could get.

Maslamah and his 80,000 Arabs duly appeared before the walls of Constantinople on 15 August while Suleyman's fleet joined them offshore two weeks later. This time Maslamah meant business, breaking with established military practice to keep up campaigning through the coming winter. Maslamah apparently entertained a hope that Leo wouldn't put up much of a fight, or even that he might agree to rule as the Arabs' puppet. The emperor actively encouraged such delusions, which made the shock to the Arabs all the greater when he revealed his real intentions. These included a devastating use of Greek Fire against Suleyman's ships; the Arabs seem to have learned little from their previous blazing encounters with this superb weapon of war.

Maslamah's decision to keep up the siege through the winter was an unfortunate one. The winter of 717–18 was unusually harsh; for weeks thick snow blanketed city and landscape. The unhabituated Arabs in their desert gear and thin tents died by the hundreds from cold and hunger, as the snow prevented them for foraging for food. According to the historian Theophanes, the Arabs ate their dead pack animals, and when the supply of those ran out, were driven to devouring their own dead, mixing the flesh with excrement and baking it. Naturally in such conditions, disease came to add its toll. Suleyman was one of the victims. His corpse and that of many others had to be thrown into the sea, as no graves could be dug in the icy ground. But in the spring of 718 it seemed that Maslamah's persistence might pay off, as a large Egyptian fleet loomed up out of the Sea of Marmara, plunging the defenders into despair. But the despair turned to relief when the fleet's Christian galley-slaves gleefully deserted to the Byzantines.

With the arrival of warm weather, help for the Byzantines arrived from another unexpected source. The Bulgars had been observing the course of events anxiously, and the last thing they wanted was a Muslim conquest of Constantinople and an infidel presence on their borders. Overcoming their past hostility to Byzantium (and larded with copious quantities of Byzantine gold), they sent an army which surprised the exhausted and weakened Arab force before the walls and killed thousands of its survivors. In August Maslamah realized the game was up and withdrew. Of the Arab fleet, those vessels that had escaped the Greek Fire were caught in storms, and reportedly just five out of the original 1,800 made it back to a home port.

Leo III's victory over the Arabs at Constantinople cannot be overestimated. He literally saved Europe – or at least most of it – from Arab conquest. The achievement is fully on a par with that of Charles Martel, the Duke of Austrasia in France, who halted the Arab Moors in a memorable encounter at Tours fourteen years later. Even Gibbon relaxes his austerity to assert that Leo 'rescued our ancestors of Britain, and our neighbours of Gaul, from the civil and religious yoke of the Koran'. Greek writers praise Leo as 'the Miltiades of the mediaeval Greeks,' referring to the Athenian general's epochal triumph over the invading Persians in 490 BC.[2] Never again would the Arabs threaten Christendom so severely (though Islam, under another ethnic group, would take up where the Arabs left off). The debacle before Constantinople signalled the impending end of the Arab Umayyad dynasty, which would totter on for three more decades under a string of caliphs, some competent, most not. Internal decay would give way in 750 of the Abbasid dynasty, which would revive the Muslim appetite for the Byzantine Empire, but with nowhere near the strength of past attempts.

Leo's stunning success provoked envy among some of the governors of the military *themes* who began to display dangerous rebellious tendencies. In response, he split up most of them into smaller units to keep them more manageable. The Byzantine navy chased Arab ships around the Mediterranean, keeping the vital Aegean sea lanes free. In 720 the emperor personally took the field with his son Constantine against an Arab army and defeated it. In civil administration he reorganized the economy and began to reform the laws of Byzantium more in line with perceived Christian principles. Here is where he had his work really cut out for him.

Though he was a fighting emperor of the first order, Leo III is known to history not so much for his military achievements as for his involvement in a major religious controversy that overshadowed his twenty-three year reign. We must not forget that in Byzantium religious ideology informed foreign policy and by extension military policy. The spirited defence of Constantinople in 717–8 was ample proof that any form of Islamic rule simply could not be countenanced by the Byzantine people, high and low. To be sure, there was plenty of trade with Muslim lands. But, unlike in our own age, money wasn't everything; when it came to belief, the ramparts were strong. But these religious ramparts, like physical ones, needed inspecting and repairing every so often, and as soon as the Arab menace dissolved, Leo turned his attention to the vexed issue of Christian icons.

Part of the ease with which the Arabs under the Umayyads had swept over large tracts of the Byzantine-ruled Middle East was that many Christian populations had viewed them as a refreshing change from the tangled and violence-tinged doctrinal controversies of which the Byzantine Empire could never rid itself. In those early days Islam was not radically different from basic Christianity; it just applied the moral rigour of the Old and New Testaments in a rather more austere way than most Christians had been used to. For example Islam, backed up by plenty of text in the Old Testament, banned all graven images. Rather like the Protestants of much later days, many Christians found this simple tenet appealing. But the problem for Byzantium was that it directly attacked hallowed orthodox practice. The holy icons were not only venerated; all too often the wood and paint and gold themselves were worshipped. The outraged purists who wished to abolish icons as barely-disguised idolatry were known as the Iconoclasts.

Early in his battles against the Arabs, Leo had become aware of the contrast between Muslim enthusiasm and Christian laxity. He must have seen some merit in the Muslim opposition to icons. In fact he had little use for the ecclesiastical world in general; he was a practical rather than a lettered man, and saw nothing to admire in the monasteries which absorbed far too many bookish young men who could be better employed on the farms, in businesses and in the army – and were tax-exempt to boot. These monks wielded extraordinary spiritual power over the common people, so in 726 Leo placed the monasteries directly under his personal control. Four years later he issued his famous Iconoclast Decree, forbidding the worship of icons. The biggest icon in Constantinople, a great golden image of Christ over the main gate to the palace dating from Justinian I, was ordered destroyed. The popular backlash was immediate; a group of manic women murdered the official in charge of the demolition, and within days, reports arrived at the palace of mutinies in the army and navy. Pope Gregory II thundered his condemnation from Rome while the Byzantine exarch in Ravenna was assassinated. In Constantinople Patriarch Germanos was sacked when he, too, raised his voice against the desecration. Protests by Saint John Damascene, a leading theologian, that the holy icons were 'the books of the unlettered,' important to ordinary people who couldn't read, were brushed aside.

The response of Leo, the no-nonsense soldier who had saved the empire, was to issue a blanket ban on icons altogether. Many thousands of them, including superb works of art, were smashed. Monks hid thousands of others under their black robes and fled to mainland Greece or inland to Cappadocia, risking arrest and possible execution if discovered. Leo sent a ship to arrest the obstreperous pope, but it sank in the Adriatic. For the next decade or so, the stunned Byzantines had to live with the puritanical Iconoclast decrees and pray before their treasured icons in secret until Leo died of dropsy on 18 June 741, aged about 60. He probably had no regrets about enforcing his puritanical version of Christianity to draw his Eastern subjects away from the lure of Islam. But far from uniting the Christian world that way, he only divided it the more.

Constantine V 'Kopronymos' (741–775) and Artabasdos (742–743)

The entry into the world of Leo's son Constantine in 718 was accompanied by a baptismal mishap rare in the annals of palace births: we are told that the royal infant evacuated his bowels into the font during the ceremony. Such an incident would probably have remained an amusing family anecdote had not an aggrieved populace had cause to remember it much later. Twenty-three years old when he assumed the throne, Constantine V had been groomed for the top job almost since that embarrassing day at the font. At age 2 he had been designated co-emperor with his father, which meant that he had fully absorbed Leo's intractable iconoclasm and was equally determined to enforce it throughout the empire. Remembering the story of his infantile defecation at baptism, his enemies dubbed him Kopronymos, literally meaning 'Name of Dung'.[3]

A year into his rule, he came up against the first determined opposition in the person of his brother-in-law Artabasdos, an official who had married into the royal family and become a rallying point for the orthodox icon-supporters. Artabasdos and the forces loyal to him struck while Constantine was on his first campaign against the Arabs, defeating an imperial force and entering Constantinople to proclaim himself emperor. The icons were brought out of hiding and restored to their places of honour in the churches and public places of Constantinople. For a year and a half the city was, in Lord Norwich's phrase, 'aglitter with gold'. But Constantine was far from beaten. Central and Eastern Asia Minor, strongholds of iconoclasm, responded enthusiastically to his call for a counter-stroke. The rival armies met at Sardis; Constantine won the fight and reoccupied his capital on 2 November 743. Artabasdos and his sons were blinded, and some of his officials executed. Patriarch Anastasios, who had backed the usurper, was flogged and paraded around the Hippodrome naked riding backwards on a donkey – and then given back his job and told to behave himself.

Artabasdos' rebellion inflamed Constantine's iconoclasm to a dictatorial degree. The orthodox populace, along with their patriarch, were completely cowed; again the icons disappeared, the grand religious mosaics torn down and replaced by secular subjects. This was probably the time that people remembered the emperor's baptismal bowel movement and used it to give him his unflattering sobriquet. He was, however, far from being a sour puritan. Our sources – admittedly mostly hostile – speak of bisexual affairs and plenty of music and partying. Yet he was an honest believer in his way and found time to write serious theological treatises in which he argued passionately against icons, the cult of saints and all the imagery that has since come to be associated with the Eastern Orthodox and Roman Catholic churches. He believed his father had not gone far enough in stamping out such practices. Giving him moral ammunition was the widespread corruption among what he despised as the 'unmentionable' clergy. Yet on the other hand, many innocent and devout priests and monks suffered humiliation, torture and death. Some monks' beards were doused with oil and wax and set on fire. However noble the motive, this was classic persecution.

Partly to ensure the loyalty of the military and partly to remedy the ravages of a severe outbreak of bubonic plague, Constantine reorganized the army into new units called *tagmata* and prepared it for a fresh drive against the Arabs in 746.[4] The Umayyad caliph Marwan II had made similar rearrangements in the Muslim forces, introducing the *kurdus*, or compact infantry cohort, for greater mobility and striking power. But the Umayyads were weak, Marwan's own days were numbered, and Constantine had no difficulty invading Syria and sending the navy to pound the Arab fleet into pulp off Cyprus. After these Arab reverses in 750 Abu-al-Abbas, who claimed a blood connection with the Prophet Muhammad, moved with a rebel army against Marwan, who along with others of the Umayyad clan was hunted down and slaughtered. Their bodies – the dying along with the dead – were heaped up to provide a table for the victory dinner of al-Abbas' general Abdullah, who feasted with his officers 'to the accompaniment of human groans'.[5] The new Abbasid dynasty at first was too preoccupied with consolidating its power to put up much resistance to Byzantium, so Constantine was able to secure more of Northern Syria.

Constantine himself was an unlikely soldier in appearance; constitutionally frail, often ill and subject to depression, he nevertheless earned his soldiers' admiration for his strong will, courage in the field and strategic talents. The Arab quiescence enabled him to turn his attention from the Middle East to fighting the Bulgars for control of the Balkans. Constantine had resettled some Syrians in Bulgaria, which aroused the Bulgars' hostility. In 755 he rode out in person, defeating the Bulgar king Kormisosh in a battle perilously close to the Anastasian Wall west of Constantinople. This campaign inaugurated a series of nine more, about which we know the basics, but little else. The Bulgars were now Byzantium's prime foe in the West, succeeding the now-gone Huns and Ostrogoths. To subdue them took up the rest of Constantine's reign. First he pacified the Slavs of Macedonia to secure his flank for a grand invasion of Bulgaria which began in 760 by an amphibious expedition of 500 vessels into the Black Sea and up to the mouth of the Danube. The imperial army was ambushed at Veregava, losing many men including two senior commanders. However, an attempt by the Bulgars to repeat that victory at Marcellae resulted in the first devastating defeat in their history.

The resulting respite for Byzantium was all too brief, as an energetic young king, Teletz, assumed the leadership of the Bulgars. Teletz spent three years putting the fight back into the Bulgar army and attacked Byzantium with all he had. Constantine this time didn't repeat the mistakes that had led to the reverse at Veregava; instead he stuck close to the Black Sea coast while 800 ships cruised offshore carrying 10,000 cavalry. On 30 June 763 Teletz attacked the emperor at Anchialos (modern Burgas). The battle raged from dawn to dusk, with heavy casualties on both sides (our scant sources do not say whether the cavalry was employed at all), until the Bulgars broke and Teletz fled the field. Constantine Dung-name returned to Constantinople in justified triumph, bringing high-ranking Bulgars in chains. During the celebrations in the Hippodrome, according to some sources, those prisoners were 'left to the mercy of the crowd', whatever that might mean.[6]

After his debacle at Anchialos, Teletz was quickly disposed of; the next couple of years saw an extended power struggle in the Bulgar kingship. Seeing weakness in the enemy, Constantine led another campaign into Bulgar territory in 764, passing through Anchialos and striking inland. This was more a show of strength than an invasion; moreover the Bulgars had strong forces guarding the main mountain passes. Of rather more use to Constantine was the spy network he had set up among the enemy. Thanks to his agents, who had access to the highest echelons of the Bulgar kingdom, and to the merciless torture of questionable tribal leaders, Constantine was able to keep track of what was going on. Over the next two years the emperor attacked the Bulgars twice more, culminating in a grand campaign that started on 21 June 766 involving the biggest Byzantine army and fleet to date. Once more Constantine appeared before Veregava; this time the sight of the imperial force was enough to cause the Bulgars to sue for peace. But before Constantine could move he received news that a storm had sunk a good portion of his fleet. He thus had no choice but to retire, trawling the waters off Anchialos for the bodies of his drowned soldiers so that they could be given a decent burial.

For the next eight years Byzantium's relations with the Bulgars are hidden behind a curtain of mystery. Constantine used the interval to concentrate once more on enforcing his iconoclast policies at home, which cannot have helped his popularity, as contemporary sources are very free with his fecal nickname, adding other epithets such as 'unholy,' 'tyrant' and 'contemptible'. It was May 774 before Constantine resumed his campaigning against the Bulgars, again by sea up to the Danube. Our sources say that this time 2,000 cavalry-laden ships took part, with the emperor himself in command of an elite squadron of red-painted imperial galleys. But at Varna, between the mouth of the Danube and Anchialos, the campaign came to an abrupt halt. The historian Theophanes claims the emperor 'lost his courage and wished to turn back'. But since that sounds too facile an explanation, what most probably occurred is that the emperor realized that the Bulgars had regained their past strength and that it might be better to make peace with them rather than marching against them ad infinitum, wasting men and resources.

He was now in his late fifties, and perhaps tired of constant warfare. His health, never robust, was probably worsening. This might help explain the astonishing naiveté which he displayed early in 775, when Telerig, the new Bulgarian king, wrote to him saying he wished to defect to Byzantium and that he required the identities of the Byzantine agents in Bulgaria who could help him escape. Incredibly, Constantine revealed the names of his spies, who were rounded up and put to death. The humiliated emperor now had no choice but to move against the treacherous Telerig. This was to be a land campaign only, without naval support. But it was August, and the long march proved too much for Constantine; his legs swelled up painfully, and he was carried back south on a litter. At Selymbria on the Sea of Marmara, consumed by fever, he was put on board a ship for Constantinople, but he expired en route on 14 September.

Leo IV (775–780), Constantine VI (780–797) and Irene (797–802)

Constantine Kopronymos' empress had been a Khazar princess, and in the chauvinistic atmosphere of the time it was natural that his son Leo, 26 at the time of his father's death, should be dubbed 'the Khazar'. Leo IV seems to have inherited his father's lack of robustness, and to have suffered from chronic illness. He paid lip service to the iconoclastic inclinations of his father and grandfather, though it seems his heart wasn't really in it. This could have been through the influence of his strong-willed Athenian wife Irene, an icon supporter, and the second powerful Athenian lady to seize the reins in Byzantium since Athenais married Theodosius II nearly 400 years before.

While Constantine V was busy with the Bulgars, conditions in Italy had moved rapidly to a Byzantine eclipse. The Lombards had taken Ravenna in 751, while three years later the Romans felt they had little choice but to throw in their lot with a new and rising power in the North West, the Franks. Pope Stephen II, no friend of the Byzantine establishment, travelled to meet the Frankish leader, Pepin the Short, and crowned him king. Pepin in return sent his troops into Italy, taking over Rome and setting up what became known as the Papal States. This final and inglorious end to Byzantine influence in Italy seemed to matter little to Leo IV, who reigned just five years. In the summer of 780 he contracted a malady that filled his face and head with sores, and in a matter of weeks he was dead.

Leo's Athenian widow Irene seized the reins as regent for her 10-year-old son Constantine VI. Events on the Bulgar front were a good omen for the beginning reign, as Telerig, oddly enough after his treachery with the spies, genuinely defected to Byzantium, to be rewarded with the title of patrician, given a wife out of the royal family and converted to Christianity. Irene, for her part, nursed a grand scheme to restore good relations with the popes – and perhaps grab back some of Italy in the process – by enforcing orthodoxy in the troublesome issue of the icons. The popes, despite their embrace of Frankish power, were still technically subject to the patriarch of Constantinople, and so Pope Hadrian I sent delegates to a grand new church council that convened in 786 in the Church of the Holy Apostles. But barely had the berobed churchmen taken their seats than soldiers burst into the church and ordered them all to clear out – the army was still overwhelmingly iconoclast, and would not allow the restoration of the icons if it could help it.

Irene was not cowed, but for the moment had her hands full with the Arabs, whose Abbasid caliph, al-Mahdi, and his fabled son Harun al-Rashid had come menacingly close to Constantinople and forced Irene to approve a heavy tribute. The units she sent eastwards to stem the Arab advance were the iconoclast ones; thus rid of them, she organized a more successful ecclesiastical council at Nicaea. After weeks of acrimonious dispute, in October 787 the Seventh Ecumenical Council restored the icons to their place in orthodox worship, though with the proviso that they should be venerated rather than worshipped outright – a distinction that meant little, if anything, to the mass of people, who duly rejoiced.

Constantine, just 17, signed the council's decrees, but otherwise he was almost totally powerless. No doubt he chafed at his mother's domination, and we see him at 18 riding out at the head of an army to the old battlefield of Marcellae to halt another Bulgar drive southwards. But the young emperor was nothing like his grandfather. The Bulgar king, Kardam, attacked the straggling Byzantines at Marcellae and routed them, capturing the imperial tent. Back in Constantinople, Irene sought to compensate for the inadequacy of her son by a bloody purge of the officer corps and officialdom. In 790 she demanded that her name take precedence over her son as monarch – in effect, making herself empress regnante and ordering the army to swear a personal oath to herself only. And just to make sure that Constantine himself would behave, she had him jailed.

The European and home units knuckled under to Irene's orders, except those of the Armeniakon *theme* in Asia Minor. Units from the Armeniakon freed Constantine from his confinement and put him in charge of the legitimist movement. We don't know whether he took over personal leadership or, what is more likely, merely did what he was told. The immediate result was that Irene was shut up in the luxury palace she had just had built for herself and her associate Staurakios, who was flogged and exiled. This did not mean, unfortunately, that the legitimate emperor of Byzantium had finally asserted himself. Irene had constantly ridiculed her son as weak and incompetent, and he did nothing to correct that impression. Easily swayed this way and that by a variety of advisers, he could never stick to a coherent policy. We may attribute the defeat at Marcellae to this quality in him; in the East his response to a raid by Harun al-Rashid was to bribe him to withdraw, further depleting the almost-bankrupt state treasury. He was also talked into restoring his mother to some measure of her former power – a catastrophic decision, as the army revolted, putting forward the emperor's Uncle Nikephoros, a monk, as imperial candidate. Irene struck back by having Nikephoros blinded and cutting out the tongues of four other uncles in case they became the foci of other revolts.

Constantine, fairly or not, was deemed at least partly responsible for those outrages. The result was that few, if any, in the army remained loyal to him. The emperor's own reaction was to flee yet further from responsible behaviour, divorcing his wife in favour of a courtesan named Theodote, who became his second wife. To the senior clergy of Constantinople this was intolerable; they had long suspected him of harbouring iconoclast sympathies, and hurled heresy charges at him. Irene, seething with revenge since her son had the temerity to confine her, also took advantage of another raid by Harun al-Rashid in 797 to commit what was equivalent to an act of high treason by giving her son false information that Harun had retreated. Constantine, who had marched eastwards to confront the Arab caliph, returned to the capital after receiving the bogus information, leaving Harun unopposed.

Irene apparently hoped that Constantine's withdrawal would bolster charges of cowardice against him. Yet her contempt of her son had grown to such awful proportions that it wasn't enough; she arranged for a squad of loyal soldiers to attack him one day as he was riding from the Hippodrome to a church. The emperor's own guard fought back, and he escaped in a boat across the Bosporus, but Irene's minions caught up with him and dragged him to the palace. There, in the very room where he had been born, a red-hot sword-point was thrust into his eyes. If this was meant to be an official blinding punishment, it was savage enough to kill him, which perhaps was the intention. He was just 27. The atrocity, for which Irene must certainly bear the blame, sent a shudder of revulsion throughout the empire. Theophanes records that 'the sun darkened, and the darkness lasted seventeen days. A thick dusk covered sea and land.' But for Irene, that was scant impediment to her insane pursuit of absolute power.

'I reign!' Theophilos cited Irene as exclaiming after she placed the crown on her own head.[7] 'The sole queen of the Romans!' But reigning would prove tougher than she thought. As Byzantium's first empress regnante, that is, in her own right and not as the consort of an emperor, Irene tried to transfer her genius for intrigue into the practice of statecraft. To hide the stain of her son's murder she abolished several taxes, but the treasury was depleted yet more by the heavy outlays to keep Harun al-Rashid pacified. Fiscal worries penetrated into the army – soldiers, after all, needed to be paid regularly to stay loyal. Then, just at the turn of the ninth century, there arrived a delegation from a Western land bearing a message that even Irene's complex mind would not have imagined – a proposal of marriage.

The suitor was none other than Charlemagne of the Franks, who had been crowned Holy Roman Emperor in Rome on Christmas Day 800, and sought, by reason of his new and exalted title, to reunite the full empire, East and West, with Irene as his consort. Charlemagne of course knew about the sordid circumstances of Constantine VI's murder, but he appeared to be confident that as a man of strong character he could control Irene; besides, in Charlemagne's domain the Salic Law prevailed, which debarred a woman from occupying a throne. Under Frankish law, therefore, the throne of Constantinople was up for grabs. Irene nonetheless was rather flattered. She was quite good-looking (though a crude image on a coin indicates she could have been overweight) and without a husband. Besides the sexual prospects, she liked the idea of extending her power and influence into Western Europe. She surely believed that she could manipulate Charlemagne, instead of the other way round. She may also have sensed that as her own people had long since turned against her, Charlemagne might be her next meal ticket. When she indicated to Charlemagne's ambassadors that she would seriously consider his proposal, she finally put her foot fatally wrong.

It would have been the marriage of the millennium if it had come off, but the great mass of Byzantine subjects, horrified at the prospect, ensured that it wouldn't. Irene by now may have been widely despised, yet everyone agreed she occupied her throne legitimately. The Salic Law did not apply in Byzantium. Charlemagne to them was just another barbarian. The people had ghastly visions, in Lord Norwich's descriptive prose, of

> the throne [being] taken over by this boorish Frank, in his outlandish linen tunic and his ridiculously cross-gartered scarlet leggings, speaking an incomprehensible language and unable even to sign his name except by stencilling it through a gold plate.

That was not all. The pope had clearly exceeded his authority in crowning a 'Roman' emperor who was not Byzantine; the passionate belief of every last Byzantine citizen was that the only true Christian emperor resided in Constantinople, as irreplaceable as God in Heaven. He (or she) was in the full sense, 'crowned by God'.[8] Yet here was Irene apparently prepared to forgo this immense privilege for the bed of a Frank! There was only one thing to do. The army leadership settled on the finance minister, Nikephoros, to take her place. On 31 October 802 officials burst into the empress' quarters with the news that her reign was over, while Nikephoros was acclaimed emperor in Sancta Sophia. Nikephoros made a show of being a reluctant successor, and Irene tried to take immediate advantage of this, going so far as to suggest that she marry him instead of Charlemagne. Nikephoros politely declined, whereupon Irene handed him the imperial crown and sceptre, commenting that 'the intentions of the Almighty are inscrutable', but adding the practical point that he would be informed of the whereabouts of the state's 'secret funds'.

1. Constantine I (the Great) [Palazzo dei Conservatori, Rome]

2. Artist's reconstruction of the Theodosian Wall [Ekdotiki Athinon]

3. Heraclius attacks Khusrau II; twelfth-century enamel [Louvre; *Der Spiegel*]

4. The Golden Gate today [C. Schug-Wille: *Art of the Byzantine World*]

5. Contemporary illustration of Greek Fire [*Der Spiegel*]

6. Krum captures Nikephoros I [Vatican Library, Rome]

7. Leo V is proclaimed emperor; Skylitzes miniature [National Library, Madrid]

8. Leo VI the Wise [National School Book Organization, Athens]

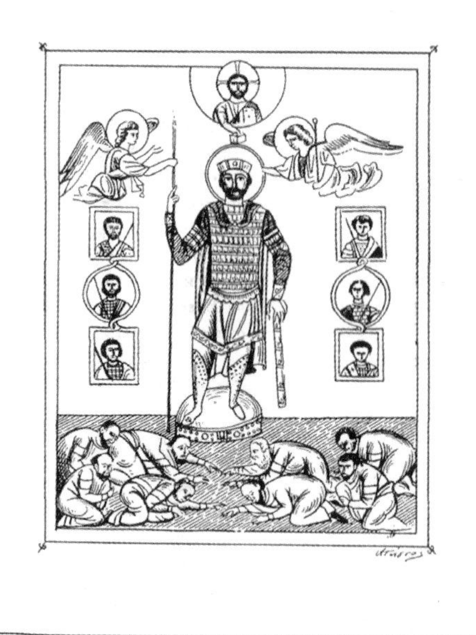

9. Basileios II the Bulgar-slayer [National School Book Organization, Athens]

10. Michael IV [Athens Numismatic Museum]

11. Mosaic depicting the Empress Zoe [Sancta Sophia]

12. The Varangian Guard; Skylitzes miniature [National Library, Madrid]

13. Emperor, possibly Romanos IV Diogenes, receiving reports from agents; Skylitzes miniature [National Library, Madrid]

14. Alexios I Komnenos (left) with Christ; twelfth-century miniature [Vatican Library, Rome]

15. Michael VIII Paleologos [*Der Spiegel*]

16. Manuel II Paleologos [National School Book Organization, Athens]

17. View of the Bosporus today [Author]

18. The interior of Sancta Sophia today [Author]

19. A Greek comic book depiction (c. 1965) of Constantine XI being struck down [Author]

20. Statue of Constantine XI Paleologos at Mitropoleos Square, Athens [Author]

The reader at this point may legitimately wonder why, since the Byzantine state ideology was that the emperor was nothing less than God's vicegerent on earth, he or she could be intrigued against and toppled so easily. The question appears vexed until we take into account the great power of the Byzantine clergy, which even more than the army reflected the views of the common people and carried huge prestige among what later ages would call an electorate. The unstated principle seemed to be that if any sovereign failed to live up to Christian rules of conduct – that is, God's commands – he or she could be legitimately removed by any means suitable. Bad behaviour on the part of an emperor, and the resulting mass unpopularity, were seen as signs that God had withdrawn His favour from that person. Though Irene, for example, was in principle 'crowned by God,' the Almighty could just as soon uncrown her through the will of the people and clergy. Before the era of votes and elections, it was as good a process as any.

Irene retired to a monastery on an island in the Sea of Marmara, but she was there only a few months before Nikephoros, not quite trusting her to stay put, moved her farther away, to the island of Lesbos. Less than a year after her removal she died, possibly worn out by remorse over many things, including the death of her son. With her perished the Isaurian dynasty. It might strain credulity that a mother, even one as power-mad as Irene, could be guilty of putting her own son to death and in so ghastly a manner. The weight of modern scholarly opinion, however, is damning. Theophanes has few doubts about her culpability. He reports that Irene was plagued by nocturnal visits by Constantine's ghost. If there was one positive result of her five years of tumultuous rule, it was the restoration of the icons, which at least temporarily left breathing room for her successor to tackle the never-ending task of defending Byzantium from the Arabs and the Bulgars.

Chapter Six

Blood on the Floor: A Cacophony of Emperors

Nikephoros I (802–811)

Nikephoros I's top priority, as a former finance minister, was to rebuild the empire's shattered economy. Reform was hugely overdue, if only in the sense that unpaid soldiers tended to be prone to thoughts of revolt. The short-term answer was high taxation, which fell heavily on the monasteries and church properties. Bitter, of course, were the condemnations in the cloisters and from the pulpits. The Studite order of monks came close to open rebellion before the emperor broke up the order and exiled them. He was now free to concentrate on military policy.

The humiliating tribute payments to Harun al-Rashid had to stop, and he told the caliph so in a letter, adding a demand that Harun actually pay back the largesse that Irene had handed him. After reading the letter the furious caliph turned it over and wrote on the back:

> From Harun, the commander of the believers, to Nikephoros, the dog of a Roman. Verily I have read thy letter, O son of an infidel mother. As for the answer, it will be for thine eye to see … Salam.[1]

Harun's answer took the form of a strong attack by 135,000 men on the Byzantine domains. Between 803 and 806 the Arabs overran Herakelia and Tyana in Asia Minor, withdrawing from the latter city only after receiving precisely the kind of tribute that Nikephoros had at first refused. This was probably the signal for a general in the Byzantine army named Bardanes Turcus – by his name, probably a Turk – to mutiny and proclaim himself emperor but he was overcome almost at once. Thus Nikephoros could turn his attention to the ever-troubled Balkans.

In 803 a powerful new leader had arisen to unite the Bulgars. This was Krum, whose origins are unknown but who quickly proved his abilities and by 807 had forged his army into a mighty hammer. Nikephoros tried to head off the new threat from the Bulgars by marching against them through Thrace, but at Adrianople he had to turn back to deal with another conspiracy. Krum figured that the Byzantine emperor couldn't even control his own military establishment, so in the following year his forces swept like a scythe onto a large Byzantine force encamped at the Strymon River and cut it to pieces. His next target was Serdica (now Sofia), which he entered by a stratagem and slaughtered the Byzantine garrison of 6,000 men.

A storm of public contempt rose up against Nikephoros, who made his position worse by clumsily trying to hide the news from the people. He had, therefore, no choice but to take the field again against Krum to redeem his tattered reputation. Nikephoros' experience had been in finance, not the military. Yet every emperor, as vicegerent of God on earth, was somehow expected to display military prowess and qualities of leadership. Military science had not reached the degree of specialization of more recent times, and so in Byzantium any patrician or leading public official could be expected to take the rank of general in time of conflict, whether or not he had any military experience or talents at all. The chief problem with this arrangement, as would be proved time and again, was that such 'political' commanders were overly dependent on professional officers who more often than not gave conflicting advice. Nikephoros had the advantage of knowing full well that wars cost money, and in the spring of 811 he instituted a new round of savage taxation. He was warned that the measure might cost him his throne but Krum was waiting, and could not be ignored.

Having taken the precaution of signing a nonaggression treaty with Charlemagne in the West, Nikephoros in the early summer gathered up all the reserves he could from the Asia Minor *themes*, and with his son Staurakios set out to measure swords with the Bulgar leader. The army that marched out of the Golden Gate must have numbered well over 100,000, yet many were green troops, poverty-stricken peasants who had joined up to earn a penny or two and were armed with just slings and cudgels and little training. Nikephoros was optimistic; a previous Greek expedition had captured and burned the Bulgars' capital, but Krum had merely made a strategic withdrawal. The news was good from the East, where Harun al-Rashid had died and his successors were absorbed in a dynastic tussle. The news was even better when Nikephoros reached the key stronghold of Marcellae and received a message from an apparently intimidated Krum: 'You have won; take what you like and leave this country peacefully.'

If there was a chance for Nikephoros to claim a diplomatic victory and go home with laurels, this was it. But his own callous nature was his doom. The so-called Anonymous Chronicle, our only reliable source for these events, says that at this point Nikephoros suffered some kind of mental disturbance. 'He was especially arrogant, and neither emerged from his tent nor gave any order to anyone.' Was this the bean-counter suddenly realizing he was out of his depth? He disciplined his son Staurakios for even daring to ask that he show his face. He did nothing to halt his more brutal troops massacring Bulgar noncombatants and throwing their infants into wheat threshers. With up to 50,000 Bulgars dead and believing Krum to be on the ropes, he followed the reckless advice of his staff and marched into the hills. He failed to take elementary precautions; Bulgar skirmishers watched his every move. On 24 July the Byzantine army entered the rocky Verbitza Pass, each end of which the Bulgars promptly plugged. Nikephoros knew he had blundered, but his generals urged an immediate attack; the emperor shook his head, realizing there was no way out 'even if we could fly through the air'.

Krum struck in the morning of 26 July. What followed for the Byzantines was one of the most horrifying defeats in military history. The great bulk of Nikephoros' army never had a chance. Whole units were butchered where they stood, or crushed when boulders were pushed down on them from the heights above; others were burned to death when the palisades were set on fire. As the Bulgar lines advanced over heaps of enemy bodies, a squad burst into Nikephoros' tent and despatched him at once, along with six of his senior officers, the commander of the Excubitors and a host of lesser officers. Most of the cavalry also perished, some of it by drowning in a river. Krum commemorated his victory at the Verbitza Pass by having Nikephoros' head stuck on a stake for a few days. Then, in one of those grisly and iconic images that stand out starkly in history, he had the skull removed, hollowed out and mounted on silver. Thus adorned, it served as Krum's drinking-cup, and no doubt an unbeatable conversation-piece at banquets. 'Thus,' says the Anonymous Chronicle, 'did Nikephoros lose his life and with it the empire's strength, through indolence and arrogance.'[2]

Staurakios (811), Michael I Rhangabe (811–813), Leo V the Armenian (813–820) and Michael II the Stammerer (820–829)

Staurakios survived the battle at the Verbitza Pass, but only just. He had received a grievous wound in the neck that severed his spinal cord. In terrible pain he was taken to Adrianople where Stephanos, the patrician in charge of the palace, proclaimed him emperor. When he could speak he bitterly blamed his father for the catastrophe. He was moved to Constantinople, but remained gravely ill, bleeding from his bladder and unable to move his legs. He was clearly in no condition to reign effectively, and on 2 October his brother-in-law Michael Rhangabe, one of the very few high-ranking survivors of the Verbitza Pass, sent him to a monastery and was crowned as Michael I. Staurakios, never free from pain, died three months later.

The precise method by which Michael I Rhangabe sidelined the suffering Staurakios and settled himself on the Byzantine throne is unclear. Some believed that his returning alive meant that he was divinely favoured in some way. He gained the important backing of the patriarch by pledging to uphold religious orthodoxy, 'not to stain [his] hands with Christian blood and respect the monks and clergy'. In the post-Verbitza political confusion he seems to have manoeuvred himself into a front-running position that was merely confirmed by officialdom.

If the Byzantines, however, were expecting a competent fighting emperor to avenge the death of Nikephoros, they would be disappointed. He looked the part: robust, according to contemporary accounts, with thick black hair and a beard. But his inner qualities, it turned out, left much to be desired. He became a puppet of the clergy who had elevated him to the throne, and spent great sums on them. Defence was quite neglected – a mind-numbing lapse in someone who had lived through a full-scale military disaster. Perhaps his strong religiosity had turned him against war. Besides, relations with Charlemagne in the West had markedly improved, despite the rebuff over Irene. But Krum came to disabuse Michael that he could have an easy time of it. In June 812 the Bulgar leader occupied Develtus on the Black Sea, cutting off a main northbound route from Constantinople and capturing much gold and silver and war matériel. After other vital Black Sea ports such as Mesembria were overrun, it became obvious that Krum would soon be astride the main north-west approach to Constantinople through the fertile Evros River Valley.

Past emperors would have sent the navy up to restore Byzantine rule through the judicious application of Greek Fire. But the navy was a shadow of its former self, having been allowed to fall into disuse. Worse, Krum had captured large stocks of Greek Fire in Mesembria, plus the equipment to spurt it through. Michael's wife Prokopia waved goodbye to her husband as he set out in May 813, riding at the head of 30,000 men through Thrace to get at Krum from the south. But he moved his forces so cautiously that the Asian units began to grumble, and when he encountered the Bulgars at the Pass of Versinicia, some twenty miles north-east of Adrianople in the Evros Valley, he remained indecisive. At the time, the Bulgars could not have had more than about 15,000 men facing him, but they were being reinforced steadily, and John Aplakes, the commander of the Macedonian division, urged a quick attack on them. Aplakes and other generals believed the superior discipline and numbers of the Byzantines would decide the issue.

But Michael seems to have been paralyzed by fears of another Verbitza, and for two weeks men and horses grew restive in the early summer heat. Disease struck and discipline broke down as many soldiers fidgeted to return to their farms for the impending harvest. Back in Constantinople the people fumed; some visited the tomb of Constantine V, he of the Dung-name, imploring him to come back to life and save the city (several claimed to have seen him jumping out and onto his horse). Aplakes' patience ran out on 22 June, when he independently ordered his 8,000-strong division to attack Krum who, in the meantime, had accumulated perhaps 20,000 men. Aplakes' move dragged the rest of the imperial force into action, converging on the Bulgars from a height overlooking the pass. Aplakes' tightly-formatted Byzantines scored an initial success, but inexplicably the emperor, in charge of the mass of men in the centre, refused to join the battle on his front, apparently content with being an observer.

Worse was to come. The Byzantine commander on the opposite wing, Leo the Armenian, not only refused to join battle but actually led his Asian division to the rear. The troops of the centre, not having any choice, also fell back, leaving the emperor isolated with his personal guard. Even Krum had to wonder what was going on. At first he thought the Byzantines might be craftily retreating to entrap him, but with Aplakes' division cut to pieces and the general himself dead, the Byzantine retreat disintegrated into a rout without any apparent cause. It is still unclear what made the imperial army lose its collective nerve at Versinicia. Personal rivalry and distrust between Leo and Aplakes probably played a part, while Michael feared both as potential rivals for the throne, an attitude that would explain his reluctance to give them free rein. One might also assume that the terrible reputation attached to Krum since he began drinking out of Nikephoros' skull intimidated Michael enough not to want to attack the Bulgars until he was completely sure the conditions were right.

With whatever little fight he had in him well and truly evaporated, Michael Rhangabe fled back to Constantinople shamed enough to abdicate at once – the will of God, he said, had been revealed, and it was against him. Prokopia, trying to play the role of the legendary Theodora, tried to rally his spirit, but was outvoted. To escape the wrath of people and army, the royal couple and their five children sought refuge in a church wrapped up in monastic garb. The three sons, however, were caught and castrated to prevent them from carrying on the male line; Prokopia and her two daughters were sent to convents. Michael himself became a monk, living for thirty-two more years in devout obscurity.

A large question mark hangs over Leo the Armenian, whose Asian units inexplicably fell back at Versinicia, ensuring one more heavy Byzantine defeat. Why, when the Macedonian wing was initially winning, did he do it? The historical evidence, when weighed, points to an attempt to discredit Michael and possibly a secret deal with Krum himself. Strengthening this hypothesis is the fact that Leo loudly proclaimed to all and sundry that he had been the last to retreat, and unwillingly at that, thereby ensuring that his own reputation was unsullied. Krum himself advanced triumphantly right up to the walls of Constantinople, to face Leo V, as Michael's hesitant general had now become. Leo had ridden into Constantinople with an entourage that included his boon companion, a fellow-officer named Michael the Amorian. After dismounting to walk into the palace, Michael followed him so closely that he inadvertently trod on the train of the emperor's cloak, almost pulling it off him. No-one thought much of the incident at the time, but Michael appears not to have forgotten it.

Krum, looking up at the mighty Theodosian Wall, realized it was near-impregnable, so to compensate, he and his troops engaged in elaborate barbarian theatrics, apparently designed to intimidate the Byzantines but earning their ridicule instead. Krum figured he could win some sort of symbolic victory by planting his lance on the Golden Gate; his request to do so was refused, so in a massive infantile tantrum he ravaged the countryside for a few days and then demanded the prettiest girls in the empire as a present. Leo may well have chuckled grimly as he learned of the demand; he believed he could outwit the crude Bulgar and accordingly invited him to a parley at Blachernai, the northern suburb where the Theodosian Wall met the Golden Horn. The secret plan was for Krum to be assassinated at the meeting. Heading the Greek delegation was John Hexabulios, who was to give the prearranged signal to act by covering his face with his hands. Perhaps the signal was too obvious, for Krum realized its possible significance at once, leaped up and ran for his horse, escaping with moments to spare.

Krum's revenge was terrible. Farm animals for miles around Constantinople were slaughtered and burned for barbarian sacrifices; countless homesteads, villas and churches went up in smoke. On his way back to Bulgaria Krum razed town after town, massacring their inhabitants; Adrianople was completely depopulated. Leo's retaliation was equally savage. Byzantine troops burst into the Bulgar garrison at Mesembria, wiping out the lot. The Greeks then marched into Bulgar lands for a new round of atrocities against the helpless civilians, seizing their children and smashing their heads against rocks. At this, Krum returned, blindly determined to seize Constantinople, whatever it took. By early 814 he had prepared whatever the art of war could boast in the way of siege engines and mangonels. Leo, for his part, ordered the wall strengthened and prepared for another siege. But Krum had, unwittingly, already met his match. It wasn't Leo, but a wound he is believed to have sustained at Mesembria. On 13 April 814, Holy Thursday in the Greek calendar, blood suddenly gushed from Krum's mouth, nose and ears, and he was dead within minutes. Whether it was the wound, a massive stroke or foul play, the Byzantines could thank God for their deliverance.

Leo V was one of those men, common in mediaeval history, who emerged from humble origins to win prominence through a combination of cunning and ruthlessness. Such men, more often than not, had a cruel streak which hardened with the assumption of supreme power. He is described as short and thick-set, with a rather loud voice, probably the legacy of years of barking orders. His courage in the field was beyond dispute, reinforcing the theory that at Versinicia he had calculated his unseemly retreat with a bigger aim in mind. With Krum unexpectedly and thankfully out of the way, Leo could now settle down to administer a long-sought period of peace for Byzantium. His main concern was to keep the army on his side, which he did by agreeing with their theological iconoclasm – not that he was particularly interested in theology himself, but he was prepared to compromise on it in the interests of the state.

For six years there was relative peace, but Leo was disturbed by the increasingly suspicious conduct of his associate Michael the Amorian, who was believed to be secretly bad-mouthing the emperor. Michael, it turned out, was doing rather more than that; in fact, he was plotting to seize the throne. When Leo questioned Michael, the latter confessed, whereupon the livid emperor ordered a particularly hideous form of execution for his erstwhile friend and collaborator – to be thrown into the furnace that heated the palace baths. What followed was a series of events that would tax the imagination of the best thriller-writer.[3] On the night of Christmas Eve 820 Michael, through a string of incredible chances, got word of his confinement to a band of supporters. While it was still dark these men disguised themselves as choristers, hiding weapons under their cloaks, and slunk into the palace chapel to join the early morning Christmas service, which Leo was due to attend. Before dawn the emperor, wearing a fur hat against the bitter cold, turned up and began chanting hymns in his loud voice. But the officiating priest also wore a fur hat, and the conspirators at first mistook him for Leo. When the conspirators pulled out their weapons and advanced on the priest he doffed his hat in terror. As the assailants momentarily hesitated, the emperor at once realized what was happening and grabbed a heavy cross from the altar to defend himself. But before he could use it his arm was sliced off, still holding the cross, to spin across the chapel floor in a trail of blood. Leo fell, and as he hit the floor another sword blow removed his head.

While all this nastiness was happening on Christmas morning, Michael the Amorian was still in shackles in his cell. His conspirators, fresh from their messy regicide, freed him and set him on the throne in the palace as Michael II. But he was still wearing his shackles – perhaps the only monarch in history to be crowned while thus hampered – but a blacksmith was presently found to strike the irons from his ankles, as the stunned palace staff looked on. Leo's headless and one-armed corpse was thrown into a public toilet and then pulled out for public display at the Hippodrome. His widow and four young sons were put on a boat for exile in the Sea of Marmara, with orders that the boys be castrated to prevent any of them from claiming the throne later; one of them died during the ordeal.

Michael II, besides being crude and ruthless, was also completely uneducated. Wits quipped that in the time it took to write his name, one could read a whole book. He also had a speech defect which the Greek term (*traulos*) translates into 'stammerer,' by which he became known to posterity, in the irreverent Byzantine fashion, as Michael the Stammerer. No doubt many remembered the incident of his stepping on Leo's royal cloak and attached a portentous significance to it. On the other hand, Michael was an eminently practical man who realized that the empire needed a more stable dynasty than the six unrelated emperors who had preceded him haphazardly over the past twenty-five years. In 821 he named his son Theophilos, aged 17, co-emperor – a clear message about where the succession should go. To extend the line further, Theophilos was married off early, to an attractive noble lady who hopefully would keep the generation machine going and bring some dynastic stability to the empire.

That dynastic plan, however, quickly came under threat. The Byzantine army was full of adventurers who, it seemed, could never take to peaceful conditions and needed something or someone to fight against all the time. While Michael had been serving Leo V in the field he had faced rivalry from an officer named Thomas the Slav. After conspiring against Michael I, this man had spent some time in self-exile in Muslim lands, returning to Constantinople under Leo V, who had given him a senior command. As both Leo and Michael had been rewarded with the imperial diadem for their exertions, Thomas the Slav naturally felt that he, too, deserved his turn as emperor. He could obtain plenty of support. The Byzantine public still shuddered over the gruesome death of Leo at the hands of Michael the Stammerer's conspirators. He was over 50 when he began to organize his forces, ingratiating himself with the peasants and poorer people by promising them lower taxes and an end to high-level corruption, and stressing his adherence to the icons. People who knew him remarked at his culture and charm, yet there was a dark and bitter undertone to his personality. To give himself an underpinning of alleged legitimacy he claimed to be Constantine VI who had somehow survived the savage blinding by his mother Irene; this claim we may safely dismiss. But more sinisterly, Thomas the Slav was almost certainly a tool of the Abbasid caliph al-Mamun, who liberally supplied him with funds and expected him to bring Constantinople under Arab control.

The fact that Thomas with a huge army of 80,000 Arabs, Persians, Goths, Huns and Slavs was able to subdue the greater part of Asia Minor within a few months tells us more about Michael's unpopularity than about Thomas' own abilities. With only two *themes*, the Opsikion and the Armeniakon, still loyal to the emperor, Thomas invested Constantinople from the landward side in December 821. It had been just eight years since the Byzantine defenders and people had fended off Krum's siege, and their resolve had not wavered. Thomas concentrated his attack on the Blachernai district where the northern wall met the Golden Horn, but it was exactly at that point that Michael's forces, remembering Krum's attempt, concentrated their strongest defence. The emperor's great catapults and mangonels, ranged along the top of the wall, wrought havoc in Thomas' camp. The emperor's teenage son Theophilos, braving the missiles, proudly held aloft fragments of the True Cross atop the wall. Thomas' large fleet, replete with stocks of Greek Fire, was supposed to have sailed up to Constantinople to coordinate with the land assault, but contrary winds kept it away.

Foiled once, Thomas the Slav tried again the following spring. This time Michael mounted the walls to appeal, despite his stammer, to the besiegers in person. Why were they fighting their brothers, he asked, at a time when Byzantium was in need of unity? Michael's message indicates that he knew Thomas was in fact serving Muslim interests, hence the appeal to the Christians in his army. Also it could have been designed to give the mistaken impression that the imperial forces were weak. If that was the intention, it worked. As Thomas's forces surged towards the wall at Blachernai, several gates opened at once, and columns of imperial troops rushed out, overpowering the attackers and inflicting heavy losses. At about the same time, the emperor's Greek Fire destroyed Thomas' naval reinforcements in the Sea of Marmara.

Thomas the Slav had barely recovered from that double defeat when the Bulgar khan Omortag, the son of Krum, thundered down into Thrace to help the Byzantines, with whom he had signed a thirty-year treaty of cooperation. Michael made a show of being unwilling to use Omortag, but covertly used him to smash Thomas' remaining forces at Herakleia (now Ereğli). Still unwilling to give up (or fearing the reaction of his paymaster Caliph al-Mamun), Thomas encamped about twenty miles west of Constantinople, just outside the Anastasian Wall. It was there that Michael rode out to settle accounts with him in May 823. Thomas tried to bamboozle the imperial troops by luring them into an ambush, and the tactic might have worked if his own men, shattered by defeat after defeat, had not become tired of the whole business and surrendered.

Thomas holed himself up in Arkadiopolis (Lüleburgaz) with a bare remnant of his once-overpowering force, subsisting on dead horses. By October his remaining few men gave him up. He was led in chains to the emperor, who stamped a purple boot on the rebel's neck in the time-honoured imperial sentence of death and ordered him to be impaled on a stake, but not before his hands and feet were hacked off. Michael's rage is understandable; Thomas the Slav's two-year insurrection had caused widespread hunger and misery in the provinces; in Constantinople itself, hordes of refugees from the devastated countryside were begging in the streets. The Byzantine navy had been decimated by wholesale desertions to Thomas' cause. Thomas' son and potential successor was also impaled, while other rebel leaders were hunted down and hanged.

Michael II was given little chance to rest. The threat from Arabs under al-Mamun may have been dealt with, but this was not the only area where the Muslims were powerful. In 756 an Umayyad prince who had escaped the Abbasids, Abd-al-Rahman, had established a powerful regime at Cordova in Spain, which had been conquered from the Visigoths forty years earlier. When Adb-al-Rahman's grandson, the amir al-Hakam I, dissolute and disliked, was attacked in the streets of Cordova by a stone-throwing mob, the amir's revenge was to crucify 300 dissidents upside down. Fifteen thousand Arab refugees fleeing al-Hakam's wrath sailed into the Eastern Mediterranean in 816, forcing their way into Alexandria two years later and seizing Crete in 825. The lack of a strong Byzantine navy was now keenly felt, as Crete henceforth became a nest of Muslim pirates who raided and terrorized the Aegean islands and Greek mainland coast. As in the Viking raids that were simultaneously taking place in the far north of Europe, monasteries were favourite objects of murder and pillage. Three times the Byzantines tried to drive the Arabs from Crete and three times they failed. At the same time, Byzantine sea power was dealt a further blow by Arab landings in Sicily.

In 824 Michael's faithful wife died, and he married the daughter of Constantine VI. She was the one who stayed by his bedside as he sickened of a kidney ailment and died in October 829. His final months had been spent grappling with that enduring bane of Byzantine rule, theological controversy. But he breathed his last content in the knowledge that he had stabilized imperial rule, ready to pass on to his son Theophilos, who had been groomed for the role for eight years and now, at twenty five, was ready to continue the defence against the Arabs.

Theophilos (829–842) and Michael III (842–867)

> One of the functions of royalty is to provide the people with a vicarious, if none the less real, fulfilment of their wishes. Kings who make a fine show are popular; and the people not only forgive, but actually commend, extravagances which, to the good Marxian, must seem merely criminal. Wise kings always earmarked a certain percentage of their income for display.
>
> Aldous Huxley, 'Waterworks and Kings' (1932)

In an era long before press photography and television turned public figures into household faces, very few ordinary people could know what their ruler looked like. This was just as well for Theophilos, who had a healthy concern for what the people thought of him, and a strong inclination to social justice. He made a habit of going forth into the streets incognito to assess popular feeling, which included checking food prices, an abiding concern of populations in all nations and in all eras. Once a week he would ride more openly across the city, willing to listen to anyone who had a problem and, if possible, remedy it. He did not hesitate to order his brother-in-law to pull down a large house that blocked the sunlight from an old widow next door, and had him whipped for good measure. These instances, plus the prior glimpse we have of him defending the wall at Blachernai in 821, paint him as the strong character, strong in both intellect and military ability, that Byzantium sorely needed at this juncture.

Theophilos (whose name means Friend of God) knew enough about statecraft to realize that the affection of his subjects needed to be balanced by a political image designed to strike awe into potential foes, which included local warlords as well as Arabs and Bulgars and Slavs. The Byzantine emperor had never ceased to be theoretically an Isapostolos – equal to the Apostles. As we have seen, his function as divinely-ordained ruler was uncontested, regardless of his own origins or character or how he came to power. Such exalted status had to be displayed, and prominently at that, for him to be able to lead his empire effectively. Theophilos appears to have been able to draw on ample state funds to be able to do it, which is surprising, given that decades of war and insurrection had almost bankrupted the state. Possibly new gold mines had been discovered in Armenia, but the source of this sudden abundance of imperial wealth remains a mystery. Theophilos had been on the throne less than a year when he sent a mission to Caliph al-Mamun bearing gold and gifts of incredible value, all designed to impress the Arab with proof of Byzantine power.

For foreign visitors to the Byzantine court Theophilos reserved the most impressive innovation of all: a plane tree made of solid gold whose branches formed a canopy over the throne and were covered with jewelled birds. By some mechanical contrivance, at a given signal the birds would burst into song while a set of golden lions and griffons around the throne would roar; this would be followed by a burst of music from a golden organ, after which the emperor would permit his diplomatic visitor to speak. The whole performance would be repeated as the visitor withdrew from the emperor's presence. One can imagine the amazement created by this fantastic arrangement – assuming, of course, that our sources are not exaggerating. Arab emissaries were the prime targets of such a dazzling display, which would have rivalled similar extravagant and expensive spectacles staged by Caliph al-Mamun.[4]

The educated and intellectual Theophilos, in fact, had much in common with the Abbasid caliph. He frankly admired Islamic art and culture and saw no reason to interrupt the sixteen years of peace on his eastern frontier. Al-Mamun would probably have had no objection himself, especially as his regime was hard put to suppress a domestic rebellion from an Islamic sect known as the Hurramites. But when the Hurramites applied to be enlisted in the ranks of the Byzantines and Theophilos accepted them and installed them in the north-eastern theme of Chaldia, al-Mamun decided that the good-neighbourliness should end. Theophilos himself defeated the first force that the caliph sent against the Byzantines in Cilicia in 830, and duly felt he deserved a triumphal procession. Waiting ten days on the opposite shore of the Bosporus to swell the number of his Arab prisoners, he sailed in magnificence up the Golden Horn. Ashore at Blachernai, he mounted his white horse to ride around the walls to the Golden Gate. First to be marched through were the columns of prisoners accompanying wagons full of war booty. There seemed to a staggering amount of gold everywhere. It was in Theophilos' breastplate and tunic, and probably in his diadem as well. It was in a crown which city dignitaries gave him as he dismounted to meet them at the Golden Gate. It was in the glittering throne set up at the palace gate to receive Theophilos after he had ridden through the flower-strewn streets and ecstatic crowds and attended the obligatory thanksgiving service at Sancta Sophia. It was in the big cross and mechanical organ flanking the throne, and in the presents to the emperor from grateful citizens' delegations, including some from the ever-active Blues and Greens.

But, as happens distressingly often in world affairs, the triumph was momentary. Al-Mamun had no intention of conceding defeat to what the Arabs still reviled as the 'Roman dogs', and mere months after Theophilos' moment of glory his army was soundly defeated in Northern Syria. The emperor dipped into his overflowing coffers to try and buy his way out of an escalation of hostilities, but the caliph was having none of it; he had never swerved in his ambition to capture Byzantium for Islam. But in the summer of 833, as he was marching to secure the northern frontiers, al-Mamun died aged 48. Theophilos enjoyed a few years' respite, as al-Mamun's brother and successor al-Mutasim was preoccupied by domestic upheavals. But by 837 al-Mutasim had consolidated his power and was in a position to renew the war. Theophilos, the 'incomparable champion' to his subjects, had just completed successful incursions into Syria and Mesopotamia, which he had celebrated with another triumphal procession in Constantinople.

Al-Mutasim set out determinedly at the head of 50,000 men and about the same number of camels. His objective was Amorion in Asia Minor, where Theophilos' father had hailed from; the name, in fact, adorned the caliph's banner, so there could be no mistake about what was in store for the city if he should take it. This was becoming personal, and Theophilos duly rode out to confront al-Mutasim, colliding with the Arab army at Damizon (near modern Tokat in Turkey). The Byzantine army had a good chance of success, had not a rainstorm broken out during the initial clash. The storm reduced visibility; when one of Theophilos' wings ran into trouble he took 2,000 men out of the centre to strengthen it. It was a bad move. In the confusion many soldiers, not seeing their emperor in the centre, feared he might have been killed and the fight went out of them. By the time it stopped raining and Theophilos showed he was still alive, the army was encircled.

Al-Mutasim, however, was having his own problems. The rain had dampened his archers' bowstrings, while the walls of Amorion turned out to be more formidable than he imagined. The Arab archers were thus unable to prevent a breakout by Theophilos who, despite heavy casualties, succeeded in organizing the defence of the city. Sturdy the wall may have been, but one spot was in disrepair, and this was duly revealed to the caliph by a traitor within the walls, a Muslim convert. For three days al-Mutasim's siege machines hammered at the spot. When the Arabs seemed to be coming close to victory and the defenders were at the point of exhaustion, a Byzantine officer named Boitzides made a secret deal with the Arabs to open the wall. The caliph's yelling troops poured into Amorion, slaughtering Christians, many of whom were burned alive after seeking sanctuary in a church. Other victims were captured as slaves and led on a horrific journey through the desert where many were left to die of thirst.[5] Al-Mutasim made good his boast, razing Amorion to the ground.

Back in Constantinople Theophilos pondered his alternatives. There seemed to be only one feasible course of action – to seek help from the only other major Christian power in Europe, the Holy Roman Empire in the West. This empire was in the hands of Charlemagne's son Louis I (the Pious), a devout ruler who might be expected to help stem the latest threat from Islam. In June 839 a Byzantine mission arrived at Louis' headquarters at Ingelheim. The initial plan was for the Byzantines to expel the Arabs from Crete while Louis did the same in Sicily and Southern Italy. But Louis was hardly in a position to act, being old and ill and having spent years fending off callous treatment by his sons. When Louis died in 840 the Byzantines turned for help to the Venetians, who weren't interested. In early 842 al-Mutasim sent an armada of some 400 dromones against Constantinople, but a storm annihilated it on the way. The caliph died before he could learn of the disaster, to be followed by Theophilos who succumbed to dysentery on 20 January aged only 38.

Theophilos' only son was just 2 when he became Michael III. This was the chance for his mother Theodora to be the regent for him, a task she conducted with the help of her capable brother Bardas, and Theoktistos, a senior civil servant. Much of her time was taken up with settling the lingering and bitter issue of the icons, with a council in 843 definitely restoring them to their honoured place in Christian worship. Theoktistos rebuilt the Byzantine navy, sending it against Crete and then against Alexandria, where it effectively employed its Greek Fire against the city as well as the Arab fleet.

As might have been expected from a boy in a protected environment dominated by his mother, Michael III was initially seen as weak-willed and pliable. But appearances deceived. He was sexually precocious at 15, but Theodora vetoed his first choice of wife, a half-Swedish girl, and forced him to marry a local debutante in whom he took not the slightest interest. Bardas, who had been relegated to the sidelines for more than a decade, sensed his nephew's suppressed hostilities. One day the teenaged emperor accosted Theoktistos in the palace grounds and sternly demanded that he, Michael, be treated as the ruler of Byzantium and not his mother. There appears to have been a brief argument before Theoktistos walked off in a huff; he had not gone far when Bardas and several officers jumped on him and dragged him to the palace entrance to the Hippodrome, where Michael gave an order for the cowering Theoktistos to be executed on the spot.

It would be a mistake to consider this act as signifying the emergence of a strong character. Rather it was an impulsive and subliminal substitute for the desire to do away with his mother; this unacknowledged mental conflict emerged in neurosis. He may also have suspected Theoktistos, rightly or wrongly, of having more than just an official tie to his mother. Whatever the case, Theodora, her power suddenly eliminated, sulked bitterly while in March 856 the Senate officially handed Michael III supreme power. He was just 16, and had a greatly exaggerated idea of his own importance, and when it came to administering the affairs of state he was by no means proved up to the job. He lived fecklessly, avoiding responsibility and leaving the nuts and bolts of running the empire to Bardas. That same year a military expedition under the royal uncle Petronas – the one whom Theophilos had ordered flogged for blocking a widow's view with his new mansion – marched across the Euphrates and retook a chunk of former Byzantine territory.

In 859 Michael rallied himself enough to take the field in person, staging a second crossing of the Euphrates that by all accounts went extraordinarily well, and taking many Arab prisoners. The Abbasid caliph at this time was al-Mutawakkil, a capable enough ruler who, however, seemed unable to stem a gradual decline in the fighting prowess of the Arabs. They were able to score their initial military successes thanks to their hardy camels and tenaciousness, but lacked the discipline needed to reverse a broken and retreating line. Cold and wet weather would dampen their morale. Al-Mutawakkil himself came increasingly under the influence of Turkish warlords brought in to bolster his state and hired Turkish mercenaries whose Islamic ardour was often in question.[6] When al-Mutawakkil tried to resist the Turks' domination they had him poisoned in 861. For the next half-century the Abbasid caliphate sank into a maelstrom of internal power struggles and civil war, as weak caliphs came and went, often at the hands of their Turkish handlers, and Byzantine arms were able to claw back large tracts of territory feared to have been permanently lost. In 863 Petronas with 50,000 men, and accompanied by the emperor, in a brilliant manoeuvre encircled the forces of Umar ibn-Abdullah, the emir of Melitene (now Malatya in Eastern Turkey), killing Umar and annihilating his mixed force of Muslims and heretic Christians. The Arab governor of Armenia met the same fate shortly afterwards.

Meanwhile in June 860, while Michael was campaigning in the East, an unexpected threat came barrelling down the Bosporus in the form of about a hundred ships manned by a people of whom the Greeks so far had heard little. These hardy men from the north in their long ships, which plundered the banks of the strait and anchored menacingly in the mouth of the Golden Horn, called themselves Rus. It was civilized Europe's first encounter with the nation that was to become the Russians – originating in Scandinavia, perhaps an offshoot of the Vikings and mixing with the Eastern European Slavs to form a growing power. The raid was the first of many attempts, stretching into our own time, by the Russians to secure access to the warm Mediterranean through the Bosporus and Constantinople.

These Russians were the equal of their Viking brethren in the art of killing and looting, and for some weeks Constantinople was terrorized. With the emperor away, the defence fell on the shoulders of the praetorian prefect, Niketas Oöryphas, who didn't have much of a physical force to rely on, but pinned great hopes – as did all Byzantines – on divine aid. Photios, the patriarch, had the miracle-working robe of the Virgin Mary carried on the walls in full view of the Russians, who unaccountably withdrew. This is one of those incidents that admit of either a divine or a secular explanation, the latter being that the Russians simply saw how strong Constantinople was and decided against moving on it.[7] Michael had been hurriedly called back, but the Russians had gone before he returned. The raid was a sobering reminder that there was no lack of non-Christian peoples ever ready to descend on Byzantium, whether in the form of the Muslim Arabs or pagan Russians and Slavs. The corollary was that if the Russians and Slavs, at least, could be Christianized, the military threat from them might be minimized, if not eliminated altogether. This was the main motive for the labours of the monks Kyrillos (Cyril) and Methodios, who spread Christianity through the Slav peoples and invented the Slavonic alphabet, based on the Greek, which the Bulgarians, Russians and Serbs still use.

Michael, when he wasn't away campaigning or trying to get his head round complex theological arguments with Pope Nicholas I in Rome, spent a large portion of his time trying to forget about the burdens of imperial rule. His youthful insecurity and moral spinelessness had never left him, and while he was still in his early twenties he sought solace in pleasures in which binge drinking played an inordinately large part. One of his pastimes was to get together an unsavoury gang and roust noisily through the streets in obscene fancy dress. In a more or less constant alcoholic stupor he ignored and then divorced his wife, sharply reducing his chances of acquiring a son and heir. Bardas still held the de facto reins of power, and it would have surprising indeed if by now he had not eyed the throne for himself.

One of Michael's rowdy companions in his street partying was a rough Armenian named Basileios (Basil). His family had been relocated to Thrace in Europe, where Krum's Bulgars had driven them on to Macedonia. At 25 Basileios had made his way to Constantinople, one of many resourceful young Balkan men out to seek their fortunes. Later accounts have him sleeping rough in the portico of a monastery church, whose abbot took one look at the ragged figure and received a divine message (said to be driven home by a mysterious punch in the ribs) that it was a future emperor huddled there, and therefore to be taken in and fed. Basileios, despite his total illiteracy and boorish manners, attracted official attention by his impressive physical strength, which included a talent for wrestling men and handling horses. There is a legend, perhaps true, that this mediaeval horse-whisperer tamed one of the emperor's skittish mounts by stroking its ear. It was even, if more dubiously, said that he shared his second wife with the emperor, being rewarded for his generosity with the post of high chamberlain.

Bardas was at once wary of this uncouth newcomer who out of nowhere had become Michael's court favourite. 'The lion,' he said, 'will end by devouring us all.' Bardas was right. Basileios had little difficulty turning the pliable emperor against his uncle, the sole obstacle to his own lust for the crown. Bardas, planning an expedition to recover Crete, got wind of a plot against his life, but Michael swore on the blood of Christ that no such thing was in the offing, so some time in April 866 both men set sail for Crete at the head of a fleet. At a provisioning halt near Miletos one morning, Bardas sat next to the emperor listening to a report; when it was over he suggested to Michael that they get back onto the ships. Before Bardas could rise, however, he thought he saw a suspicious movement and reached for his sword. It was the last move he ever made, as Basileios had got his own sword ready rather sooner.

Was Michael a party to this assassination? The answer is probably yes. We are told that he reacted in a stunned way, though that could well have been theatrics. The emperor's line – doubted by many in high places – was that Bardas had been executed for supposedly plotting to kill him. The immediate result was that the expedition to Crete was scrubbed (it may have been concocted in the first place simply to get Bardas out of the way) and soon Michael was back in Constantinople with Basileios at his side – in a more literal sense than anyone could have imagined. In Sancta Sophia Michael solemnly proclaimed Basileios, 'who has delivered me from my enemy and holds me in great affection', co-emperor and seated him on a throne identical to his own.

Basileios' rise had been meteoric – from stable-hand to co-emperor in just nine years! Michael, glad that someone ruthlessly capable was handling day-to-day imperial affairs, abandoned himself to dissipation. But soon the two men began to disagree over vital issues. On the evening of 24 September 867 Basileios slipped away from a drinking party at the Saint Mamas Palace and broke the lock on Michael's bedroom door; the emperor, staggering to his bed later, didn't notice, and as he snored away, Basileios and a handful of conspirators overpowered the door guard and burst into Michael's chamber. One of the plotters lost his nerve at the last moment and managed only to chop off Michael's hands, but his fellows finished the job. As they and Basileios fled down the Golden Horn to the main palace, Michael's mutilated body was left to bleed wrapped in a horse-blanket. 'With such servility and crime the letterless son of a peasant established the longest of all Byzantine dynasties.'[8]

Chapter Seven

The Macedonians

Basileios I the Macedonian (867–886) and Leo VI the Wise (886–912)

In the long history of human leadership, time and time again we find a personality who, having given little promise of greatness or nobility in the early years, changes radically after having greatness and nobility thrust upon him. Such a one was Basileios I – conventionally named the Macedonian. It seems that the restless energy which he had previously expended in intrigue, violence and murder channelled itself into higher deeds when his circumstances changed. Like many newly-minted emperors before him, he inherited a state in need of repair in many sectors and tackled them decisively.

In line with the dimensions of his ego, Basileios set his sights on reuniting the Eastern and Western empires. Two centuries of intermittent conflict with the Arabs had convinced him that Christian Europe needed to be a single power again. To achieve this required the consent of the popes of Rome, who were at that time the single most powerful individuals in the West, steering the policy of the Holy Roman Empire. The illiterate Basileios knew little and cared less about doctrinal complexities but saw the advantages of reconciliation with the papacy. Strengthening his hand was the final conversion of the Bulgars to Christianity under Khan Boris (later renamed Michael), and a relaxation (albeit temporary) of tensions in that quarter.

But it had been three centuries since Justinian I's attempt at unification, and in culture, language and mentality the Eastern and Western empires were as far apart as ever. Holy Roman Emperor Louis II (the German) had been mulling over giving his daughter Hermingarde to Basileios' son Constantine, but when Niketas Oöryphas led a fleet to Bari to help the Franks besiege the Muslims there, he found the Franks outnumbered and drunk into the bargain. Ill-feeling on both sides mounted until Louis, in a paroxysm of wrath, sent envoys to Constantinople demanding that he be recognized as *Imperator Romanum*, outranking even the Byzantine emperor!

Basileios properly ignored this outrageous claim, while the navy under Oöryphas patrolled the Adriatic Sea and cleared it of Muslim and Slav privateers. Bari itself was brought back into the Christian fold, marking 'the beginning of the end of the Moslem menace to Italy'.[1]

Yet Arab fleets were very active in the Southern and Eastern Mediterranean. An Arab fleet from Crete penetrated into the Sea of Marmara in 881, to be consumed by Greek Fire (one wonders why the Muslim mariners hadn't learned their hard lesson by now). Oöryphas resumed the naval offensive, pursuing the Arab pirates into the Saronic Gulf near Athens and over the Isthmus of Corinth into the gulf of the same name. After a period of neglect the Byzantine navy was again a rising power, the mistress of the Eastern Mediterranean. It had the services of another capable admiral, a Syrian named Nasr, who chased the pirates from the West Greek islands and Southern Italy.

Basileios himself took the field against the Arabs twice, during a ten-year war from 871 to 882. A personal victory alongside his brother-in-law Christophoros was followed by thrusts deep into Syria, though a serious defeat at Tartus temporarily checked him. Caliph at the time was al-Mutamid, much preoccupied by domestic conflicts including a revolt of black slaves which developed into full-scale war. This did not mean that the Eastern frontiers of Byzantium ceased to be in danger. The Abbasid caliphate may have been disintegrating, but in its place a host of petty local Islamic dynasties had sprung up, all of them eyeing the Christian empire as well as the central power in Baghdad. Basileios could not afford to relax his vigilance in that sector. But in the meantime he had to make at least one serious stab at regaining Italy.

Though he had alienated the popes and Louis II, Basileios' naval mastery of the Adriatic helped him seize Benevento in the Italian peninsula and Otranto on the heel of Italy. These victories, and more, are attributed to the sound generalship of Nikephoros Phokas, the first appearance of the Phokas military family that would supply a generous quota of soldiers to the empire, as well as a few emperors. Basileios' attempt to emulate the great Justinian extended to an ambitious building programme that made Constantinople the jewel of the world – a combined London, Paris and New York of its time.[2] The Balkan and Slav peoples were being converted to Christianity apace, and the haughty popes of Rome were receiving the snub the Greeks believed they deserved. Then in September 879, at the height of Basileios' triumphs, personal disaster struck: his beloved eldest son Constantine, who was to have united East and West by marrying Hermingarde, died suddenly of causes unknown to us. For any parent that is a terrible blow, but for a ruler intent on a continuing a dynasty it is especially grievous. For all his toughness of character, Basileios never recovered from the loss. His behaviour became increasingly erratic. Consumed by pathological guilt feelings over the death of Constantine that fed a growing paranoia, he delved into the occult. He beat his second son, the 16-year-old Leo, bloody for maintaining an erotic liaison of which he did not approve and went so far as to put him behind bars for three months. There was a story that Basileios freed his son only after the imperial parrot got on his nerves by continually squawking 'Poor Leo!' – no doubt echoing much popular sentiment.

We know tantalizingly little about how Basileios I met his end in the summer of 886. It is universally accepted that it was a classic royal 'hunting accident', but that is about as far as certainty goes. An elaborate report circulated that the emperor, 74 and not in prime condition, rode towards a large stag drinking at a stream, intending to kill it. The stag, however, charged his horse, unseated Basileios and caught the emperor's belt in its antlers. It ran for miles into the woods, dragging the emperor along. He was eventually found by his Turkish bodyguards, unconscious and still fastened to the stag, which was grazing peacefully. When he came to he appeared to be in a state of disorientation, raging that the guard who had cut him loose from the stag deserved death for lifting a sword against his emperor. His stomach, however, had been punctured and on 29 August he died in agony – but not before wondering aloud whether Leo had a hand in it.

The dying Basileios may not have been wrong. Leo hated and feared his father and would have ample reason for despatching him. Basileios in his turn would have thought little of having Leo executed, especially after the boy's highly-gossiped affair with the daughter of the Armenian courtier Stylianos Zautses, who just happened to be the head of the rescue party that went looking for Basileios after the stag dragged him off, and could have concocted any tale to disguise what might have been a plain assassination. The jigsaw pieces as we have them fall into place, yet we have no firm indication one way or another. We may fairly conclude that Basileios I, who attained power through intrigue and murder, left it by the same route.

There has always been a question mark over the paternity of the smart and studious 20-year-old who inherited the throne as Leo VI. Most authorities are inclined to believe he was a genuine offspring of Basileios I, but two pieces of circumstantial evidence argue that he could conceivably have been the son of the previous emperor Michael III. The first is the undisguised contempt that Basileios had for him, in contrast to his late adored elder son Constantine. The second is that one of Leo's first acts on assuming the throne was to transfer the remains of Michael III from their resting place at Chrysopolis to the imperial mausoleum in the palace grounds. Was this the act of a secretly devoted son, or simply a symbolic reversal of Basileios' foul murder of Michael?

If Leo was indeed Basileios' son, no two men could have been more different. Leo was intellectual and a born scholar, yet not nerdy. He was fascinated by learning and science of all kinds, a trait which earned him his sobriquet of 'the Wise'. A fourteenth century miniature in the University Library of Bologna shows him with shoulder-length dark hair and a full beard, tinkering in wide-eyed wonder with a contraption that looks like a heating brazier topped by some kind of fan. According to the mediaeval chronicler Bishop Liutprand of Cremona, he took a page out of Emperor Theophilos by occasionally going through the streets incognito in search of some injustice to correct. One night a police patrol arrested him for vagrancy and locked him up for the night. The shock of the officer in charge the next morning can be imagined. But far from punishing the policeman, Leo rewarded him for doing his duty properly.

As his ally Stylianos Zautses was promoted to Master of the Offices, a kind of prime minister of the realm, Leo strove to control the aristocratic families and put some order into the ever-fractious church administration. In 899 a general synod restored relations with Rome. Leo applied his workaholic mind to codifying the complex of Byzantine laws that needed upgrading three centuries after Justinian I. But some of Zautses' ideas, especially in the foreign and military sphere, turned out to be less than wise. This was odd for an emperor who was believed to be the most intelligent to occupy the throne so far. But Zautses was Leo's mistress' father, and therefore had to be accommodated.[3] Zautses' first mistake was to meddle in the affairs of Bulgaria. In 889 the newly-Christianized King Boris was shunted into a monastery by his vicious pagan son Vladimir, whose attempt to bring back the bad old ways was cut short by his enraged father, who abandoned his cloister and took back the reins of government. Vladimir was blinded and replaced as king by his younger brother Symeon, a professed friend of Byzantium. But Zautses could not leave well enough alone. In 894 he altered commercial agreements with Bulgaria to favour the port of Thessalonica – the second city of the empire – over the Black Sea ports, dealing a grievous blow to Bulgarian trade.

Symeon retaliated by invading Thrace, and Leo had no choice but to mobilize the army, which was already occupied on two widely-separated fronts, Southern Italy and the Arab East. General Nikephoros Phokas and the ranking admiral (or *drungarios*) Eustathios blockaded the mouth of the Danube. Leo sought help from the Magyars, a barbarian tribe on the northern fringes of Bulgaria, who swept down on the Bulgars. Symeon countered that by recruiting another tribe called the Petchenegs to fall on the Magyars from their rear. The Magyars dissolved in disorder, migrating to present-day Hungary, where their descendants still are. After a short truce Symeon's army resumed its offensive against the Byzantines, whom he trounced with great slaughter at Bulgarophygon (now Babaeski). Nikephoros Phokas had since been recalled and replaced by an incompetent commander. One of the very few survivors of the Byzantine army was so affected by the disaster that he spent the rest of his life atop a pillar near Corinth as Saint Luke the Stylite. And the Bulgars regained their commercial privileges.

The holocaust at Bulgarophygon so depleted Byzantium's military manpower that six years later Taormina, the last Byzantine outpost in Sicily, fell to the Muslim amir of the island, the bloody Ibrahim II. Leo's forces had initial success in the east, at Tarsus and in Armenia in 902. But disaster loomed closer to home. In 904 a renegade Greek, Leon of Tripolis, burst into Thessalonica with a fleet of Arab pirates, slaughtering thousands of people and taking away 30,000 of the survivors in chains. As a reprisal Leo earmarked Tarsus, the Arabs' key trading port in the Eastern Mediterranean and a rival to Alexandria, for destruction. The reprisal was to be conducted by Himerios, who had succeeded Zautses as chief policymaker, in conjunction with Andronikos Doukas, the commander of the Kibyrrhaiote *theme* in what is now Southern Turkey. Himerios was to take a powerful fleet to Attaleia (now Antalya) and join Andronikos Doukas for an overland march to Tarsus.

It didn't quite work out that way. Doukas was one of those senior commanders who owed more allegiance to his own military aristocratic class than to any emperor whom, in his own estimation, he could easily replace. Instead of helping Himerios, whom he considered his inferior socially and militarily, he saw no point in going on with the campaign. Himerios, to his credit, pressed on with the force he had and sacked Tarsus. Andronikos Doukas' traitorous reaction was to transfer his allegiance to the Arabs. Apparently willing to overlook this overt treachery, Leo wrote secretly to Doukas offering him his old job back. The caliph at the time was the 11-year-old al-Muqtadir, whose advisers discovered the letter and feared Doukas might be won over. The boy-caliph and his advisers ordered Doukas to either convert to Islam or forfeit his head. The Greek chose the former, but was jailed anyway.

As a scholar and writer, Leo the Wise may not have been cut out for service in the field. But he nonetheless made a large contribution to military science by compiling his Short Instruction of the Tactics of War, more often known as the Taktika. The work, rather dryly written and cumbersome in its terminology, is divided into twenty chapters with twelve appendices. It delves in detail into every military issue, from the definitions of strategy and tactics to effective generalship, officer training, weapons, horses, discipline, logistics, transport, camping, preparations for battle, sieges, stratagems, naval warfare and the need for a professional soldier to constantly study his subject. In the Taktika Leo takes a page out of the Muslim doctrine of jihad, or holy war, and urges Christian powers to adopt the same principle.[4]

Leo's family life, however, was not happy. He had not the slightest romantic interest in his wife Theophano, who lived the life of a nun inside the palace, forswearing all sexual relations. For an emperor who needed a son and heir, this was not the ideal arrangement, but she made things easier for him by becoming ill, wasting away and dying in 897. Once the lavish funeral was over Leo sought out his real love, his permanent mistress Zoe Zautsaina (or daughter of Zautses). Very conveniently, Zoe's own husband left this world at about the same time, and so Leo and Zoe were wed in 898. The joy was short-lived. Zoe produced a daughter but died the following year of an unspecified illness. Besides the grief it produced in the emperor, Zoe's death gave him a legal problem to deal with, as church rules forbade the emperor from marrying a third time. Yet such was the urgent need for an heir that the ban was overlooked; theoretically, his younger brother Alexander could have produced a legitimate heir, but he was a sickly alcoholic and considered unlikely to live very long himself. And the great majority of the Byzantine people heartily wished for dynastic stability.

Overriding canon law and the grumbles of the clergy who damned third marriages as 'legal fornication', Leo wed a very attractive young woman from Phrygia named Eudokia Baïana who had been among a group of debutantes paraded before the twice-widowed emperor in what was now a time-honoured practice of empress-selection. For a few months, matters seemed to be proceeding promisingly, until on Easter Day 901 Eudokia died giving birth to the much-needed baby boy – who himself succumbed shortly afterwards. For Leo grief was piled upon grief, not least because if the Byzantine clergy frowned on third marriages, fourth ones were totally beyond the pale – 'bestial polygamy' in the ferocious ecclesiastical definition. So Leo had no choice but to live in sin with his fourth consort, Zoe Karbonopsina (whose name means 'coal-black eyes'), the daughter of the general Himerios. In September 905 Zoe delivered herself of a baby boy who looked sickly but survived, ending the emperor's extraordinary run of bad matrimonial luck. But how to baptize the child, when Leo and Zoe were legally unmarried? Thanks to a pliant patriarch, Zoe agreed to briefly leave the palace to enable the law to be bent just enough so that the boy could be baptized in Sancta Sophia as Constantine.

But Leo's family problems were far from over. To the intransigent clergy, young Constantine was a bastard and hence ineligible for the throne. Leo got round that one by collaring a simple priest to perform a marriage ceremony of sorts. The church establishment went purple with fury but could do little except callously advise the emperor, now that he had the heir he needed, to get rid of Zoe, 'as we dismiss a ship when her cargo is discharged'. But Leo was not called the Wise for nothing. When the patriarch denied him entrance into Sancta Sophia as a cardinal sinner he secretly turned to Pope Sergius III for support. A measure of peace returned to the imperial household, but the clergy continued to thunder. To make sure of the succession, little Constantine, dubbed Porphyrogennetos – born 'into the purple', i.e. the russet-walled birth chamber in the palace – was named co-emperor in his second year.

Fate left a sharp sting in the tail for Leo the Wise. In late 911, while still in his mid-forties, he sent his father-in-law Himerios and the navy to try and recapture Crete from the Arabs. Himerios faltered before the massive Arab defences, having little to show after six months in action. During that time the emperor's health broke down. Receiving the news, Himerios raised the siege and set sail for home. On the way, off the island of Chios, he was ambushed by an Arab fleet under the renegade Leon of Tripolis. Most of the Byzantine fleet was destroyed; Himerios was one of the few survivors. Leo, gravely ill, did not need the shock of the news of the disaster; he died on 11 May 912.

Alexander (912–913) and Constantine VII Porphyrogennetos (913–959) including Romanos I Lekapenos (920–944)

Young Constantine was 7 when his father passed away, and too young to effectively rule, so thoughts turned to Leo's younger brother Alexander. In favour of Alexander was the church's dismissive attitude to Constantine as an illegitimate bastard, and so the brother was given his turn.[5] That turn, however, was as vicious as it was mercifully brief. Alexander, aged 41, was something close to certifiably insane. He made a habit of appearing riotously drunk in public places and mocking holy symbols, giving the church a nasty surprise and adding the suspicion of paganism to his sins. He got it into his head that a bronze boar in the Hippodrome was his other self and, as Lord Norwich elegantly puts it, 'had it provided with new teeth and genitals in an attempt to remedy the extraordinary wear and tear that he had inflicted on his own'. He kicked his sister-in-law, the widowed empress Zoe, out of the palace and threw her father Himerios into prison.

In one of his drunken paroxysms Alexander deigned to receive an embassy from the Bulgar king Symeon congratulating him on his accession. Alexander replied by bawling at the emissaries that he would no longer pay tribute to Symeon to keep the peace in the Balkans. Symeon duly noted the response and prepared for war. Meanwhile, Alexander meddled madly in ecclesiastical affairs, throwing the entire church into turmoil. His sexual excesses had worn him out prematurely and probably contributed to his collapse from a stroke – either playing polo in the summer heat after a heavy meal or while sacrificing to his alter ego the bronze boar – in June 913. Zoe returned to the palace determined to push her son for the succession. We are told that Alexander recovered consciousness just long enough for him to confirm Constantine as his successor, and died two days later.

Constantine VII Porphyrogennetos began his reign with a lot stacked against him. At seven, he could not hope to counter the hostility of the formidable Patriarch Nicholas, the head of the church, who still considered him the fruit of sin. Moreover, Nicholas was the chief regent, and in that capacity had no hesitation in having Zoe's head shaved and packing her off to a convent. Nicholas also plotted with the army commander-in-chief, Constantine Doukas, to depose the boy. But when Doukas attempted his coup with a picked squad, another of the regents named John Eladas counterattacked with a militia. During the fight Doukas' horse slipped on the paving stones and its rider was thrown; before he could rise, a single sword stroke removed his head – yet another example of a technique that appears to have been highly developed in Byzantium. Patriarch Nicholas, in a panicked attempt to divert suspicion from himself, ordered the massacre of hundreds of soldiers who had been under Doukas' orders, impaling them along the Bosporus and blinding and whipping many others.

Putting an end to this spasm of insane violence was the appearance of Symeon with a vast army in the plain before Constantinople. As de facto head of the Byzantine state, Nicholas decided on diplomacy. Viewing the smoke from the devastated farms and homestands in the plain west of the capital, and the refugees streaming in through the gates, Nicholas agreed to Symeon's offer to talk things over. Religious rather than military considerations determined the outcome. Symeon had little chance of breaching the massive walls of Constantinople; but on the other hand Nicholas needed the allegiance of the Bulgarian church. Young Constantine dined merrily in the company of the Bulgar king's two sons and seems to have been promised a daughter of Symeon as his future wife.

The occasional banquet apart, Constantine's life was not a happy one. He missed his mother terribly; the sight of his pale and slight figure shuffling tearfully about the palace was heart-rending. But he was destined not to be desperately sad for long. The patriarch began to be seen for what he was, an unholy tyrant. In 914 he came under growing suspicion for his willingness to treat with Symeon and was sidelined. Zoe Karbonopsina was brought back from her cloister and appointed chief regent for her son. With Zoe in firm control, aided by a capable group of officials and officers known as the 'Council of Eunuchs,' Nicholas was told in no uncertain terms to stick to his pulpit.[6] For the next six years Zoe Karbonopsina provided the vital underpinning for her son's reign. When Prince Ashot of Armenia sought Byzantine help after his country was ravaged by the Muslims, she sent him back with a Greek army that brought Armenia back into the Christian fold. At the same time, a Byzantine army defeated an Arab force at Capua in Italy.

There was no way that Zoe would ever agree to Constantine's marrying the Bulgar Symeon's daughter. Symeon's hopes of securing a foothold towards the Byzantine throne thus thwarted, he made a show of force before Adrianople. Zoe countered with an offensive that drove the Bulgars off. She arranged with her general John Bogas to entrap Symeon in a pincer movement, with the navy ferrying Petchenegs southward across the Danube in conjunction with the army moving north from Constantinople. It would have worked had not the naval commander, Romanos Lekapenos, failed to do his assigned job of bringing the Petchenegs across the river. There was talk that Lekapenos had been bribed by Symeon. The Byzantine army, alone and unsupported before Anchialos on the Black Sea coast, was butchered almost to a man by the Bulgars on 20 August 917.

An inquiry found Romanos Lekapenos guilty of desertion, but somehow he avoided the blinding that would ordinarily have been his punishment. Zoe sent another army into Thrace against the Bulgars, but this one also came to grief. These defeats cost her popularity, and to keep herself in power she contemplated marrying Leon Phokas, the aristocratic general who had commanded (and lost) the campaigns against the Bulgars. Phokas was brought into the palace as a close adviser until she could make up her mind about him. But though wealthy and good-looking, he was not widely liked, and the inevitable fears arose that he might want the throne for himself. Then, quite unexpectedly, young Constantine himself was heard from.

Now 13, he was proving to be a pubescent youth of high intelligence and a certain quality of character, but uncertain health. Observing the course of events closely had been his tutor Theodore, who one day wrote to Romanos Lekapenos asking for protection against the supposed ambitions of Leon Phokas. Zoe may have got wind of this, as she ordered Lekapenos to disband his fleet. The admiral responded by arresting her envoy as he came aboard the flagship. Zoe Karbonopsina called a meeting of her regency committee, but found it hostile to her. Patriarch Nicholas saw his chance to oust her; he may have drafted the proclamation that Constantine was made to read, stripping his mother of her post as chief regent. But the young emperor still loved his mother, and succeeded in preventing her from being sent back to the convent.

Leon Phokas and Romanos Lekapenos prepared to battle for control of the imperium. In March 919 Lekapenos sailed with his fleet into the small harbour just south of the palace and marched into the imperial precincts – the gates were unlocked, it was said, by the emperor's tutor Theodore. He underpinned his coup d'état with a touch of legitimacy by marrying his daughter Helena to Constantine. Across the Bosporus Leon Phokas prepared to fight. We are told that a camp prostitute carried out propaganda work for Lekapenos among Phokas' troops by displaying a letter purporting to show that Lekapenos enjoyed the complete confidence of the emperor. Phokas' support melted away; he was caught, blinded and jailed. Some weeks later he was put on a mule and paraded around the Hippodrome before a jeering crowd.

Romanos Lekapenos began the next stage of his rise to power by getting rid of Zoe Karbonopsina, accusing her of trying to poison him (we cannot know if it was true) and hastening her delayed return to the convent. Then there was the imperial tutor Theodore, who had at first regarded Lekapenos as his pupil's saviour, but had quickly changed his mind. Theodore was arrested while at dinner and exiled to his country home in Asia Minor. Constantine, powerless to halt the banishment of his mother and trusted friend, was forced to proclaim Lekapenos Caesar in September 920 and three months later crown him officially as co-emperor. Constantine Porphyrogennetos, senior in theory but very much junior in age and practice, was never more alone than now.

Romanos I – as Lekapenos now was – buttressed his position by raising the art of nepotism to a new height, even for Byzantium. Hardly had he begun to warm his throne than he raised three of his three young sons (the fourth, destined for the clergy, was castrated) to be co-emperors, giving Byzantium no fewer than five simultaneous sovereigns along with the ignored Constantine. His motives were a mixture of ambition and caution, conducted with the cunning of his Armenian peasant origins and lack of formal education. That he rose quickly through the ranks of the navy from seaman to commander of the Samian Theme on the east coast of the Aegean Sea in less than twenty years argues for a certain level of brain power as well as an ability to handle people without violence. He saw trickery as a more effective weapon. On the other hand, his religious faith prevented him from disposing of Constantine VII, as many a lesser usurper would have no hesitation in doing.

This does not mean that Romanos did not wish that somehow Constantine was not there. He firmly believed his own family was far better fitted than the weakened Macedonian house to rule Byzantium. Romanos tried to buy off Symeon with tribute, but the Bulgar king brushed aside the offer. Romanos got the Serbs to harry the Bulgars, but that didn't work as well as was hoped, and Symeon invaded Byzantine territory, reaching the Bosporus north of Constantinople in 922. But he knew he could not hope to break through the formidable walls of the city, so he sent an embassy across the Mediterranean to a breakaway Arab state in what is now Tunisia ruled by the Fatimids, a dissident Muslim clan that was challenging the central caliphal authority, to provide him with a fleet. The Fatimid imam, Ubaydullah al-Mahdi, eager to flex his muscle in the region, seems to have agreed in principle. While the Bulgarian envoys were returning they were intercepted by the Byzantine navy and jailed; the Arabs with them, however, were treated very well and sent home laden with money and gifts which ensured that nothing more would be heard from Ubaydullah al-Mahdi.

Thwarted momentarily, Symeon suggested a summit conference. Romanos agreed, and an elaborate security operation was planned in which the two kings would confer on either side of a fence placed across a pier built over the northern tip of the Golden Horn; Symeon would arrive by land while Romanos would go by sea. No one was taking any chances at the big meeting that took place on 9 September 924. Romanos approached his adversary carrying the mantle of the Virgin Mary as a sign that he wished to negotiate in earnest. The first thing he asked Symeon was why he was so intent on making war on Byzantium. 'Today you live and tomorrow you are dust,' the emperor said, lecturing the Bulgar on certain inescapable realities. What did Symeon want? Was it money? All he needed to do was ask. He urged Symeon to embrace 'a peaceful, bloodless and untroubled life' and to cease 'destroying fellow-Christians'.[7]

According to our Greek sources (there is no corresponding Bulgarian account), at that moment a couple of eagles flew over the domes and roofs of Constantinople, and one of them was seen to wheel off westwards towards Thrace. In those portent-filled times the birds were seen to symbolize Romanos and Symeon, with the latter destined to go back home. Symeon did not say much; we are told that once he received a promise of a hundred luxury silk robes a year he got back on his horse and rode off. Romanos had carried himself off with the aplomb of a true Roman emperor. Symeon lived for three more disillusioned years, giving himself the title of Tsar (Caesar) of the Romans and Bulgars for comfort, but everyone knew the claim was an empty one. 'He can call himself the Caliph of Baghdad for all I care,' Romanos deadpanned when he heard of it.

With the Bulgars taken care of, Romanos turned his attention to the East, which was chronically in a state of intermittent friction, with Muslim statelets and powers fighting themselves and Byzantium. For this he turned to an extremely competent general named John Kurkuas who had recently been appointed commander-in-chief of the army after a period of devoted service to Romanos. Hailing from what is now Georgia, Kurkuas knew the wider region very well. By 932 he had cleared most of Armenia and the region around Lake Van. But in 941, after dealing with the latest Arab resurgence in Syria, Kurkuas received a panicked message from Romanos to return home – the Russians had struck again. For the past eighty or so years, since their first fearsome invasion from the Black Sea, they had been silent. Now they were back with over 1,000 ships under Igor, the Grand Prince of Kiev. The Byzantine navy, too, was away; all that remained in the shipyards were fifteen old hulls destined for the breakers. These were hastily refitted and packed with quantities of Greek Fire. Under Theophanes, an aristocratic official, they sailed up the Bosporus just in time to see the Russians approaching from the Black Sea on 11 June 941. Theophanes was the *Protovestiarios*, or Keeper of the Imperial Wardrobe. But his naval talents outshone his sartorial ones as, without waiting for Igor's armada to sail any closer, he attacked with his Greek Fire. The effect of this remarkable weapon on the Russians can hardly be exaggerated. As the first Russian ships went up in flames the rest turned and made for the Southern Black Sea shore. There the Russians perpetrated atrocities on the Christian population, including piercing the skulls of priests with iron rods.

Theophanes' resolve held up the Russians long enough for the regular navy to turn up, along with Kurkuas from the East with Bardas Phokas, an elderly general and father of Leon Phokas. Theophanes was able to blockade the Russians, who tried to break out but again were decimated by the flame-throwers of the Greeks. Within minutes Prince Igor's fleet and the great majority of his men were incinerated. Just ten Russian ships out of some 1,000 are said to have survived. Theophanes, the hero of the hour, was given a promotion. The Russian prisoners appear to have been executed, to great public approval. Prince Igor attempted another invasion three years later, but this time, probably remembering the Greek Fire, he pulled back after consenting to a handsome payment. Soon afterwards, Kiev and Constantinople signed a commercial treaty. On Igor's death his widow Olga converted to Christianity and became a firm friend of Byzantium.

After the Russian interruption John Kurkuas continued his brilliant successes in the East, re-establishing Christian control over large parts of Syria and what is now Southeast Turkey. He achieved a major foreign policy coup by getting the Muslims in Edessa to hand over a purported image of Jesus imprinted on a cloth. This sacred relic was delivered to Constantinople, where with great solemnity Theophanes received it to hand on to Romanos. But the emperor, meanwhile, had sunk to a shadow of his old self. It often happens that outwardly strong and active men, once their powers have waned and have ceased to feel useful, develop a morbid fear of death. This is what seems to have happened to Romanos, who was now over 70 and obsessed by thoughts of the end of life. As if in divine punishment for his usurping the throne, the sons he had appointed as Caesars (one of the three had since died) had proved to be not only worthless but dangerous, as their intrigues had got Kurkuas dismissed from his command. Physically ill as well as mentally tormented, Romanos slipped helplessly into a life of prayer, repentance and good works which he hoped would extend his earthly life and earn him points in the next. When, in a burst of good sense, he confirmed Constantine as outranking his sons, they lifted their father from his sick-bed in December 944 and shipped him off to a monastery on an island in the Sea of Marmara.

And what of the sad and neglected young man who all this time had lived unobtrusively in the palace, bearing the title of Constantine VII Porphyrogennetos? Keeping a low profile through the twenty-four years of Romanos I's rule was the best thing he could have done. His people had not forgotten him, and as Romanos' sons made themselves unpopular and Romanos himself declined, they fondly recalled the legitimate scion of the Macedonian dynasty who by all accounts had behaved like a perfect gentleman throughout. But Constantine had keenly felt every single slight inflicted on him, and hadn't forgotten them. Moreover, he was very likely on the Lekapeni brothers' hit list. After Romanos' removal a militant crowd gathered in front of the palace demanding to see Constantine, who appeared at a window showing signs of having been roughed up.

Under pressure of overwhelming public opinion the Lekapeni brothers agreed that Constantine should be, in fact as well as in name, senior emperor, while plotting to assassinate him. He got wind of the plot, aided by his resolute wife Helena – another Theodora-figure of the kind that Byzantium threw up surprisingly often – and had the brothers arrested and sent off to join their father in his monastery. Bishop Liutprand of Cremona, an important source for the events of this era, reports that old Romanos received them with heavy sarcasm. But there would be no peace for Romanos or his sons. The ex-emperor was tormented by nightmares of hell, including one on the night when his elder son was killed trying to escape. In spring 946 the monastery witnessed the strange sight of Romanos chanting the Kyrie Eleison (Lord Have Mercy) in the presence of a crowd of monks, confessing aloud all his sins and submitting to a flogging from a novitiate. Two years later he was dead, his final days comforted with assurances that the sins that he had accumulated trying to run the Byzantine Empire efficiently, and as bloodlessly as possible, for a quarter of a century had been forgiven.

Constantine VII was now free to reign unhindered. He was now about 40, tall and well-built, blue-eyed and with an abundant black beard. A woodcut and a gold medallion which bear the few known likenesses of him show a long, thin face dominated by melancholy eyes. Denied the chance to administer the state for so long, he had excelled in scholarship instead. In 952 he issued a major work on political science, *De Administrando Imperio*, in which he minimized the importance of war as an instrument of national policy. Diplomacy and, where necessary, bribery, were preferable ways of keeping the peace and Byzantium prosperous. This was true, he believed, even for the Petchenegs, the barbarian tribe that now had become Byzantium's most serious potential foe. The Petchenegs, Constantine wrote, echoing his father Leo the Wise, were 'fiercely covetous of those commodities that are rare among them, and shameless in their demands for generous presents'.

Constantine, for all his scholarly attainments, maintained a healthy interest in the military. His choices for senior appointments in the army and navy were generally good ones. He rehabilitated the Phokas family, putting Bardas Phokas (son and namesake of the Bardas Phokas who had helped repel the Russians) in command in the East to replace John Kurkuas. Bardas Phokas was put out of action early by a wound, but his son Nikephoros Phokas, his successor in command, took Adana, securing the pass through the Taurus Mountains into Syria. General John Tzimiskes, another of the able soldiers whom the emperor had picked, took the strategic city of Samosata.

Constantine also examined the chances of an alliance with the Holy Roman Empire, now in the hands of Otto I (the Saxon), with a view to possibly regaining control of Italy or at least parts of it. Otto's chief envoy, Bishop Liutprand of Cremona, was given the full dazzling treatment at his reception in Constantinople in 949. One reason why the imperial throne was so coveted by all manner of relatives and usurpers was the sheer extravagant magnificence it lent to the occupant, for all the world to see and marvel at. The technology for this purpose had advanced since Theophilos' golden songbirds of a century before. They were crude compared to what surrounded Constantine Porphyrogennetos when dignitaries came to call. A bigger golden tree with more mechanical coruscated birds overshadowed the huge throne, which could be raised to the ceiling like a lift, so that the emperor could gaze down on the foreigner from on high. On either side of the throne stood metal lions which, as the nonplussed Liutprand observed, 'beat the ground with their tails and emitted dreadful roars, their mouths open and their tongues quivering'. After such intimidation, an envoy would then be wined and dined in luxury, entertained by acrobats who would do credit to a modern circus. This, truly, was the pinnacle of Byzantine magnificence and power, a pinnacle that would never be reached again.

Constantine made sure his military establishment was a solid one, guaranteeing landholding rights to the smallholders who made up the bulk of the soldiery in war, while staying in the good graces of the aristocracy to which the senior officer class belonged. In September 959, however, he was showing signs of fatigue. He was 54, by no means old, but his health had never been robust and moreover, much of his energy was now being taken up with that bane of almost all his predecessors, church disputes. The clergy had never forgotten the emperor's father's alleged criminal polygamy, and many as a result continued to consider Constantine illegitimate. The emperor travelled into Asia Minor to seek advice from friendly clerics and visit the warm springs at Bursa for a persistent fever that had been troubling him for some time. While calling at a monastery on Mount Olympus, he took a turn for the worse; the monks there advised him to prepare for the end.[8] He managed to return to Constantinople where he died on 9 November. There were the inevitable rumours that he been slowly poisoned, but in the absence of any sounder evidence, they may be discounted.

Romanos II (959–963), Nikephoros II Phokas (963–969) and John I Tzimiskes (969–976)

Constantine Porphyrogennetos' eldest son Romanos inherited the empire at 21, with everything going for him. He also inherited his father's intellect and his mother's good looks, but little else. His main concerns were partying, hunting and playing polo and, when the crown descended on his head, a manipulative commoner named Theophano, the daughter of a Greek innkeeper, whom he fell in love with and married. Theophano's family came from the area of Sparta, and her own character partook fully of the tough traditions of that ancient military city. Even sober commentators had to admit that Theophano was one of the prettiest women of her day, and when she became empress at 18 had no hesitation in banishing any female competition, including Romanos' mother and sisters, to oblivion in convents, personally overseeing the obligatory shaving of their heads.

Totally besotted, Romanos allowed Theophano to sack any official she chose. One who managed to keep his job was the high admiral of the fleet (*drungarios*), Iosif Bringas, who assumed military responsibility for the empire. Bringas decided that the time was ripe for Crete to be recaptured from the Muslims, and in early 960 he prepared a massive amphibious operation that would involve more than 50,000 troops, including Russians and axe-wielding Scandinavian Varangians. They would sail on 1,000 transports to be supported by more than 300 supply vessels and 2,000 specialized Greek Fire-squirters. In command he placed Nikephoros Phokas, the most capable member of a leading military family that had given Byzantium at least three generations of soldiers.[9]

Nikephoros Phokas was a general's general – tireless, fearless, physically strong, highly intelligent and above all, considerate to his men. He was deeply religious to the point of sociopathy, associating off duty with no one but holy men, and a strict vegetarian to boot. On 13 July the great fleet loomed over the north coast of Crete and swept inland, taking the Arab defenders by surprise. The Arabs fought with fanatical courage, but in the end were overcome by the Byzantine cataphract heavy cavalry. Early in the advance on

Chandax (later Candia, now Heraklion, the chief city of Crete), a Russian detachment under General Patsilas indulged too freely in the heady Cretan wine and was slaughtered almost to a man. Nikephoros Phokas bulled his way up to the great walls of Chandax and for eight long months hammered away at the defenders as the winter set in and few supply ships could get through the bad weather. The Byzantines suffered severely from cold and hunger, but Phokas maintained their morale. The Arabs appealed for help elsewhere in the Mediterranean Muslim world, but none came. After a relief fleet arrived from Byzantium in February 961 the siege began anew. In less than a month the Greeks burst into Chandax, wreaking their revenge by three days of indiscriminate butchery; a favourite sport was to impale Arab babies on lance points. Nikephoros Phokas, to his credit, appealed to his troops to tame their savage urges, but few would listen.

Crete was under Christian control again after 136 years, for which Romanos and Theophano attended an elaborate thanksgiving service in Sancta Sophia. But the name on everyone's lips was that of Nikephoros Phokas, who shortly afterwards sailed up the Golden Horn for the imperial couple to receive him. But if the general thought he would be the figure of honour at a victory procession through the city, he was mistaken. If not Romanos himself, no doubt Theophano was deeply suspicious of this victorious soldier. Nikephoros Phokas had to be content with a lesser celebration in the Hippodrome, without the parade and not even on horseback. And hardly had the cheers of the crowd died down than he was sent east to tackle a rising Arab leader named Sayf al-Dawlah. Nikephoros could thus be useful and conveniently away from Constantinople at the same time.

At precisely the time Nikephoros Phokas' expedition had been sailing for Crete, Sayf had led 30,000 Arabs across the border from Syria, plundering and killing. The local forces of Leon Phokas, Nikephoros' brother, were heavily outnumbered, but he waited until Sayf made his leisurely withdrawal back south through the Taurus Mountains.[10] There, in a funnel-shaped pass, the Byzantines loosed a cascade of boulders onto the unsuspecting Arabs, killing more than half of them. Sayf, after fighting heroically, turned and fled with 300 surviving horsemen. Nikephoros Phokas, after concluding the Cretan mission, hastened east to join his brother; together they took fifty-five enemy towns in three weeks, advancing to Aleppo, Sayf al-Dawlah's headquarters. Within a matter of days Aleppo had fallen, to great slaughter, and Sayf had fled yet again, leaving behind all his fabled wealth.

In the spring of 963 the Phokas brothers were leading their victorious army home when, on 15 March, Romanos II died aged 25. We are not given the cause of this untimely demise, though perhaps inevitably Theophano came under suspicion of having poisoned him. Such rumours, as we have seen, arose regularly after the unexpected death of an emperor, and so far we have nothing to further substantiate them. The case against Theophano can probably be dismissed; she had given birth to her fourth child two days before, and despite her tough and often merciless character stood to gain nothing from her husband's death. Moreover, she had made a legion of enemies, and with Romanos gone she appealed for protection to the only figure she could trust – the general who had given her husband his great victories in the West and East.

There followed a game of cat-and-mouse between Theophano and Nikephoros on the one hand, and High Admiral Iosif Bringas on the other. Bringas believed he had a better right to the throne than the popular general, but he was outwitted in the game of intrigue and had to sourly watch Nikephoros' triumphal procession and attendant celebrations in the Hippodrome. But what were Nikephoros' motives? He seems to have genuinely wished to retire from soldiering and devote the rest of his life to prayer and meditation on Mount Athos. He had second thoughts after suspecting, probably rightly, that Bringas was plotting to murder him. Nikephoros sought sanctuary in Sancta Sophia, publicizing the threat and getting the people on his side. After Easter, he returned to his command on the Eastern front.

Who reigned during this confused intermezzo? Technically, Theophano held the throne in place of her two sons, 6-year-old Basileios and 3-year-old Constantine. Theophano felt she wasn't up to the job, especially with two royal princes to protect, so she is believed to have made a secret deal with Nikephoros to make him co-emperor. Why, then, did he return to the East when he did? The answer is almost certainly that it was a ploy to deceive Bringas. Nikephoros, for his part, was content to bide his time until summoned by the empress, but Bringas forced his hand by asking two other generals, Romanos Kurkuas and John Tzimiskes, to replace him by underhand means. Tzimiskes, however, was Nikephoros' ally and spilled the plot to him. There could now be no doubt about what Nikephoros had to do. On 3 July 963, outside Caesarea in Cappadocia, as the army watched and cheered, his generals raised him on their shields and proclaimed him emperor of Byzantium.

Nikephoros Phokas was not what might be called a handsome man. He was short and stumpy, with a large head and small eyes and hardly any neck to speak of. His years of campaigning in the field had given him a heavily-sunburned swarthy complexion that seemed not to sit well with Liutprand of Cremona, who judged his appearance 'Ethiopian'. Also, according to the bishop, he never had his royal robe washed. Such characteristics may help explain Bringas' deadly hatred of him, a hatred which he put to good use during Nikephoros' march to Constantinople. When the general and his army arrived at the Asiatic shore of the Bosporus he found Bringas waiting for him with his own hastily-raised force; Bringas had also taken the precaution of holding the Phokas brothers' father, the veteran general Bardas Phokas, as hostage. The old man, however, escaped from confinement and sought refuge in Sancta Sophia. Bringas pursued him there personally, but had to retire under the insults of the furious crowd. On the second attempt Bringas seized Bardas, but when he sent a squad of Macedonian troops to the church, the mob set upon them.

Thus began a generalized riot that came close to consuming Constantinople. For three days the mob rampaged until a eunuch son of the late Romanos Lekapenos called Basil, the commander of the Russian and Varangian Imperial Guard, got together about 4,000 palace and Guards staff to restore order.[11] In fact, they began by looting and burning Bringas' house. On 16 August, Basil, known as 'the Bastard' (Nothos) for his illegitimate birth (though his character might merit that description as well), led the navy down the Golden Horn and across the Bosporus to carry the new emperor to his palace. Nikephoros Phokas sat in a gaudily-decorated warship on a silver throne under a golden shade. Disembarking at the Hebdomon (Seventh) Palace outside the west wall, he changed into his royal robes, mounted a white horse and rode slowly through the Golden Gate, stopping only to pray to an icon of the Virgin, to be formally crowned Nikephoros II in Sancta Sophia.

Bringas survived the turmoil but was exiled for his sedition. John Tzimiskes was elevated to commander-in-chief of the army in the East. The new emperor's next move surprised almost everyone – he married Theophano, still in her twenties, and as extraordinarily beautiful as she was clever. But could she have had romantic feelings for the lumpish Nikephoros who was not a woman's man in any case, concerning himself solely with spiritual and ascetic occupations? Historians have concluded that the marriage was a purely political one, made after Theophano was made to seclude herself for a month in a fortress – probably to avoid the gossip that would have arisen if they had shared the palace. Then Nikephoros' own dormant romantic instincts awoke and fastened themselves on Theophano. Despite his piety, he defied the Byzantine church establishment when it ruled Theophano's second marriage illicit under canon law and ordered him to put her aside under threat of excommunication. Nikephoros tearfully swore that he never had sex with Theophano, but insisted on staying married to her.

Nikephoros Phokas, in the end, was more comfortable on campaign. The year after his accession he returned to the Eastern front, which he believed he had a God-given trust to keep free from the Muslims. To the Greeks even today he is the 'White Death of the Saracens', superior to all other Muslim-battlers. He seized the port of Tarsus on the Syrian coast, while his general Michael Bourtzes took Antioch, which became Christian again after more than three centuries. General Niketas Chalkoutses landed on Cyprus and cleared the island of Muslims. The emperor asked the patriarch to bestow the honours of martyrdom on all his fallen men, but the clergyman refused on the logical grounds that as it was a soldier's job to kill, even the defence of his land and faith could not absolve him from the basic sin. As for the Arabs, their resistance was at its lowest ebb; after the disaster at Aleppo Sayf al-Dawlah had died, a broken man. With the Arab enemy neutralized, Nikephoros turned west, intending to deal with the Bulgars, whose new tsar, Peter, was greedy for Byzantine gold. When Peter's envoys arrived at the palace to collect the annual tribute the emperor drove them off, lambasting the Bulgars as 'a race of filthy beggars, triple slaves and sons of dogs'. To complete the ignominy he had them whipped. Nikephoros knew this would mean war, but with the bulk of the army occupied in the East, how would it be conducted? His solution was to pay Prince Svyatoslav of Kiev to move against the Bulgars, which that rapacious and power-hungry Russian prince was all too eager to do.

Relations with the Holy Roman Empire were also tricky. Emperor Otto I still hankered after a marriage alliance with Byzantium, but how could Nikephoros countenance any ties with a heretic monarch who was usurping the one and only title to Roman Empire held by Constantinople? When Bishop Liutprand of Cremona arrived in Constantinople at the head of the mission to press Otto's request, they were lamentably ill-treated. But, Byzantine diplomats suggested, a Greek princess might be available for Otto's son if Byzantium could reoccupy large portions of Italy. Otto rejected the proposal. As for Liutprand, after his treatment his hatred of the Byzantines was fully confirmed. This contempt would feed a great gulf of prejudice opening between the Western and Eastern empires, which by now had drifted so far apart in language, creed and mentality as to erase any hope of reunion.

Nikephoros never had any social graces. As a soldier he was brilliant, but as a diplomat he was worse than zero, as his treatment of Liutprand showed. His one concern was to eliminate Byzantium's infidel foes, and if he had confined himself to that task he might have earned a better place in Byzantine history. But while he was emperor he seems to have forgotten his earlier devout humility and, faced with the inevitable evils of politics and domestic intrigue, he turned into a tyrant. The only beneficiaries of his rule were the soldiery and the senior officer class – the only people with whom he could feel comfortable. Against him were ranged the church, still smarting over his marriage to Theophano, and much public opinion, which saw the powerful military families enriching themselves at the expense of everyone else. On Easter Day 967 a brawl between some Armenian soldiers and Thracian sailors got out of hand; later that day, as the emperor took his seat in the Hippodrome the crowd feared that he might order his troops to attack them, as in the old days of the Blues and the Greens. Nikephoros surely intended nothing of the kind, but the purely ceremonial appearance of troops triggered a panic; hundreds died in the rush to escape, while Nikephoros sat there impassively.

Some weeks later a mob, blaming him for the deaths, encircled him as he was returning from a church service. His guard saved him only with difficulty. Two women, a mother and daughter who are believed to have been relatives of Hippodrome victims, were arrested after throwing bricks at Nikephoros from a roof; the following day, both were burned alive. This was about as unpopular as an emperor could get. The story circulated that one day an ugly monk approached him and put a scrap of paper in his hand. The message on it was that he would die within a few months. The terrified emperor had a private security palace built connecting the main palace with the Bukoleon harbour. Ever more mystically religious, he slept on a panther-skin on the floor rather than a bed. To get a potential rival out of the way he relieved John Tzimiskes of his command. But Tzimiskes had no intention of staying put. Though short of stature, he was a far better-looking man than Nikephoros, and it wasn't long before he had captured the heart of none other than Theophano. The empress talked her husband into recalling Tzimiskes, who was, however, kept no nearer than the Asian shore of the Bosporus. To Tzimiskes this was a laughable barrier, and he often crossed secretly to enjoy nocturnal trysts with her in a corner of the palace. The next step, of course, was to get rid of Nikephoros.

Tzimiskes and Theophano laid their plans carefully. Joining the conspirators was Michael Bourtzes, the conqueror of Antioch, and Basil the Bastard, who had helped deal with the threat from Bringas. What followed was the stuff of Hollywood. One snowy night in December 969 the chief conspirators disguised themselves as women, secreting themselves in Theophano's quarters. The emperor, though, was uneasy; plot security seems to have been poor and a priest warned him his life was in imminent danger. But an official who was in the plot reassured him. As a blizzard howled outside the palace walls, Theophano wondered whether Tzimiskes would be able to cross the Bosporus to join her. Eventually, with some difficulty he made the crossing and just before midnight, emitting a whistle as a signal, he was drawn up by a rope into Theophano's quarters.

Nikephoros had spent the stormy evening alone reading devotional literature and praying, before wrapping himself in an old hair shirt and drifting off to sleep on the floor. When the conspirators entered his chamber he woke with a start, just in time to receive a sword slash across the face from an officer, Leon Balantes, who had aimed for the neck. Bleeding heavily, he called on the Virgin Mary to save him as he was dragged to the foot of his bed. There, as his former general Tzimiskes looked on, he cowered on the floor as his assailants kicked him and ripped out parts of his hair and beard, all the while screaming imprecations at him. The emperor's front teeth were knocked out and his jaw smashed; finally one of the conspirators finished him off with a sword-stroke.

The Imperial Guard learned of the assassination by the sight of Nikephoros' head being dangled out of a palace window. The rest of his body lay in a bloody heap below. The Varangians knew better than to contest the issue at this late stage and at once transferred their allegiance to John Tzimiskes, who himself lost no time in ransacking the imperial wardrobe and decking himself in the suitable attire, including the purple boots. The following day dawned over a mist-shrouded city under curfew and numb with shock. At its close, the broken and headless body of Nikephoros II was carried on a stretcher to the Church of the Holy Apostles and placed in a sarcophagus.

For John Tzimiskes the way now seemed clear to ruling Byzantium in tandem with his amour Theophano (his own wife Maria had conveniently died shortly before). But here Patriarch Polyeuktos stepped in and banned a third wedding for the empress. Tzimiskes was put on the spot. He was given a choice similar to that faced by Britain's King Edward VIII in 1936 – throne or wife. He couldn't have both. So, unlike Edward, Tzimiskes opted for the throne. Theophano, in shock, was led off to confinement in a monastery on an island in the Sea of Marmara. When she tried to escape she was exiled to

Armenia, but not before managing to confront Tzimiskes one last time and, as the great scorned woman, shower ferocious insults on him before being dragged off by attendants.

Free to concentrate on matters weightier than an ex-girl friend's wrath, John Tzimiskes needed to mollify the public distrust over the dastardly method by which he had come to power. His confident manner, fair hair and penetrating blue eyes helped him win popularity; moreover, he was wealthy enough to donate a good part of his fortune to relieve famine-stricken farmers and maintain a lepers' hospital on the Asian side of the Bosporus which he regularly visited, even tending the patients himself. He therefore had the people behind him when the Russians under Prince Svyatoslav of Kiev in 970 made another all-out attempt on Constantinople. The short-term Russian aim was plunder; the longer-term aim, which was not to waver over the next ten centuries, was to secure the sole outlet to the warm Mediterranean Sea.

Tzimiskes chose to stay in the capital while he sent more members of the Phokas military family – his brother-in-law Bardas Skleros (the Hard) and Petros Phokas, a nephew of the late Nikephoros, reputed to have immense physical strength – as generals to lead an army of 12,000 men against Svyatoslav, who had at least twice that number, including Magyars and Petchenegs. Near Adrianople Skleros cleverly manoeuvred his forces so as to lead the Russians into a trap. The Petchenegs fell into the trap first and were massacred; a few days later the main forces clashed at Arkadiopolis. Byzantine chroniclers report formidable feats of heroism by the Greek generals; we are told that Skleros personally slashed a mounted Viking down the middle, the two halves of the hapless man falling apart on either side of his horse. As the Russians fell back, Tzimiskes could plan how to dispose of the Russian threat for good.

The army of the East, temporarily free of Arab pressure, was brought back, re-trained and re-equipped. In spring 971 Tzimiskes was ready to take the field against Svyatoslav, but at the last minute was confronted with a mutiny led by the brothers Leon and Bardas Phokas who had escaped from their confinement. When an attempt by Tzimiskes to defuse the mutiny by diplomacy failed, he detached Bardas Skleros to the rebel camp to bribe as many mutineers as he could. The use of money thus averted what could have become a civil war without so much as a bloody nose. Hardly had that crisis been overcome than the emperor, uncomfortably aware that he was technically a usurper, moved to marry into the Macedonian dynasty. His bride for this purpose was Theodora, one of the late Romanos II's five sisters who had spent a dozen years in a convent and was not much to look at. But she was a bona fide royal, and therefore Christmas 971 was a time of great rejoicing in the palace, especially as Holy Roman Emperor Otto I was about to receive the long-awaited Greek bride for his son, the future Otto II. Her name was Theophano, and it would be titillating if she were the same Theophano who played such a tumultuous role in the lives of three Byzantine emperors. But this Theophano, just 16, was probably a niece of Tzimiskes. She and young Otto were married by Pope John XIII in Rome in April 972. Theophano was at first apprehensive of the huge change in her life; she needn't have worried, as she was treated well and proved an ideal consort to Otto II, bringing Greek and Byzantine civilization to the Saxon court and helping improve ties between East and West.

In late April 972 Tzimiskes bowed his head in prayer in an ornate little oratory that Romanos I had built in the vicinity of the palace as a private chapel. Emerging, he mounted his horse bearing aloft a large cross. This cross contained a fragment of the True Cross set in gold – a sign, if any were indeed needed, of the fundamentally religious character of Byzantium's military campaigns from Constantine the Great onwards. Byzantium's thousand-year military history, in fact, was one huge crusade, not only against the Muslims in the East and South but also against pagan foes in the West and North which needed to be subdued by the forces of Christ, hopefully to render them less hostile. The emperor rode at the head of a procession to a grander service at Sancta Sophia, where he prayed for victory over the obstreperous Russians, who had to be finally brought to heel. And this time he would see to it personally that they were. Astride his horse, he saw off the navy, which pulled out of the Golden Horn on its way into the Bosporus and Black Sea, and that same hour rode west at the head of his army.

In his glittering armour and sumptuous tunic, the emperor was a formidable sight. The Byzantine troops in Thrace, languishing under a drunkard of a general, revived their hopes on seeing him. Passes and defiles where past Byzantine armies had met disaster were now encouragingly free of foes. This was because Svyatoslav of Kiev naively expected the Greeks to be preoccupied with celebrating Easter in Constantinople instead of marching. He was quickly disabused when Tzimiskes' army hurled itself on him near the old Bulgar capital of Preslav. Though caught by surprise, the Russians rallied and put up a stout resistance. But Tzimiskes had not spent the past couple of years drilling his troops incessantly for nothing; one of his innovations was a crack regiment known as the Immortals, whom he had personally trained and kept by his side.[12] When it seemed that neither side could gain the advantage, the Immortals were let loose on the Russian left, which broke at once, taking the rest of the army with it. Mass flight was accompanied by a killing spree that lasted well into the night. When morning broke Tzimiskes rode over acres of Russian bodies to the gates of Preslav, calling on the town to surrender. The defenders refused. The Byzantines brought their catapults and mangonels into action, bolts of Greek Fire flew smoking over the walls and the infantry began an assault by ladder. We are given the name of a young soldier, Theodosios Mesonyktes – probably still in his teens as he is described as 'beardless' – as being the first man over the wall. The rest of the Greeks surged behind him, but were brought up short in front of the inner citadel which seemed impregnable. The emperor then ordered Preslav burned; the largely wooden buildings went up at once, and only a handful of Russian defenders escaped the twin killers of flame and sword.

As for Svyatoslav, he was trying to hold off the Byzantine fleet at Dristra, a town on the Danube (now Silistra, on the border between Bulgaria and Romania). After destroying Preslav Tzimiskes marched to cut off Dristra from the south, while the fleet blockaded it from the river. Svyatoslav held out valiantly for months, but as supplies were running dangerously low, on 24 July 972 he made a desperate sally that caught the Greeks by surprise. For some time the issue was in doubt until the Greeks staged a mock retreat that lured the Russians to their destruction. The emperor himself swore – and who are we to doubt him? – that he glimpsed the form of a warrior saint, Theodore Stratelates, on a white horse battling in the lines; many other soldiers claimed to have shared the vision.[13] Before the day was out Svyatoslav sued for peace.

The Prince of Kiev expressed a desire to meet the Byzantine emperor for a frank talk. The historian Skylitzes describes the Russian as white-robed and shaven-headed except for two long strands of blond hair, arriving at the meeting place in a boat which he rowed himself. The talk seems to have been civil enough, centring on Svyatoslav's request that Kiev might restore trade ties with Constantinople. Tzimiskes agreed, and the Russian got back in his boat. It was as he was riding back home through the land of the grasping Petchenegs that they ridiculed him for not bringing them the Byzantine booty he had promised. The ridicule hardened into contempt, and then murder. Svyatoslav's skull, like that of the unfortunate Nikephoros I, was made into a drinking cup for his killer.

The vision of Saint Theodore Stratelates that Tzimiskes claimed to have seen in the thick of the battle at Dristra moved him to rename the town

Theodoropolis. When he marched into Constantinople in August, the crowds went wild. Dazzling as always in his burnished armour, he rode behind an icon of the Virgin Mary, to which he gave due credit for his victory; the icon itself was placed in a gilded carriage pulled by four white horses. Behind the emperor, on foot, came the legitimate tsar of the Bulgars, Boris, and his family – not exactly as prisoners but as something scarcely more exalted, as vassals. Boris was forced to abdicate his tsardom in exchange for the title of *magister*. But Bulgaria was only temporarily prostrated.

As the history of Byzantium showed many times, the elimination of a threat in one theatre was accompanied by a resurgent problem in another. Hardly had John Tzimiskes rested from the Bulgarian triumphs than the Muslim Fatimid regime in Egypt, which had supplanted the old Abbasid Arabs as the main foe in the East, expanded dangerously into Syria. In the spring of 974 Tzimiskes marched south-east, but had to detour into Armenia to deal with a dynastic dispute. There he gained an extra 10,000 experienced troops with which he pacified the region around Antioch, and could easily have gone on to take Baghdad, but two things, the approach of winter and a crisis with the papacy in Italy, called him home in a hurry. This crisis, of no concern to us here, was resolved within a year, and Tzimiskes was free again to return to face down the Egyptians in Syria.

His true aim, in fact, was to recapture Jerusalem for Christendom. The three centuries since Heraclius were too long for the centre of the Christian faith to remain in infidel hands. Tzimiskes' religious fervour was never in doubt – while lightening his subjects' tax burden, he had replaced the image of the emperor on Byzantine coins with that of Christ – and it carried great weight in his more prosaic strategic considerations. His campaign started out superbly. One by one the Syrian strongholds fell to him like ninepins – Emesa (Homs), Baalbek, Damascus itself, the onetime seat of the feared Muslim Umayyads, then Tiberias and Nazareth, all places made sacred by scripture. 'The nations trembled at the wrath of Tzimiskes,' wrote a contemporary chronicler, 'as the sword of the Christians mowed down the unbelievers like a scythe.' Tzimiskes was within but breathing distance of the supreme goal, Jerusalem, when illness forced him to cut short his triumphal progress and return home.

The illness, whatever it was, may have been genuine. Or he may have been the victim of one of those mysterious and slow-acting poisons that every so often were said to have despatched Byzantine royals. The circumstantial evidence for the latter is strong, as no fewer than three major writers of the time openly blame Basil the Bastard, the palace high chamberlain, whom the emperor suspected of corruption on a grand scale. Tzimiskes seems to have been about to order a major investigation into this official when he fell ill with a variety of symptoms including severe myasthenia and bleeding from the eyes. He had to be carried into Constantinople on a litter, living just long enough to deposit in Sancta Sophia two holy relics he had brought from the Holy Land – a pair of sandals which Christ had worn, and a lock of John the Baptist's hair. On 10 January 976 he died aged 51, praying to the last. He had bequeathed all his possessions to the poor.

Chapter Eight

The Bulgar-Slayer and Lesser Figures

Basileios II Bulgaroktonos (976–1025)

The sword that fell from John Tzimiskes' hands was taken up by Basileios, the elder son of Romanos II and the strong-minded Theophano, who as a warrior was destined to far surpass his predecessor. Just 18 when he was crowned Basileios II, he had already by that age displayed his basic character, which was bluff and simple yet perceptive and energetic. Not for him were the tiresome rituals of palace and state, the book-learning of princes and the glittering worlds of art and culture. Short and well-built, fair-faced and with light blue eyes, he seemed more at home strolling about town in simple work clothes which seldom saw a washtub. He was a Byzantine version of Shakespeare's Henry V, wild and a bit of a roustabout while a mere prince, but maturing and sobering up quickly once the crown of responsibility was lowered onto his head.

As far as anyone knows, Basileios never married. For an emperor who was expected to produce at least one heir, this was strange. There is, of course, a possibility that he was gay. He shunned not only women but also immoderate eating and drinking. He was a devout man, given to moderation in all things. These habits served him well as he would all too soon have to fight to keep his throne in the time-honoured Byzantine tradition going back to late Roman times. The army was always prepared to topple a young or weak emperor and install some popular and experienced general in his place. Technically the Macedonian dynasty, after the interludes of outsiders Nikephoros Phokas and John Tzimiskes, was still the reigning house. But Basileios II knew he had to work to maintain it. His first foe was his predecessor's chamberlain and purported poisoner, Basil the Bastard. This man had been used to wielding power behind the throne and was not about to surrender it to an 18-year-old shavetail. The grizzled general Bardas Skleros, who had served under and idolized Tzimiskes, also had little time for the new emperor. Skleros mobilized his army in the East, seized the military treasury and marched to the Bosporus, expecting the youth to meekly surrender.

The youth didn't, largely because Basil the Bastard didn't want Bardas Skleros sticking his nose in. Basil was still fairly well in control of the levers of state and able to send the navy to trounce Skleros' ships in the Golden Horn and call on the services of the reliable general Bardas Phokas. This officer, languishing in a monastery after his abortive attempt to unseat Tzimiskes, was handed back his armour and ordered to Caesarea to raise an army loyal to the Macedonian dynasty. There followed a three-year civil war, with neither side gaining any real advantage in the field. Phokas then took a page out of the lines of Homer to replay a scene probably not witnessed since the Trojan War: he challenged his adversary Skleros to single combat to the death to decide the issue.

The years of enforced monasticism had not dulled any of Bardas Phokas' fearsome fighting qualities. 'Anyone who received a blow from him was already a dead man,' wrote one awed chronicler. Skleros could not but accept the challenge, and in spring 979, as thousands of soldiers watched, the two generals thundered at each other on horseback in a deadly joust. Skleros thrust first with his sword, but Phokas deflected the blow which sliced an ear off Skleros' horse. Before Skleros could react, Phokas brought his own sword down on his head, unseating him and grievously wounding him. Skleros survived, but defected to the Arabs. For six years he plotted a comeback, dreaming of the day when he, too, would don the purple. Bardas Phokas, of course, was the hero of the hour, but precisely on that account, Basileios was not reassured. Now 21, he was no longer in need of powerful chaperones. The first to go was the feared and corrupt Basil the Bastard, who probably owned more land in the whole Byzantine Empire than anyone else. Basil's sacking broke his spirit, and he died soon afterwards.

The civil conflict between Phokas and Skleros whetted the appetite of the Bulgars, who every so often, after a calm period of alliance with Byzantium, would fall under the sway of a hostile tsar with expansionist tendencies. This time it was Tsar Samuel, who dreamed of conquering and uniting under Bulgarian rule the whole Balkan Peninsula to the southernmost point of Greece. Few could predict how long this latest trial of strength with the Bulgars would last. It opened with a wave of aggression, with Bulgar armies sweeping unstoppably down into the Peloponnese; from the Adriatic to the Aegean, from Ambrakia in the West to Thermopylai in the East, Samuel's bands raided and pillaged and brought settlers in their wake, permanently altering the ethnic make-up of the mainland Greeks. The large Central Greek town of Larissa was besieged until its inhabitants were reduced to cannibalism, the survivors being sold into slavery.

This atrocity, committed in 986, moved Basileios to personally lead the imperial army to strike at the heart of the Bulgar tsardom, its capital Sardica, and force the Bulgars to hasten back north. He was within striking distance of the city when he decided to wait for his rearguard before the final push. It was a disastrous decision. The delay gave Samuel time to rush to the scene and take positions in the mountains surrounding Trajan's Gate, near where Basileios was encamped. For three weeks the Byzantines sweltered in the heat beating off enemy raids and running out of supplies, so on 17 August the emperor ordered a withdrawal – back through Trajan's Gate and straight into a carefully-laid Bulgar ambush. The Greeks' casualties were appalling. Basileios was left with a mere handful of troops who shuffled back home in ignominy. The emperor brooded long and hard over his failure. But he took it as a salutary lesson, and vowed that the next time he faced the Bulgars, he would be far better prepared.

A development in one region often acts as the trip-wire for another elsewhere. Living the oriental life in Baghdad, Bardas Skleros learned of Basileios' disaster and believed his day in the sun was at hand. He had not taken that terrible wound from Bardas Phokas for nothing. He talked the Abbasid caliph Al-Tai, immensely wealthy but a puppet in the hands of a Shia military caste, into giving him men and money to march on Constantinople. Starting off in 987, Skleros found some support among the Anatolian landowners who held Basileios responsible for the debacle in Bulgaria. But his old adversary Bardas Phokas had also entered the lists to claim the throne for himself. To join forces against Basileios the two men, either personally or through intermediaries, agreed to make one of those sweeping territorial deals harking back to Constantine the Great and his successors. They would split the empire between them, Phokas getting the West and Skleros the East. But Phokas, whose cunning matched his physique, had no intention of sharing power with anyone. Skleros, his guard foolishly down, was seized and confined. Basileios, in mortal danger from Phokas, had only one course of action open to him, and that was to ask for help from Prince Vladimir of Kiev. Vladimir, a callous ruler and sexual predator to boot, agreed to send 6,000 Norse Varangians to help the emperor, but in return demanded the hand of Basileios' sister Anna. The idea of giving a Byzantine princess to a pagan chieftain filled many with horror, but Basileios consented, as Vladimir, for all his faults, had shown sincere signs of wishing to convert himself and his people to Christianity.

Several months passed, in which the imperial navy – as well as freezing weather – kept Phokas' forces at bay until the Norse ships arrived from

Russia; the Vikings, with Basileios at their head, sneaked across the Bosporus at night, surprising the rebel camp. While the navy hurled salvoes of Greek Fire from the sea, the Norsemen waded into Phokas' men, their great battle-axes dripping with blood. Phokas' commanders were executed, while the rebel leader himself made plans to blockade the Hellespont at Abydos. The emperor and his navy followed him there, where on 13 April 989 Basileios led his Vikings in an attack. Phokas caught sight of Basileios riding splendidly up and down the lines, exhorting his hulking Noresemen to greater efforts. He remembered how he had snatched victory from probable defeat thirteen years before when vanquishing Bardas Skleros in a one-on-one joust, and thought he might pull off the same trick once more.

During a lull in the fighting, Phokas leapt onto his horse and galloped straight at Basileios, his sword drawn, 'like a hurricane,' according to one eyewitness. Basileios calmly waited for him, his own sword in his right hand and an icon of the Virgin Mary in his left. When Phokas was mere yards away, he appeared to be overcome by a dizzy spell. He stopped his horse, swayed a few moments, and then toppled to the ground. When Basileios reached him he was already dead, most likely the result of a massive stroke.[1]

The other pretender, Bardas Skleros, had ceased to be a danger. Old and blind, he agreed to meet Basileios in Bithynia, just across the Sea of Marmara. The emperor could hardly believe that the doddering figure having to be led around by attendants was the terrible enemy he had feared for so long. After Skleros was ordered to remove his purple boots – only true emperors could wear those – he was treated to a cordial banquet of forgiveness. Seeing considerable promise in Basileios, still only about 30, he let the emperor have the benefit of sage advice that rivals Machiavelli in its practicality and validity, even in our time (though few would now have the courage or resolve to follow it). In short, Basileios was advised to keep his regional governors and generals on a tight leash and occupied with fiscal and administrative problems to stop them plotting, to confide in only a very few trusted people and – doubtless in reference to the many baleful occasions in which strong-minded Byzantine women ran things – to keep women out of policy conferences. The emperor took the advice very seriously.

Vladimir of Kiev, meanwhile, was getting impatient. He hankered after his royal bride and occupied the Byzantine colony of Cherson in the Crimea to press his claim. The public mood in Constantinople was anxious. The appearance of a bright comet in the skies – always unsettling to the mediaeval mind – was followed by a devastating earthquake that seriously damaged Sancta Sophia and countless other buildings. In the middle of all this poor

Princess Anna was packed off weeping to a husband of whom she could have heard little that was good. She needn't have fretted. Vladimir kept his side of the bargain and was duly baptized a Christian in the Dnieper River, the opening move in the creation of the Russian Orthodox Church of today. Moreover, taking his baptism seriously, he renounced his old irresponsible ways, ditched his four previous wives and unnumbered mistresses, and was by all accounts a decent husband to Anna.

Basileios hadn't forgotten the Bulgars, but before he could deal with them he had to quell an incipient revolt in Armenia. From there Basileios moved back west to Thessalonica, where he sought out the priest who had baptized him, a saintly fellow who promised to pray for him daily. Thus buttressed, the emperor consolidated Byzantine positions in Northern Greece. The imperial army was now arguably at the pinnacle of its efficiency. Basileios had drilled it almost to perfection, to be able to fight in all weathers. Tight organization was everything. In the presence of the enemy the emperor kept his forces in a solid mass for instant communication between the source of command and the various wings, and heavy and light cavalry and infantry. Rules of engagement were extremely strict. Any soldier ignoring them and trying to perform his own heroics was severely punished. In every spare moment Basileios himself would regularly draw up the troops on parade and minutely inspect whatever they wore or carried; the men grumbled, but at bottom they knew that he cared for them as he would his children, if he had had any. Tsar Samuel, for his part, watched and waited.

In 995 a crisis in Syria demanded Basileios' attention. The Cairo-based Fatimid dynasty caliph, al-Aziz, sought to claw back Aleppo into the Muslim fold. Al-Aziz, a humane and popular ruler who treated Christians well, represented the height of the Fatimids' power and prestige. A Fatimid general, Manjutekin, trounced a Byzantine army on the banks of the Orontes River, placing Antioch in grave danger. In Constantinople the emperor could raise up to 40,000 reservists, but the march through Asia Minor would be a long one, and there was no time to waste. Therefore, instead of foot-slogging, the soldiers would ride. Every man received two mules, one to ride on and the other as a reserve. Basileios led them personally, and in just over two weeks they appeared before Aleppo that was under siege by Manjutekin's Muslims. The sight of some 17,000 troops in Basileios' vanguard was enough to make Manjutekin retreat, but the emperor arrested his general Michael Bourtzes for losing the encounter at the Orontes. Antioch was safe for the time being. Al-Aziz died the following year, to be succeeded by a half-mad son who was not a military threat.

New Year's Day 996 opened with a shock to the Byzantine system. Basileios, on the throne now for twenty years, had demonstrated his prowess on the battlefield and in the halls of state. Now he placed on himself a new mantle, that of social reformer. In a decree issued on that day he declared war against an internal enemy, 'the Rich who amass their wealth at the expense of the Poor'. In his sights were the great Anatolian landowners who had been adding to their estates through fraud and theft for many decades. This arrogant aristocracy was a potential threat to imperial power and the cause of growing class hatred that could only enervate the army, as the great mass of soldiers came from the peasant class. The Muslims made good propaganda hay out of this inequality: was this the famed Christianity of Byzantium? Basileios, with backing from the great mass of the people, cut the ground out from under the landed aristocracy in one blow. The mighty Phokas family, for example, lost most of its assets virtually overnight. The peasant families whose lands had been stolen by the wealthy were especially grateful.

A messy dispute with Holy Roman Emperor Otto III, whose mother had been the Princess Theophano, over the papal administration in Rome had absorbed Basileios' attention for a few years, during which, however, he kept a keen eye on Tsar Samuel and the Bulgars. Bulgaria was always important to Byzantine security as the main overland link to Central and Western Europe. The seaport at Thessalonica in Northern Greece, one of the empire's main trading entrepôts, was always vulnerable to Bulgar ambitions. As we have seen, as long as Bulgaria's kings remained Christian and friendly towards Constantinople, the emperors could relax; but when someone like a Krum or a Samuel arose to beat the war drums, the alarms went off. In 996 Samuel's forces seized Thessalonica and threatened the Adriatic coast as far as Dalmatia. The only immediate solution for Basileios was to enlist the aid of the Doge of Venice, Pietro Orseolo, to protect the Byzantine provinces in Dalmatia as proxy governor. In return Orseolo's son gained a Greek royal bride whom he wed in the palace in Constantinople (though both were to die of plague within a few years).

The millennium year of 1000 found Europe in the full flower of feudalism, though with centralizing national forces slowly gaining ground. Otto III neglected his native Germany in a vain attempt to recapture Italy; he partly succeeded, but died at 22 along with his policy. Two-thirds of Italy, including Lombardy, Tuscany and the Papal States, were nominally under Holy Roman Empire rule except for the independent outpost of Venice; the southern third, including Sicily, was under Norman control. The papacy itself in Rome was at its lowest ebb ever, sinking into a pit of corruption and faction. In France the Capetian dynasty tried to pull the kingdom together but found itself thwarted by powerful feudal nobles and the English. These latter, under the weak Saxon king Aethelred the Redeless, were about to undergo a second Danish conquest under Canute with its attendant turmoil. No power in Western Europe, therefore, had the inclination or power to venture militarily as far as the Eastern Mediterranean.

In Eastern Europe the Slavs were now the dominant ethnic group. The Bulgars had embraced Slavic culture, all but erasing their Turkic origins. The Russians, based in Kiev, were still weak but well on their way to forging a solid Christian state, the precursor of modern Russia. On the other side of the Mediterranean the Muslim Fatimids of Egypt were in the hands of a deranged caliph and soon to dissolve into quarrelling factions. Therefore Basileios could afford to take his time preparing his ultimate blow at Tsar Samuel. The Bulgars had been repulsed in a key battle at the Spercheios River in Greece in 996, thanks to the competent leadership of General Nikephoros Ouranos, one of a new line of senior officers trained by Basileios. The conflict simmered in the mountains and defiles of Northern Greece until in 1014 Basileios led an army to settle accounts once and for all with Samuel.

Mindful of his humiliating defeat at Trajan's Gate twenty-eight years before, the emperor proceeded with caution northwards from Serrai through the Strymon River Valley. Samuel, knowing the efficiency and solidity of the Byzantine army, did not risk an ambush but blocked the valley at Kleidion, forcing the emperor into a long detour.[2] The Bulgars' position at Kleidion appeared unassailable. One of the emperor's generals, Nikephoros Xiphias, offered to take a detachment through the woods on one side of the defile to fall on the enemy from the rear – a copy of the tactics the Persians had used to flank the pass of Thermopylai in 480 BC. Basileios initially didn't want to take the risk, but the more he thought about it, the less he could come up with any better idea, so Xiphias led his picked men around the Bulgars' position, timing his attack on their rear with a frontal assault by Basileios and the rest of the army. Surprise was complete. Embattled on two fronts, the Bulgars broke and some 14,000 of them were mown down. Samuel himself barely escaped with his life, his son hauling him onto a horse to get him away.

Thousands more Bulgars were captured, and if we are to believe the prevalent accounts of the battle, Basileios inflicted on them a terrible deterrent: he blinded no fewer than 15,000 of the poor wretches, leaving a single eye in every hundredth man who would be able to lead the rest home. When Samuel saw the dreadful procession arriving at his palace in Prespa, the shock was such that he collapsed of a stroke, dying a couple of days later. Serious historians from Gibbon onwards are almost unanimous in repeating this story, chiefly, one suspects, because of its horror value. Yet the sources for it – like all sources for the events before and after the battle of Kleidion – are scant. The chronicler John Skytlitzes devotes to it a narrative thread, which appears to be the basis of all later versions. Greek accounts range from the apologetic to outright denial that the great Basileios ever did such a thing.

If it indeed happened, it was a war crime of the first magnitude. From what we know (or think we know) of Basileios' character, it's quite possible. War changes and hardens men, and reveals the hidden beast in us. If the emperor's war aim was to intimidate and terrorize the Bulgars once and for all, the blinding of the prisoners achieved it perfectly. Yet much is left unexplained. The logistics involved must have been considerable. How many specialist troops with sadistic tendencies would it have taken to efficiently deprive thousands of men of their sight – probably by the crudest of methods? For any army, that would seem to be a tall order. And would not many Greek soldiers witnessing or participating in the atrocity be traumatized by it? We have no such evidence one way or the other. Most surprising of all, we see no surge of chauvinist revenge among the Bulgars at large, as might be expected after so monstrous an act against them. Basileios himself took out some insurance by subsequently treating the Bulgars well, reducing their taxes and opening up possibilities for royal intermarriage. We may conclude that some such atrocity on the prisoners was carried out, though perhaps not on the scale as was later reported.

Basileios returned in triumph to Constantinople graced with a new and enduring epithet – *Bulgaroktonos*, or Bulgar-slayer. Though startling in English, the word in Greek conveys rather less harsh overtones, rather like referring to an insecticide, and no doubt the Byzantine people viewed his act as akin to ridding the earth of vermin.[3]

Samuel's son Gabriel Radomir carried on the struggle for a year or two more, but he was murdered by a rival, and so in 1018, after an intermittent war lasting forty-two years – exactly the length of his reign so far – Basileios made his formal entry into the Bulgar capital. From there he rode south into Greece. At Thermopylai he came on the whited bones of the Bulgars who had fallen there twenty-three years before, and then south to Athens where he climbed the Acropolis and prayed in the Parthenon, which was then in use as a church of the Virgin Mary, to thank God for victory.

When he bowed in prayer in the Parthenon, Basileios was 60, a good age at which to take stock of a career. He could justifiably take pride in his military achievement, which pushed back the frontiers of the Byzantine Empire to their greatest extent since Justinian I. From the Danube to Syria, from Italy to Armenia and the Caspian Sea, the Christian empire preserved Western Europe from barbarism and Islam. Already, his chroniclers were hailing him as the greatest emperor ever up to that time, outshining even Constantine the Great. None of this, however, went to his head. Still a bachelor, Basileios lived a frugal and sober life. As befitted a soldier, he dressed plainly, avoiding the showy display of imperial purple. His speech was laconic and sometimes abrupt, yet not without a dour sense of humour, and he had little time for art and culture. People who talked to him noticed that he had a habit of twirling the ends of his moustache when agitated – a sign that his mind was always active.

Foreign emergencies continued to call him out of the palace. In 1021 he rode to quell an incipient revolt in the Caucasus, in the process organizing eight new military *themes* from Antioch to present-day Azerbaijan. Once that was done, Southern Italy beckoned. The region was under threat from the Lombards and Normans, who were halted by the Byzantine general Basileios Boioannes and driven back to the Alps. Yet part of Sicily remained under Muslim rule, an obstruction to Mediterranean sea trade. Basileios and Boioannes began planning for an invasion of Sicily, but just before Christmas 1025 the emperor died. We are not told how he passed away, but it was probably unexpected. He had stipulated that he was to be buried as a simple soldier at the main parade ground outside the walls, a wish that was granted.

Constantine VIII (1025–1028), Romanos III Argyros (1028–1034), Michael IV the Paphlagonian (1034–1041), Michael V Kalaphates (1041–1042), Zoe (1042), Constantine IX the Dueller (1042–1055), Theodora (1042 and 1055–1056) and Michael VI the Soldier (1056–1057)

Basileios the Bulgar-slayer's younger brother Constantine was his very antithesis in both appearance and character, so much so that many doubted they were brothers at all. Whereas Basileios was shortish, coarse and uncultured, and seemingly uninterested in women, Constantine was tall, every inch a royal, and very partial to female company. Technically he ranked as co-emperor with his brother, but had done little or nothing to make use of such an exalted position. In his youth he cared nothing for military or state affairs, and everything for the high life. Basileios may well have encouraged this tendency as keeping a potential rival out of the way. But in one of the surprises of history, we see him in 989, as a young man leading the vanguard of the imperial army against the rebel Bardas Phokas at Abydos. Just before the momentous encounter with Basileios, Phokas had noticed the young Constantine riding fearlessly by his brother's side, carrying a long lance.

But thirty-six years had passed since that day, and at his accession Constantine VIII was pushing 60, past the age for the strenuous hunting and athletics that had absorbed his younger years, and debilitated with gout. His mind was keen and he could be diplomatically charming when he wished. But such was his basic weakness of character that the throne and its responsibilities basically terrified him. His behaviour became (if it was not already) quite unpredictable. One day he might order an execution or blinding based on the flimsiest rumour, and the following day be consumed with blubbering remorse. Cruelty seemed to be his way of dealing with his moral fears. The army remained loyal to the memory of Basileios, and hence to him. But the big landowners of Asia Minor took advantage of his weakness by repossessing the properties Basileios had wrested from them in the cause of social justice, reducing much of the peasantry again to serfdom.

This unflattering picture may be a little one-sided. It comes mainly from Michael Psellos, an erratic genius of a scholar who is our main source for the period. Psellos, writing some decades later, was still too dazzled by the achievements of Basileios the Bulgar-slayer to have anything good to say about anyone coming after him, and what he did write was probably based on hearsay. Compared to his late brother, Constantine may indeed have been rather lazy and not inclined to great exertions on behalf of his empire. He spent much of his time feasting, gambling, watching strip shows and experimenting with gourmet cookery, but that didn't necessarily make him an execrable ruler. Oddly enough, Arab sources treat him with better respect. Moreover, his conduct in the field at Abydos demonstrates that he had some steel in him.

One day in November 1028 he fell ill. Of what, we don't know. But the illness turned out to be terminal, and he realized he had to name a successor. His offspring were three daughters; the middle one, Zoe, had been destined to wed Holy Roman Emperor Otto III, but he died, and she had spent the intervening quarter-century fretting sexlessly in the palace. The third daughter, Theodora (the eldest had long since taken the veil and was out of the picture), was smarter but uglier, with no love lost for her sister. Zoe therefore was in line for the succession, but according to the laws then in force, she had to find a husband who would become emperor. The influential civil service took a hand in the matter and nominated Romanos Argyros, an elderly noble senator who had the office of imperial prefect, something equivalent to the mayor of Constantinople. Argyros had long been quite happily married, but the exigencies of state came first. Argyros and his wife were dragged before the dying Constantine and given a harsh choice: Romanos must either divorce and become emperor, or be blinded. His wife decided the issue by tearfully consenting to the divorce and cutting off her hair before retreating to a convent.

As for Zoe, she couldn't be happier. Nearing 50 and past childbearing age, she at last had her coveted husband. No longer would she languish manless in the women's quarters. Two days later Constantine breathed his last, and Zoe became the empress of Romanos III Argyros. Unexpected supreme power went to this ex-senator's head with a rush. Tall and good-looking, cultured and a good speaker, he made the most of his role. Notes the waspish Psellos: 'his idea of his own range of knowledge was vastly exaggerated.' This syndrome included a belief that he was the equal of the great Roman emperors of old, which naturally led to an obsession with obtaining an heir. Both he and Zoe wasted a great deal of time and money on quack sexual stimulants and black magic to get her tummy to swell, but as anyone of common sense could have told them, it just wasn't going to happen.

Romanos Argyros' delusion of being a warrior-king was put to the test in 1030, when he marched against Aleppo, whose emir had not provided any *casus belli*. Romanos' own senior officers saw no sense in a Syrian campaign that had no valid military purpose. But he had his heart set on his own victory procession through Constantinople, and had already ordered the special crown he would wear for it. Then the realities of war hit him. His army had hardly entered Syria when a howling horde of Muslims, scimitars flashing, ambushed the Byzantines in a defile. Romanos barely managed to make his escape, which was so quick as to arouse astonishment in the Arabs. On the heels of Romanos the Muslims advanced into the Byzantine military *theme* of Teluch, near Antioch.

In command of the imperial garrison there was General George Maniakes, a young giant of a man who did not scare easily. Described as very tall, with 'a voice like thunder and hands that seemed made for tearing down walls', Maniakes showed he was a good actor as well as soldier. When 800 Muslim cavalrymen invested his camp with the disinformation that the emperor had been killed, Maniakes pretended to be overwhelmed. As evening was coming on he promised the besiegers that he would surrender his entire garrison first thing in the morning; to show his good intentions he sent the besiegers copious amounts of wine. The wine worked just as Maniakes expected it would, and that night all 800 Muslims were slain where they slept in drunken stupors, their noses and ears removed for good measure. Maniakes tracked down Romanos in Cappadocia and flung a sack full of Arab noses and ears at the feet of the delighted emperor. Maniakes was promoted to governor-general of the Upper Euphrates Valley, from where over the next two years he scored signal victories over the Arabs and reconquered Edessa.

Apparently having learned the lesson that soldiering was not for him, Romanos Argyros spent the next few years trying to reform the imperial finances, but all he accomplished was to worsen the plight of the poorer classes. Also unhappy was Zoe, who chafed under her husband's stinginess; moreover, he had begun deserting her for a younger mistress. One day in 1033 a handsome young man, the son of a senior civil servant, was presented at the palace. As soon as Zoe set eyes on this man, Michael Orphanotrophos, she fell hopelessly in love with him – precisely as his ambitious father had planned. A full-blown sexual relationship ensued, despite the nearly four decades' difference in their ages. Making things easier for Michael was his appointment as the emperor's personal health attendant and masseur. When Romanos eventually cottoned on to the truth, Michael denied the whole thing. But Romanos had been slowly sickening, and by early 1034 those around him thought he looked like 'a walking corpse'.

There is a strong case that Zoe, amply making up with Michael Orphanotrophos for her sexless younger years, wished to be rid of her rickety old man as soon as possible. One day shortly before Easter, as Romanos was putting in some laps in the sumptuous palace baths, he called for his attendants to dry and dress him. They came, but instead of doing as he bade them, they held his head under water. When his body went limp, they thought he was dead and left. But shortly afterwards he was found, still in the water, calling feebly for help. Zoe came running, and in Psellos' account, made 'a great show' of grief and concern and ran off, seemingly to get more help. Romanos gasped for breath, sicking up some kind of 'dark, coagulated matter' before expiring.

This account by Psellos has been widely accepted. But Romanos could have died of a heart attack or stroke while bathing, or fallen victim to one of those slow and devastating poisons that crop up with depressing regularity in these pages. Yet the circumstantial evidence against Zoe is considerable. Lending weight to the conspiracy charge is the fact that barely was Romanos' body cold and covered up than Zoe donned the imperial diadem and jewelled imperial robes and seated herself grandly in the coronation hall of the palace, sceptre in hand. She wasn't alone; young Michael sat beside her, similarly got up, for all to see. The couple rode side by side in Romanos' funeral cortege. In the crowd was Psellos, barely out of his teens, who looked upon the face of the late emperor in his open casket and noted the unnaturally swollen and pallid countenance that suggested a poisoning. 'What would a queen in love not do for her lover?' he would write later.

It ought to have been obvious to Zoe that Michael had wanted her only for sex, and now that he was Michael IV (surnamed the Paphlagonian, from his Asia Minor birthplace), he needed someone who would give him an heir. Therefore, trouble was brewing from the first. Zoe considered herself the real ruler; but Michael, to his credit, had no intention of playing the toyboy, and before 1034 was out Zoe found herself once more confined to the women's quarters of the palace under strict guard. But Michael, despite his youth and erotic vigour, had never been in the best of health. He suffered from epilepsy and had his throne screened off in case anyone should witness his fits. He also developed dropsy that cramped his bedroom style. The third affliction to beset him was the worst – a tortured conscience. He spent hours in anguished prayer and made a point of often giving up his bed to poor, sick monks and holy men.

Along with this spiritual convulsion came a sort of maturity. Michael made a genuine effort to govern effectively and wisely. Yet he was overshadowed by his scheming and ruthless elder brother John Orphanotrophos, who though dressed humbly like a monk, kept his finger on domestic intelligence and the levers of power. John appointed his brother-in-law Stephanos, a lowly shipyard worker, to the post of commander of the navy for a long-postponed expedition to recapture Sicily. It was high time, in the opinion of the majority of Byzantines, to bring that island back into the Greek Christian fold. Taking advantage of civil conflict among the Muslim overlords of Sicily, the expedition sailed in 1038 under the terrible George Maniakes and including the trustworthy Varangian Vikings under Harald Hardrada. The force swept into Messina and advanced to Palermo, fighting all the way. But after Palermo was taken in 1041, it all began to unravel. Maniakes had no use for Stephanos, the emperor's brother-in-law, and insulted him grossly, which earned Maniakes a charge of treason and a spell in a dungeon. The Muslims took advantage of the disorganization to reconquer all of Sicily except Messina.

The news further dispirited the people of Constantinople, who meanwhile had been informed that their young emperor was dying. Michael the Paphlagonian was still in his twenties, but epilepsy and dropsy had consumed him terribly. His legs had developed gangrene and the slightest movement sent him into agonies. While monks and priests all over the empire prayed for him daily, he was taken several times to the tomb of Saint Demetrios in Thessalonica on which he would throw himself in prayer. As Michael was childless, his ever-watchful brother John Orphanotrophos cast about for a successor. He found one in Stephanos' son Michael, who worked as a caulker in the shipyards, and the dying emperor and Zoe agreed.

But Michael IV, despite his grave disabilities, wanted to be a fighting emperor before he died. The Bulgars had raised their hostile heads again, under Peter Deljan, a grandson of Tsar Samuel, and had invaded Greece proper. Somehow, despite contrary advice from all directions, Michael got the army together and led it into Bulgar territory. One night in camp he became so ill as to almost give up the ghost. But the following morning, writes Psellos, he got into his saddle and, 'to the wonder of all who saw him, rode to the rear and formed up the divisions into a coherent force'. At that point Deljan chose to quarrel with the other Bulgar leaders; the Byzantines made short work of their forces. Against all expectations, Michael made his triumphal entry into Constantinople in 1041, though Psellos amid the cheering crowds saw that he swayed on his horse and 'looked as if he were at a funeral'.

On 10 December he knew the end was near. He was taken to the monastery of Saints Kosmas and Damianos where he doffed his imperial garb and put on a simple monk's habit.[4] To his grieving brothers he appeared serene, though he refused to see Zoe when she turned up. He had ordered a pair of sandals, but they weren't ready, so held up by a couple of monks, he limped barefoot into the monastery chapel for Vespers. There he collapsed, out of breath with the effort, and died in his cell shortly afterwards. He was not yet 30. Whatever the superficial pridefulness of his youth, Michael IV had somewhat redeemed himself in his final months.

John Orphanotrophos was now the undoubted master of Byzantium, and it may be wondered why he did not seize the throne for himself. He figured that his nominee, the shipyard worker Michael, the son of Stephanos, would be inexperienced and hence pliable. He may simply have been one of those who prefer pulling the strings behind the scenes rather than visibly assuming the purple, where he would be vulnerable. The man who would shortly become Michael V Kalaphates (the Caulker) cannot have been much more than about 20. When the elderly Zoe gave her blessing, he was crowned.

Michael V, writes Lord Norwich, was an 'unpleasant young man' who 'possessed no particular qualities of character or intelligence to recommend him beyond the lowliest of his subjects'. He was also a total slave of Zoe, but displayed a degree of spirit by standing up to the domination of John Orphanotrophos. But before John could act to neutralize Michael, he was called to the palace. The boat bringing John from his estate was about to dock when he was unceremoniously bundled onto another boat that drew alongside and sent directly into exile. Beset by a complex over his humble origins, Michael Kalaphates began to purge the aristocracy. Distrusting his own personal guard of Anglo-Saxons and Vikings, he replaced them with a subservient corps of Slav eunuchs. The emperor's big mistake was to try and get rid of Zoe, even though she was his adopted mother and he would not have become emperor without her. He may have feared one of those slow poisonings at her hands; the old lady was arrested and charged with trying to kill the emperor. After a travesty of a trial her hair was shorn and she was shipped off to a convent on Prinkipo Island. But the common people of Constantinople, stirred up by the clergy, protested violently; Zoe, for all her flaws, was a member of the great Macedonian dynasty, the niece of the revered Basileios II, and could not be treated so shabbily.

Psellos, who by now was employed as a palace functionary, was in the outer premises dictating to a secretary when he heard 'a noise like thunder' rolling over the rooftops. Psellos dropped what he was doing, jumped onto his horse and headed for the city centre to be confronted by a murderous mob 'with madness in their eyes', wielding all manner of weapons including axes, swords and stones. Men, women and children, and inmates from the opened jails, joined in the march on the palace in a popular insurrection as frightening as it was sudden. No guard could possibly stop them. Within minutes the entire imperial complex had been torn down in a fury of destruction; even the children clawed at the masonry with their little hands. The entire contents of the buildings were looted. The emperor's uncle Constantine, fleeing from the ruins of his own quarters, came upon a terrified Michael trying to hide, alone and unprotected. The mob could be mollified only by bringing Zoe back. While a mission sailed to Prinkipo Island, Constantine and a small force fought off the insurgents all day, until in the evening Zoe arrived. She was re-robed in the purple and led to the royal box of the Hippodrome to show herself to the people.

The mob hesitated, distrustful as long as the despised Michael Kalaphates was reigning. Then someone – we are not sure who – had the brainwave of bringing in Zoe's younger daughter Theodora as a compromise sovereign. Theodora had been in a convent for fifteen years but was still a member of the royal family with equal rights to her sister. Yet she was most unwilling to swap the peace and quiet of sisterhood for the dangers and vanities of the palace, so she had to be forcibly dragged to Sancta Sophia where, dressed in the unfamiliar imperial robes, on 19 April 1042 she was crowned empress regnante of Byzantium to the resounding cheers of the populace. It was understood that she would reign jointly with Zoe, the only time in Byzantine history when two women occupied twin thrones in their own right, and not as wives of emperors.

Michael knew the crack of doom when he heard it. He wanted to escape on a ship but his uncle Constantine was all for staying and fighting to the last and urged Michael do so as well, as befitted a true emperor. Michael stayed, to be unexpectedly reinforced by the arrival of General Katakalon Kekaumenos from Messina. That night Kekaumenos and the palace guard fended off constant attacks by the insurrectionists, whose fury and determination now knew no bounds. The following morning the rebel assault on Michael in the palace began in earnest, from three directions. Some 3,000 rebels fell against the well-armed but outnumbered Imperial Guard. The next day the rebels overcame the Guard and swarmed over what was left of the palace, baying for Michael's blood. Disguising themselves as beggars, ex-emperor and uncle managed to board a boat which took them to the refuge of Saint John's monastery at Stoudion, a few miles down the coast.

With Theodora as the people's new idol, Michael did not have long to enjoy his refuge, which was soon discovered and surrounded. Psellos tried in vain to restore some order with a Guards detachment. When the rebels began knocking down the monastery walls he forced his way into the monastery chapel to find Michael 'on his knees, clutching the altar … barely recognizable in [his] sordid rags, [his] face transformed by mortal fear'. Psellos himself had no love for Michael, but wept at the pitiable sight. Terrified out of his wits Michael might have been, but he had enough presence of mind to realize why all this was happening. 'God is not unjust,' he muttered in Psellos' hearing. 'I am guilty of grave crimes and must now suffer the punishment.'

For the rest of the day Michael and his uncle stayed at the altar, the mob hesitating to burst into the holy sanctuary. In the evening a senior official arrived, claiming to be an emissary from Theodora allowing them a safe-conduct back to the city. Michael suspected, correctly, that it was a ruse and refused to move. The official then ordered his armed escort to physically drag Michael and his uncle, kicking and screaming, from the chapel, put them on donkeys and take them to the palace. On the way they were met by a heart-stopping sight – the executioner and his squad sharpening their instruments of death. Michael almost swooned with terror and cried loudly to God for deliverance. Constantine, for his part, seemed rather braver. But it was not death which awaited the pair. Constantine went first – to have his eyes put out with cold steel, and without uttering so much as a groan. To Michael, it was a fate hardly better than execution. Crying and struggling, he was held down while his own eyes were stabbed out. He was allowed to live out the rest of his miserable life on a monastery on the island of Chios.

Did Theodora really offer Michael and Constantine a safe-conduct? The evidence is contradictory. She could not hope to have a secure rule as long as Michael Kalaphates was in the picture; the people of Constantinople would not have stood for it. The fact that the emperor was not executed but 'merely' blinded indicates that she did not want to pour blood on blood, and possibly turn her predecessor into a martyr. Zoe, too, had to be placated if she were to share the throne; she was jealous of her cleverer younger sister and needed to be disabused of any hankering after Michael. Whatever Theodora's motives, a bloody convulsion in Byzantine royal history was allowed to subside.

The two sisters ruled uneasily side by side. Zoe, still attractive, plump, blonde and bubbly, was the very antithesis of the slimmer and tighter-mouthed Theodora. Verdicts on their rule differ according to the preferences of the chronicler. Zoe probably spent a lot of state money, and launched a witch-hunt into the misdeeds of the previous reign. Yet the advice against women in positions of power which Basileios II took to heart appeared to bear itself out. Neither sister proved able to control the civil service. The thoughts of Zoe in particular turned yet again to marriage. Theodora, for her part, had done happily without men for half a century and wasn't about to change her ways now. Two candidates for Zoe's hand were considered and rejected. The third was a rich and good-looking noble named Constantine Monomachos (= Dueller). For political reasons he had been exiled on Lesbos, but reports of his wealth, sophistication and good looks were enough for Zoe. One can imagine Constantine's amazement as he was released and put on an imperial ship for his wedding and coronation in Constantinople on 11 June 1042. Monomachos took his place in the roster of Byzantine emperors as Constantine IX.

He wasn't much of a success, as he soon fell under the spell of his elderly and free-spending wife. But while confined on Lesbos he had acquired a mistress, who now moved to the capital to be with him. Zoe, now less interested in sex, appeared not to mind when her husband publicly revealed his long-term affair. The girlfriend's name was Sklerina; she was the granddaughter of the general Bardas Skleros and attractive to the point at which even the cynical Psellos was quite captivated. She also got on the good side of Zoe and Theodora, but to the public at large she was merely an interloper. The people of Constantinople had become quite fond of the old sisters, 'our mothers,' and resented any other female coming to upstage them. They needn't have worried. Within a couple years Sklerina was dead of some pulmonary ailment, perhaps severe asthma or an oedema. Or she may have been poisoned.

Sklerina's death was a severe blow for Constantine, who made little pretence at governing effectively. The well-to-do were allowed to buy off their military service, swelling the coffers for Zoe's extravagances. One man who decided to do something about it was George Maniakes, who after laying waste large parts of Southern Italy and Sicily in an orgy of destruction and slaughter, was recalled. Maniakes, on the old Roman model, had his adoring men proclaim him emperor and marched on Constantinople. At Ostrovo in Bulgaria he was killed while fighting an imperial army sent to stop him. Maniakes' head was exhibited on a spear in the Hippodrome. Hardly had that threat been dealt with than the commander of the army garrisons in Thrace and Macedonia, Leo Tornikes, made his own move on the throne. Tornikes, a proud aristocrat, was seeking revenge for a public humiliation by the emperor. Raising the standard of revolt at Adrianople, Tornikes claimed that Constantine was dead and that Theodora wanted him, Tornikes, as a consort. The line appears to have been believed, and in September 1047 he and his force appeared before Constantinople.

There they found that Constantine was very much alive, though crippled by progressive arthritis and, some said, a lack of courage. But he did have the spirit to show himself to the besiegers at a window of the Blachernai Palace, with Zoe and Theodora by his side. As he stood there an arrow came whizzing by, just missing him. He was quickly led away, but returned to the window the following morning. That same day an advance guard of Tornikes smashed its way past a defensive work in the northern section of the wall, killing many defenders and sending the rest racing rearwards in panic. Then Tornikes sat back and awaited what he thought would be an invitation 'to be led up to the palace preceded by flaming torches', according to Psellos. It didn't happen. Tornikes waited a day and a night, but instead of a welcoming committee he was confronted by the sight of the defending soldiers rushing back to their posts, the whole population of Constantinople solidly behind them. Constantine also added his bit, which consisted of a dose of time-honoured bribery aimed at Tornikes' men. The revolt disintegrated; Tornikes was captured and blinded.

Constantine the Dueller, however, is remembered for one of the pivotal events of history that occurred towards the end of his reign – the final split of the Eastern and Western Christian churches. A military history need not dwell on the complex theological and political causes of the Great Schism of the Churches of 1054. Suffice it to say here that it confirmed a rift between the two halves of Europe that had been developing for centuries, and deprived Byzantium of the faith-based alliance of the Western European powers. From now on the Roman Catholic and Eastern Orthodox churches would go their own ways. It was a change that would eventually spell the doom of the empire. Constantine was distressed at the schism, seeking solace in the monastery near his beloved Sklerina's grave. He was in constant pain from his arthritis, which he tried to assuage by daily baths. One day he caught a chill and died from its complications in January 1055, joining Zoe, who had left this world two years earlier. 'That,' noted the contemporary historian George Kedrenos, 'was the beginning of decline for the Romans.'[5]

By the time Theodora was left to reign alone she was 77 and childless. Eight months later, in August, she contracted acute appendicitis. Psellos and what was in effect an inner cabinet conferred to pick a successor who would not display too much character and occupy the throne as little more than a figurehead while the generals and senior officials ran the show. It was not an unreasonable aim, as Theodora and the half-dozen Macedonian dynasty emperors preceding her had not had very impressive records. The choice fell on an old aristocrat named Michael Bringas, of a family that had included the senior admiral Iosif Bringas, Romanos II's chief minister a hundred years before. Psellos was disappointed in the choice, whom he judged as 'less qualified to rule than be ruled'. Yet Theodora appeared to give her consent; hours after Michael Bringas' coronation she died – the tail end of the great Macedonian dynasty.

Psellos was certainly correct about the character failings of the man who was now Michael VI, surnamed either the Soldier (by his supporters) or the Old Man (by his detractors).[6] To the latter group was added the army and senior officer corps after Michael lined up those officers who expected to receive a commendation in the Easter honours for 1057 but instead received an embarrassing and public tongue-lashing for having 'lost Antioch' among other supposed failures. Two generals in particular who were thus reprimanded, Isaac Komnenos and Katakalon Kekaumenos, were outraged at the manifestly unfair charges. It was clear that the emperor was violently prejudiced against the military – a fatal attribute in one charged to defend the empire against foes and potential foes in all directions.

Naturally, the plotting for a military coup was set in motion. The church leadership, anxious for the empire's future, eagerly seconded the plot. Isaac Komnenos appeared to be the most suitable candidate for emperor. He initially ruled himself out, but his fellow conspirators insisted, reminding him of the sting of his public humiliation. Komnenos soon found himself at the head of a mass movement by the army in Asia and perhaps a majority of Byzantine public opinion. He was given the old Roman *imperator* acclamation by being raised on a shield. Moreover, he possessed the iron character and presence to impose his will on the movement. By August 1057 he and his force had reached the Asian shore of the Bosporus, ready to storm into Constantinople.

Komnenos was encamped in the rolling hills west of Nicomedia, but the general may have underestimated Michael, whose forces attacked vigorously on 20 August. Komnenos himself was briefly encircled by a squad of big-boned Varangians and Russians and nearly killed, but eventually his numbers prevailed. The emperor now had no choice but to negotiate. Psellos was one of three envoys picked to go to Komnenos' headquarters and parley. He found the general seated on a high couch, elaborately robed and braided, backed up by an amazing and intimidating array of warriors, from beefy armour-clad officers to garishly-attired Asians, some of them sporting war-paint. Many were armed, casually resting battle-axes on their shoulders, apparently ready to use them at a moment's notice. But Psellos, despite the array before him, was a competent negotiator and by nightfall had got Komnenos' agreement to act as Caesar and wait until Michael's death to replace him. Michael, for his part, agreed to reverse several unpopular decisions on military appointments. But events in Constantinople outran the negotiations. Hardly had Psellos and Komnenos firmed their deal than news arrived that, practically while they were talking, the Senate had overthrown Michael who, probably threatened with blinding or worse, abdicated to a monastery, that last home of many an emperor. He had enjoyed the throne for just a year.

Chapter Nine

Rear-Guard Heroism: Romanos Diogenes

Isaac I Komnenos (1057–1059) and Constantine X Doukas (1059–1067)

Isaac I inaugurated what would eventually become the great Komnene dynasty. He got to work from almost the very first moment he set foot in the palace. In the military sphere he disbanded most of his army, and applied his organizing talents to cleansing the civil service of incompetent imperial favourites. He was appalled to the find the treasury depleted by decades of waste and theft, and partly refilled it by confiscating the ill-gotten estates of the corrupt ones. Yet he had one great rival, in the person of Patriarch Michael Keroularios, one of the architects of the great schism of 1054 with the Roman Catholics. The prelate had the great mass of people on his side, and when Isaac deemed that the prelate needed to be brought down a peg or two, deposing him on trumped-up charges, the majority of Byzantines, and of course the church, came to hate the emperor with a passion.

Not that he particularly cared. When the Magyars and Petchenegs attacked Byzantine territory from the north, the army held them off with little trouble. On the third day of the encounters Isaac himself rode to the scene, to find that his enemies had decided that discretion was the better part of valour. In daily life he was a workaholic, playing as well as working hard, and sleeping little. He loved to hunt, and he was thus occupied in the autumn of 1059 when he caught a fever. Within a few days he was hardly able to walk, yet insisted on riding unaided to the palace. Psellos saw him as a 'towering cypress violently shaken by gusts of wind'. Once at home, Isaac failed rapidly, but had to deal with the succession. He had no living son and – probably on Psellos' advice – picked an aristocratic scholar named Constantine Doukas. After personally giving Doukas the nod he was carried to the monastery of Saint John at Stoudion where he died shortly afterwards.[1]

Psellos was delighted that his old friend and fellow-intellectual Doukas had now been elevated as Constantine X. The Doukas family was an old one, a pillar of the Byzantine military aristocracy. The family had hankered after the throne for a long time, and now its time seemed to have come. But if Psellos hoped that Constantine would carry on where Isaac had left off, and pump some military vigour back into the empire, he was disappointed. Constantine preferred scholarly debate to military affairs. The army as a result was neglected. Apparently fearful of military coups, he clipped the powers of the senior officers and slashed army funding. Most destructively, he allowed many peasant-soldiers of the provinces who had been the backbone of Byzantium's armies to buy off their terms of service and hire foreign mercenaries to replace them. At one stroke, the patriotic-religious motives that had, at least since Heraclius, helped the Greek Byzantines fight bravely in the field against all manner of infidels were pulled out from under the soldiery.

What, in the late eleventh century, were the Byzantines fighting for? Preserving trade routes by sea and land was, of course, important as always. But until now those prosaic needs were overshadowed by the overwhelming requirement to preserve the Orthodox Christian faith against Muslim and other aggressors, and where possible, expand the faith as a buttress against future threats. This was the Age of Faith. It would be centuries before secular nationalism replaced religion as the driving force of international politics. In Eastern Europe there were no such things as fixed borders and flags and national citizenships. There was the Holy Christian Byzantine Empire, embracing all ethnic groups accepting the official faith. That had been enough to fire the courage and loyalty of the soldiery. But it seems that a malaise had fallen on the upper echelons of Byzantine society. The recent bewildering succession of emperors and empresses, the layers of intrigues within intrigues, and the gratuitous violence accompanying changeovers of power had eroded many people's faith in the old ideology. It was the army that suffered the most – and at precisely the wrong time.

For some time the Byzantines had known about the Turks, an Asian people that had appeared east of the Caspian Sea, sucked into the region after the elimination of the Mongols. They had penetrated slowly to the northern and eastern fringes of the empire, at times proving to be useful allies against foes such as the Bulgars and Magyars. By the eleventh century the Turks had embraced Islam and expanded their influence over the decadent remnants of the Abbasid caliphate in Baghdad to the point at which the caliphs were mere puppets of Turkish military overlords. In 1055 one of those overlords, Tughrul Bey, imposed himself as sultan and effective ruler, relegating the caliph al-Qaim to a merely ceremonial and religious role.

Tughrul Bey was a descendant of the Oghuz clan originating in the steppes of Turkestan, a fresh and warlike people whose vigour was personified in Tughrul's nephew and successor, Alp Arslan (= Hero-Lion). His clan became known as the Seljuks, after Seljuk, Tughrul's predecessor who had united them into a striking force. Alp Arslan saw rich pickings in the weakened Byzantine Empire. He had considerable military talent, and used it effectively by capturing Ani, the capital of Christian Armenia, in 1064. In the ensuing years Alp Arslan tested his strength against the Eastern Byzantine garrisons, scoring a notable success by sacking Caesarea in Cappadocia. Because of poor morale in the Byzantine army, for which the emperor's mismanagement can be blamed, Alp Arslan met with scant resistance.

The loss of Armenia, a key Byzantine ally for centuries, stung Constantinople into action. In 1067, the year of Alp Arslan's attack on Caesarea, Constantine X died of an unspecified ailment. There was some confusion as to who should succeed him; his own Doukas family naturally demanded that it be one of their number. But when news of Caesarea arrived at the capital, many wanted a tough military man. The decision was actually made by Constantine's widow Eudokia, who was prepared to marry (breaking a pledge to her dying husband) whoever would prove most fitting to step into the imperial purple boots. And she had a distinct preference – a distinguished member of the Anatolian military aristocracy named Romanos Diogenes. The Senate and church concurred. Romanos Diogenes was in exile at the time, serving a commuted death sentence for some anti-palace intrigue; but Eudokia seems to have arranged a pardon, and thus he was called to the palace for an interview. The empress took a liking to him at once, for both personal and political reasons. He was on his way to Cappadocia when a message recalled him with orders to wed Eudokia and head the state.

Romanos IV Diogenes (1068–1071)

Romanos IV was crowned on the first day of 1068. He was a handsome man, in his middle forties, impressive of bearing and with combat experience against the Petchenegs to his credit. Something he had done in Bulgaria had turned Constantine X against him, but whatever it was, it was forgotten in the general desire to present a strong front to the advancing Seljuk Turks. He was a man of courage and nobility of spirit, traits which often bring with them a certain arrogance. We don't know how he came by his surname of

Diogenes – perhaps it was a version of Digenis, a term denoting mixed birth and common in Asia Minor, rather than harking back to the ancient Greek cynical philosopher of the same name. From the first, he had a lot to contend with, including the implacable hostility of the Doukas family, which felt cheated out of a birthright, and Psellos himself, who preferred to hide away in a cloister than help the new emperor in anything. A subtle power play was at work here: Romanos represented the old military-based aristocracy, what the French would later call the *noblesse d'epée* (nobility of the sword), that was under growing challenge by the so-called *noblesse de robe*, or nobility based on wealth or scholarship, of which the Doukas family and Psellos were typical representatives.[2]

Romanos opened his reign with two years of expeditions to the East, where he had to contend not only with the obvious enemy but also with constant intrigue on the home front as well as the demoralization of the army that suffered from irregular provisioning and seemed always on the point of mutiny. Romanos spent 1070 in the capital settling arrears of pay for his soldiers and training new units. He was able to do this thanks to a shaky truce with Alp Arslan, who didn't yet have the nerve for a more substantial clash with Byzantium. The emperor raised at least 70,000 men, and possibly more, for a grand expedition to dislodge the Seljuks, and set out in March 1071.

Romanos considered the alternatives of either striking deep into Seljuk territory to draw Alp Arslan into battle or playing a defensive game, beefing up the border posts and laying waste the countryside to deprive the Seljuk sultan of provisions. A conclave of generals decided against the latter course on the grounds that it would entail unnecessary destruction and alienate the local people. So an offensive it would be – but where exactly? Romanos doesn't seem to have given it much thought. One obvious objective was the fort at Hliat on the north shore of Lake Van, athwart Alp Arslan's lines of communication. The area was generally well-fortified, though the Seljuks occupied the fortress of Manzikert to the north.

Romanos' behaviour during the long march eastwards left much to be desired. To his officers and men he became increasingly distant, ostentatiously shunning fraternization. When his tent-pole broke he was haunted by what it might portend; then an unexplained fire killed his best horses. His arrogance worsened into a chronic bad temper; when a soldier was arrested for stealing a donkey the emperor ordered his nose cut off despite the poor soldier's appeal for divine intercession. We may conclude, without being too far off the mark that Romanos was in the throes of some kind of depression, caused partly by the distrust of his own senior staff.

To do some justice to the emperor, that staff was not such as to inspire excessive confidence. The two senior generals were Joseph Tarchaniotes, commander of the army's eastern wing, and Nikephoros Bryennios, commanding the western. A Norman knight, Roussel de Bailleul, led a contingent of about 500 'bloodthirsty and undisciplined' Frankish mercenaries, while a smattering of Oghuz Turks and Petchenegs served as foils for the Seljuk cavalry. An officer named Michael Attaliotes served as senior military judge; a writer by profession, he is our best source on subsequent events. Among the imperial advisers was what Attaliotes described as an 'ugly dwarf', a deserter from the Seljuks who could supply intelligence. As emperor and army passed through each military *theme* the recruitment process kicked in smoothly.

Alp Arslan was in the process of extending his control over the last remaining bastion of Shia Islam, Fatimid Egypt, when he received a message from Romanos suggesting a renewal of the truce. Romanos wanted the fortress of Manzikert back. Alp Arslan is believed to have consented in return for some Byzantine positions in Syria. But the message may not have got back to Romanos, who repeated the offer six weeks later, rather more insistently. We are not in a position to know what precisely happened. Was the emperor's offer a bluff designed to lull the Seljuk sultan into a false sense of security? Alp Arslan had hesitated to measure swords with Byzantium directly. Now, however, he had little choice but to cut short his plans for Egypt and wheel northwards to face Romanos. Raising troops from Azerbaijan, including 10,000 Kurdish cavalry, he gathered up about 30,000 men and led them in search of the Greeks in the depths of Armenia.

The Byzantine force outnumbered the Turks by at least two to one. But Romanos vitiated that advantage by the cardinal error of dividing his army in the presence of the enemy. One section under Tarchaniotes moved against the Seljuks to the north of Lake Van, while the larger section under Bryennios cleared the Muslims out of Manzikert with little resistance. Tarchaniotes is a mysterious figure; scholars theorize that he strongly opposed dividing the army and let himself be routed in an initial clash with the Seljuks just to prove the emperor wrong. Also, was the long arm of the Doukas family reaching out to foment mutiny in the ranks?[3] If that was the case, it certainly had its effect, for when the first Turkish detachments probed Romanos' position at Manzikert, Tarchaniotes was essentially out of the picture. On 24 August the emperor sent a foraging party in the direction of Hliat. The party ran into a mounted Seljuk detachment and was cut to pieces. In response, he sent Bryennios with a stronger but still inadequate force, and Bryennios had to call for reinforcements. Romanos seems to have been irritated at this, and unwilling to deploy troops piecemeal. He sent another detachment under the Armenian general Basilakios who knew little about how to deal with fast-moving mounted guerrillas like the Seljuks, and allowed himself to be outmanoeuvred and captured. When Bryennios rode out with the Byzantine army's right wing he found a considerable number of Seljuks waiting for him and withdrew in some haste, taking a wound in the back of the neck and a couple of arrows in his armour for his pains.

Romanos probably only now realized that the Seljuks in the area were more numerous than he had thought. Moreover, the time-honoured solid formation and tactics that had served the Byzantines so well in the time of Basileios II against the Bulgars were now almost useless against the Seljuks. Neither could the loyalty of some of the allies be counted on, as most of the Oghuz contingent deserted to their fellow-Turks the following day. If this was an ominous sign of things to come, Romanos appeared not to heed it. When Alp Arslan sent an embassy to his camp proposing a truce, the emperor dismissed it brusquely as an attempt by the Seljuks to buy time. According to Attaliotes, who was present at the encounter, it was a wrong move. Unfazed, Romanos ordered the army in motion against the enemy in the morning of 26 August.

The army marched in two lines between four and ten men thick, infantry and cavalry intermixed, with two wings on the sides; the rear line was organized flexibly so that portions of it could move to help either wing. In front rode Romanos with his imperial guard. The one glaring absence was the cataphract cavalry under Tarchaniotes and now nowhere to be found. De Bailleul's Normans had also vanished. Commanding the left wing was Bryennios, with Theodore Alyates in charge on the right, together which those Oghuz and Petchenegs who had not deserted. Andronikos Doukas commanded the rear. Romanos' initial plan was to send Bryennios on a leftward sweep to outflank the enemy, to be followed by the emperor; as the Seljuks rushed to that sector, the Byzantine right under Alyates would take the enemy in the rear and crush them against Bryennios and the emperor. Any resistance would then be taken care of by Doukas' reserves. It was not a bad plan. But the question remains: why did Romanos set it in motion while lacking fully half his army, including the cataphracts? The explanation can only be that the emperor woefully underestimated the enemy. There was not the slightest doubt about his personal courage; he had no hesitation in throwing himself into battle like an ordinary soldier. But a commander needs something more than just valour, however commendable.

The area around Manzikert was a parched wilderness on the side of an extinct volcano, with hardly any trees to speak of. The north-west slope of the volcano was cut up with gullies and dry stream beds, and here thousands of Alp Arslan's horsemen, commanded by the chieftain Taragi, were drawn up in a roughly rectangular formation, ready to pounce. Observing the action was the sultan himself from a safe distance. As the Byzantine army closed in, he read a message from Caliph al-Qaim to the troops exhorting them to 'fight for the faith of Allah, the justice of the faithful and the soldier's paradise'. It was Friday and the Muslims had just been at prayer, as had the Byzantines, their priests assuring them of the rightness of their cause. Romanos addressed a few unremarkable words to the men, promising them financial as well as spiritual rewards. As the morning wore on, the Greeks made slow and rather unsteady progress, held up continually by hit-and-run attacks, towards the heights on which the Seljuk camp stood. Romanos and the centre slowed up their advance, probably so as not to get too far in front of Bryennios on the left and to be able to move in his direction when the time was right. But as the enemy's strikes became sharper, it was harder for the army to keep its lines intact. The result was that the wings fell back, leaving Romanos and the front line exposed in the centre. But Romanos and the front line persevered, capturing the Seljuk camp in the early afternoon.

The Byzantines so far had suffered few casualties and were confident of victory. But the Seljuks had made only a tactical withdrawal. Moreover, the Greek wings and Doukas' reserve line had been left far behind. The emperor and the men with him were tired; the unfamiliar terrain seethed with unseen threats. Provisions and water were in short supply. The logical thing for Romanos to do would be pull back, but to where? Bryennios and Alyates were occupied with continuous Seljuk attacks on their fronts and could not come to the emperor's aid. Doukas was still nowhere to be seen. Some time in the late afternoon Romanos decided to risk a pullback, but the move was uncoordinated. On the right the troops saw the centre streaming back and assumed a fight had been lost.

At this moment the Seljuks struck decisively, smashing Alyates' wing, whose troops ignored the emperor's frenzied calls for them to rally under his own banner. As the enemy pressure on the centre became overwhelming, Romanos tried to change the battle order from line to column, a move that only made the confusion worse and got the whole army surrounded. Romanos himself was at his best in the encounter. Bryennios wrote later:

> The king, all alone, abandoned and bereft of all help, bared his sword against the enemy, killing many and compelling many others to flee. Encircled by a host of enemies, he received a wound in his arm … his horse was shot by arrows, it slipped and fell and took its rider with it.

Though he had received a spear wound in the left shoulder and was horseless, Romanos fought on. Charging Turks seemed to be everywhere, driving the Greeks rearwards like panicked sheep, killing them and trampling them under their horses' bloody hooves. Great clouds of dust made effective communication impossible and fuelled the general panic – 'a tragic sight,' thought Attaliotes, 'beyond any mourning or lamenting.'

The Armenians were among the first to flee. In his desperation Romanos may well have glanced towards the rear and wondered where Andronikos Doukas and his reserves were. Doukas, in fact, was well within earshot of the battle, but was staying put. The more charitable explanation is that Doukas saw what was unfolding and decided not to throw more men into the fire. The less kind – and more likely – theory is that he simply wished to be rid of Romanos and refused to help him. The Doukas family, as we have seen, regarded Romanos as a usurper, the occupant of a throne rightly theirs. The verdict must be that in an hour of mortal peril, Doukas served his emperor thoroughly treasonably.

Manzikert was not an especially bloody battle for its era; its significance lies in its outcome rather than its physical losses. The imperial army suffered a severe blow not so much in casualties as in morale and territory. Suffering the heaviest casualties was the Imperial Guard, with an estimated loss of 10 per cent killed and wounded and about 20 per cent captured. The Seljuks, moreover, neglected to follow up their victory and appeared unsure of how to go about it. By nightfall Taragi, the commander of the main Seljuk force which had lost at least 4,000 men, had not apparently given the order to continue the pursuit, and thus the great bulk of the Byzantine force managed to escape to the fortress of Manzikert.[4] But beyond mere tactical considerations, the result of Manzikert was that the Seljuk Turks made themselves masters of a great deal of Asia Minor and the Byzantine Empire suffered a blow from which it would not recover.

And neither would Romanos. All that night he lay wounded among the dead and dying, to be discovered in the morning by a Seljuk soldier looking for booty. He was led before Alp Arslan, who learned from Basilakios, also captive, who the illustrious prisoner was. The sultan ordered Romanos to kiss the ground in front of him in a gesture of ritual subjection and placed his foot on the bowed emperor's neck. But once that symbolic humiliation was over, Alp Arslan revealed his noble side. He embraced the wounded emperor with the philosophical words, 'That's life,' and gave him some food. According to Bryennios, Romanos was kept a prisoner in near-ideal conditions for about a week, going for walks with the sultan and discussing the recent momentous battle like two gentlemen. Alp Arslan was unfailingly polite and chivalrous, though he allowed himself some salty comments on the conduct of the emperor's own soldiers who had deserted him in the crunch. He is reported to have asked Romanos what he would do if the roles were reversed, if he were the prisoner and Romanos the victor. 'I'd torture and kill you and expose you in the streets of Constantinople,' Romanos undiplomatically replied. To which Alp Arslan retorted that he had reserved a worse punishment for the emperor – 'I'm setting you free.' Romanos readily agreed to a treaty of peace with Alp Arslan by which all prisoners were at once exchanged, the Byzantine state was to pay a million and a half gold pieces to ransom its emperor, and the deal to be cemented by a marriage between a daughter of Romanos and a son of Alp Arslan.

News of Manzikert threw Constantinople and its administration into consternation. Empress Eudokia in particular was on the spot, under pressure to approve a successor to Romanos who, though alive, could no longer remain a credible head of state. Already he was being blamed for the apocalypse at Manzikert – not least by the treacherous Doukas family, which saw its way to the throne opening up. The sentiment was shared by Attaliotes, the staff officer, who blamed the emperor as 'the prime factor in our failure … irrational exuberance, neglect and petty jealousies drove the reasoning of him and his staff … his worst adviser was his own hesitancy'. Duly freed, Romanos made his way north to Armenia, where he changed out of his Turkish attire, spent some days recuperating and began the process of getting together his own ransom. It was while he was preparing to return to the capital that he got the news that he had been deposed.

Michael VII Doukas (1071–1078) and Nikephoros III Botaneiates (1078–1081)

The Doukas family had acted with alacrity. Its senior member, John Doukas, the ranking Caesar, brought back his son Andronikos (the same who had stood aloof at Manzikert), put him in charge of the Imperial Guard and sent it rampaging through the palace proclaiming Michael, the son of Constantine X and Eudokia, as the new emperor. John himself, with another armed retinue, burst into Eudokia's quarters, seized her and exiled her to the Hellespont. John had judged his candidate cannily; Michael, while a genuine royal and a Doukas, was also a pliable man who could be expected to do the family's wishes.

As Michael VII was crowned in Sancta Sophia, Romanos attempted to put together the remnants of his army to reclaim his throne. The new regime in Constantinople sent out forces to stop him; among the commanders was his nemesis Andronikos Doukas, who defeated Romanos at Adana after the ex-emperor had suffered a similar discomfiture at Dokeia (Tokat). Romanos thus gave himself up to the very man responsible for his catastrophe at Manzikert, but if he expected clemency he did not get it. Though Romanos agreed to drop his claim to the throne and enter a monastery, Doukas treated him abominably, forcing him to ride a mule for some 500 miles to Kotyaion (Kütahya) while ill with a persistent dysentery that could have been an attempted poisoning.

At Kotyaion Romanos was dragged roughly to his place of punishment. The blinding was entrusted to an inexperienced Jew who botched the job horribly, plunging the iron into the victim's eyes as he writhed and screamed in agony, held down by heavy shields with men standing on them. Looking 'like a decaying corpse', according to Attaliotes, 'with his swollen face riddled with worms and a horrible stench about him,' he lingered a few days longer until he died. 'At no time did he utter any curse or blasphemy, continuing always to give thanks to God, and bearing courageously whatever befell him.' Back in Constantinople Michael Psellos heartily approved – after all, by his own admission, not only had he issued the order for the blinding, but he had also written to the wretched emperor callously congratulating him for losing his sight – 'a sure sign that the Almighty had found him worthy of a higher light'.[5]

Michael VII foolishly tore up the treaty between Romanos Diogenes and Alp Arslan, which could have settled relations with the Turks. Alp Arslan was assassinated thirteen months after Manzikert, and his son and successor Malikshah, who was soon to prove the Seljuks' greatest sultan, sent human waves of Turkoman tribesmen into the entire eastern half of Asia Minor – 30,000 square miles of previous Byzantine territory that had supplied the empire with much of its food and many of its best soldiers. The region became known as the Turkish sultanate of Rum (= Rome). To deal with the drastic loss of revenue, Michael debased the Byzantine currency, driving up inflation and public discontent along with it.

Predictably, Michael totally lost control of the situation. Nikephoros Bryennios, who had fought alongside Romanos Diogenes at Manzikert, and Nikephoros Botaneiates, the septuagenarian commander of the Eastern army, were soon in keen rivalry to topple the weak emperor. When a grain shortage sent the price of bread soaring and triggered riots in March 1078, Botaneiates was first on the scene as the purported saviour. A frightened Michael quickly abdicated. But Nikephoros III Botaneiates, after his coronation, proved no better than his feckless predecessor. He had his rival Bryennios blinded, but apart from that rather unnecessary act, let the state slide downhill fast. He may have been a competent soldier in his prime, but he was no statesman and spent great sums on his cronies. As there was no lack of military men still angling for power, it was only a matter of time before one of them would act. At Easter 1081 a young general named Alexios Komnenos, the nephew of Isaac I Komnenos, burst into the city with a loyal force that proceeded to loot and pillage until Botaneiates slipped over to Sancta Sophia in an old robe, agreed to abdicate and proceeded to the obligatory monastery (where he duly complained about the compulsory vegetarian diet). The empire held its breath to see how this young officer, all of 24, would work out.

Chapter Ten

The Komnene Revival and The Crusades

Alexios I Komnenos (1081–1118)

There was not a day to be lost. Malikshah had extended and consolidated the Seljuk domain to include Byzantine cities perilously near to the capital such as Ikonion, Nicaea and Chrysopolis. The Turks' settlements were actually within sight of the city walls. In the West the situation was equally dire. The weakness of the Byzantine state had encouraged the Normans to smother, one by one, the last Byzantine outposts in Sicily and Southern Italy under the steamrollering leadership of Robert Guiscard. One of Alexios' first acts was to decide who was the more immediate menace, the Seljuks or the Normans. In charge of the Sultanate of Rum was Suleyman, a cousin of Alp Arslan, who appeared not to be aggressive, and so as Alexios firmed a truce with the Seljuk, he prepared to attack the Normans who were making no secret of their desire to master Byzantium itself.

Even before Nikephoros Botaneiates was forced out, Alexios had inserted himself firmly into the palace environment by gaining the favours of Eudokia who, in the well-tested tradition of empresses regnantes and otherwise, knew a lot of what was going on through her own personal spy network. There may well have been a romantic element here, as what woman would not have preferred the young Alexios over the elderly and dithering Botaneiates? The upshot was that she formally adopted the young general as her son. This in turn had gained Alexios the support of the Doukas family. In appearance Alexios resembled several of the vigorous soldier-emperors we have come across: stocky in build, with heavy brows and penetrating eyes. He lacked height, but when he sat on the throne he somehow had a way of impressing people – not the least his own soldiers, who were ordered to stop meddling in politics and settle down in their barracks. They would soon have enough work to do. The military establishment he inherited was not quite to his liking; he was uncomfortably aware that it contained too many barbarians whose loyalty was never certain. He believed himself at least partly responsible for this state of affairs, and thus to expiate his supposed sin he slept on the floor with a stone for a pillow for six weeks and wore a rough sackcloth under his robes.

Before Alexios could move on Byzantium's foes, a peculiarly embarrassing situation had to be dealt with. No one, possibly not even he, quite knew what the precise relationship was among him, his adoptive mother Eudokia and his teenage wife Irene Doukas. Eudokia insisted on playing a central role in palace affairs to such an extent that poor Irene – all of 15 – couldn't even be at her husband's coronation. The Doukas family fumed and threatened, and eventually Eudokia was persuaded to retire by a promise that Constantine, her son by Michael VII Doukas, would be made co-emperor, a pledge that cost Alexios nothing. The emperor was now free to confront Robert Guiscard, who by 1081 had landed his Normans on the Epiros coast at Buthroton (now Butrint in Albania), directly threatening the overland route to Constantinople.

Robert Guiscard was a classic warlord, who looked and acted the part. Massively built, with a voice like thunder and a will to move continents, he was a Norman version of Alexander the Great, without the latter's culture and with an overdose of villainy. After capturing Southern Italy and eradicating the last Byzantine outposts in that land, it was hardly surprising that he would entertain notions of becoming the new Roman emperor. Somehow Michael VII had not seen that as a threat; he actually suggested that his son marry one of Guiscard's daughters. The Norman warlord took up the offer with alacrity, sending his daughter Helena, barely out of infancy, to be schooled in the Constantinople court and the Orthodox faith in preparation for her eventual nuptials. But it was not to be. When Michael VII was toppled by Nikephoros III Botaneiates, the marriage deal was off and Guiscard prepared for war.

Alexios was far better prepared than either of his two predecessors to counter the Norman fleet when it sailed from Brindisi and Otranto across the Adriatic, overcoming the garrison at Corfu and establishing a bridgehead at Dyrrachion (now Dürres). The way seemed open for Guiscard to march over the Via Egnatia, a Roman road built 800 years before to enable Rome's legions to march to the Middle East.[1] Then a Venetian fleet allied to Byzantium turned up and burned the Norman fleet to a crisp with Greek Fire. But it still took a Greek force under George Paleologos to hold off Guiscard until Alexios himself could arrive on the scene. Combat was joined outside Dyrrachion. Alexios placed himself in front centre, directly opposite

Guiscard. Making up most of the Imperial Guard was a body of English Anglo-Saxons who had sought refuge in Byzantium after losing the Battle of Hastings, and wanted nothing better than another crack at the hated Normans. Robert Guiscard was flanked by his huge blond son Bohemond and his equally formidable wife Sichelgaita who would make a habit of 'charging magnificently into the fray, her long blonde hair streaming out from beneath her helmet, deafening friend and foe alike with huge shouts'.[2]

Guiscard's Apulian cavalry on the Norman right seems to have opened the battle with a charge that broke against the furious, axe-wielding English. At that point, according to a widely-believed account, Sichelgaita screamed at the fleeing cavalrymen, calling on them to stand and fight like men. To at least one Greek she was like an incarnation of the goddess Athene, seizing a spear and jabbing at the retreating men, turning them around, a scene out of a combination Homeric epic and Norse myth. Then the Norman left wheeled round with a deadly new weapon against which the battle-axe was almost useless – the crossbow. The Anglo-Saxons, in their eagerness to fight, had become separated from the main imperial army and were cut down where they stood; the few who survived were burned to death after seeking refuge in a chapel.

Alexios personally had plenty of fight in him, but the same cannot be said for much of his army. The Englishmen of the Guard had been one of his few reliable units. The Byzantine army had yet to fully recover from the shock of Manzikert ten years before. Battle-weariness, outright cowardice and treachery enervated the Byzantine effort early in the campaign, forcing Alexios to break it off and withdraw disconsolately to Ochrid nursing a head wound. Hot on his heels was Guiscard, who had little trouble taking Dyrrachion and later the Greek mountain town of Kastoria, where he decided to winter after taking the surrender of its English contingent. The following spring, however, Guiscard was called back to Italy by a challenge from Holy Roman Emperor Henry IV. On the way he vowed not to shave until he could return to Greece for the real object of his lust – Constantinople.

Until the Byzantine army could get its breath back, Alexios employed that most effective Byzantine diplomatic weapon – money, of which Henry IV received copious amounts while Guiscard's nephew Abelard was in Constantinople actively intriguing against his aggressive uncle. The emperor himself stayed in Thessalonica raising troops. But the money spent on diplomatic bribery depleted the treasury, so he strong-armed the church into melting down its enormous accumulations of sacerdotal gold and silver, the first time it had done so since Heraclius half a millennium before. The clergy grumbled, but Alexios was able to pay his growing army. Bohemond, meanwhile, had marched through Epiros and was threatening Thessalonica from the south. In spring 1083 Alexios blocked his way at Larisa, the main market town of the Thessalian Plain.

The Normans opened the battle with a general dawn attack on the Byzantine main force, which they thought was under the command of Alexios. But the emperor, leaving command of the main force to George Melissenos and Basileios Kourtikos, had sneaked behind the Norman lines during the night with a picked unit. Melissenos and Kourtikos had specific orders to feign a disorderly retreat, which they did at the proper moment, luring the Normans on and allowing Alexios and his force to overrun the Norman camp, inflicting heavy losses and capturing much material. Bohemond was forced to withdraw to Kastoria, all the way suffering a steady attrition of his weary and unpaid soldiers who accepted the Greeks' offer of rich rewards for desertion. By the end of the year only a couple of Western islands remained in Norman hands. But Guiscard, meanwhile, having sacked Rome in May 1084, returned to Greece with blood in his eye. A new attempt to take Corfu almost came to grief at Venetian hands, but Guiscard's bullishness carried the day. Despite the fact that he was pushing 70, he had high hopes of reconquering all of Western Greece, but while he was on the island of Kephalonia he died of typhoid.[3]

Hardly had the Norman menace been disposed of than the Petchenegs, that troublesome tribe that had been stirring up tension on the northern fringes of the empire for at least 200 years, loomed up anew. The news encouraged the Seljuk emir of Smyrna, Chaka, who controlled the East Aegean coast, to raise a fleet and move on Constantinople from the sea in 1090. Alexios by that time had managed to rebuild the neglected navy, which drove back Chaka's attempt. The Petchenegs proved rather tougher to handle. The emperor here brought financial diplomacy into play, bribing the Cumans, a nomadic Turco-Balkan tribe living in what is now Ukraine, into raising an army against the Petchenegs.

On 28 April 1091 Alexios and the Cumans faced the Petchenegs at the mouth of the Maritsa (now the Evros) River on the Aegean. According to the emperor's daughter Anna Komnene, our prime source for this era, when Alexios called his men for evening prayer, they fixed little wax candles to the tips of their spears, 'lighting up the heavens with the gleam of many stars'. The next day, those spears were put to rather deadlier use; almost the entire Petcheneg force, including women and children camp followers, was extirpated from the face of the earth. Besides giving Alexios a fresh dose of popularity at home, the terrific slaughter intimidated other potential foes of Byzantium, and incidentally proved once more the truism that, contrary to popular perception, nice guys don't make heroes. When the emperor returned to the capital he was cheered to the skies.

Also cheering Alexios was news that the 1054 rift between what became the Roman Catholic and Greek Orthodox churches looked as if it might be healed (though it gapes as wide as ever to this day). Both Alexios and Pope Urban II made honest efforts to reconcile; but probably neither man was prepared for the momentous events about to spring on Europe and the Middle East. In 1071, the year of Manzikert, the Seljuk Turks had wrested Jerusalem from the tolerant Fatimid regime, seriously cramping what until then had been a growing tourist trade in Western pilgrims to the Holy Land. Alexios appealed for papal aid to stem the Turkish menace, an appeal which Urban II amplified into a call for a holy war during an address to a conclave of nobles and clergy at Clermont in France. He also spared a thought for the Byzantines. 'The kingdom of the Greeks is now dismembered,' by the Muslims, he warned. The time to reverse the Muslim tide was now. '*Dieu li volt*!' thundered the French peasants, burghers and knights in reply. 'God wills it!' The cry was echoed in a million souls all over Western Europe; ordinary men of town and field, oppressed by feudal routine, poverty and the general dullness of life, found release in the twin, if incompatible, promises of spiritual salvation and material plunder. Not a few criminal elements, high and low, were only too eager to join in, and thus began the Crusades.

Our concern here is with the Crusades' military effect on Byzantium rather than the Muslim world. The pope might be sympathetic to Byzantium, but what to make of his concurrent claim to be Europe's big Christian leader, overshadowing the emperor? Had not Byzantium itself been fighting for the cross for hundreds of years? At first there appeared to be little overt threat. The First Crusade got underway in the late summer of 1096, consisting of about 30,000 foot soldiers and perhaps 4,500 cavalry who poured into Constantinople on their way east, 'outnumbering the grains of sand on the sea-shore,' according to Anna Komnene. They included Bohemond, the son of the late Robert Guiscard, who had matured into a carbon copy of his larger-than-life and sinister father. As for Alexios, he was stunned to see this host, together with its women and children, seething through the city. The higher-ranking Westerners invited to the palace were stunned at the opulence and civilization they were treated to, but the lower ranks had a different view.

> The masculine, half-barbarous knights of the West despised these subtle and cultured gentlemen of the East as heretics lost in effeminate luxury; they looked with astonishment and envy upon the riches laid up in the churches, palaces and markets of the Byzantine capital, and thought that fortune should belong to the brave.[4]

Even the hard-nosed Gibbon, no lover of Byzantium, was compelled to admit that the majority of these first Crusaders were 'savage beasts, alike destitute of humanity and reason'. After two anxious weeks Alexios managed to get them ferried across the Bosporus. Crossing into Asia Minor, the Crusaders seized Nicaea back from the Turks, aided by Alexios who sent twenty Greek ships to cut off the Seljuks' retreat by sea. The emperor had given the Franks plenty of advice on how to fight the Turks and had seconded an officer named Tatikios to march with the Crusader army as intelligence adviser. The Crusaders moved on to Armenia to help the local Christians recapture their own homes from the Seljuks. They seized Antioch with little trouble and Alexios was on the way to officially reclaim the city for Christendom when news reached him that the Muslims had retaken Antioch, besieging the Crusaders within, and so he saw no point in continuing. The siege was soon broken, but the Franks never quite forgave the Greeks for not turning up. In 1099 the Crusaders moved on to seize Jerusalem where they butchered as many of the inhabitants as they could while weeping in holy joy.

Alexios' attitude to the initial success of the First Crusade was equivocal. He of course rejoiced at the news of the seizure of Jerusalem, but had begun to fret at the presence of so many semi-barbaric Westerners within the empire. The Greeks and Latins, socially and psychologically as well as theologically, had drifted far apart. Antioch was now in the rough hands of Bohemond, who to the Byzantines was quite as much an alien as the neighbouring Muslims were. There was some relief when the Danishmends, a Turkish tribe, kidnapped Bohemond in 1100 and kept him in a castle for three years. But by this time fresh Crusaders were coming to North Syria in successive waves, overcoming anyone in their way, whether Christian or Muslim.

In April 1104 the Franks suffered a devastating blow at Harran, essentially ending the First Crusade. But Bohemond was not finished. Freed in 1103, he managed to get to Italy two years later, intent this time on war with his old enemy, Byzantium itself. Alexios' apparent abandonment of the Crusader cause during the siege of Antioch gave him the excuse he needed. He was warmly received by Pope Paschal II, King Philip I of France and

King Henry I of England, all of whom pledged troops with which he set sail in autumn 1107. Bohemond's forces landed at Dyrrachion, repeating his father's expedition of more than twenty years before; and just as on that occasion, Alexios thwarted him. The town proved difficult to invest, while the Byzantine navy cut off his communications with Italy. After a hard winter, as Bohemond's force wasted away from hunger and disease, Alexios turned up with the imperial army and forced Bohemond to surrender. The Norman leader promised meekly to recognize the emperor as his true overlord and hand Antioch back to the Greeks. He never recovered from the shame, dying in Italy three years later.

Alexios and Byzantium had gained a valuable reprieve. While the Franks were otherwise occupied in the Middle East, the emperor used the reprieve to increase the royal household and its privileges, a tactic guaranteed to neither do his popularity any good nor keep the state coffers full. The debased currency was put on a stable footing to maintain army payments, but at the cost of unpopular taxation. The army resorted to forcible impressment of the peasantry to keep its numbers up, a tactic that reduced the number of tillers of the soil and resulted in food shortages which added to the public complaints. The emperor's own view was that those same peasants would be doing a better job defending their compatriots from rape and slaughter by foreign foes. But that argument failed to carry much weight, and Alexios found himself widely despised. His response was to try and reform the entire administration and church. There was the usual diplomatic bickering with the church of Rome, which seems to have cost him his health, as in summer 1112 he fell seriously ill.

Either before or after his illness he marched to head off a Turkish thrust into the Gallipoli Peninsula, following it up with a victory over 50,000 Turks near Nicaea the following year. These were just the opening moves in what was to become a near-continuous crisis, with Alexios wearily compelled to counter repeated Turkish raids. In 1116, now about 60, he decided to dislodge Sultan Malikshah of Ikonion. On his way east he was slowed up by masses of homeless Greeks seeking protection with the army. It was while the emperor was wondering what to do about this humanitarian problem that Malikshah attacked his forces at Philomelion, only to suffer an ignominious defeat. Back in Constantinople, Alexios' last months were darkened by court and family intrigues; soon he developed serious respiratory problems and an ugly swelling of the mouth and throat. On 15 August 1118 he called his son John to his bedside to hand him the imperial ring and advise him to hasten to Sancta Sophia and get himself proclaimed emperor, which he did. Alexios passed away that same evening, with few of his subjects fully realizing how he had guarded the empire from Eastern and Western marauders.

John II Komnenos (the Good) (1118–1143)

From the outset of his reign John Komnenos was well-liked by his subjects, who rewarded him with the sobriquet Kaloioannes, or John the Good. But the sentiment was not shared by his historian elder sister Anna Komnene, who had idolized her father and moreover considered herself the rightful empress-presumptive. Anna put about the story that John grabbed the ring from his dying father's hand and led an armed mob to Sancta Sophia to get himself crowned. He also, according to his sister, stayed away from Alexios' funeral because he felt insecure. It may have been a simple case of sibling rivalry getting out of hand, as Anna was accused of plotting to have her brother assassinated at the funeral. With what we know of John's character, such callousness seems unlikely, while the murder plot theory tallies ill with what we know of the scholarly Anna.

John II was nearly 30 at his accession, well-educated, brave in the field and blessed with an equitable and forthright personality. A diplomatic visitor noted that he was short and dark-complexioned like an Arab. Not for him were the executions and blindings ordered by previous emperors. He disposed of the hostile Anna by despatching her to a convent where she would write her magnum opus, the *Alexiad*, a fruitful source of information on Alexios I Komnenos' reign. Sober and religious, he was a stickler for good manners at court, including simple dress and simple food and sober conversation. 'Few emperors like John Komnenos sat on the Greek throne of Byzantium,' avers one modern Greek authority. 'He proved to be an enemy of profligacy and tried to inculcate those values in Greek society, giving the example from his palace.'[5] He also was keenly aware of the ever-present Turkish menace and lost no time personally marching against the Turks in the first full year of his reign, clearing them out of a couple of strongholds in what is now Southern Turkey. But he was soon obliged to hurry back north, where the Petchenegs had so far recovered from their holocaust at the Maritsa River at the hands of Alexios I nearly thirty years before as to be pressing into Thrace again.

It was in the field that the serious-minded John, like a true Komnene, found his vocation. He held faithfully to the old imperial doctrine that he was God's soldier, firmly believing that 'the Empire had been bestowed on him by the Almighty as a sacred trust'. With the energy thus supplied by that fervent belief, John entered into almost constant campaigning. He wed a Hungarian princess named Piriska both for love and for the advantage of an alliance with the Hungarians to guard his north-western frontiers. The West, in fact, was quiescent; the Normans in Italy and Sicily fell into disorganization, while the popes in Rome were in the midst of a supreme tussle for power with the Holy Roman Empire. The Petchenegs were the only dissonance in this desirable state of affairs.

John and the imperial army met them in 1122 at Beroe (near Stara Zagora in modern Bulgaria). The Greek cataphract cavalry attacked and took some prisoners, but failed to seize the main enemy camp where the Petcheneg chariots were pulled up in a defensive circle. John himself, lightly wounded in the first clashes, saw his cavalry accomplishing little and prayed to the Virgin for guidance. Rising from his knees, he ordered his horsemen to dismount; with them and his faithful axe-wielding Varangian Guard of Englishmen (since replenished after their decimation at Dyrrachion), he charged the Petcheneg position. Masses of Petcheneg prisoners were captured, to be offered land in return for a pledge of military service in the Byzantine cause, an offer many took up. Thanks to the twin blows of a decisive attack and generous diplomacy, the Petchenegs bowed out of history.

Hardly had the Petchenegs been dealt with than a wilier and wealthier foe raised its mailed fist. For some time the Venetians had been actively trying to dominate East Mediterranean sea trade at the expense of Byzantium. Originally the beneficiaries of trade privileges, the Venetians had progressively abused these privileges to the point at which when they came up for renewal in 1122, John refused. The Venetians, he said, would henceforth be subject to the rules of trade competition like everyone else. The Doge of Venice, Domenico Michiel, arrogantly led seventy-one warships out of the lagoon city to show the Greeks who was boss of the Mediterranean. The force besieged Corfu for six months against determined resistance, before being called to Palestine to help Crusader King Baldwin II of Jerusalem who found himself in a tight spot, having been captured by the Muslims. But the Venetians were aggressively active elsewhere, occupying several strategic Aegean islands and forcing John to restore their privileges.

This was the time when Hungary, the land of the emperor's wife's birth, came under the reign of Stephen II who accused Byzantium of harbouring a rival claimant to his throne. John realized there was a necessary battle to be fought over this, and in 1128 he personally brought it about on the banks of the Danube, supported by the navy which had sailed up by the Black Sea. Stephen happened to be ill when John surprised his force at the Haram fort, smashing it fairly completely. A near-simultaneous uprising by the neighbouring Serbs was successfully tackled almost as an afterthought.

But it was the East, now dominated by the Danishmend Turks in Central and Eastern Anatolia and by the Christian Crusader kingdoms in Syria and Palestine, which was John's chief focus of attention. John could not see the Crusaders as his natural allies, especially as the Venetians were proving to be their chief suppliers, enriching themselves and their tiny republic in the process. The Crusader kingdoms themselves were weakened by rivalries among their aristocratic elites, while the lower orders were assimilating themselves into the Middle Eastern way of life. But the emperor could receive no comfort when the Muslim Danishmends massacred the Crusader army of King Bohemond II of Antioch in 1130, sending the young king's head to Caliph al-Mustarshid in Baghdad. For the next five years John led almost annual campaigns against the Danishmend leader, the Emir Ghazi, almost effortlessly recapturing the previously-Greek communities of Western Asia Minor. It was enough to earn him a great, swaggering triumphal entry into Constantinople, the first the city had seen for about 150 years. Silver-caparisoned white horses awaited him at the Golden Gate to carry him on his chariot; but he humbly elected to walk, allowing the host of prisoners, his troops and senior officers to proceed first among the cheering throngs standing on wooden risers lining the route to Sancta Sophia. He himself came last, on foot, holding aloft a cross in order to show who truly deserved the credit for his victories; in the place of honour in the chariot rested the icon of the Virgin Mary that never left his side on campaign.

The following year the Emir Ghazi died, putting a brake on Danishmend aggression. John employed the lull to sign a treaty of mutual aid with Holy Roman Emperor Lothair III as a hedge against threatened aggression from the Normans in Italy and Sicily. But King Leo of Lesser Armenia chose this time to begin expanding at the expense of both the Byzantines and the Franks, and John marched a large and battle-tested army south-east to Cilicia to stop him. Leo's force melted into the Taurus Mountains and on 27 August 1137 John arrived before Antioch determined to wrest this key city back into the Byzantine fold. The city's government had been weakened by a complex dynastic struggle and its new ruler, Raymond of Poitiers, was sadly out of his depth. It took just a few days of pounding by the Greek siege engines to make Raymond sue for terms. John insisted on unconditional surrender; the Muslim threat to the Crusader states was mounting by the day, so Raymond capitulated and the Byzantine double-headed eagle flag again fluttered over Antioch – a victory remarkably bloodless by the standards of the time.

The way was opening for John to realize what by now must have been his ultimate ambition: to seize Jerusalem from the Franks and encircling Muslims, and bring back the Holy Land under the sole rightful Christian empire. The first stage in this plan was to capture Aleppo, with the help of Raymond and the obstreperous young Count of Edessa, Joscelin II of Courtenay. But Aleppo was strongly held by a Seljuk warlord named Zengi, an energetic and thoroughly unscrupulous leader, so John bypassed that city and laid siege to Shaizar, a town on the Orontes River considerably to the south. John pressed the siege vigorously; eyewitnesses claimed he was everywhere at once, instantly recognizable in his shiny helmet, helping aim the great catapults, urging on the line troops to greater efforts and tending to the wounded. The contrast could not be greater with his two Frankish allies Raymond and Joscelin who stayed safely in the rear playing dice.

During the siege the emperor received a delegation from the emir of Shaizar offering to surrender the city and hand back a ruby-encrusted cross that Romanos Diogenes had lost at Manzikert. John accepted at once, as reports were reaching him that Zengi was on the march against him. Back in Antioch John had to put up with a brief but ineffectual revolt of the Franks against the ruling Greeks, but by about the end of 1138 he was back home in Constantinople, more popular than ever. Yet John always had to watch his back. If it wasn't his brother Isaac and nephew John conspiring against him, it was some Byzantine warlord or other, such as Constantine Gabras of Trebizond, who briefly allied with the Danishmends but was put down by John himself. In 1140 a sortie against the Danishmend leader Mohammed came to grief after John failed to dent the great fortress of Neocaesarea and his nephew John defected to the enemy, embracing Islam. John's youngest son Manuel was among those who fought gallantly, but high Byzantine casualties forced John to break off the operation.

Shortly afterwards Mohammed conveniently died, and so John was again free to pursue his main objective – Syria and eventually Jerusalem. Zengi was busy trying to seize Damascus from the Franks. In spring 1142 the imperial army, with John and his four sons at its head, snaked down through the mountains of Anatolia to Attaleia (Antalya) on the south coast. There, in high summer, the emperor's eldest son and heir-apparent Alexios sickened of a fever and died. The second and third sons, Andronikos and Isaac, escorted Alexios' body to Constantinople by sea. Andronikos never made it, dying from apparently the same ailment that killed his brother. Shattered in spirit, John nonetheless pressed on to Antioch where he demanded that his inconstant ally Raymond give up the city. Raymond stalled on various pretexts, so John decided to teach him a lesson, sending parties to raid Frankish estates as a small taste of what he could expect.

The decisive thrust at Raymond in Antioch, however, would have to wait until the following spring, when the weather would be improved and the men rested. All appeared to be ready in March 1143, when John rode out into the Taurus Mountains for a spot of hunting. Somehow one of his own poisoned arrows scratched his hand; at first he ignored the wound, but septicaemia set in. Knowing he was dying, John with admirable calm set about organizing his succession. On Easter Sunday he received Holy Communion. Then, in a scene reminiscent of the last hours of Alexander the Great, he opened his bedroom door to anyone in the camp who wished to talk to him. The next day he handed out food and presents to his bravest soldiers, and announced his successor. It was to be the younger brother Manuel, whose calm and reasonable nature he felt to be better for the empire than the elder but more irascible Isaac, whose loyalty, moreover, had been in question. As Manuel knelt by the bedside, John weakly raised himself to place the imperial diadem on his head and the purple imperial robe on his shoulders. Within three days John II Komnenos was dead, moments after having received the last rites. He was 53.

John's task, like that of his immediate predecessors, had been to maintain the Byzantine Empire as an administrative unity amidst international chaos. The Muslim world was fragmented, in turmoil and constantly aggressive. In continental Europe the Bulgars, Magyars and Normans all had covetous eyes on the wealthy East. The Holy Roman Empire and the papacy were seriously at odds, with the petty German fiefdoms and Italian commercial cities mere pawns in that game. In France the kings had yet to assert themselves against the fractious nobility. Only in England, under William the Conqueror and his successors, do we find the evolving centralized monarchy of which Byzantium was the model at the other end of Europe. John II can take credit for maintaining his empire along similar lines, at great personal effort. In his military career he had personally conducted no fewer than twenty-five sieges. In Lord Norwich's judgement, 'no Emperor had ever worked harder, or sacrificed himself more consistently, for the good of his Empire.'

Manuel I Komnenos (1143–1180)

Manuel Komnenos inherited his father's reasonableness and military talents. He had displayed the stuff of which he was made during the fighting in front of the fort at Neocaesarea, and now put it to good use making sure that his elder brother Isaac in Constantinople did not seize the throne first. He despatched the grand domestic, John Axuch, to the capital post-haste, with the authority of a regent. Axuch arrested Isaac before he could act, preparing the way for Manuel's return to Constantinople in August and the first chance for his people to assess him. They saw a remarkably tall, if slightly stooped, young man, swarthy like his father, but far handsomer and with a refreshing zest for life.[6] Much of this zest took the form of an inveterate talent for womanizing, as his two wives and several mistresses (including, we are told, a niece) would attest. But if that was his besetting flaw, it was probably the only one, as in civil administration and military affairs he proved quite as capable as his father and grandfather. He built a new palace at Blachernai, near the northern corner of the city wall, which to one French visitor seemed 'the fairest building in the world … pillars and walls half covered with gold and jewels that shone even at night'.[7]

In 1145 Zengi captured the Frankish stronghold of Edessa, forcing Raymond to seek aid from Manuel to hang on to Antioch. Manuel sent money, Zengi hesitated to provoke Byzantium into renewed action, and Antioch was saved. Zengi was assassinated the following year. The fall of Edessa, however, sent a shock through the West. Saint Bernard of Clairvaux, echoing the actions of Pope Urban II half a century before, whipped up the Second Crusade, joined by no less than French King Louis VII and Holy Roman Emperor Conrad III. Manuel's first inkling of this renewed crusading fever came in the form of a letter from Louis VII notifying him of the new armies that would soon come flocking out of the West. The emperor was less than enthusiastic; even though he admired Western chivalric practices and customs (and was appreciated by the West in return), he had no such regard for the average rough French or German soldier. Memories were still fresh of the chaos in Constantinople caused by the First Crusade.

Manuel's trepidation was more than justified. The Crusader armies, swelled by the inevitable criminals, louts and fugitives from justice and family, cut a destructive swathe over Thrace and the approaches to Constantinople; the imperial detachment that Manuel had sent to escort them had to quell their excesses by force several times. Conrad III, for his part, seems to have harboured a desire to see the great capital in order to assess his chances of conquering it (and eliminating a rival Christian emperor); he brushed aside Manuel's request that his army bypass Constantinople on its way into Asia Minor by crossing at the Dardanelles. The French were also on their way, making themselves despised in the Balkans, arriving at the walls of the city in October 1147. Manuel could see only one way to thwart the possibility of conquest by the Crusaders, and that was to secure a truce with the Turks in Asia Minor. Louis VII, meanwhile, was wined and dined and flattered – and fed an ingenious bit of disinformation according to which the Turks were massing large forces and therefore, the Crusaders needed to cross into Anatolia as quickly as possible. Louis and Conrad took the bait and it was with huge relief that the Greeks ferried the French and Germans across the Bosporus.

At about this time a new king of the Normans in Sicily, Roger IV, had begun raiding the Byzantine territories of Greece, starting with Corfu. His expedition commander, a turncoat Greek Muslim named George of Antioch, inundated mainland Greece where many people welcomed him as a relief from oppressive Byzantine taxation. But he also removed all prospects of future prosperity from Southern Greece by rounding up all the area's renowned silk workers and taking them to Sicily. At one stroke, a major industry and source of revenue was eliminated. Calling Roger 'a dragon, an enemy of all Christians', Manuel dusted off old plans to reconquer Sicily and Southern Italy. In April 1148 a refurbished imperial fleet of some 500 galleys and double that number of troop transports under the emperor's brother-in-law Duke Stephanos Kontostephanos, carrying 30,000 men under Axuch and led in person by Manuel, was ready to sail west.

The expedition almost never got started. Several emergencies in the East, political uncertainty in Venice which had been enlisted as an ally, and freak storms in the Aegean held up the sailing until autumn, when the Byzantine and Venetian fleets joined up to blockade Norman-held Corfu. Early snow in the Pindos Mountains blocked Manuel's progress, so he wintered in Thessalonica. There he met the sick and dispirited Conrad III whose army had been all but annihilated at Dorylaion. Louis VII had fared hardly better; he reached Jerusalem, but at the cost of huge casualties, immense suffering among his men, and the contempt of his wife. Manuel, who had medical skills, treated Conrad personally in the palace at Constantinople and made a firm friend out of him, securing a German pledge to join forces against Roger IV's Normans.

In spring 1149 Manuel's army and navy blockaded Corfu. The closely-built main town was hard to invest by sea, while the well-armed defenders had stored up months of supplies. The Venetian allies, perhaps losing patience, staged an elaborate prank by which they took over the imperial flagship and dressed a black Ethiopian in imperial robes, staging a mock crowning on the deck. The stunt was meant to deride Manuel's dark skin, and he quite properly never forgave the Italians for the crude insult. Corfu soon fell – at the cost of Kontostephanos' life – and now Manuel found himself the object of hostility from the French, who blamed the Greeks for their difficulties in the Holy Land. By now all of Central Europe was roiled by the great power struggle between the Holy Roman Empire and the powerful popes of Rome. Manuel braced himself for the repercussions from this, but by 1155 the scene had changed dramatically; Conrad, Pope Eugene III and Roger IV were dead, and Conrad's successor, Frederick I Hohenstaufen (Barbarossa), a towering figure in European history, had forced his way into Rome and imposed his will on Pope Adrian IV (the Englishman Nicholas Breakspear).

Manuel observed all this with a wary eye. As Frederick Barbarossa was an unknown quantity, he sent two generals, Michael Paleologos and John Doukas, across to Italy to sound out the diplomatic possibilities. By chance they found Frederick at Ancona, disheartened after the Romans had expelled his forces. Though he was willing to join up with the Byzantines against the Normans, his weary barons would have none of it. But Paleologos found a kindred spirit in Count Robert of Loritello, a Norman intent on toppling his bosses in Palermo. With Paleologos providing the ships and money, and Count Robert the men, Bari was taken and the main Norman force defeated with some savagery. The news encouraged Pope Adrian to make common cause with Manuel, and Greek and papal forces marched south in triumph. It seemed that Byzantium might finally realize Justinian's old dream.

It was not to be. Paleologos' arrogance alienated Robert of Loritello, who took himself off in a huff. Then Paleologos died, but despite the efforts of Doukas, the old cooperation could never be quite replaced. The imperial-papal forces confronted the Normans at Brindisi on the heel of Italy, to be all but wiped out on 28 May 1156. Doukas was thrown into jail in Palermo. Byzantium reeled from this major setback; Manuel felt he had no choice but to approach the victorious Norman king, William of Sicily, who by now had the blessings of the pope. The emperor played a risky double game, wooing William while secretly trying to stir up trouble among the rebel Norman barons in Italy. His emissaries did the job expertly, securing the release of John Doukas and regularizing relations with William. This left Manuel free in 1158 to tackle again the single greatest foreign policy problem of the empire – the Muslim presence in the East.

There was plenty of unfinished business in the region. The Second Crusade had evaporated in blood and humiliation. Reynald of Châtillon, the latest prince of Antioch, attacked and pillaged Byzantine Cyprus, capturing the emperor's nephew who commanded the island's garrison and slicing off the noses of Greek priests. Manuel, his blood well and truly up, marched with a large army down into Cilicia opposite Cyprus; Reynald, in abject panic, stood in sackcloth outside the emperor's camp at Mopsuestia (near modern Iskenderun). He was led barefoot and bareheaded into Manuel's imposing presence, surrounded by the blond hulks of the Varangian Guard. Manuel deliberately took his time deigning to notice Reynald, and when he finally did, he ordered Antioch to be immediately surrendered, which it was.

Manuel made his grand entrance on horseback into Antioch on Easter Day 1159, preceded by his Varangian Guard shouldering their battle-axes and accompanied by King Baldwin III of Jerusalem. The emperor wore a coat of mail covered by a purple robe, and a pearly diadem on his head. Reynald walked by the horse's side, giving himself something to do by adjusting the stirrup straps. During the eight days of partying that followed, Manuel jousted with his fellow royals and applied his medical expertise to Baldwin when he broke his arm while hunting. But if the Franks expected that they and the Greeks would now join forces to expel the Muslims from Syria, they would be disappointed, as Manuel now judged it wise for political reasons to show his face again in the capital and, moreover, the Seljuk Turks in Anatolia seemed to be the more immediate problem. Their bumptious sultan, Kilij Arslan II, needed subduing if the imperial route to Antioch was to be kept safe.

Manuel moved on Kilij Arslan personally as part of an elaborate strategy involving simultaneous attacks by John Kontostephanos up from Cilicia with a contingent from Reynald of Châtillon, and a pincer movement by Nur-ed-Din of Aleppo, a descendant of the Turk Zengi, who had become an ally for the occasion. Faced with this array from the four directions of the compass, Kilij Arslan capitulated without a fight. In return, Manuel did all he could to dazzle him with wealth and generosity while keeping him a guest-prisoner in the palace. During one of the entertainment events a member of the sultan's entourage tried to fly with the aid of air that he said was trapped in his large coat pockets, jumping from a springboard high above the Hippodrome. As a measure of the callousness of the day, the crowd roared with laughter as the body was lifted up and carried out. It was more humiliation for Kilij Arslan. But Manuel had preserved the route to the Holy Land.

The good relations between Manuel and Baldwin of Jerusalem were not to last. In 1159 the emperor's German-born wife died, and he cast about for a replacement. Baldwin was led to believe that his pretty cousin Mélisende would be the new bride, and she might well have been, but Manuel preferred blondes and declared his preference for her sister Marie, who wed the emperor in September 1161. A few months later Baldwin sickened and died. Meanwhile, fresh problems arose in Hungary where a new king, Stephen III, was upsetting previous deals over Croatia and Dalmatia, where Byzantium had continued interests. Manuel crossed the Danube to chastise the Hungarians; it took him three years until the general Andronikos Kontostephanos pacified the region.

The reasserting of Byzantine control over Croatia and Dalmatia worried the Venetians on the other side of the Adriatic Sea. The worry turned into fury when Manuel in 1171 was talked into arresting 10,000 Venetian colonists who until then had enjoyed trade privileges in Constantinople after complaints by the Greeks that the wealthy Italians were abusing their social position. In Venice Doge Vitale Michiel feverishly prepared for war and led 120 ships eastwards; when the fleet reached Euboea (Evia) in Greece it was met by emissaries from Manuel who urged that both sides talk it over rather than fight. Michiel accepted. While his fleet was still in the Aegean, plague struck, killing thousands of troops. Moreover, the Venetian envoys to Constantinople were ill-treated and kicked out. Michiel returned to Venice a broken man, to be knifed to death in the streets by a furious mob.

By now the Central European political scene was dominated by the struggle for power between Frederick Barbarossa and the popes in Rome. This gave Manuel a chance to restore relations with the Catholic Church and, hopefully, reunite Christendom. But he failed to appreciate with what suspicion he was regarded in the West, and the depth of the theological rift between the Catholic and Orthodox churches, not to mention the endemic distrust between Italian and Greek. Besides, his main attention was focused always on the East, where by 1173 Kilij Arslan seized several Danishmend territories. Diplomacy broke down, and in summer 1176 Manuel marched on the Seljuk domain. Before the army arrived at Ikonion it was met by envoys from Kilij Arslan who proposed a peace favourable to the Byzantines. The senior officers urged acceptance, as progress through the Cappadocian Mountains would be hard going with the constant threat of ambush. But a few young hotheads clamoured for combat, and Manuel sided with them. On 17 September 1176 the army passed the fortress of Myriokephalon (the Thousand Heads) and entered a long defile where Kilij Arslan's forces were waiting unseen.

It was as Manuel's army was strung out for some ten miles that the Turks surged down from both sides of the valley. Their first victims were the transport mules, whose bodies blocked any movement backward or forward. Manuel appears to have been stunned, but not so Marie's brother Baldwin of Antioch, who charged into the enemy with his Franks and perished along with them. The emperor called an emergency meeting at which he urged flight. Voices were raised, and soldiers outside the tent heard Kontostephanos, the commanding general, protest loudly at this loss of spirit. Manuel was shamed into staying, but the next day saw new and overwhelming attacks by the Seljuks. Manuel began to fear the worst when, during a lull, an emissary from Kilij Arslan offered peace plus the gift of a fine horse for the emperor. Manuel was only too happy to agree. The Byzantine defeat at Myriokephalon has been compared to the disaster at Manzikert just over a century before. Manuel was wounded and many of his men lost, and the way was now open, if Kilij Arslan wished, for a full-scale Seljuk attack on Constantinople. But the Turk hesitated, probably unsure of the outcome after his own serious losses. Manuel was not quite beaten; in the next few years he conducted raids against Seljuk outposts, but they were never more than nuisances.

Manuel was now pushing 60, but like the other Komnenes before him, believed he had plenty of fight left in him. In March 1180 he celebrated the marriage of his 10-year-old son Alexios to Princess Agnes of France, a year younger. But soon afterwards he became ill; probably he never recovered from the humiliation at Myriokephalon. As a medical man, he may have been aware of his approaching end, for a few months after the wedding of his son and heir-apparent he exchanged his imperial robes for a monk's rough habit and died shortly afterwards. On his tomb was placed a heavy stone which he had personally carried on his back from Ephesus on one of his campaigns – it was the stone on which Christ's body was believed to have been placed after being taken down from the cross.

Alexios II Komnenos (1180–1183) and Andronikos I Komnenos (1183–1185)

Manuel I Komnenos was perhaps the last true friend the West had in Byzantium, as after his death relations deteriorated alarmingly. His son Alexios II reigned through his regent mother, the Empress Marie, but in the first few years he turned out to be vain and dim-witted, addicted to games and 'vicious pastimes', while Marie formed an attachment to a ne'er-do-well 'chief adviser' who spent most of his day in bed. The Orthodox population, moreover, had never quite taken to the 'foreigner' Catholic Marie. The general unhappiness found a focus in Alexios' cousin Andronikos Komnenos, an elderly and charismatic general and lusty womanizer whose dubious fame had echoed around Antioch. In 1182 Andronikos raised an army and marched on Constantinople, where he received a hysterical welcome that exploded into violence as Latins everywhere were hunted down and murdered. The general Andronikos Kontostephanos was seized and blinded. Marie and Alexios were captured. The poor 13-year-old Alexios was forced to sign his mother's death warrant after which 'the foreigner' was strangled. A few weeks later Alexios met the same grisly fate and his body was thrown into the Bosporus.

Thus began the cruel but mercifully brief reign of Andronikos I Komnenos. Not content with executing the hapless Alexios, he married the boy-emperor's child bride even though he was 64 at the time! Andronikos' idea of effective rule was to bludgeon and terrorize the state mechanism and public into submission. True, he was merciless against corruption and high-level abuses, and reduced taxes on the poor and slashed waste. But he had a ghastly talent for personally torturing his victims to death. The chief object of his hate was the military aristocracy. Small wonder that many of that class escaped to the West, where reports of Andronikos' savagery gained wide circulation – especially in Norman-held Sicily, where William II saw his chance to strike at the empire.

William held what he thought was a trump card up his sleeve – a youth in his court claiming to be Alexios II. This boy was almost certainly an impostor, but the Norman king may well have believed his tale, and thus in June 1185, amid stringent security, a massive Norman army of some 80,000 men sailed in more than 200 ships from Messina across the Adriatic under the command of Count Richard of Acerra. The force had no trouble landing at Dyrrachion, the starting point of the Via Egnatia, along which the Normans marched without hindrance until they appeared at Thessalonica, the second largest entrepôt of the Byzantine Empire. The imperial governor of Thessalonica, David Branas, could well have put up an effective resistance to the invasion but in the eyes of a contemporary he was 'weaker than a woman [and] more timid than a deer'.[8] Moreover, Branas was away from the city at the time. The local German colony opened the gates, and the Norman-Sicilian horde swarmed in. At least 5,000 civilians were butchered in a paroxysm of ethnic and religious hatred. Norman soldiers urinated on the floors of ruined Orthodox churches and burned the sacred icons in their campfires. When some order was restored, the masses of unburied bodies triggered an epidemic that killed about 3,000 more people.

Leaving the stunned city of Thessalonika behind, the Norman-Sicilian army headed east towards Constantinople. Imperial detachments could do little more than helplessly observe its progress, thanks to Andronikos' own inability to figure out what to do. The news from Thessalonica stunned the people of Constantinople, already terrorized by their emperor's cruelties. When Andronikos sent an emissary to arrest a cousin named Isaac Angelos, the latter slew the emissary and ran to Sancta Sophia to rally a desperate resistance. Joining him were members of the Doukas family who knew they were playing their last card and that if the insurrection failed, they were all as good as dead. The cowed population responded with gusto; after an all-night vigil in the candlelit Sancta Sophia crowds surged through the capital unbarring the jails and calling on everyone to join the revolt against the hated Andronikos.

Inside the church there were scenes of intense drama. A church warden took what was believed to be the old crown of Constantine the Great from its place of honour above the altar and put it on Isaac Angelos' head. Isaac shrank back, not at all confident that the revolt would succeed and fearing execution if it failed. But John Doukas, the latest patriarch of that family, offered his own bald head for it. He was stopped by a great shout from the assembled people, who cried out that they wanted a younger man on the throne. The mob, meanwhile, had reached the palace, where Andronikos ordered his archers to fire volleys into the attackers. But they seemed to be slow to obey, so he grabbed a bow himself and began shooting recklessly. At that point, the truth seems to have dawned on him. Throwing aside the bow, as well as his imperial purple attire, he donned a shapeless cap as a disguise, gathered up his 'bride', 13-year old Agnes of France, as well as his rather older girlfriend Maraptika, and shepherded them onto a galley. The boat had not sailed far up the Bosporus when it was seized. As the mob thoroughly razed the palace, looting its treasures and not sparing even highly sacred relics, the emperor, Agnes and Maraptika were led before Isaac.

The two blameless women, who behaved with great dignity, were set free. But gruesome things were in store for Andronikos. He had a thick chain fastened around his neck and was at first cast into a dungeon, where one hand was cut off, his eyes put out and he was deprived of food and water. A few days later, blind, maimed, famished and crazed with thirst, the wretched figure was placed on a camel and paraded through the streets to face the full murderous fury of his erstwhile subjects. Shrieking insults, they hurled everything they could at him, from stones to excrement. One woman threw a bucket of boiling water over him. Andronikos was then hung upside down. He was heard to mumble agonized prayers of self-pity, and put his one remaining hand to his mouth as if to drink the blood away, after which he mercifully expired.

Chapter Eleven

Angeli and Latins

Isaac II Angelos (1185–1195 and 1203–1204), Alexios III Angelos (1195–1203), Alexios IV Angelos (1203–1204) and Alexios V Mourtzouphlos (1204)

The Angeli were a family that had only recently climbed to the top layer of Byzantine society, thanks to the love-marriage of a daughter of Alexios I with a family member. The Angeli hailed from Philadelphia in Lydia, the West Anatolian province made famous by Herodotus in his account of the wealthy Croesus. Despite its name, however, the bulk of the family of Angelos would prove to be definitely un-angelic.

Isaac II, despite his initial reluctance to don the purple, started out well enough. The Normans were steamrollering across Thrace under Richard of Acerra, convinced that the route to Constantinople would be a walkover. Accordingly, their guard was down. Isaac appointed the capable Alexios Branas to mass the entire Byzantine army to block Richard's way while the fleet waited in the Sea of Marmara. Branas and his newly-heartened men fell on the unprepared invaders at Mosynopolis and drove them back a considerable distance. As the Norman army was licking its wounds at the Strymon River, Branas struck again with spirit. Many Normans and Sicilians drowned in the swollen Strymon; thousands more were cut down as they fled. Richard of Acerra was captured and the pseudo-Alexios II blinded. In Thessalonica the population turned on their erstwhile killers and killed in return. Only a tiny fraction of the Norman-Sicilian force made it back to the Adriatic.

But Europe's attention soon turned again to the Middle East. Among the Turkic tribes who had allied with the Seljuks were the Kurds, who quickly attained positions of power in the Seljuk domains of Anatolia. A Kurd named Ayyub ibn-Shadhi ended up as governor of Damascus. Ayyub's son Salah ad-Din followed in his father's footsteps, becoming commander of the Syrian Muslim forces in 1169. Salah ad-Din, however, was out for bigger things, namely, control of the whole Muslim world. For this he needed to secure Egypt, but before he could do that he had to protect the northern approaches to Palestine. In 1182 he overcame several domestic rivals to reign supreme in the Islamic domains. Five years later he almost annihilated the armies of the Crusader states in the bloody battle of Hattin (one of the victims was Reynald of Châtillon). That same year Salah ad-Din rode triumphantly into Jerusalem and Europe resounded to the contracted version of his name: Saladin.

Saladin's conquest of Jerusalem triggered the Third Crusade, in which England's Richard I and Philip II Augustus of France personally took part (Frederick Barbarossa drowned in a river en route). The English and French kings appeared to be incapable of working together, thus Richard was left alone to try and dislodge Saladin from the holy city, but by 1192 he had to admit failure. Saladin cut by far the best figure in this affair. 'Few Islamic princes can be named who, like him … were concerned only with the well-being of their dynasties and subjects.'[1] To his defeated foes he was the supreme gentleman. The crusading spirit would sputter on for another century or two, but as the twelfth century drew to a close, it was plain that the Frankish kingdoms in the Middle East were finished. Yet the Crusades had in store one more nasty surprise for Byzantium.

Isaac Angelos proved to be an incompetent and wasteful administrator, letting the army and navy decay while more and more of the rising tax burden was spent on palace entertainments and the sale of senior civil service jobs. The prospect of a German Crusader host descending on Constantinople scared him so much that he jailed the envoys who had come to negotiate arrangements for Barbarossa's crossing into Asia Minor. Faced with Barbarossa's towering rage, Isaac relented. But he had little time for anything else, because on 8 April 1195 his elder brother Alexios toppled him in a coup d'état and administered the standard blinding to keep him out of future mischief.

Unfortunately, Alexios III Angelos was scarcely better. He seems to have badly underestimated the mortal threat to Byzantium that was gathering like a thundercloud in the West. The Germans never forgot the gratuitous insult to the envoys of the late Barbarossa, but for the present, Saladin was the prime target. Of ships there were plenty. The reassertion of Muslim control over the Palestinian seaboard had seriously cramped the Venetian traders' style, so the aged, blind but astonishingly energetic Doge of Venice, Enrico Dandolo, agreed to supply fifty galleys and transports for some 35,000 mounted knights and foot soldiers in return for half of whatever territory they could seize. When the fleet assembled in Venice in June 1202, the great majority of Crusaders had no idea where they were going. They had at first been told Palestine, but then the destination changed to Egypt; at that, two-thirds of them went home. This left the expedition leaders unable to afford what Venice was demanding to transport the army. In the midst of this impasse, wily old Dandolo suggested that if the force were to sail into the Adriatic and raid Zara in Dalmatia (now Zadar), in Hungarian possession, the money might be raised. And so Zara it would be. Dandolo himself sailed in the lead with 480 ships. Inside a week, Zara was sacked. Then came the fatal factor, and it came from within Byzantium.

The blinded ex-emperor Isaac, languishing in jail, had a son named (confusingly) Alexios, who escaped to the West to seek help in restoring his father to the throne. The request reached the ears of Dandolo, who agreed to defray the cost of the necessary expedition and contribute 10,000 men into the bargain. Pope Innocent III strongly disapproved of such shenanigans involving a fellow-Christian power. 'But,' writes one brilliant commentator, 'the greatest and most powerful of the popes could not make his voice heard above the clamour of gold.'[2] Dandolo and Venice had everything to gain and little, if anything, to lose. In June 1203 the Crusader fleet sailed up to Constantinople, but unlike earlier occasions it was there to take the city rather than bypass it. The soldiers were dazzled by the size of the city and its opulence and no doubt planning how much of its contents they could seize and haul home.

At the time, Alexios III had been reigning for eight years, during which his venality and incompetence had reduced the Byzantine navy to a few rotting hulks. He watched the Crusaders and the young pretender Alexios pitch camp across the Bosporus and appropriate the area's entire wheat crop. The emperor made a half-hearted attempt to negotiate, but the gesture was rebuffed. He tried to resist a Venetian landing in the Golden Horn, but fled before a fight could be joined. The Venetians cut the great defensive chain that had stretched across the mouth of the inlet and destroyed what few Byzantine warships they found.

But the land walls of Constantinople were a different proposition, lined with the Byzantine cohorts to contest every inch of the assault, which began on 17 July. The English and Danish stalwarts of the Varangian Guard beat off the first Frankish attack in the Blachernai area, the weakest part of the fortifications. But Dandolo displayed the most astounding physical energy for his 80-odd years, not to mention his virtual blindness: standing in the prow of his ducal galley he exhorted his men, cowering under the rain of defenders' arrows, to a successful amphibious landing. Soon afterwards, the Franks were through the wall, capturing twenty-five towers and setting fire to the Blachernai quarter. Alexios III secretly fled the city with his bags of treasure, leaving his family behind.

Senior palace officials felt they had no choice but to lead the blind Isaac out of his jail cell and back onto the throne, and install his son alongside him as Alexios IV. Dandolo and the Venetians professed themselves satisfied, but the Byzantine people were far from it. First, Alexios sharply raised taxes to fill the empty state treasury and give the Venetians their promised money. Second, the Orthodox clergy had no intention of submitting to the arch-heretic Pope Innocent III. Third and most serious, a few Frankish soldiers burned a mosque in the city's Muslim quarter; the fire soon spread to devour a large part of the city. Dandolo, for his part, was not at all certain that Isaac and Alexios would pay their considerable debts to his republic, and concluded that nothing short of a full-scale occupation of Constantinople would balance Venice's books.

The Senate, clergy and people of Byzantium, provoked to the boiling point, gathered in Sancta Sophia to depose Alexios IV. The news was brought to him that night by a senior chamberlain named Alexios Doukas who roused him out of bed, pretended to help him escape by wrapping him in a cloak – and led to him a dungeon where he was strangled with a bowstring. (Isaac was probably put to death about the same time.) After this nefarious achievement Alexios Doukas – surnamed Mourtzouphlos, or the Frowner, because his bushy black eyebrows lent a permanent scowl to his features – was crowned Alexios V. The new emperor wasted no time reinforcing the city defences, and the public spirit revived. Dandolo's response was to launch his all-out assault on 9 April 1204 along the stretch of wall lining the eastern shore of the Golden Horn. For several hours the Franks and Venetians could make no headway against the hail of Greek catapult fire. Three days later the Venetian landing craft were strengthened, and thanks to a helpful northerly wind, blown right under the walls where a gate was breached. Alexios Mourtzouphlos galloped around the city rallying his men, but the defenders were too demoralized by the breach to listen. As the Crusaders poured in, Alexios escaped with the women of his family to Thrace.

That day was one of the most dreadful in Constantinople's history. The so-called Crusaders engaged in an orgy of theft, sacrilege and slaughter. No work of art, however ancient and venerable, was left unvandalized. Libraries were invaded and sacked; the great bulk of the plays of Sophocles and Euripides were destroyed, leaving only the paltry examples we have today. The invaders desecrated churches and smashed their holy relics, looting whatever they could find in Sancta Sophia and defecating on the floor. They set a prostitute on the patriarchal throne and made her sing rude songs 'hurling insults at Jesus Christ'. The streets were filled with bloody bodies; neither the old nor women were spared. House after house went up in flames. The stunned Greeks were quite right to wonder how such barbarians could call themselves Christians, who 'carried the Cross on their shoulders, the Cross upon which they had sworn to pass through Christian lands without bloodshed, to take arms only against the heathen'.[3]

The Latin emperors: Baldwin I of Flanders (1204–1205), Henry of Hainault (1206–1216), Peter of Courtenay (1217), Yolanda (1217–1219), Robert of Courtenay (1219–1228) and Baldwin II (1228–1261) (including John of Brienne (1231–1237))

As the Venetians and Franks divided the immense spoils – and the Fourth Crusade's creditors were finally satisfied – Dandolo engineered the election of Count Baldwin of Flanders and Hainault as puppet emperor of Byzantium under the thumb of Venice and the Roman Catholic Church. Innocent III, to his credit, had flatly forbidden that any harm should come to Constantinople, and was appalled by what had happened. But he was also a realistic ruler, as he came to see that a Latin Constantinople could prove a valuable bulwark for an eventual reconquest of the Holy Land. And so he gave his reluctant endorsement to the seizure.

The Byzantine Empire at this point consisted of Constantinople and its environs, Thrace, the Asia Minor coast of the Dardanelles and Bosporus and the islands of Chios, Lesbos and Samos. The rest of the Byzantine heartland, including much of Greece, was divided up among various Frankish nobles. Thessalonica was given to Boniface of Montferrat, an ally of Dandolo, whose Venetians controlled the rest of the Asia Minor coast, Crete, Euboea, the Central Aegean islands, parts of the Peloponnese and the port of Dyrrhachion in Epiros. Boniface shortly afterwards made himself master of most of the Greek mainland. Otto de la Roche, a French noble, became Duke of Athens, while an Italian, Marco Sanudo, styled himself Duke of the Aegean.

Baldwin I was soon called upon to emulate the exploits of his more glorious Greek predecessors, which proved to be his downfall. Late in 1204 he moved against the symbol of Greek resistance in the person of Theodore Laskaris, a son-in-law of Alexios III, who held a swathe of Byzantine territory from the Black Sea to the Aegean, including the Asian side of the Bosporus. Baldwin crossed the strait and defeated Laskaris' forces at Poimanenon, and could well have mopped up the Greek presence then and there had not the Bulgars gone on the warpath in response to a call by the Greeks of Thrace who were suffering under the Latin occupiers. Tsar Kalojan, in fact, was promised the throne of Constantinople if he could drive the Latins out. Baldwin marched to meet him, suffered a devastating defeat at Adrianople in April 1205, was taken prisoner and tortured to death. The irrepressible Dandolo, who had eccentrically styled himself 'Lord of a Quarter and Half a Quarter of the Roman Empire', was present at the fight, and survived to lead the remnants of his beaten army home. Unsurprisingly, worn out by his battlefield exertions, the octogenarian Doge died a few weeks later and was buried in Sancta Sophia, where he still lies.

The throne passed to Baldwin's brother Henry of Hainault, who managed to save Constantinople from the Bulgars, with the reluctant help of the Greeks. The Bulgars in retaliation ravaged Greek territories, though Tsar Kalojan was murdered at the walls of Thessalonica.[4] Henry of Hainault worked to diplomatically consolidate his occupation throne against the presence of Theodore Laskaris to the south by negotiating with Kaikosru, the Seljuk sultan of Ikonion. Henry tackled Laskaris at the Rhyndakos River in 1211 and defeated him, but had to wheel about to face another Bulgar incursion before he could follow up the victory. Despite his status as a foreign occupier, Henry of Hainault was not disliked, and took the trouble to respect the Greeks and their church. But when he died unexpectedly in Thessalonica in 1216, just 40, there was no offspring to succeed him. The Frankish leaders elected Henry's brother-in-law Peter of Courtenay as emperor.

Peter was in France at the time, and when he received the news of his elevation he set out for Constantinople in high spirits. He never got there. First, he wanted Pope Honorius III to crown him in Rome, which the pope reluctantly did (though outside the walls, so as not to invest the event with too great a significance). Then he set sail with 5,000 men on a fleet of Venetian vessels for Dyrrhachion as the first step in what he hoped would be a conquest of the Despotate of Epiros, an independent Byzantine principality that had sprouted in Western Greece. But Dyrrhachion was too strong for Peter; he was captured and cast into prison, and probably murdered.

Peter's wife Yolanda, the late Henry's sister, and their children had sailed separately. She arrived in Constantinople to find herself empress regnante by default, and just in time to bear a son named Baldwin. Yolanda took steps to make peace with Laskaris, but didn't live long enough to see the results; she died in 1219, leaving the throne to her eldest son Robert, an enigmatic and most unattractive figure, whose stupidity was matched only by his viciousness. Robert of Courtenay was talked into attacking the increasingly strong independent Byzantine principality of Nicaea which in 1222, after Laskaris' death, passed into the hands of his able son-in-law John Doukas Vatatzes. At Poimanenon, where Laskaris had been vanquished two decades before, Robert's army was in turn crushed. From then on Robert sank into a depraved life of women, drink and theft. One night a few barons burst into his bedroom, knifed his latest girlfriend across the face and drowned her mother. Robert sailed to Rome to complain to the pope about this unseemly conduct by his own barons; the pope told him, in essence, to learn to fight his own battles. He was on his way back to Constantinople when he died in the Peloponnese in January 1228.

Here was a chance for the Latin and Greek royal families to reconcile. As Robert had no children and his younger brother Baldwin was a minor, the barons in Constantinople had the idea of elevating Theodore Laksaris' widow Maria to the throne as regent for Baldwin. But that window of opportunity soon slammed shut as Maria soon died. The barons eventually realized that there was a senior crusader kicking about with nothing to do – John of Brienne, a middle-grade French knight from Champagne who had led the ill-fated Fifth Crusade. During that campaign John had suggested a cautious approach in Egypt, but he had been overruled, with the result that his army had been routed on the Nile in August 1221. He had been the pretender to the throne of Jerusalem, buttressing his claim by marrying his daughter to Frederick II Hohenstaufen, the wunderkind of Europe at the time. But as Frederick himself was after Jerusalem, John was shunted into obscurity, from which he was rescued by Pope Gregory IX's suggestion that he fill the vacant seat of Constantinople.

John of Brienne was now well over 60, and needed some prodding to serve as emperor-regent for 11-year-old Baldwin II. At length, convinced that it would be worth his while, he sailed from Rome to be crowned in Sancta Sophia in late 1231. Four years later, John's fighting qualities were called upon when a combined force of Bulgars under Tsar John II Asen and Orthodox Greeks under John Doukas Vatatzes (see below) encircled Constantinople by land and sea to force out the Latins. John of Brienne, despite his age, fought valiantly in the front line, gaining a year's respite for his regime. The following year the Orthodox forces attacked again. But John of Asen, never a very reliable character, fearing that the Greeks would be the bigger threat to Bulgaria than the Latins were, suddenly switched sides. By 1237 John of Brienne was dead and Tsar John Asen was attacking Greek forts in Thrace.

Baldwin II inherited a Latin 'empire' that was little more than the city of Constantinople itself. His principal adversary, John Doukas Vatatzes, was growing in power. John Asen died in 1241, as a Mongol horde under Batu Khan thundered into Eastern Europe and the Middle East, forcing Bulgar, Turk and Arab alike to give them their full attention. The teenaged Baldwin spent four years in Italy trying to raise money; he returned with 30,000 men who promptly went back home when the money was not forthcoming. Western and papal interest in the Latin kingdom was waning, as Baldwin learned the hard way when he went cap-in-hand to Europe, calling on Frederick II, Pope Innocent IV, Louis IX of France and Henry III of England. None of these monarchs were even remotely interested. The barons of Constantinople were reduced to selling whatever ecclesiastical relics had escaped the looting of 1204, and even the lead from the palace roof, to rapacious Venetian buyers.

Baldwin II struggled on until 1260, when the Byzantine emperors-in-exile (see below) were now ready to pounce on his rickety kingdom. Only the Venetians were willing to help, and they very grudgingly. Venice's great sea trading rival, Genoa, had already sided with the Greeks. In the early hours of 25 July 1261 a small Greek detachment under Alexios Strategopoulos slipped through an undefended postern gate, killed the guards on the wall and opened a main gate to the rest of the army. Hardly any Latin troops were on hand to resist. Baldwin was rudely awakened in his palace at Blachernae and ran through the city, pursued by the Greeks, to the main palace. Nursing a wounded arm, he jumped into a Venetian merchant ship moored at Boukoleon harbour and sailed to the island of Euboia off the Greek mainland. The Latin population was treated well – in contrast to the brutalities the Greeks had suffered at their hands in 1204 – and sent packing on boats.

The Byzantine emperors-in-exile: Theodore I Laskaris (1204–1222), John III Doukas Vatatzes (1222–1254), Theodore II Laskaris (1254–1258) and John IV Laskaris (1258–1261)

The fifty-seven year Latin domination of Constantinople was a travesty of Byzantium, a foreign body in the region. The semi-barbarian Frankish barons contributed nothing to Byzantine history in art, culture or politics (quite the contrary, in fact), and their military record (apart from a brief and shining performance by John of Brienne) is lamentable. So it is with some relief that we find Greeks back in control of Byzantium even though Latin rule had left it a small geographical fraction of its former self, and almost bankrupt.

Three of the four men who served as Greek emperors-in-exile were all fighters. (The fourth, John IV Laskaris, was too young, as we shall see.) We have seen how Theodore I Laskaris, the son-in-law of Alexios III and first emperor-in-exile, measured swords with the Latins from his stronghold in Nicaea, at first unsuccessfully. However, he was careful to keep in place the old Byzantine state mechanism, replete with Orthodox patriarch, for the day, he never doubted, when the Byzantines would rule in their capital again. But the Seljuk Turks in the East were a constant menace, and in 1211 Theodore rode to meet Sultan Kaikosru's invasion of Nicaea. The two armies met at Antioch on the Meander River.[5] Theodore's force of about 3,000 included some 800 Latins, plus a detachment of German ex-Crusaders seeking employment. New Scandinavian and Russian recruits had beefed up the reconstituted Varangian Guard. The heavy cavalry was almost completely Western, supplemented by Cuman light horse specializing in mounted archery. Opposing them were the Seljuk ghulam, or heavy cavalry consisting of freed slaves whom Kaikosru used as a bodyguard, plus at least 20,000 foot soldiers. In the Seljuk sultan's train was the deposed Alexios III, hoping to get some sort of throne back.

Though Theodore gave the Seljuk sultan ample warning of his arrival, the Seljuks were hard-pressed to defend the two towns they occupied, Antioch and Philadelphia (Alaşehir), which meant splitting their forces. The Byzantines set up a fortification to be defended by a core of Latin and German cavalry backed up by local infantry on the wings. Theodore himself remained in the rear to coordinate operations. At the sound of the trumpets the two armies rushed each other in the confined space of the Meander valley. The Byzantine-Latin cavalry punched a hole in the Seljuk line, but advanced too far in its enthusiasm and found itself surrounded. A ferocious melée ensued, in which the Byzantines were slowly pushed back. But Theodore, who had now joined the fight and the Varangian Guard, formed a screen in front of the fort. Kaikosru got the emperor in his sights and charged him furiously, knocking him off his horse. What happened then is in dispute. Muslim sources claim Kaikosru chivalrously allowed Theodore to remount before continuing the duel. Considering the savagery of the battle, however, that appears unlikely. Greek sources say as the grounded emperor rolled to escape the sultan's sword-thrusts, a German killed Kaikosru's horse. The sultan fell to the ground, probably hitting his head, as he was unconscious when the same German despatched him. Their sultan dead, the Seljuks fled. (As for Alexios III, he was captured and – of course – sent off to a monastery.)

The realm of Nicaea was not the only Byzantine territory in active resistance to the Latins. On the southern shore of the Black Sea the grandson of Andronikos I of ill-repute, yet another Alexios, set up the so-called Trebizond (now Trabzon) Empire under a branch of the Komnenes. This territory prospered but was never a significant threat to the Latins. In Western Greece another Komnene noble, Michael Angelos Doukas Komnenos, established the Despotate of Epiros based at present-day Arta. Michael and his successor, his brother Theodore, cleared the Latins out of Dyrrhachion (disposing of Latin emperor-designate Peter of Courtenay in the process) and Thessalonica. Theodore then claimed full legitimacy as emperor of Byzantium, but during a battle with the Bulgars in 1230 he was captured and blinded.

When Theodore I Laskaris died in 1222 he left no sons, so the succession by seeming default fell on the husband of his eldest daughter, John Doukas Vatatzes, who became John III. One of Vatatzes' first acts was to transfer the capital and palace to Nymphaion (now Mustafa Kemalpaşa), near the south shore of the Sea of Marmara, a better strategic location. He husbanded his strength over the years until he could fulfil his late father-in-law's wish to retake Constantinople. To give himself room, he decided to settle accounts with the rival kingdoms in Thessalonica and Epiros. By deft diplomatic footwork he neutralized the rivalry from those quarters, though in 1253 he had to take a large army across to Northern Greece to force his will.

Despite his abilities, however, John Vatatzes was ill. He was subject to epileptic fits that sometimes interfered with his sanity. On one occasion he ordered his general Michael Paleologos to be tortured with red-hot irons for some imagined conspiracy, only to rescind the order and promote him to senior commander. In 1254, after a successful thirty-two-year reign, John III Doukas Vatazes – revered locally as a saint – died, to be succeeded by his 32-year-old son Theodore II Laskaris. This second Theodore showed every sign of being quite as capable as his father and uncle; he was intelligent, a capable administrator and brave in the field. Yet he also inherited his father's epilepsy, and in a more pronounced form. The malady could have exacerbated his deadly jealousy of the military aristocracy personified by the brilliant and still-young Michael Paleologos, who again came under paranoid suspicion and sought refuge with the Seljuks. For a time Paleologos kept up his battlefield skills helping the Seljuks against the marauding Mongols, who seized and sacked Baghdad in 1258.

Theodore ably led several campaigns against the Bulgars, but could never quite get out from under a cloud of public mistrust. Like his father, he recalled Paleologos and gave him a command in the Balkans which, however, was too small for him to do anything effective with. The general was unable to halt offensives by the Despotate of Epiros and was arrested and jailed for his pains. His arrest shocked the military command and convinced it that Theodore was no longer fit to rule. They may well have been about to topple him when the emperor's epilepsy forestalled them. In August 1258 a sudden severe attack struck him down. He remained coherent long enough to name his young son John, 8, as his successor. His chamberlain, a despised and low-born figure named George Muzalon, was to act as regent until John came of age. Muzalon's appointment was too much for the aristocracy, who had him and his brother cut to pieces in front of the altar during a memorial service a week later. The conspirators now turned to the one person whom they could trust to keep Byzantium-in-exile a going concern: Michael Paleologos.

The Paleologi were a distinguished family, related to the cream of the Byzantine aristocracy, the Doukai, Angeli and Komneni. A George Paleologos had served Alexios I as general and ambassador. Michael's wife Theodora was related to the late emperor John Doukas Vatatzes. This pedigree, plus his own youth and talents, raised Michael onto the traditional shield in November 1258, to be crowned emperor alongside young John IV Laskaris. Michael's first concern was to pacify the independent-minded Greeks in the Balkan Peninsula; his brother John Paleologos employed smart tactics to neutralize a far larger force of opponents including Prince William of Villehardouin who ruled Achaia in the Peloponnese (around the modern city of Patras). General Alexios Strategopoulos captured Arta, the seat of the Despotate of Epiros.

In 1260 Michael took personal command of the army for the first major attempt to retrieve the capital. We have seen how Strategopoulos broke through a postern gate to lead the Greek army back into the city, sending the hapless Baldwin II scurrying for his life. At the time Michael was 200 miles away; asleep in a camp. His elder sister, who used to lull him to sleep as a child with songs of how he would grow up to one day take back Constantinople, tickled his toes to wake him up with the news. He dared not believe it until the messengers brought him Baldwin's abandoned imperial finery as proof. On 15 August 1261 Michael VIII Paleologos made his entry into the cheering city through the Golden Gate, just as his sister's lullaby had foretold. He proceeded on foot, behind an icon of the Virgin Mary said to have been painted by Saint Luke himself, to Sancta Sophia to be crowned. The people rejoiced and the church bells tolled far into the night. It would be pleasant to thus round out the story of the recovery of Constantinople, but a jarring note intrudes. Michael, though co-emperor with John IV, never seems to have given the boy another thought. Simply put, John was blinded on Christmas Day, his eleventh birthday, and confined in a castle for the rest of his natural life.

Chapter Twelve

Constantine Goes Down Fighting

Michael VIII Paleologos (1261–1282)

Though he was acclaimed emperor in 1258, for historical convenience we may place the official start of Michael VIII's Byzantine reign at the recovery of Constantinople in 1261 and his crowning in Sancta Sophia, while leaving a tiny corner of history for the hapless John IV whose sad fate was wholly undeserved. If Michael considered himself a second Constantine the Great, which we are told he consciously did, it would be on the basis of his literal conquest of Constantinople from a foreign occupier and, in a sense, its refounding as Byzantium's capital.

How feasible could such a refounding be? Europe in the thirteenth century was in a phase of rapid change from the High Middle Ages into something more fluid. The Crusades and their ultimately futile outcome had changed many political and spiritual facts on the ground. The Holy Roman Empire was battling for supremacy in Central Europe with the popes who were at the peak of their power, though that power would soon wane dramatically. England had developed into strong centralized monarchy with France struggling to get there, though both countries were too absorbed in their long-running dynastic and territorial feuds to pay much attention to the East. Europe's economy was changing fast, as the vigorous Italian city-republics of Venice, Genoa and Pisa pioneered international business and banking and accumulated capital that the rest of Europe's rulers borrowed for their wars. For Venice especially, what remained of Byzantium – the western terminus of the great Asian trade routes – was a prize worth playing a long game for.

Michael VIII Paleologos was nobody's fool. His contemporaries acknowledged that he had some of the flaws that often accompany a strong character – 'selfish, an inborn liar, vain, cruel and rapacious'.[1] But he excelled as a strategist and diplomat, and that, in military and power terms, is how he may be judged. His first task was to repair the damaged and neglected capital, especially its walls. The most vulnerable point had been where the wall runs down to the Golden Horn by the Blachernai palace. He settled into that residence to oversee the reinforcement work. The plan was to erect a strong double fortification in that sector facing the sea to make it hard for an attacking fleet to land. He replaced the chain that had blocked the mouth of the Golden Horn while inaugurating a crash naval rebuilding programme. By now the Genoese had replaced the Venetians as Constantinople's main Italian commercial colony; soon many native Greeks who had fled during the Latin occupation came filtering back to repopulate the deserted districts, and also to provide potential recruits for the army and navy. Michael also set up a wide-ranging military intelligence service.

In foreign policy, the emperor knew he had to buttress the ragged western frontiers of the empire. The main obstacle here was the French Principality of Achaia. Its overlord was Charles of Anjou, the younger brother of the Crusader King Louis IX of France, who also ruled Sicily and Southern Italy. During the Latin occupation of Constantinople Charles had mastered the coasts of Epiros and got himself crowned King of Albania. In Rome Pope Urban IV seethed with fury at losing Constantinople to the despised Greek Orthodox 'schismatics' and plotted revenge. But in his call for a fresh crusade he had few takers, as Michael's spies already knew. The pope hated the German Hohenstaufen emperors almost as much as he hated the Greeks. Thus Michael was left pretty much alone to retake as much of the Peloponnese as he could, including Achaia. But treachery on the part of Prince William of Achaia forced the emperor in 1263 to send the newly-built fleet against the Aegean islands held by the Franks and over to the Peloponnese itself. The fleet sacked Kos, Naxos and Paros and sailed on to the rock of Monemvasia to march on ancient Sparta and north to Achaia. There the local Greek garrison commander in Frankish service sallied out and vanquished the imperial army whose commander, the emperor's brother Constantine, barely escaped with his life. At about the same time, a Venetian fleet smashed a Genoese fleet off the small island of Spetsai. Michael blamed Genoese ineptitude for this reverse; in fact, the Genoese trading colony in Constantinople was proving treacherous, to be duly expelled en masse.

His back to the wall, Michael contemplated striking a deal with the pope. He proposed that the Catholic and Orthodox churches end their bitter divorce in the interests of joint action against the Franks and Germans – not to mention the ever-present Muslim Turks in the East. While waiting for a reply, he had the sad experience of sending his brother Constantine back to Achaia for another crack at the Franks and seeing him crushed again. The defeat was partly the result of a mass desertion by 5,000 Seljuk horsemen who had been unpaid for half a year – another telling example of how ready money can be more important to an army than the best weaponry. By the time the papal emissary, Bishop Nicholas of Crotone, arrived in the capital, Michael was pretty much prepared to give the pope what he wanted, but Urban's death in 1264 gave the Orthodox a reprieve.

Charles of Anjou, the very antithesis of his saintly brother Louis IX, was aggressively carving out domains in Sicily and Naples. Urban's successor as pope, Clement IV, backed this blatant raiding expedition. When Charles, whose reputation for cruelty and callousness was well known, occupied Corfu and some points on the Western Greek mainland, Michael became seriously concerned. He was right to be, for Charles' ultimate aim was to restore Latin rule in Constantinople, and this time, a pope was cheering him on. Some nifty diplomatic footwork was called for here, and Michael proved equal to it. Fences were mended not only with the Genoese, but also with the Venetians, who needed support against Charles as well as the Turks. The emperor approached Louis IX with a proposal to contribute a Greek contingent to a new crusade, a proposal which the French king eagerly took up. Then, in what must have been an excruciating and massively unpopular decision, Michael agreed to submit the Orthodox Church to Rome in return. Hardly was the ink dry on the initial documents than Louis hastened to Tunisia for this paltry Eighth (and last) Crusade, to be followed by none other than his grasping brother Charles. Senior Greek clergy pursued Louis there to get the agreement signed, but he sickened with typhoid fever and died soon afterwards, purportedly murmuring, 'Jerusalem, Jerusalem'.

Now the judgement on Charles of Anjou was also about to fall. After his brother's death he scored some success against the Muslims in Tunisia, but when his fleet returned to Sicily to winter in the port of Trapani a severe storm smashed it to bits with huge loss of life. Michael shed tears of joy when he heard the news; this was truly a miracle, of the kind that had saved Constantinople many times in the past. But in the religious sphere, he felt he couldn't press his luck too far. Because of 'the overriding need to avert the perils by which we are threatened', as he told his officials, he felt a reconciliation with the papacy was still necessary. A sympathetic pope, Gregory X, now occupied the throne of Saint Peter, and in July 1274 the Catholic and Orthodox churches were formally reunited after a 220-year break.

Michael didn't count on the mass contempt that his move aroused in the Greek populace, or if he did, felt he could risk it in the interests of peace. There was not an Orthodox believer or clergyman who did not smart under the belief that their proud church was knuckling under to semi-barbarous papal heretics. Demonstrators darkened the streets of Constantinople; many fled to other Greek domains rather than submit to the hated pope. The emperor tried to enforce the law, harshly punishing dissident priests and monks who resisted. Imperial forces were sent to harass Charles of Anjou's outposts in Greece and take back some of the Aegean islands. Much of the credit goes to a Venetian in the emperor's service, one Licario, who proved to be a brilliant naval commander, though, sadly, that is all that is known about him.

Through the 1270s Michael toyed with the idea of joining a Western crusade to clear Asia Minor of the Turks, but there was always the wild card of Charles of Anjou who could never be trusted. Meanwhile, a new and determined pope, Nicholas III, made no secret of his desire to enforce every last letter of the treaty of union and keep the Byzantine emperor under his thumb. In a dramatic meeting of Orthodox clergy, Michael urged them to remain patient, but they had little time for him. The emperor could only hope that imperial successes in the field in Greece and the Balkans might tilt the balance of power back in his favour. But by August 1280 Charles of Anjou's 8,000-strong army under Hugh the Red of Sully had established a strong bridgehead at Dyrrhachion and was pushing eastwards along the Via Egnatia. As the army besieged the Byzantine stronghold of Berat in Albania, Michael gathered what reserves he could, and after an all-night vigil in Constantinople, sent them to Berat. While Hugh was riding to reconnoitre the Greek position his horse was shot from under him and he was captured. His men, believing him dead, panicked. The Greeks then bore down on the Franks, took many hundreds prisoner and led them in chains to Constantinople for the people to jeer at.

Charles of Anjou was nothing if not persistent. Now the strongest ruler in Europe, he maintained alliances with the pope, Venice, Serbia, Bulgaria and the independent Greeks of Epiros. In spring 1282 he had put the final touches to a huge war fleet of 4,000 ships and 27,000 knights ready for the assault on Constantinople, when the people of Sicily – taxed and burdened beyond endurance to provide for Charles' great project – rose up in a bloody insurrection known as the Sicilian Vespers. Frenchmen anywhere on the island were massacred. The Byzantium campaign was, of course, shelved, and Charles was forced to evacuate Sicily. Well might Michael believe that yet again the Almighty had stretched forth His hand to save the realm; yet he, too, had a hand in the success, as for some time Greek agents had been active on the island stirring up anti-Angevin sentiment, not the most difficult task in the circumstances.

With Charles of Anjou disposed of, Michael could personally campaign in Asia Minor to keep the Turks at bay. He succeeded, but the exertion and previous anxieties over Charles of Anjou had taken their toll on his health. He was now 60, but despite his wife's pleas for him to settle down to a quiet life, he felt he had to go to Greece to pacify a dissident potentate in Thessaly. He would have the help of 4,000 Mongol Tartars lent by the Great Khan of the Golden Horde. He boarded a ship at Selymbria to take him to Thrace, but a storm cut short the voyage and he was compelled to ride overland. The ordeal overtaxed him, and on 11 December 1282, in the little village of Pachomia, he died. On his deathbed he named as successor his son Andronikos.

Andronikos II (1282–1328), Andronikos III (1328–1341) and John V (1341–1391) [including John VI Kantakouzenos (1347–1354), Andronikos IV Paleologos (1376–1379 and John VII (1390)]

We will pass over in haste the next half dozen or so Byzantine emperors, who presided over a rapid political and military decline. Andronikos II's first act was to bury his father in secret. Though Michael had accomplished the supremely important task of recovering Constantinople from foreign occupation, his subjects and clergy had never forgiven his agreement with the Roman Catholics, and it was quite unlikely that they would approve a Christian burial for him.

Quite aware of his subjects' feelings, Andronikos re-established his Orthodox credentials. But in the military sphere he was a disaster. As by now the drastically shrunken Byzantine state was desperately short of cash, he disbanded regiments of experienced foot-soldiers and mercenaries, relying instead on undisciplined semi-brigands. The navy was the biggest victim of the cost-cutting; in fact, it was to all intents and purposes scrapped, to the great delight of the Genoese and Turks, who became the eager employers of jobless Greek sailors. The Seljuk Turks, however, had long passed the prime of their power. They were now Mongol vassals, giving way to other, as yet unconquered, Turks who were being swept westwards by the Mongol advances. These, fired by the urge for jihad, had a long tradition of border skirmishing with the Christian lands. The most ambitious clan was that of the Osmanlis, led by Osman, who by 1300 had carved out a state in north-west Asia Minor, within a day's ride from Constantinople. Wherever Osman's hordes rode, they left a wake of devastation, horror and despair; the roads were crammed with refugees and lined with the bodies of the old and ill.

Andronikos' attention was occupied elsewhere. The Serbs under Stephen Urosh II had taken Skoplje (modern Skopje). The independent statelets in Greece were still unruly. The emperor's generals were disappointed by his weakness and at least once plotted to unseat him. In 1296 the Byzantines watched helplessly as a Venetian fleet ravaged the coast, following up the attack a year later by a raid into the Golden Horn, a stunt repeated in 1302. These raids forced Andronikos into granting the Venetians sweeping commercial rights. That same year the emperor's son Michael lost a battle against the Turks at Magnesia (east of present-day Kuşadası) largely because the army had little stomach for a fight.[2] Then a band of mercenaries called the Catalan Company offered its services to him for one month.

The Catalan Company was the brainchild of a German-born pirate named Roger de Flor who demanded a high price for his services. Andronikos accepted, but didn't like the way the 6,500 well-paid Catalans brawled bloodily with the Genoese in the streets of Constantinople. Roger de Flor was then politely asked to take his men across the Bosporus, where he scattered the Turks as far as Philadelphia and plunged on right to the borders of Syria. The Catalan Company was one of the most effective fighting forces ever seen anywhere, but that was precisely the danger for Byzantium. Roger de Flor owed allegiance to no one but himself. After Asia Minor, Andronikos needed him to stem a Bulgar invasion in Thrace, where he received a message that his services were no longer needed. Did the emperor have no more money to pay the Catalans? He hadn't paid them for a year. Was the report of a Bulgar invasion a piece of disinformation designed to bring the adventurer back west and dispose of him? Roger went to Adrianople to appeal to Michael, but while there was murdered during a banquet. The Catalans then proceeded to an orgy of massacre and pillage across Northern Greece, ending up in Athens where in March 1311 they smashed the defenders under Duke Walter of Brienne and set up their own state that was to last seventy years.

The remainder of Andronikos II's reign was filled with tribulations, both political and family-dynastic. One source was his eldest grandson Andronikos, who was growing into a juvenile delinquent. During a night-time brawl over a girl he killed his own brother (by mistake, it was claimed). The news was responsible for the death of his father. There followed a year of civil war during which the emperor, now 60, tried to hold back the claim of the younger Andronikos, who was gathering strong forces at Adrianople. The challenger had the services of the talented noble and military aristocrat

John Kantakouzenos as well as his own influential Paleologos family, and pressured Andronikos II into accepting a dual rule, with his grandson reigning simultaneously in Thrace. For the next five years both Androniki, grandfather and grandson, observed an uneasy coexistence as the younger Andronikos was crowned Andronikos III in Sancta Sophia in February 1325. One evening in spring 1328 Andronikos III and Kantakouzenos led a squad with scaling ladders to the section of wall near Constantinople's Romanos Gate; safely over the top, the squad opened the gate to the force they had gathered. But no violence proved necessary, as the rudely-awakened Andronikos II agreed to abdicate.

The great majority of Byzantines were glad to see the 30-year-old Andronikos III take over. He had his faults, but was also a strong and fighting character. When in the year after his accession the Osmanli – whom we can now call the Ottoman – Turks strengthened their position at Brusa and moved up to besieging Nicaea, Andronikos and Kantakouzenos had to act. The Ottoman emir was Orkhan, the son of Osman, who was encamped within a three-day ride from Constantinople near the village of Pelekanos. There Orkhan confronted the imperial army on 10 June 1329; though the Turks had more men, the Byzantines stood off two strong attacks at the cost of heavy casualties. In the evening Kantakouzenos figured that the Turks would bring up more men and suggested a discreet withdrawal. Early the next morning, as the pullback was under way, a few Greek detachments broke off to fight the pursuing archers. It was the worst thing they could have done, as Andronikos felt compelled to turn back to rescue his own men, and he and Kantakouzenos found themselves encircled by the enemy. The emperor was hit in the leg, but managed to ride back to the main force; just as he arrived, his badly-wounded horse fell dead. The sight of Andronikos on a stretcher spooked some of the army, but his wound turned out to be not serious.

But the army could not long sustain the loss rate suffered at Pelekanos, and Andronikos' concern was to stem further Turkish advances by diplomacy rather than fighting. The Byzantine Empire now was a tiny fraction of its former self, limited to Constantinople and its European environs, and parts of the Aegean islands and Northern Greece. Nicaea fell to Orkhan in 1331, and Nicomedia in 1337. The Ottoman emir was able to score those successes partly because he was a wise and tolerant Muslim, allowing the conquered Greek Orthodox populations to continue their worship unhindered. The situation in the Aegean was more encouraging for Andronikos, as he had rebuilt the navy and was seriously challenging Venetian and Genoese-held islands. Then Pope John XXII added his bit by floating the idea of a new crusade. But it never got underway, and it is highly unlikely that Andronikos would have had anything to do with it if it had. For some time now many Byzantine Greeks had been viewing the infidel Muslim Turk with rather less horror than the heretic Roman Catholic. The Ottoman Turks were merciless at war, but in times of peace they for the most part treated their Christian subjects with consideration as 'People of the Book', that is, the Bible. Islamic sharia law laid it down that fellow-believers in God such as Christians and Jews deserved to keep their faiths as long as they paid their taxes and stayed orderly.[3] The Greek experience of the Catholic powers, on the other hand, had been one of uninterrupted extreme prejudice, arrogance and brutality. This uncomfortable fact, more than any other, was to sign the death warrant of the Byzantine Empire.

Theology, in a way, also terminated the life of Andronikos III. In June 1341 he presided over a particularly acrimonious ecclesiastical council in Sancta Sophia; in the evening, quite exhausted, he repaired to a nearby monastery for some peace and quiet. The next day he developed a fever which grew worse, and on the fifth day of his illness he died, at just 42. The event thrust Byzantium into a dynastic crisis of sorts. Andronikos had two sons, but he had not taken the trouble to designate either of them co-emperor, which would have set the seal on the succession. Besides, they were still young boys. As it would have been unseemly to ignore the elder boy, 9-year-old John, John Kantakouzenos assumed de facto power in the name of the titular heir, who took the title John V Paleologos. It was an uneasy and patchy deal, designed primarily to keep the house of Paleologos in power.

Kantakouzenos found his hands full almost at once, having to deal with simultaneous attacks by the Turks, Serbs and Bulgars, all of which sensed weakness in Byzantium. He was successful in repelling all these threats, but his domestic foes were more formidable, led by the widowed empress Anne of Savoy, who had always resented Kantakouzenos' closeness to her husband. Anne's faction rose in revolt, burning the imperial palace and placing Kantakouzenos' family under arrest. Kantakouzenos received the news at Didymoteichon in Thrace and, with the army backing him to the hilt, sped back to Constantinople to punish the insurrectionists. On the way he was proclaimed emperor in the traditional shield-raising manner, to rule jointly with the young John V.

But social conditions in what remained of Byzantium had been worsening. As the realm shrank it lost revenues. The streets of the capital teemed with penniless refugees and unemployed workers. The military aristocracy, on the other hand, was piling up wealth from outright theft and corruption. The city prefect, Alexios Apokaukos, tapped the boiling public resentment and led an uprising that presaged the great Peasants' Revolt in England of forty years later. The insurrectionists seized control of Adrianople and Thessalonica, terrorizing the upper classes. In Constantinople Kantakouzenos' sumptuous palace was sacked and its considerable contents in food, silver and gold confiscated. His mother was subjected to fatal tortures. He himself, for good measure was excommunicated by the patriarch.

To save his skin, Kantakouzenos took the only option open to him – to seek a foreign ally. He found one in the person of King Stephen Dushan of Serbia, who was only too glad to expand his influence into Byzantium. Both men struck a deal at Pristina in Kosovo in July 1342. But as Kantakouzenos was on his way back to Constantinople he came upon the rebels blocking his way at Serres. While besieging that city his army was devastated by plague – possibly an initial phase of the Black Death of several years later. Three-quarters of the soldiers perished. Kantakouzenos' position appeared hopeless, but towards the end of the year he received aid from the Turkish emir of Aydin, Umur, who figured that he might be owed a favour in the future. Over the following months Kantakouzenos' support in Greece grew, while Umur's 200-ship fleet deterred Apokaukos from extending the rebels' power at sea.

In Constantinople the widowed empress Anne of Savoy and the young John V felt abandoned. Conditions in the city were as dire as ever. While Kantakouzenos was away, Anne's sole hope for support lay in Pope Clement VI and the Venetians. The latter demanded so much protection money that Anne was forced to pawn the Byzantine crown jewels, which duly vanished into the greedy Venetian maw, never to be seen again. Even that huge sacrifice – for which she has been vilified by Greek writers ever since – was in vain. Neither pope nor Italian paid her appeal the slightest heed. Her support in the civil service and military had drained away to Kantakouzenos. Apokaukos, the insurrection leader, turned paranoid, arresting anyone on the slightest suspicion of disloyalty to the cause. One day as he was inspecting work on a new prison being built to house his opponents, someone seized a workman's axe and struck off his head, which was then stuck on a spike on the prison walls for all to see. Apokaukos' remaining bodyguard was massacred and the revolt collapsed.

The way was now free for John VI Kantakouzenos to re-enter the capital. His ally Umur was in no position to help, as his fleet had been decimated at Smyrna by a papal force, so he turned to the Ottoman emir Orkhan. The

Turk promptly fell in love with Kantakouzenos' daughter Theodora, whom he married and allowed to keep her Christian faith. But Kantakouzenos was still not so sure of his status. Anne was not exactly fond of him, though he took care to always acknowledge her son, the 14-year-old John V, as senior emperor. On the night of 2 February 1347 he slipped unobtrusively into the city. The Golden Gate, the traditional grand entryway in the West wall, had been bricked up for security, but Kantakouzenos and 1,000 men found a narrow gap and squeezed through. Anne of Savoy was in terror for her life, but a week later Kantakouzenos showed his good faith by formalizing his joint rule with John V (though he was not formally crowned until May) and ruling out any reprisals for the recent civil conflict. Another daughter of Kantakouzenos was given to John V as a wife.

All these petty and confusing power manoeuvres were a symptom of the fact that the empire, or what remained of it, was in a parlous state. The imperial treasury was bankrupt. Hardly had Kantakouzenos been crowned than the Black Death hit crowded Constantinople, carrying away an unknown but large percentage of the population including Kantakouzenos' youngest son. The capital's food supply was at the mercy of Genoese merchants and any foreign aid donated by outside powers such as the Grand Duchy of Muscovy went to pay for mercenaries. Beyond the Western frontier the Serb king Stephen Dushan sought every opportunity to topple the shaky empire. The Genoese were hard bargainers, and Kantakouzenos realized that the only way to tame them was by rebuilding the Byzantine navy. But before that programme could get started, the Genoese navy launched a general assault on the walls from the Golden Horn; the entire remaining population of Constantinople rose as one to resist them – even the lowliest servants were taught the use of weapons – and the Genoese were whipped back with heavy casualties. This victory heartened the people enough to be able to contribute to the shipbuilding programme with timber from the woodlands of Thrace carried overland by ox-trains. The eastern shore of the Golden Horn was fortified, capped by what was known as the Tower of Christ.[4]

In spring 1349 the new navy was ready, but the same cannot be said of the officers and men who manned it. An initial attack on the Genoese ships in the Golden Horn came to grief, first in a squall and then by an inexplicable attack of mass panic among the crews. Many crewmen jumped overboard to either drown or be killed by the Genoese, who captured the emperor's brand new ships. The crowds watching from the shore were seized with an equally unreasoning terror, turning tail and trampling one another as if 'some evil genius', to quote a Greek observer, was at work. To this day, the shocking debacle of 6 March 1349 lacks any reasonable explanation; most likely the causes were the colossal inexperience of the Greek crews and general nervous exhaustion among the people.

The Genoese, to their credit, agreed to pay Byzantium a healthy war indemnity and promised to be good boys in commerce. This freed both co-emperors to move to thwart the designs of Stephen Dushan in Macedonia; together they entered Thessalonica, where John remained to rally the population, while Kantakouzenos regained some key outposts in the Balkans. For the next few years Kantakouzenos juggled various problems arising from an outbreak of hostilities between Venice and Genoa, whose rival fleets actually battled it out in the Golden Horn. Kantakouzenos backed the Venetians, who turned out to be the losers.

Dynastic rivalry emerged to end Kantakouzenos' career. His son and heir-apparent Matthaios distrusted John V; when their respective forces came to blows at Adrianople, Kantakouzenos made the disastrous decision to use Turkish mercenaries against the younger emperor, formally depose him, and exile him to the island of Tenedos in April 1353. But the patriarch refused to confirm Matthaios as formal heir, excommunicated his father (for a second time), and sailed to Tenedos to revive the 21-year-old John's spirits. That same year a terrible earthquake hit Thrace, eradicating hundreds of towns and villages. That event, more than anything else, gave the Ottoman Turks the opportunity to cross into Europe and essentially repopulate large tracts of once-Greek land. The Ottoman emir, Süleyman Pasha, rebuffed Kantakouzenos' call for some of Gallipoli to be returned on the grounds that it had been given to the Turks 'by an act of Allah'.

Disheartened by his unending run of bad luck, and feeling control slipping away, Kantakouzenos could only watch helplessly as John V's supporters sprung the young co-emperor from his island prison and spirited him back to the capital. On 22 November 1354 John greeted delirious crowds and messaged Kantakouzenos proposing to restore their joint rule and even to acknowledge him as senior emperor. Kantakouzenos consented; but it was far too late now for him to recover even a shred of popularity. The cares of office and command had worn him down. The mass incursion of the Turks into Thrace had been the last straw. The streets of Constantinople echoed to violent demonstrations denouncing him. So on 4 December he took the only honourable way out. In his palace he did something he had wanted to do for a long time: he doffed his imperial attire, put on a monk's habit and abdicated the throne. From now on he would be known as the monk Joasaph.

John V, having seen off John VI, was now sole ruler of Byzantium, and still only 23. The Serb Stephen Dushan was dead, carried off by medical misfortune at the height of his powers. This left the Ottoman Turks as the main foes of the empire, and unlike Kantakouzenos, John was in no mood to accommodate them. The Muslims had to be expelled from Europe and Byzantium, and for this to happen, Western aid was needed. In what was a restoration of Byzantium's traditional Christianity-oriented foreign and military policy, John wrote a long and earnest letter to Pope Innocent VI. But the pope was interested solely, it seems, in dragging the Byzantine emperor back into the Catholic fold. The emperor's Orthodox subjects were not surprised; the papacy was crafty and unreliable anyway, and they chided their emperor for stooping to ask its help.

John was now mature enough to take military matters into his own hands. The Turks, steamrollering across Southeast Europe, pressured the Bulgars to join them on a move against Byzantium. To forestall this, John captured Anchialos on the Black Sea coast; but that was merely a stopgap until he could secure the support of King Louis I of Hungary (known to Hungarians as Louis the Great). Breaking therefore with all tradition, he decided to travel outside the boundaries of the empire not as a warrior – as all the fighting emperors had done until then – but as a supplicant. It availed him precisely nothing. Louis, totally under papal influence, demanded that John become a Catholic; on top of that he kept two of the emperor's sons hostage while John himself was captured by the Bulgars on his way home and kept in confinement for six months, to be released thanks to his Catholic cousin Amedeo of Savoy.

In return for this favour, John felt he had to concede something to Rome. Knowing full well that his subjects would bitterly despise him for it, John personally declared his allegiance to the pope. The monk Joasaph – formerly John VI Kantakouzenos – was brought out of holy retirement to lead the negotiations on the Greek side. On 18 October 1369, in Rome, John V kissed the feet of Pope Urban V on the steps of Saint Peter's. In Venice he agreed to cede the island of Tenedos to the Venetians. But the clergy and people at home seethed with fury at the imperial sell-out; their opposition was focused by the emperor's eldest son and heir-apparent Andronikos, who refused to give up the island, strategically placed in the mouth of the Dardanelles. In retaliation the Venetians kept John a virtual prisoner. Andronikos was advised to sell some imperial treasures as a ransom, but he refused. Eventually money was raised from other sources and John returned to Constantinople in 1371, despised by his people as a heretic Catholic.

Worse was to come. The Ottomans had a new and vigorous sultan, Murad, who trounced the Serbs at the Maritsa River, after which nothing lay between him and Byzantium. The only way John could deal with this was by essentially becoming Murad's vassal. Just how this happened is far from clear; what we do know is that in 1373 he was campaigning alongside the Turks in Asia Minor. His father's adherence to the Catholics and now the Turks was too much for Andronikos. His insurrection was short-lived; he was partly blinded, jailed and stripped of his right to the succession. But the Genoese had been secretly hoping for Andronikos' success as he would have reduced the influence of their arch-rival Venice. They helped spring Andronikos from jail and burst into Constantinople with the aid of Turkish infantry and cavalry. Once there, he had his father seized and thrown into a notorious dungeon with his younger son Manuel. About a year later, in October 1377, as it became apparent that few were prepared to fight for John, Andronikos was crowned as Andronikos IV.

Andronikos' two years of rule were notable for their confusion. The Genoese and Venetians bickered over Tenedos, while Sultan Murad forced Andronikos to hand over Gallipoli that had been in the hands of Amedeo of Savoy. John and Manuel languished in jail for a while, but both were freed, most likely with the aid of the Turks to whom John promised Philadelphia, the last Byzantine city in Asia Minor, and a hefty tribute. On 1 July 1379 John returned to the capital, and this time it was Andronikos IV's turn to pack up in a hurry along with his father, the ex-John VI who had to be content with being plain Joasaph again.

The rest of John V's incredibly chequered 50-year reign can be briefly summarized. Andronikos died in 1385, leaving John to govern more or less in peace. But to govern precisely what? The empire had been reduced to four small states. Only Manuel, based in Thessalonica, put up a brave personal fight against the encroaching Turks, but they were now too numerous to be stopped. In September 1383 they converged on Thessalonica and besieged it. The siege lasted three and a half years, after which the defenders could hold out no longer. Despite Manuel's exhortations, the city surrendered to the Turks in 1387. Manuel himself, bitter at the failure of the Catholic and Western powers to come to his aid, had taken care to sail off before he could be captured. The Serbs made one last attempt to stave off Murad's hordes but were decimated at the terrible battle of Kosovo in 1389. Murad himself was assassinated by a Serb noble just after the battle, to be succeeded by his son Bayezid, of equal or greater ability than his father, and considerably crueller.

Bayezid – soon to be known ruefully as Yıldırım (Lightning) – eyed Constantinople greedily. It was widely believed that the Prophet Muhammad had foretold the capture of 'the city where two continents meet, resembling a ring adorned with two sapphires and two emeralds'. He himself took the title Sultan of Rum, that is, Rome. While the sultan was thus occupied, the late Andronikos' son John plotted with the Genoese to depose his namesake grandfather, with Bayezid's blessings and aid. In 1390, in a confusing and tangled series of events that need not be detailed here, John V's grandson John set himself up as John VII, only to be driven from office – with the help of the Knights of Saint John of Rhodes – a few months later.

Bayezid had his own grand agenda, and had no hesitation in ordering both Manuel, John V's younger son, and ex-John VII to join him on campaign in Anatolia. As vassals of the sultan, they had little choice. Bayezid drove home the harsh point by commanding John V to demolish the Golden Gate fortifications, otherwise Manuel would be blinded. The emperor, old before his time (he was now 58) and utterly depressed looking back on fifty years of imperial futility, acceded, but lost the will to live, dying in February 1391. The verdict of history on the long-suffering John V and Kantakouzenos is not a generous one. Both are censured chiefly for allowing the Ottoman Turks to overcome Anatolia and Southeast Europe. But given the straitened circumstances of the empire, what choice would they have had? It was either that or domination by the popes, and at this juncture the Turks were judged to be the lesser evil.

Manuel II Paleologos (1391–1425) and John VIII Paleologos (1425–1448)

Manuel II succeeded to the throne determined somehow to put some spine back into the state. He felt keenly the hopes of his people when he entered the capital on 7 March 1391. Unlike his predecessor, he was prepared to knuckle under to neither Turk nor Catholic. We learn that he had a commanding presence, combining brain and brawn, which impressed even Bayezid, out of whose sight he had managed to slip unnoticed. The sultan, of course, would have preferred the more pliable ex-John VII, but he comfortably controlled almost everything outside the city limits of Constantinople and could afford to let Manuel play at being an emperor. Besides, Manuel remained Bayezid's official vassal, and was compelled to accompany him on an expedition along the Black Sea coast alongside ex-John VII. It broke the emperor's heart to have to ally himself with the Turks while witnessing his own Byzantine subjects massacred and driven from their homes. Back in Constantinople in February 1392, he married Helena, a Serbian princess, to strengthen his Christian links. The wedding itself was a touching reminder of Byzantium's faded Orthodox glories.

> At that moment, as the mosaics glinted gold in the candlelight … and the coronation anthem echoed through the Great Church, it hardly seemed to matter that the true regalia were in pawn to the Venetians; or that the Emperor whose semi-divinity was being so loftily extolled had in fact returned only a month before from a campaign on behalf of the infidel Sultan.[5]

The following year Bayezid ordered Manuel to join him in putting down a rebellion in Bulgaria. All the sultan's other Christian vassals had been called up as well, which caused Manuel to strongly suspect that Bayezid wanted to do away with them all. The sadistic and mentally unstable sultan was certainly capable of it. Manuel returned to Constantinople with all speed, resolved to fortify the city as best he could and withstand anything the sultan could throw at him. The humiliating vassalage, he decided, was history. Bayezid replied by besieging Constantinople, but because he had no navy to speak of, the city held out for eight years. Venetian ships were able to filter in supplies by sea while the resourceful Constantinopolitans grew food in their own gardens and allotments, tearing down old cottages for firewood.

The Turkish advances in Eastern Europe triggered another call in the West for a crusade. The popes and most of Western Europe's powers raised about 100,000 men who sailed down the Danube. In September 1396 at Nikopolis (near the modern Romanian town of Turnu Magurele) this army blundered into the main Turkish force under Bayezid himself and was virtually annihilated. The sultan himself observed the beheading of no fewer than 10,000 prisoners. After that grisly diversion he turned his attention anew to Constantinople. Halfway up the Bosporus on the east side he began building a large castle to dominate the waterway and block the already scant food supplies from the north. Poor people died of hunger in the streets. Manuel himself, in every spare moment, would pray quietly to Christ to spare his thousand-year capital from the Turk. He also decided on yet another appeal to the West. The emperor despatched diplomatic missions to Pope Boniface IX and the kings of England, France, Aragon and Poland, plus two more to Muscovy and Kiev. The pope and King Charles VI of France were enthusiastic; Richard II of England, however, was in no position to help as he was on the point of being deposed by Henry Bolingbroke, and thus the English had more pressing matters to attend to.

Charles VI sent Marshal Boucicault, a veteran of the Nikopolis 'crusade' and thirsting for revenge, with six ships and 1,200 men; the force butted its way through the thin Turkish blockade to Constantinople. Manuel appreciated the gesture, but knew he would have to raise far more allied help than that, so in December 1399 he set out to tour the Western capitals, accompanied by his wife Helena and Boucicault. It would mean an absence of some two years, during which Manuel constantly worried about the home front. The emperor's first stop was Venice, where he received a tumultuous welcome – the Italians had now finally woken up to the grim reality of the Turkish advances – and moved on to Milan, feted all the way. On 3 June 1400 he entered Paris on a white horse which the French king had given him for the occasion. Eyewitnesses noticed the confident way he mounted the horse, and 'manly chest and yet firmer limbs under a long beard', a man 'indeed to be worthy of imperial rule'.[6]

The pomp and circumstance were impressive, but the results meagre. Charles VI was in no mood for any more crusading; moreover, he was mentally ill and subject to alarming fits. Manuel hoped for better results from England, but had to tarry at Calais for two months until Henry IV returned from putting down a Scottish revolt. On Christmas Day 1400 Henry welcomed 'the Emperor of the Greeks' with great reverence with a banquet in Eltham Palace. Manuel indeed made a powerful impression in his spotless white imperial robes and his innate dignity. Yet those in the know could not help pitying him. Adam of Usk, a lawyer in Henry's court, was saddened to see 'this great Christian prince … driven by the Saracens from the furthest East to these furthest Western islands … O God, what dost thou now, ancient glory of Rome?'[7]

Manuel himself was impressed with Henry, 'most illustrious both in form and judgement [who] with his might astonishes all'. The churchgoers of England had raised some £4,000 – a huge sum at the time – to aid the Christian empire. Seven weeks later Manuel was back in Paris, deep in making plans with the pope and the French. Word had arrived from the Far East that the Mongols were on the warpath again, this time under a warlord named Timur of Kesh, a descendant of the feared Jenghis Khan. Might this Asian leader finally clip off the thorn of Bayezid? But throughout 1401 nothing definite could be decided. Popes and kings, including Henry IV, could not quite make up their minds. Manuel continued to hope that some military aid could be squeezed out of the Western powers, and stuck doggedly to his task for another year at least.

The dire reports from Asia were right. Timur of Kesh – also known to history as Timurlane (a corruption of Timur the Lame) – was surging into Eastern Anatolia. In spring 1402 Timur's hordes appeared on the central Anatolian plain of Ankyra (now Ankara) where Bayezid was waiting for him. The sultan's Ottomans and auxiliaries were no match for the Mongols, who swept all before them. Bayezit was captured and at first treated well, but after trying to escape he was shackled in chains and placed in a litter enclosed by a grille carried on two horses.[8] The sultan's Serbian wife was forced to wait on tables naked. Not surprisingly, Bayezid could stand no more than eight months of this humiliation and died of a stroke, or, as the English poet Christopher Marlowe imagined, by beating his head against the bars.

On news of the battle of Ankyra, Manuel had started out for home, hugely relieved that Byzantium's worst foe was suddenly no more. But if he hoped Timur might help him, he was disappointed, as in 1403 the Mongol warlord died of a fever while attacking China. At a stopover in Venice, Manuel learned that Bayezid's son and successor, the easy-going Süleyman, who 'preferred the conference table to the battlefield', had reversed his father's policy and actually agreed to become a vassal of Byzantium. Once home, Manuel banished ex-John VII for some unknown misdeed, but the dispute was soon patched up, with John being given Thessalonica to govern.

Süleyman was just one of four sons of Bayezid, and the other three wanted his job. Civil war among them raged through the first decade of the fifteenth century. Ex-John VII died in 1407, apparently leaving no heir, to be replaced by Manuel's youngest son Andronikos, just 8, as a preliminary to recovering as much of Greece as he could under imperial control. Three years later Süleyman came to grief, strangled by his ruthless brother Musa. Yet again Constantinople found itself ringed by Turks. The Byzantine navy, again a force to be reckoned with, kept the main sea lane to the Aegean open. To counteract Musa, Manuel enlisted the aid of the sultan's sensible brother Mehmet, who in June 1413 ferried his army across the Bosporus on Byzantine ships to drive Musa from the capital's environs and defeat him in battle in Serbia – and naturally, to have him strangled in his turn.

Mehmet I appeared to sincerely want peace with the Greeks. In despatches he referred to Manuel as 'my father the Emperor' and pledged to do whatever he commanded. Relieved on the Eastern front, the 63-year-old Manuel felt he had enough energy remaining to try and recapture as much of the Greek mainland and Peloponnese as he could. At the Isthmus of Corinth, the narrow land link between the Peloponnese and the mainland, his army rebuilt a wall that had spanned the neck in ancient times. Completed in less than a month, it was dubbed the Hexamilion, or Six-miler, to serve as a bulwark against any eventual Turkish move on the Peloponnese, which the emperor envisaged as a huge Byzantine fortress to command the sea lanes of the Eastern Mediterranean.

Manuel also pinned hopes on prospects of the reunion of the Catholic and Orthodox churches, more out of strategic than any doctrinal motives. The Council of Constance, called to heal a devastating rift within the papacy, included clergy from the Orthodox Church. Manuel arranged the marriage of his son John to a French Catholic princess who, we are told, was so unattractive that John could not abide to sleep with her; she in consequence spent her lonely life holed up in the women's quarters and then in a convent in Italy. The unhappy girl, however, did legitimate John's elevation to co-emperor, along with a growing share in state decision-making. Mehmet I proved a faithful ally of Byzantium, though there was always a question mark over long-term Turkish plans. In May 1421 the sultan was visiting Manuel on the Asian side of the Bosporus when he died suddenly of causes still unknown; 'hunting accident' and dysentery have been mentioned, as well as poisoning, though a plague epidemic is known to have struck Constantinople about that time.

Mehmet's successor Murad II might well have continued his father's conciliatory policy towards Byzantium, but John of the ugly wife had other ideas. There was never any lack of anti-Turkish feeling in the capital. Manuel would have none of it, but he was overruled by John, who wanted to champion the cause of an Ottoman pretender waiting in the wings on the island of Lemnos. Murad trounced this pretender by force of arms, but smarted under the not unjustified impression that the Byzantines had double-crossed him. Perhaps it was time to teach the perfidious Greeks a lesson.

In the summer of 1422, as the people of Constantinople watched from the walls, a great earthwork was raised along the whole length of the walls on the outside. On top of this the Ottomans raised siege engines and began hurling missiles into the city. The entire population, led by John, resisted stoutly. Murad had with him an imam supposedly descended from the Prophet who claimed to have divine knowledge that Constantinople would fall on a 24 August. On that day the Turks threw everything they had at the walls, but the defenders held firm. Disappointed that the prediction had failed to materialize, Murad eventually raised the siege. In fact, he had little choice, as his 13-year-old brother Mustafa – secretly in Byzantine pay – had been stirring up sentiment against him. Young Mustafa escaped to Constantinople, but hardly had he arrived when Manuel suffered a debilitating stroke. John took over de facto rule, though soon afterwards Mustafa was betrayed to Murad, who applied the regulation strangling to him.

By now the Ottomans were besieging Thessalonica. The ailing Manuel saw no choice but to hand the city over to the Venetians, which he did on 14 September 1423. John sailed for Venice and Milan hoping to raise some sort of crusade to defend Thessalonica, but returned disappointed, as neither the papacy nor any Western power would even consider it. Europe had its own regional issues to handle. Manuel was now very ill and confined to his bed, but his mind was quite clear and very much au courant with political developments. He and John would conduct often-acrimonious discussions, and he feared his son had impracticably grandiose ideas about uniting East and West; he told an adviser that what the empire needed now was not so much a visionary as 'a good manager'. In June 1425, on his seventy-fifth birthday, Manuel donned a monk's habit to live out his remaining twenty-five days in holy peace. He was deeply mourned by his people.

The Byzantine people, in fact, had much to mourn about. Their empire had long been one in name only, confined to Constantinople itself.[9] Even within the city walls, plague, destitution and emigration had denuded large districts and turned them into vacant land. The dwindling population – perhaps as little as 50,000 – was but a shadow of the great metropolis of the past. Crime and fraud soared as people tried to survive. It was obvious to locals and visitors alike that Byzantium, slowly strangled by the giant Muslim noose around its capital, was breathing its last. Only the Orthodox Church retained its strength as the social glue of the Greeks, and as their political situation declined, their faith paradoxically grew stronger and more resolute. John VIII, who succeeded his father, found it out the hard way.

Things at first went well for the new emperor, who with his brother Constantine took back parts of the Peloponnese. But this minor military success was no match for the vigour of Sultan Murad II, who at the end of March 1430 burst into Venetian-held Thessalonica, massacring thousands and carrying off more into slavery. Epiros and Albania fell to him like dominoes. In Italy, a worried Pope Eugenius IV agreed to meet the emperor at Ferrara to discuss cooperation. John set out for the conference in November 1437, with 700 delegates, while his younger brother Constantine was left to hold the fort at home. In Venice the doge, Francesco Foscari, gave John an elaborate reception that included cheering crowds, bands and pennants.

At Ferrara, however, negotiations proved difficult, with the pope haughtily insisting on precedence in protocol and the emperor every so often going off on hunting trips. When an epidemic hit Ferrara in 1438, the Greeks for some reason stayed healthy, adding to the Italians' mistrust.

Theology entangled the issue. The papacy had never abandoned its claim to be the sole mediator between God and man, and brought into play abstruse arguments to support its cause, which the Orthodox stoutly opposed. Weeks were spent in fruitless wrangling. The conference moved to Florence; by February 1439 John and the Greeks were thoroughly worn out; the Orthodox Patriarch Joseph, over 80 and suffering from heart disease, died of the stress. John figured that if the price of Western help turned out to be nothing more than lip service to the pope's ecclesiastical claims, then so be it. Still, he had to employ more than a little arm-twisting to get his fractious delegation to agree, which it finally did on 5 July 1439.

With the Decree of Union under his arm, John returned to Constantinople to find himself thoroughly reviled from all sides. To make matters worse, his beloved second wife had just died. Members of the delegation who signed their subservience to Rome were attacked in the streets. John's own brother Demetrios led a short-lived attempt to dethrone him. As for Pope Eugenius, he was more concerned about the apparently unstoppable Turks than what the Orthodox thought of him; Murad's forces were now surging into Transylvania and on the doorstep of Hungary. In summer 1443 a papal crusade led by King Ladislas of Hungary and Poland, Hungarian general John Hunyadi and George Brankovic of Serbia set off down the Danube Valley to join up with a Venetian fleet that would sail through the Bosporus and into the Black Sea in order to cut off the Turkish presence in Europe. An Albanian guerrilla leader, George Kastriotes (better known as Skanderbeg), would stir up resistance behind the Turkish lines. The result was of no use to the Greeks whatsoever. Murad realized what was afoot, and craftily secured a ten-year truce with Hungary and Serbia. This placed the sultan in a position to decisively smash Hunyadi and what remained of the pope's forces on the Black Sea coast in November 1444.

To John, it seemed as if his years of worry, compromise and unpopularity had all been for nothing. He had become a vassal of Murad, and could do little about it; after the sultan's victory over Hunyadi protocol demanded that the emperor welcome and congratulate Murad. Not so his brother Constantine, who made himself useful in Greece attacking Turkish garrisons where he could. But the only result was a new wave of incursions by the Turks, who devastated everything in their path. Worn out and depressed, John VIII died on 31 October 1448, aged only 56. His ragged remnant of an empire would outlive him by just five years.

Constantine XI Paleologos (1448–1453)

The reader at this point may well have the impression that the implosion of the Byzantine Empire, which once extended from the Alps to the Euphrates and was now confined to a handful of square miles, was a rather rapid development. The necessary telescoping of events in this single-volume narrative could be misleading. In fact, to the Byzantines of the mid-fifteenth century the days of the great Macedonian dynasty, of Basil the Bulgar-slayer, were as far back in the memory as Henry VIII is to Britons of the twenty-first century; Constantine the Great was as far back as William the Conqueror is to us. The decline was excruciatingly slow and tortuous.

John's brother Constantine was in Greece when the emperor died. Their younger brother Demetrios, however, had a head start on him and rushed to the capital to be crowned. Demetrios enjoyed some popularity as a leader of the anti-church-union party, but the empress dowager Helena (widow of Manuel II) pulled rank as de facto head of state until a new emperor could be crowned. She flatly preferred Constantine for the honour and carried much public opinion with her. With a certain chagrin, one feels, Helena was compelled to get Murad's seal of approval, though it was a mere formality. Constantine XI was crowned in Mystra, a flourishing Greek community and centre of learning perched on Mount Taygetos overlooking ancient Sparta, on 6 January 1449, arriving in the capital on a Catalan galley in March.

Constantine, like his father, was what a later generation would stereotype as 'tall, dark and handsome'. At the time of his coronation he was 44, with the reputation of a good soldier and administrator. He was no intellectual giant, but was known for his rigid honesty and good temper. The suffering Constantinopolitans may have genuinely welcomed him, but at the outset he laboured under one huge disadvantage. Ever since his father had caved into the papacy and signed the hated Act of Union, the emperor of Byzantium had lost his timeless status as God's vicegerent on earth. In military terms, by this time it probably mattered little, but in moral terms it removed a key pillar of his legitimacy in the eyes of many of his subjects. Constantine, for all his undoubted noble qualities, was in effect a mere king of a tiny city-state. And as such he was called upon to confront the most powerful wave of fanatical Muslim expansionism the world had ever seen.

Murad II may have exerted himself overmuch in his relentless absorption of the Balkans. As early as 1444 he had attempted to retire, but had been called back in 1446 as few had much faith in his impetuous and headstrong son Mehmet. In February 1451 Murad suffered a fatal stroke. Mehmet was only 19 and had so far not shown any great sign of exceptional ability, but he was widely resented in the administration for his arrogance and unwillingness to listen to wise advice. He was extremely well-educated but his character was shot through with streaks of that secretiveness and ruthlessness that any Ottoman ruler needed to survive. Portraits of Mehmet show a determined face dominated by piercing dark eyes and a large hook nose over red lips, reminiscent of 'a parrot about to eat ripe cherries'.[10] He liked his drink and was enthusiastically bisexual. He was monomaniacally preoccupied by the old supposed dictum of the Prophet that '70,000 sons of Isaac' would take Constantinople, whereupon the Last Judgement would sound, and how he could bring that about. After spending the first few months of his reign putting down the inevitable local rebellions attendant on a change of sultan, Mehmet began work on a castle on the European side of the Bosporus at the narrowest point of the strait, and expanded the already existing one on the Asian side. This new fortification, the Rumeli Hisar (Roman Castle) and its opposite number, the Anadolu Hisar (Anatolian Castle), formed a chokehold on Constantinople's northern sea lifeline.[11] When the emperor sent envoys to protest, Mehmet had them beheaded. It was as effective a declaration of war as any. Constantine addressed a last desperate appeal to Rome for aid, hinting that he was prepared to bypass the divisive ecclesiastical issue, but Pope Nicholas V was adamant: accept the supremacy of Rome or suffer the consequences – which did not need to be spelled out. As viewed from secure Rome, Constantinople was a tiny flickering point of light about to be snuffed out by waves of infidels; if anyone was going to head the Christian resistance to the Muslims, it would have to be the pope rather than an emperor who had next to nothing left. It was a logical point of view, but of course the Greeks in extremis could not bring themselves to accept it. To hand over a thousand-year Orthodox realm to the heretic Catholics would be unthinkable – it was often heard, even among educated Byzantines, that if worse came to worst, 'better the sultan's turban than the pope's mitre'.

Constantine, like many on both sides, at first seriously underestimated Mehmet. He believed he could get some diplomatic mileage out of harbouring at court an Ottoman pretender, Prince Orkhan, a distant cousin of the sultan, with a small private force of Turks. The emperor unwisely demanded that Mehmet contribute to the maintenance of Orkhan and his band, compounding the error with half-hearted attempts to foment rebellion by other Turkish clans. Mehmet, for his part, speeded up work on Rumeli Hisar, which was completed on the last day of August 1452. The sultan, whose headquarters were now at Adrianople, promptly marched with the army right up to the walls of Constantinople; for three days he studied them in detail, leaving those in the city in no doubt of his intentions. The garrisons in the two castles inspected every ship that passed up and down the Bosporus; a Venetian galley that refused to stop was sunk by a single cannonball; its crew were beheaded and its skipper impaled.

The incident threw the Byzantines into near-panic. On 12 December the emperor attended a solemn service of intercession in Sancta Sophia. Not many people were present; few were willing to share the church service with those who favoured union with the Catholics. Constantine was still hoping beyond hope for help from the West. But despite favourable noises emerging from Pope Nicholas, the powers of Western Europe were too embroiled in their own affairs to be able to divert massive military resources so far east. All that winter, the emperor could do little more than hope and pray.

Mehmet made his siege preparations with single-minded ruthlessness. 'Give me Constantinople!' he roared one evening at his terrified vizier. By January 1453 he had decided what to do. The Ottoman Turks had finally acquired a trump card, and that was a powerful navy. The Byzantine navy was long gone, as the wooded lands that grew ship timbers had fallen under Turkish or Venetian control. The Turks could field about 130 warships, of which about half were light, swift *fustai*, designed for manoeuvrability. Mehmet correctly figured that the Venetians and Genoese, until now the strongest maritime powers in the Mediterranean, when it came to a crunch would lack fighting motivation; as long as they could keep their trading colonies in Constantinople they didn't care who ruled there. Starting in March, the Ottoman navy began assembling off Gallipoli. At the same time Dayi Karaca Bey, the commander of the sultan's European forces, was ordered to snuff out all remaining Byzantine outposts in the Balkans.

Mehmet, in fact, plays a more dynamic part in the drama of the fall of Constantinople than Constantine, whose main activity consisted of appealing in vain to the West. Pope Nicholas agreed in April to send a paltry five galleys in aid, but the Venetians delayed their own contribution to the point at which when their ships arrived at Constantinople it was already too late. Fortunately, there were some Catholic individuals of noble spirit who placed Christian solidarity above self-interest and volunteered to fight for the emperor. Among them were the leader of the Venetian colony in the city, Girolamo Minotto, and two Venetian sea-captains, Gabriele Trevisano and Alviso Diedo, who converted their merchantmen into warships 'for the honour of God and the honour of all Christendom'. A ship's surgeon, Nicolo Barbaro, began writing a diary of operations. From Genoa came seven professional soldiers with at least 700 volunteers; chief among them was Giovanni Giustiniani, an acknowledged expert in walled defence.[12]

Of all the past sieges of Constantinople, that of April 1453 was the most formidable, and the one that would prove fatal. Mehmet had at his command 80,000 Ottoman Turks and Balkan auxiliaries, against which Constantine could muster a mere 7,000, including the foreign volunteers and monks pressed into military service, to defend fourteen miles of wall. Against the 130 Ottoman ships, just twenty-six were afloat on the Greek side, of which ten were commanded by the emperor and the rest Italian. To the watchers on the walls, the first Turks came into view on 2 April, Easter Monday. After an initial fruitless skirmish against their advance guard, Constantine ordered the gates closed. A thick metal chain resting on wooden floats was placed across the entrance to the Golden Horn as a protective boom. Three days later Mehmet himself arrived with the bulk of his army. He was more confident than ever because, in addition to his navy, he had bought the latest military technology Europe could supply, in the form of artillery.

Cannon had been used in Europe for at least a century, but by the middle of the fifteenth century important advances in gun efficiency had been made. The Turks had proved apt pupils in the science of artillery. A Hungarian cannon-maker named Urban had approached Constantine the year before offering his services to the emperor, but withdrew his offer when Constantine told him he couldn't afford it, so he went over to the Turks, who agreed to pay him four times his asking price. Urban claimed to able to make a supergun that would 'blast the walls of Babylon itself'. The first gun was cast within three months and proved its worth by sinking the Venetian ship that tried to run the Rumeli Hisar blockade. Mehmet then ordered a gun twice the size of the first. When it was tested in January, the noise terrified the people of Adrianople, and the ball travelled a mile. A delighted sultan ordered the monster cannon to be drawn by fifteen pairs of oxen to the walls of Constantinople.

Constantine himself, not daring to tell anyone how outnumbered his forces were, joined army and people in repairing the walls and organized the distribution of weapons. He had words of encouragement for everyone he met, especially when Urban's huge gun lumbered over the horizon, and rainstorms and earth tremors stoked dread among the people. The vulnerable

Blachernai sector in the north was strengthened by a moat running beneath the wall. The defence was formally organized on 5 April. Constantine and his best Greek troops took up position at the Fifth Military (Saint Romanos') Gate in the north-west, where the wall crossed the Lykos River; to his right stood Giustiniani at the Charisian Gate, but when Mehmet's tent was seen going up directly opposite the emperor, he moved closer to Constantine's position. Minotto and the three Bocchiardo brothers, Antonio, Paolo and Troilo, headed the defence at Blachernai, while the Catholic Archbishop Leonard of Chios, sent as part of a token papal force, guarded the spot where the wall joins the Golden Horn. Doctrinal differences were now finally cast aside in the overarching need to repel the Muslim.

To the emperor's left was the Genoese Maurizio Cattaneo, defending the stretch of wall that included the Fourth Military Gate. Theophilos Paleologos, a relative of the emperor, stood at the Third Military Gate with a Greek force. Next came the Venetian Filippo Contarini, defending the stretch of wall from the Pegai Gate to the Golden Gate, including the Second Military Gate. Demetrios Kantakouzenos commanded the detachment between the Golden Gate and the sea. Jacopo Contarini, the brother of Filippo, was in charge of the sea wall abutting the Stoudion quarter. Prince Orkhan and his Turks were tasked with defending the main harbours on the Marmara shore, helped by a volunteer Catalan force under Péré Julia, the Catalan consul. Placed on the western shore of the Golden Horn were Cardinal Isidore, a former Metropolitan of Kiev, at the south end of the boom, and Diedo and Trevisano to his left. Two detachments under Loukas Notaras and Nikephoros Paleologos were kept in reserve. The emperor is believed to have mixed up his ethnic units in this way as to secure maximum cooperation and avoid 'nationalistic quarrels'.[13]

Looking out from his post, Constantine thought that a little psychological warfare might be in order. At his suggestion, about 1,000 of Trevisano's strikingly-clad Venetian seamen paraded in full regalia along the wall. Whatever impression the display made is not recorded, as Mehmet replied by issuing a formal ultimatum to Constantinople: surrender or be shown no mercy. Either way, the Greeks had little faith in infidel promises; to a man, they agreed to resist. Mehmet opened operations by bombarding the wall near the Charisian Gate, causing considerable damage which was partly repaired during the night. On 9 April the Turkish ships tried and failed to break through the Golden Horn boom. The Ottoman cannon resumed their devastating fire on 12 April; Urban's huge gun could only be fired seven times a day, but each of those shots sent the thousand-year-old Theodosian masonry flying like shards of pottery. At night Giustiniani and many ordinary people laboured to plug the gaps with anything they could find. At sea the Turks were less successful. Their ship cannon lacked the elevation to do much harm to the tall Christian galleys and when the Turkish fleet found itself in danger of encirclement, it had to withdraw.

For the first few weeks of the siege Giustiniani was life and soul of the defence in the central sector. The defenders took heart on 20 April when three Genoese galleys promised by the pope turned up, accompanied by a large transport carrying vital grain. Mehmet barked at his admiral-in-chief, Süleyman Baltoğlu, to stop them or pay for his failure with his head. At first the Genoese ships pressed on undaunted, brushing aside the ineffectual Ottoman resistance, but a sudden current pushed them landward and Baltoğlu saw his chance. But the superior discipline of the Genoese crews, commanded by the brilliant Greek captain Phlatanelas, held fast; to those watching the battle, only the masts of the Christian ships were visible above a writhing sea of Muslim vessels.

The desperate Turkish admiral, knowing full well what awaited him if he lost, rammed his flagship into the grain transport. But Phlatanelas brought his Greek Fire into play, pouring it by the gallon onto the Ottman ships; the Greek and Genoese sailors hacked off the hands of Turkish sailors who tried to seize their vessels, and threw them into the bloody sea. Phlatanelas ordered all four ships lashed together for a better defence. Mehmet, beside himself, roared ineffectual curses at his admiral, and more than once rode his horse into the sea as if that way he could affect the battle. When it seemed as if the sheer weight of Turks would prevail, a sudden northerly breeze filled the Christian sails. The ships swept the Turks aside and gained the shelter of the boom. Baltoğlu, trying to ignore the sultan's imprecations from the shore and not to think of what his fate would be, ordered a withdrawal. He was saved from execution only by testimony from his officers that he was a truly courageous commander and had done all he could. He had been wounded in the eye by friendly fire from one of his own ships. For punishment he was flogged and sent to live out the rest of his days in obscure poverty.

The naval debacle convinced Mehmet that he had to seize the Golden Horn. He thought up an ingenious plan to transport his fleet from the middle reaches of the Bosporus overland, over a ridge corresponding roughly to today's Taksim Square and Istiklal Caddesi, and into the inlet from its eastern shore. On 22 April the first of some seventy ships were hauled up the 200-foot ridge by teams of oxen, as drums rolled, trumpets blared and the crews flew all their flags just as if they were at sea. Constantine called for Giustiniani to discuss tactics. An Italian sea-captain, Giacomo Coco, proposed to head a mission to burn the ships, but the plan was compromised as the Venetians and Genoese quarrelled over who should share the glory. Coco's team was approaching the Ottoman ships at night when Turkish guns opened fire and sank them. Coco was killed and forty Christian seamen were captured, to be slaughtered the next day. In revenge, the Greeks butchered 260 Turkish prisoners on the walls, in full view of the enemy.

As food supplies in the city ran low, Constantine ordered a fast ship to sail into the Aegean to find out what had happened to the flotilla promised by the Venetians. The ships were indeed on their way, but had been ordered to stay at Tenedos while its commander gathered intelligence about the Turkish fleet. The real reason for the delay appears to have been Venetian reluctance to measure swords with the Ottomans and a corresponding hope that by the time the flotilla reached Constantinople the issue would have been decided one way or the other. Inside the city, acrimony between the Venetians and Genoese reached new levels. 'The war outside is enough for us,' Constantine told them. 'For the pity of God do not start a war between yourselves.' The emperor nursed a faint hope that somehow he could come to an accommodation with Mehmet, but those hopes evaporated after secret feelers to that effect were rebuffed. Constantine's advisers suggested he escape the capital and carry on the fight from outside, much as the emperors had done under the Latin occupation. No, he replied, if Constantinople were to die, he would die with it.

Throughout the first two weeks of May the Turkish guns continued to hammer at the walls, concentrating on Guistiniani's sector to the left of the Blachernai Palace. The Turkish ships holed up in the Golden Horn tried to break the boom chain twice, but failed. The Scotsman Grant managed to undermine a Turkish sapping operation that was trying to weaken the wall from beneath; sappers from both sides, in fact, conducted an unseen but fierce underground war that was won by the Greeks thanks to information provided by a tortured Turkish officer. Great ingenuity was exerted by attackers and defenders alike in tunnels, explosives and siege engines. But Constantine could not relax. He was keenly aware of a dark prophecy among the people that as the first Constantine was the son of Helena, so would be the last. On 25 May the holiest icon of the Virgin was carried around the city; at one point it tumbled to the ground and, as we are assured by all writers, became inexplicably heavy and could be raised only by the greatest effort. The procession was then aborted by a ferocious thunderstorm with torrents of hail. The following day, a highly unusual spring fog blanketed the whole city – it was muttered that the Divine Presence was veiling His departure. That evening a strange light was seen on the dome of Sancta Sophia. Mehmet saw it, too, and interpreted it as a sign from Allah that his wish would be granted.

The sultan made one last attempt to gain the city peacefully. He sent a renegade Greek to the emperor offering two alternatives: either Constantine pay him a large annual tribute or the people of Constantinople should abandon the city with their families and possessions; Constantine refused. Two days later the 21-year-old sultan – overriding the advice of his vizier and senior officers who thought the attempt on Constantinople foolhardy – informed his army that he would distribute all the Greeks' treasures among them, and that once they were through the walls, they would have three days in which to kill and pillage to their hearts' content. The answering roar of 'Allahu akbar!' (God is great!) could be heard for miles.

Monday 28 May was a day of rest for the Turks, who were ordered to conserve their strength for the great assault scheduled for the morrow. Mehmet gave his senior officers a pep talk and made the final arrangements for the battle order. Inside the city church bells tolled and relics and icons were paraded around, especially at the weaker parts of the walls. There was no division between Orthodox and Catholic now – all were united to save the last bastion of Eastern Christendom. Constantine gave a speech in which he professed to be willing to die for his faith and his city. He urged his hearers, Greek and Italian, to remember the heroes of ancient Greece and Rome and emulate them in the face of the enemies of Christ. When he finished speaking he spoke to each one present in the chamber and embraced them, begging forgiveness if he had ever offended any one of them. At nightfall the people of Constantinople, as if pushed by an invisible hand, converged on Sancta Sophia for a solemn service of intercession. Orthodox and Catholic alike took confession and administered Holy Communion. 'At this moment,' notes Runciman wryly, 'there was union in the Church of Constantinople.'

At some point during the service the emperor walked out, got on his horse and rode to the Blachernai Palace in the darkness. There he said his farewells to his servants and staff, again asking forgiveness for any wrong he might have done them, before making a final inspection of the walls with his private secretary, George Phrantzes. Back at Blachernai both men dismounted and climbed a tower at the Caligarian Gate. They heard the dull hubbub of the enemy preparations, the gun wagons creaking as they were brought up to within range of the wall. Looking west, they could see the flickering lights on the Turkish ships in the Golden Horn. For about an hour the two men remained atop the tower, then Phrantzes went home, never to see his emperor again.

Ninety minutes after midnight, the Ottomans launched their attack, galvanizing into action the whole defence line along the walls. The clamour reached the worshippers in Sancta Sophia, who scattered, the fighting-age men to the walls, the younger women to help in the rear echelons. The city echoed to the uproar, punctuated by the frantic ringing of church bells and the occasional sinister boom of Urban's supergun. First to go in were the crack Ottoman irregulars known as Bashi-Bazouks, whose disorganized human waves in the central sector were eventually repulsed. Constantine joined Giustiniani in making short work of the Bashi-Bazouks, but there was no rest for the weary, as Mehmet next sent in his more disciplined and better-armed Anatolian divisions under Ishak Pasha. These were fanatical fighters who made strenuous efforts to scale the wall in the southern sector but were beaten back with heavy losses in vicious hand-to-hand combat atop the scaling ladders. Just as Ishak's men were about to retire, a lucky shot from Urban's cannon demolished a good length of the defenders' stockade. Several hundred yelling Muslims rushed into the gap, but were cut down by the emperor and his guard.

Mehmet fumed again, this time sending his prized Yeni Cheri, better known as Janissaries, into the fray. The Janissaries were Christian boys taken by force from their families in Greece and the Balkans and brought up as fanatically militant Muslim warriors. Unlike the previous units that had attacked in a rush, the elite Janissaries advanced to the central sector in perfect discipline and order to the sound of martial music. The sultan did them the honour of marching at their head, stepping aside as the Janissaries reached the defensive ditch in front of the stockade. They came up against solid Greek resistance and for an hour, locked in combat, they could make no progress at all. But farther north the defence was weakening. The Bocchiardo brothers in the Blachernai sector had been using a small postern gate abutting the palace, the Kerkporta, to make sallies on the enemy. But after one such sally someone forgot to bar the gate, and several dozen Bashi-Bazouks rushed inside. These were quickly detected and would have been neutralized had not Giustiniani at that moment staggered back, hit by a Turkish arrow that holed his breastplate. Shaken and in great pain, he asked to be taken to the rear. Constantine tried to persuade him to stay, fearing the effect on morale in that sector, but the Italian's spirit was broken. As Giustiniani was carried to a Genoese ship, his fellow-Genoese gave up the struggle and fled.

Constantine galloped up to the Kerkoporta, but could do nothing about the Turks surging through. Returning to the central sector, he helped fight off determined waves of Janissaries. Yet Mehmet was exultant. Seeing an Ottoman flag flying over the Kerkoporta, he believed the city was his at last. And so did Constantine. The emperor must have known his final moments were at hand. When the Janissaries finally overcame the desperate Greek defence, Constantine stood facing them, sword in hand, in the Fifth Military Gate. At his side, willing to defend him to the last, were his cousin Theophilos Paleologos, one John Dalmata, and a Spanish noble named Don Francisco of Toledo, one of those excellent souls who appear momentarily in history like a blazing star, but about whom nothing else is known. The four of them kept their position as panicked Greek troops retreated into the city. 'I'd rather die than live!' cried Theophilos, and threw himself into the Ottoman hordes. At this, the emperor flung off his imperial robes and insignia. 'The city is falling and I live still?' he cried, and followed his cousin, along with Dalmata and Don Francisco. None of them were ever seen again.

Epilogue

The dawn of 29 May 1453 broke on the Ottoman hordes surging through Constantinople in a hell of slaughter and destruction. They burst into Sancta Sophia, where the service was still in progress, dragging off young men and women in the congregation as slaves. Four thousand civilians died in the three days of looting. The Greek Orthodox Church was, however, allowed to keep on functioning, and it lives still in a shabby corner of what is now Istanbul. To this day it regards itself as the shadow of the defunct Byzantine Empire; the Orthodox ecumenical patriarch's glittering ceremonial robes are direct derivatives of the imperial attire.

Many Greeks cling to an old belief that someday another Constantine will appear to take back The City, though in this globalized age few would openly admit it. Yet even today, in modern Greece it is still frowned on to call the city Istanbul; even the mass media faithfully term it Constantinople. A few romantic hopes were placed on King Constantine II, when he assumed the Greek throne in 1964, that he might be the one to reclaim the heritage of eleven Constantines before him. There is no evidence to suggest that he ever took it seriously, as Greece and Turkey have been North Atlantic Treaty Organization allies since 1952. Politically and militarily, Byzantium is history. Yet spiritually, it lives on. Like the popes of Rome, the Orthodox patriarchs have no military divisions. Yet that is perhaps precisely why they are still there.

Constantine XI Paleologos, the last emperor of Byzantium, ended his life as he wished, fighting for his city, people and faith. Several soldiers claimed to have seen him fall and his head hacked off by a Janissary. Mehmet himself wished to know what had become of his adversary. Several bodies were displayed to him, and he was reported to have recognized Constantine by the imperial insignia on the socks. He is said to have chivalrously given the body back to the Greeks for burial, and for centuries an unremarkable grave in the Vefa quarter of Istanbul was believed to be the last emperor's last resting-place. The exact location of the grave has long been forgotten. An alternative story, that the sultan had Constantine's head displayed on a pike, and then stuffed and sent to other Muslim leaders, may safely be discounted.[1]

But there is more. In Saint Leonard's Church in Landulph, Cornwall, there is an inscribed plaque over the last resting place of one 'Theodoro Paleologvs' who died in January 1636 and is described as hailing from Pesaro, Italy, 'descended from ye imperiall lyne of ye last Christian Emperors of Greece,' the great-grandson of the 'second brother to Constantine Paleologvs … last of yt lyne yt raygned in Constantinople'. The plaque states that he married one Mary Balls and had five children by her.[2] 'How we would love to believe it,' writes Norwich, admitting a maddening lack of further evidence. Yet by that same token, why should we not believe it? The Pesaro connection seems to be a genuine one; a Theodore Paleologos was convicted of attempted murder there in the early seventeenth century and moved (or escaped) to England. There he met Mary Balls, whom he married in Yorkshire when she was already pregnant. A son, Ferdinand, emigrated to Barbados and had a son named Theodoros who returned to Britain and lived in Stepney. This second Theodoros' sole offspring appears to have been a girl named Godscall Paleologus, and with her, in East London about 1695, the imperial trail peters out. So almost certainly a trickle of the blood of the last fighting emperor of Byzantium runs in British veins today.

Notes and References

Prologue

1. From *Reveries on the Art of War* (1732), quoted in Barbara Tuchman, *The Guns of August* (New York, Dell 1962) p. ix.
2. Quoted in Norwich I, p. 25.

Chapter One

1. Stephenson, pp.127–38.
2. As named in Gospel of John. The other three evangelists mention merely 'one of the followers of Jesus' as committing the act.
3. Durant III, p. 646.
4. Durant III, p. 641.
5. Cyprian, cited by Durant III, p. 665.
6. A story circulated by Geoffrey of Monmouth in the twelfth century that Helena's father was one Coel, the founder of Colchester – the nursery-rhyme Old King Cole – can safely be discredited.
7. The adjacent suburb of Rome is called Labaro, after the Greek *labaron*, or standard of Constantine.
8. Christian writers made much of the parallel with the drowning of Pharaoh's forces in the Red Sea, which had parted to let Moses and the Israelites through. Cf. Exodus 15:21, where Miriam exults, 'The horse and his rider hath he thrown into the sea' – a c. 900 BC fragment of verse that is the oldest known text of the Old Testament.
9. The Arch of Constantine became a fortification in the historically-unaware Middle Ages and then part of the Frangipane family mansion. In the eighteenth century it was restored and the jumbled surroundings cleared. Now it straddles the northern end of the Via di San Gregorio.
10. Quoted in Durant III, p. 659.
11. Pitton de Tournefort, Voyage du Levant, v I, Lettre XI (Amsterdam 1718.)
12. 'New York on the Bosporus' is how German Byzantinist Andreas Müller describes Constantinople. See 'Byzanz' in Der Spiegel Geschichte, 1/2014.
13. Eunapius, quoted in Stephenson, p. 200.
14. Quoted in Sherrard, p. 22–3.
15. Emperor and Caesar Flavius Constantinus Pius Happy Victor and Triumphant Chief Pontiff, Four-times Chief Vanquisher of the Germans, Twice Chief Vanquisher of the Sarmatians, Twice Chief Vanquisher of the Goths,

Vanquisher [once] of the Dacians, Tribune for 33 Terms [years], Consul for Seven Terms, Emperor for 32 Terms, Father of the Country and Chief Consul. (In Stephenson, p. 235.)

16. In Stephenson, pp. 228–235.
17. Not to be confused with Eusebius of Caesarea, Constantine's biographer and the source of the speech.
18. The church had been rather shoddily built, and some years later Constantine's remains were moved to safer quarters to the church of Saint Acacius the Martyr. Their subsequent fate is an enduring mystery.
19. Simon Sebag Montefiore, *Jerusalem* (London, Phoenix 2011) p. 143.
20. Constantine's middle son Constantius is usually given the numeral II since his grandfather Constantius Chlorus is regarded as Constantius I, though Chlorus was a Roman rather than a Byzantine Augustus.
21. Stephenson, pp. 294–6.
22. Norwich I, pp. 88–90.
23. Durant IV, p. 136.
24. It was said that the court Magi held the royal diadem over the appropriate part of the queen's anatomy in a symbolic pre-birth coronation. Without the benefit of ultrasound technology, they nevertheless claimed they knew it would be a boy.
25. Durant IV, pp. 15–6.
26. Gibbon/Trevor-Roper, p. 259.
27. Greek historians dub him the Parabates, or violator (of Christian law).

Chapter Two

1. Quoted in Norwich I, p. 103.
2. Not counting Constantine II, Constans and Valentinian I, who were either absent or ruled only in part.
3. Jordanes, quoted in Durant IV, p.24.
4. Norwich I, p. 121.
5. Greek historians also dub Theodosius II the Small (Mikros), a title which conveys a degree of deprecation to contrast with his grandfather, the Great.
6. Quoted in Norwich I, p. 154.
7. This 'Battle of the Nations' is often cited as having been fought at Châlons-sur-Marne.
8. Literally, commander of a thousand, roughly equivalent to a brigade commander.
9. Ferguson, W. K. *A Survey of European Civilization*, Vol I, Third edition (Boston, Houghton Mifflin, 1962) p. 114.
10. The last Romulus was later given the condescending title Augustulus, or Little Augustus.
11. The story is related by Ioannes Kedrenos and Zonaras. Zeno has exercised a certain fascination in more recent times. An English Jesuit wrote a play about him that was performed in Rome in 1643, while the German playwright Friedrich Dürrenmatt featured him in his 1950 play Romulus the Great.
12. Norwich I, p. 187.
13. Dhu Nuwas' followers claimed he rode his horse into the sea and disappeared.

Chapter Three

1. Much titillating ink has been spilled over Theodora. Those eager for more details will find plenty in Procopius' scurrilous Secret History, which is riveting, but best taken with a quantity of salt. Gibbon reports her response to the Nika rioters as 'The throne is a glorious sepulchre.'
2. According to Procopius, Theodora was deeply involved in this sexual intrigue, perhaps as a means of derailing any imperial ambitions that Belisarius may have had.
3. A legend that Belisarius was reduced to sitting at the Pincian Gate in Rome, blind and with a begging-bowl in hand, is almost certainly spurious. More probably, he is said to have built the church of Santa Maria in Trivio, where a stone records that he built it to expiate a sin – probably his removal of Pope Silverius for allegedly preferring the Goths over the Byzantines.
4. Most histories refer to him as Tiberius II (adding the name Constantine), as the second Roman emperor after the first Tiberius who reigned in the time of Christ.
5. I use the Greek spelling rather than the traditional Maurice, as by now the Byzantine Empire was fast losing its last Latin vestiges and was becoming Greek. Emperors' names will be rendered in Greek spelling from now on, except for those too familiar to change, i.e. Constantine, Justinian, Heraclius, Michael and John.
6. The Avars continued to dwell in the lands north of the Danube, where they were a potential threat to the stability of Central Europe until Charlemagne achieved a crushing victory over them in 796. Their name thereafter disappears from history.

Chapter Four

1. Montefiore, p. 162.
2. These holy items were preserved by Khosru's Christian wife Shirin in Ctesiphon.
3. George of Pisidia, quoted in Norwich I, p. 190.
4. The Greek Orthodox hymn *Te Hypermacho* (To the Champion, i.e. the Virgin Mary) was written to commemorate the victory, and is still sung in Greek churches on patriotic occasions. Regrettably, the writer is unknown, as it is a supreme example of Byzantine ecclesiastical poetry.
5. A legend arose later that as the emperor approached the gate it mysteriously walled itself up, opening only when Heraclius humbled himself by casting off his rich robes. (Montefiore, p. 165.)
6. Hitti, pp. 24–5.
7. Alamundarus is the Greek form of al-Mundhir. I have preferred the Greek version to prevent reader confusion with the al-Mundhir of the Lakhmids.
8. Quoted in Hitti, p.144.
9. Daniel 7:1–8.
10. By comparison, United States defence expenditure in 2013 was about 19 per cent of the national budget.

11. The term moira derived from the ancient Spartan mora, or basic fighting unit, and has passed into modern Greek usage as the term for an air force squadron.
12. The assassination sparked a devastating rift in the Muslim world that plagues it to this day. Ali continues to be revered among Shia Muslims, as opposed to the Sunni (orthodox) Muslims who do not recognize the mystic legitimacy of his descendants to rule the Muslim world.
13. The English word arsenal derives from the Arabic term for shipyard, *dar al-sina'ah*.
14. Norwich I, p. 323n. Greek historians call the weapon 'liquid fire' (*hygron pyr*).
15. Some authorities, notably Ostrogorsky, dispute this.
16. Norwich I, p. 338.

Chapter Five

1. The Arabs claim that Leo agreed to accept the caliph's money to march on Constantinople.
2. Gibbon/Trevor Roper, p. 488; Vourazeli-Marinakou, p. 112.
3. A rough equivalent in twenty-first century transatlantic usage might be 'Shithead'. Such liberties with royal nomenclature might seem to us shockingly *lèse-majesté*, yet it highlights an underlying public irreverence that was always just beneath the surface of the Byzantine absolute monarchy, and which an emperor tampered with at his peril.
4. Tagma is the modern Greek term for battalion. *Tagmatarchis* = major. But the Byzantine *tagma* must have been rather larger than a modern battalion, probably the strength of a regiment.
5. Hitti, p. 285–6.
6. Quoted in Yannopoulos, p. 17.
7. If the phrase in English happens to resemble Irene's name, that is purely a linguistic coincidence.
8. A principle still strong three centuries later, when Anna Komnene asserted it in her memoir. Komnene, p. 388.

Chapter Six

1. Quoted in Hitti, p. 300.
2. Quoted in Yannopoulos, p. 32.
3. A riveting detailed account is found in Norwich II, pp. 28–30.
4. The contraption has fascinated generations of writers. In his 'Sailing to Byzantium', the Irish poet William Butler Yeats refers to it as 'such a form as Grecian goldsmiths make/ Of hammered gold and gold enamelling/ To keep a drowsy Emperor awake'.
5. Just forty-two captives survived the ordeal. For seven years they stoutly resisted pressures to convert to Islam and willingly died for their faith by having their heads cut off on the banks of the Tigris River. Among them, despite his own apparent conversion, was Boitzides. The Greek Orthodox Church commemorates the Forty-two Martyrs of Amorion every 6 March.
6. Brockelmann, pp. 132–3.

7. According to another much-circulated story, Photios dipped the holy robe into the sea, which promptly whipped up into such a fury that the Russians' ships were smashed to bits.
8. Durant IV, p. 429.

Chapter Seven

1. Hitti, p. 605.
2. See Müller, op. cit. '[I]n the whole of that city, there now survives of [Basileios'] work not one stone resting on another.' (Norwich II, p. 97.) Istanbul, Constantinople's present successor, is a wholly different place in culture and architecture.
3. Leo was officially married to the pious but burdensome Theophano for at least four years, and had a young daughter with her, but he never paid her much attention otherwise.
4. The full text can be found in G.T. Dennis (ed.) *The Taktika of Leo VI* (Dumbarton Oaks, Washington DC, 2010).
5. Some Greek historians discount Alexander entirely, relegating him to a mere temporary regent. See Vourazeli-Marinakou, p. 142.
6. Castration was not necessarily the grim fate we would consider it today. Many of the most capable men in the empire were castrated in youth to prepare for careers in the civil or military service. This was to ensure that they would not be distracted from their high duties by the need to provide for a family. It was also an effective remedy against nepotism for a eunuch, of course, could not pass on his position to a son. See Norwich II, p. 130.
7. Quoted in Norwich II, p. 139.
8. The present Ulu Dağ in Turkey, not the more famous Mount Olympus in Greece.
9. Not to be confused with his grandfather Nikephoros Phokas who had regained Southern Italy nearly a century before.
10. Again, as in the Phokas family, this Leon Phokas is not to be confused with his uncle and namesake who lost the battle at Anchialos half a century before and was blinded as punishment.
11. In reality Basileios, but since there is a risk of confusing him with later emperors named Basileios, we will here call him Basil.
12. The name was probably not a conscious imitation of the elite Persian unit of the same name that took part in the Battle of Thermopylai in 480 BC.
13. There is some uncertainty about whether Theodore Stratelates (= army leader), a native of Asia Minor who died for his faith, was a sanctified soldier or militarized saint. Whatever the truth, he became one of the most revered saints of the later Byzantine era. (T. Papamastorakis in 'Military Saints', Kathimerini newspaper, 27 October 2002.)

Chapter Eight

1. Basileios' icon, known as the Nikopoeia, or Creator of Victory, is most likely that which now hangs in the Basilica of Saint Mark in Venice. See Norwich II, p. 242n.

2. Also known as Cimbalongus. Kleidion gained military fame again in April 1940 when the German XXX Corps, invading Greece, knocked out Greek and British positions there in Operation Maritsa.
3. No fewer than fifteen thoroughfares in Athens, and many more in other Greek cities, are called Basil the Bulgar-slayer Street. The practice has lately given rise to a minor internet war between Bulgarian and Greek bloggers, but nothing diplomatic (yet).
4. The doctor brothers beatified by the Greek Orthodox Church for their charitable healing.
5. It must always be borne in mind that the Byzantines themselves, though they spoke Greek and were brought up in Greek culture, never called themselves Greeks (or Hellenes). That was a name reserved for the ancient pagans. The Byzantines remained, to the end, *Romioi*, or Romans – a term by which many modern Greeks still refer to themselves in colloquial speech. To the Arab Muslims the European Greeks are still *al-Rumi*; to Turkish Muslims they are *Rum*.
6. Despite his sobriquet of Stratiotikos (= Soldier), he was probably never in the military, but held the post of civil administrator of the army – a sort of defence minister.

Chapter Nine

1. Some claim that Isaac I was not physically ill but stepped down in a fit of depression, though most modern authorities accept Psellos' version as given here.
2. For this interpretation see Markesinis, B, *The Duality of Genius* (Athens 2010) p. 299.
3. Markesinis surmises that Psellos had a hand in weakening Romanos' forces, a charge which, if true, smacks of high treason. (See Markesinis, p. 299.)
4. See Haldon, p.126 et seq, for a discussion of casualties.
5. The paraphrase is Norwich's, in Norwich II, p. 357.

Chapter Ten

1. After many centuries of neglect, the Via Egnatia (Egnatia Odos in Greek) was recently resurrected into a six-lane motorway crossing northern Greece. It remains a prestige commercial and business address in the city of Thessaloniki.
2. Norwich III, p. 19.
3. The place where Robert Guiscard breathed his last is called Fiskardo, a local corruption of the name Guiscard.
4. Durant IV, p. 590.
5. Vourazeli-Marinakou, p. 165.
6. A twelfth-century miniature in the Vatican Library shows him as conspicuously dark-faced, in sharp contrast to his blonde French wife Marie.
7. Quoted in Durant IV, p. 650.
8. Niketas Choniates, quoted in Norwich III, p. 148.

Chapter Eleven

1. Brockelmann, p. 229.
2. Durant IV, p. 603.
3. Norwich III, p. 179.
4. Sometimes called Skylogiannes, or John the Dog, by the Greeks, who suffered as much as the Latins did from his depredations.
5. Now Yamalak, and not to be confused with the Antioch of North Syria.

Chapter Twelve

1. Durant IV, p. 652.
2. Sometimes referred to as Michael IX, as he was co-emperor.
3. See Sherrard, p. 99.
4. Now the landmark Galata Tower.
5. Norwich III, p. 351.
6. Quoted in Norwich III, p. 361.
7. Quoted in Runciman, p. 1.
8. The widely reported story that Bayezid was shut in an iron cage like a circus animal is corrected by Hitti, p. 701, as the result of a mistranslation of the original Arabic report.
9. However, four Paleologi ruled semi-independent domains in the Peloponnese, which could in a sense be considered as forming part of the empire.
10. Description in Runciman, p. 58.
11. A good view of them both can be had today from the Upper Bosporus Bridge.
12. Among Giustiniani's men was one Johannes Grant, believed to be a Scotsman. See Runciman, p. 84.
13. Runciman, p. 94.

Epilogue

1. Runciman, pp. 143–4.
2. Quoted, with photograph of the plaque, in Norwich III, p. 447.

Sources and Further Reading

Asbridge, Thomas, *The Crusades* (London, Simon & Schuster UK, 2010)

Belezos, Dimitris, *Byzantine Army* (Athens, Periskopio, 2006) (in Greek only)

Brockelmann, Carl, *History of the Islamic Peoples* (New York, Capricorn Books, 1960)

Browning, Robert, *Justinian and Theodora* (London, Gorgias Press, 2003)

Dennis, G.T, *The Tactica of Leo VI* (Dumbarton Oaks, 2010)

Durant, Will, *The Story of Civilization, Volume III: Caesar and Christ* (New York, Simon & Schuster, 1946) (cited in footnotes as Durant III)

Durant, Will, *The Story of Civilization, Volume IV: The Age of Faith* (New York, Simon & Schuster, 1950) (cited in footnotes as Durant IV)

Eusebius, *Life of Constantine* (Oxford, 1999)

Gibbon, Edward, *The Decline and Fall of the Roman Empire* (London, Phoenix Books, 2005) (a one-volume condensed version edited by Hugh Trevor-Roper, cited in footnotes as Gibbon/Trevor-Roper)

Haldon, John, *Warfare, State and Society in the Byzantine World* (London, UCL Press, 1999)

Hitti, Philip K, *History of the Arabs*, 9th edition (London, Macmillan, 1968)

Komnene, Anna, *The Alexiad* (Penguin Classics, 2003)

Mango, Cyril, ed. *Oxford History of Byzantium* (Oxford, 2002)

Norwich, John Julius, *Byzantium: The Early Centuries* (Penguin Books, 1990) (cited in footnotes as Norwich I)

Norwich, John Julius, *Byzantium: The Apogee* (Penguin Books, 1993) (cited in footnotes as Norwich II)

Norwich, John Julius, *Byzantium: The Decline and Fall* (Penguin Books, 1996) (cited in footnotes as Norwich III)

Procopius, *History of the Wars*, e-book available free at www.gutenberg.org

Runciman, Sir Steven, *The Fall of Constantinople 1453* (Cambridge University Press, 1967)

Shepard, Jonathan, ed. *Cambridge History of the Byzantine Empire* (Cambridge, 2009)

Sherrard, Philip, *The Greek East and the Latin West* (Limni Evia, Denise Harvey, 1995)

Stephenson, Paul, *Constantine: Roman Emperor, Christian Victor* (New York, Overlook Press, 2009)

Vourazeli-Marinakou, Eleni, *History of the Middle Ages* (Athens, School Book Publication Organization, 1962) (in Greek only)

Yannopoulos, Nikos, *Byzantine-Bulgarian Wars* (Athens, Periskopio, 2007) (in Greek only)

Byzantine Emperors 313–1453

** Fighting emperors in the field*

Late Roman period

Constantine I (313–337)*
Constantine II (337–340)*
Constantius II (337–361)*
Constans (337–350)*
Julian (361–363)*
Jovian (363–364)
Valentinian I (364–375)
Valens (364–378)*
Gratian (375–383)*
Theodosius I (379–395)*
Valentinian II (383–392)

Early Byzantium

Arcadius (395–408)
Theodosius II (408–450)*
Marcian (450–457
Leo I (457–474)
Leo II (474)
Zeno (474–491)*
Basiliscus (475–476)
Anastasius I (491–518)
Justin I (518–527)
Justinian I (527–565)
Justin II (565–578)
Tiberius II (578–582)
Maurikios (582–602)*
Phokas (602–610)
Heraclius (610–641)*
Constantine III (641)
Heraklonas (641)
Constans II Pogonatos (641–668)*
Constantine IV (668–685)*
Justinian II Rhinotmetos (685–695, 705–711)*
Leontios (695–698)
Tiberius III (698–705)
Philippikos Bardanes (711–713)
Anastasius II (713–715)
Theodosius III (715–717)
Leo III (717–741)*
Constantine V Kopronymos (741, 743–775)*
Artabasdos (742)
Leo IV (775–780)
Constantine VI (780–797)*
Irene (797–802)

Middle Byzantium

Nikephoros I (802–11)*
Staurakios (811)
Michael I Rhangabe (811–813)*
Leo V Armenian (813–820)*
Michael II Stammerer (820–829)*
Theophilos (829–842)*
Michael III (842–867)*
Basileios I Macedonian (867–886)*
Leo VI Wise (886–912)

Constantine VII Porphyrogennetos (913–959)
Romanos Lekapenos (920–944)
Romanos II (959–963)
Nikephoros II Phokas (963–969)*
John I Tzimiskes (969–976)*
Basileios II Bulgaroktonos (976–1025)*
Constantine VIII (1025–1028)
Romanos III Argyros (1028–1034)*
Michael IV Paphlagonian (1034–1041)*
Michael V Kalaphates (1041–1042)
Zoe (1042)
Constantine IX Dueller (1042–1055)
Theodora (1055–1056)
Michael VI Soldier (1056–1057)
Isaac I Komnenos (1057–1059)*
Constantine X Doukas (1059–1067)
Romanos IV Diogenes (1067–1071)*
Michael VII Doukas (1071–1078)
Nikephoros III Botaneiates (1078–1081)

Late Byzantium

Alexios I Komnenos (1081–1118)*
John II (1118–1143)*
Manuel I (1143–1180)*
Alexios II (1180–1183)
Andronikos I (1183–1185)
Isaac II Angelos (1185–1195, 1203–1204)*
Alexios III (1195–1203)
Alexios IV (1203–1204)
Alexios V Mourtzouphlos (1204)*

Latin emperors

Baldwin I of Flanders (1204–1205)*
Henry of Hainault (1206–1216)
Peter of Courtenay (1217)
Yolanda (1217–1219)
Robert of Courtenay (1221–1228)
Baldwin II (1228–1261)
John of Brienne (1231–1237)*

Emperors-in-exile

Theodore I Laskaris (1204–1222)*
John III Doukas Vatatzes (1222–1254)*
Theodore II Laskaris (1254–1258)*
John IV Laskaris (1258–1261)

Michael VIII Paleologos (1261–1282)*
Andronikos II (1282–1328)
Andronikos III (1328–1341)*
John V (1341–1391)*
John VI Kantakouzenos (1347–1354)*
Andronikos IV Paleologos (1376–1379)
John VII (1390)
Manuel II (1391–1425)*
John VIII (1425–1448)
Constantine XI (1448–1453)*

Index

Abd-al-Malik, 100–101, 105
Abd-al-Rahman, 129
Abelard, 198
Abu-al-Abbas, 112
Abu-Bakr, 90
Abu-Tammam, 90
Adam of Usk, 243
Adrian IV (Nicholas Breakspear), pope, 210
Aethelred the Redeless, 171
Aëtius, 54
Agapitus I, Pope, 70
Agnes, Princess, 213, 215
Alamundarus, 89
Alaric, 42, 45–9, 51, 59
Al-Ayyub al-Ansari, 98
Al-Aziz, 169
Alboin, 74
Alexander, Emperor, 143–5
Alexander the Great, 23, 33, 87, 197, 207
Alexios I Komnenos, 195–203, 216, 226
Alexios II Komnenos, 213–14
Alexios III Angelos, 217–20, 220, 224–5
Alexios IV Angelos, 218–19
Alexios V Mourtzouphlos, 219
Alexios of Trebizond, 225
Alexios, son of John II, 206
Alfred the Great, 23
Al-Hakam I, 129
Al-Harith II, 89
Ali, 96
Al-Mahdi, 115
Al-Mamun, 128–9, 131–2
Al-Mundhir, 89
Al-Muqtadir, 142
Al-Mustarshid, 205
Al-Mutamid, 139
Al-Mutasim, 132–3
Al-Mutawakkil, 134–5
Al-Numan, 90
Alp Arslan, 187–8, 190–4
Al-Qaim, 186, 191
Al-Qutami, 89
Al-Tabari, 95
Al-Tai, 167
Al-Walid I, 103
Alyates, Theodore, 190–1
Ambrose, Bishop, 40–1, 43
Amedeo of Savoy, 239–40
Ammianus Marcellinus, 32, 34, 36–7
Amr ibn-al-As, 92, 95
Anastasios, Patriarch, 111
Anastasius I (Flavius Anastasius), 60–2, 67
Anastasius II (Artemios), 105, 107
Andronikos I Komnenos, 213–15, 225
Andronikos II, 232–4
Andronikos III, 233–5
Andronikos IV Paleologos, 239–41
Andronikos, son of John II, 206
Andronikos, son of Manuel II, 244
Anna, wife of Basileios II, 167, 169
Anne of Savoy, 235–7
Anthemius, 48–51
Antonina, 71
Aplakes, John, 124
Apokaukos, Alexios, 236
Arbogast, 42–3
Arcadius, 43, 46–9
Ardabur, 55
Ardashir, 28
Ariadne, 55, 57, 60
Aristotle, 29
Arius, 15, 27
Artabasdos, 107, 111

Asclepiades, 59
Ashot, 146
Aspar, 54–5, 57
Asparuch, 99
Ataulf, 49, 51
Athenais (Eudokia), 50, 53, 64, 115
Attaliotes, Michael, 189–90, 192–4
Attila, 51–4
Ayyub ibn-Shahdi, 216
Axuch, John, 208–209

Bahram Chobin, 77
Baïana, Eudokia, 143
Balantes, Leon, 159
Baldwin I (of Flanders), 220–1
Baldwin II (of Constantinople), 221–23, 226
Baldwin II of Jerusalem, 204–205
Baldwin III of Jerusalem, 211
Baldwin of Antioch, 212
Balls, Mary, 259
Baltoglu, Süleyman, 253
Barbaro, Nicolo, 250
Bardanes Turcus, 120
Bardas, brother-in-law of Theophilos, 133–4, 136–7
Basilakios, 190, 192
Basileios I the Macedonian, 136–41
Basileios II Bulgaroktonos, 155, 165–74, 179, 181, 190, 248
Basiliscus, 54–5, 57–9, 69
Basil 'the Bastard', 156, 158–9, 163, 165–6
Batu Khan, 223
Bayan I, 78
Bayezid, 240–4
Belisarius, 67–73
Bernard of Clairvaux, Saint, 208
Bessas, 72
Bleda, 51–2
Bocchiardo brothers, 252, 256
Bogas, John, 146
Boioannes, Basileios, 173
Boitzides, 133
Boniface IX, Pope, 242
Boniface of Montferrat, 220
Bonos, 86
Boris, Khan, 138, 141, 163
Botheric, 41
Boucicault, Marshal, 243
Bourtzes, Michael, 157–8, 169
Branas, Alexios, 216
Branas, David, 214
Brankovic, George, 247
Bringas, Iosif, 153–4, 156, 159, 183
Bryennios, Nikephoros, 189–91, 193, 195
Buddha, 23
Byzas, 16–17

Caligula, 102
Callinicus, 73–4
Canning, George, viii
Cattaneo, Maurizio, 252
Chaka, 199
Chalkoutses, Niketas, 157
Charlemagne, 117–18, 121, 123, 133
Charles VI of France, 242–3
Charles of Anjou, 229–32
Clement IV, Pope, 230
Clement VI, Pope, 236
Coco, Giacomo, 254
Conrad III, Holy Roman Emperor, 208–10
Constans I, 23–6
Constans II Pogonatos, 95–7, 99
Constantia, wife of Licinius, 13–14
Constantina, wife of Maurikios, 80
Constantine I (Flavius Valerius Constantinus,) vi, 1–3, 5–23, 26–28, 36–7, 64–5, 82–3, 161, 167, 173, 215, 228, 248, 254
Constantine I, Pope, 105
Constantine II, 13, 23–5
Constantine II of modern Greece, 258
Constantine III, 93–4
Constantine IV, 97–9
Constantine V Kopronymos, 109, 111–15, 124
Constantine VI, 115–17, 119, 128, 130
Constantine VII Porphyrogennetos, 144–8, 150–3
Constantine VIII, 173–5
Constantine IX the Dueller, 181–3
Constantine X Doukas, 185–7
Constantine XI Paleologos, 246–59
Constantine, brother of Basileios II, 155

Constantine, son of Basileios I, 138–41
Constantine, son of Michael VII, 197
Constantine, uncle of Michael V, 179–81
Constantius II, 23–32
Constantius Chlorus, 5, 7–9
Constantius, husband of Galla Placidia, 56
Contarini brothers, 252
Crispus, 8, 13–14, 21, 27
Croesus, 216
Cyril, Bishop, 26

Dalmata, John, 257
Dandolo, Enrico, 217–21
Daniel, Prophet, 92
Daniel the Stylite, 58
Darius I, 21
Darius III, 87
Dayi Karaca Bey, 250
De Bailleul, Roussel, 189–90
De Flor, Roger, 233
De la Roche, Otto, 220
Deljan, Peter, 178
Delmatius, 24
Demetrios, brother of John VIII, 247–8
De Saxe, Maréchal, vi
Dhu Nuwas, 64
Diedo, Alviso, 251–2
Diocletian, 4, 7–9, 16, 18
Domentziolos, 80
Dorkon (horse), 85, 97
Doukas, Andronikos, General of Leo VI, 142
Doukas, Andronikos, General of Romanos IV, 190–4
Doukas, Constantine, Army Chief under Leo VI, 145
Doukas, Irene, 197
Doukas, John, General (11th century), 193
Doukas, John, General (12th century), 210, 215
Doukas, Theodore, of Epiros, 225
Durant, Will, vii

Edward VIII of England, 159
Ela Atzheba, 64
Eladas, John, 145
Eudokia, wife of Constantine X, 187, 193–4, 196–7
Eudoxia, daughter of Theodosius II, 50
Eudoxia, wife of Arcadius, 46–8
Eugenius III, Pope, 210
Eugenius IV, Pope, 246–7
Eugenius, Emperor in the West, 42–3
Euripides, 219
Eusebia, wife of Constantius II, 30
Eusebius of Caesarea, 2, 18, 22
Eustathios, 142
Eutropius, 46–7

Fabia, 82
Fausta, 10, 12, 14, 21, 23
Flavius Ablabius, 24
Foscari, Francesco, 246
Francisco of Toledo, 257
Frederick I Hohenstaufen (Barbarossa), 210, 212, 217
Frederick II Hohenstaufen, 222–3

Gabras, Constantine, 206
Gabriel Radomir, 172
Gainas, 47–8
Gaiseric, 54–7
Galerius, 5, 7–10, 12, 16
Galla Placidia, 49, 51, 56
Galla, wife of Theodosius I, 42
Gallus, 26–7, 29
Gelimer, 69–70
George of Antioch, 209
George of Pisidia, 87
George, Prince, vii
Germanos, Official, 79–80
Germanos, Patriarch, 110
Ghazi, 205
Gibbon, Edward, vii, 5–6, 14, 17, 22, 29, 33, 73, 75, 98, 109, 172, 201
Giustiniani, Giovanni, 250–4, 256
Grant, Johannes, 254
Gratian, 39–40
Gregory II, Pope, 110
Gregory IX, Pope, 222
Gregory X, Pope, 230
Gregory, General, 95
Grimuald, 96
Guiscard, Bohemond, 198–202
Guiscard, Robert, 196–200

Hadrian I, Pope, 115
Halimah, 89
Hardrada, Harald, 177
Harmatius, 58
Harry, Prince, vii
Harun al-Rashid, 115–17, 120–1
Helena, daughter of Robert Guiscard, 197
Helena, daughter of Romanos I, 147, 151
Helena, mother of Constantine I, 3, 7–8, 14, 21, 23, 64, 254
Helena, wife of Julian, 30–1
Helena, wife of Manuel II, 242, 248
Henry I of England, 202
Henry III of England, 223
Henry IV (Bolingbroke) of England, 243
Henry IV, Holy Roman Emperor, 198
Henry VIII of England, 248
Henry of Hainault, 221
Heraclius, Emperor, 81–8, 90–5, 163, 186, 198
Heraclius, father of Heraclius, 55
Heraclius, General, 80–1
Heraklonas, 93–5
Hermingarde, 138–9
Herodotus, 216
Hexabulios, John, 125
Himerios, 142, 144–5
Homer, 166
Honoria, 53–4
Honorius III, Pope, 221
Honorius, Emperor in the West, 43, 46, 48–9, 51, 56
Hormisdas, Pope, 63
Hormizd II of Persia, 28
Hormizd IV of Persia, 77
Hugh the Red (of Sully), 231
Hunyadi, John, 247
Huxley, Aldous, 130
Hypatius, 67

Ibrahim II, 142
Ibuzir, 102–103
Igor of Kiev, 149–50
Illus, 58–9
Innocent III, Pope, 218–20
Innocent IV, Pope, 223
Innocent VI, Pope, 239
Irene, 115–19, 128
Isaac I Komnenos, 184–5, 195
Isaac II Angelos, 215–19
Isaac, brother of John II, 206–208
Isaac, General, 72
Ishak Pasha, 256
Isidore, Cardinal, 252

Jengis Khan, 243
Jesus Christ, 3, 19, 22–3, 83, 164, 220, 242
John I Tzimiskes, 152, 155, 158–65
John II Asen, Tsar, 222–3
John II Komnenos, 202–207
John III Doukas Vatatzes, 222–3, 225–6
John IV Laskaris, 224, 226–8
John V Paleologos, 235–40
John VI Kantakouzenos (Joasaph), 234–41
John VII, 241, 244
John VIII Paleologos, 245–8
John XIII, Pope, 161
John XXII, Pope, 235
John Chrysostom, 48
John Damascene, Paint, 110
John, General, 71–3
John, nephew of John II, 206
John of Antioch, 81
John of Brienne, 222–4
John of Ephesus, 75
John the Baptist, 164
John the Hunchback, 59
Joscelin II of Edessa, 206
Joseph, Patriarch, 247
Jovian, 36–8
Judas Iscariot, 87
Julian 'the Apostate' (Flavius Claudius Julianus), 27, 29–36, 38
Julius Constantius, 24
Justa, 59
Justin I, 62–6
Justin II (Flavius Justinus), 74–6, 89
Justina, 40
Justinian I (Flavius Petrus Sabbatius), 64–74, 78, 82–3, 89, 110, 138–9, 141, 173, 210
Justinian II Rhinotmetos, 99–105, 107

Kaikosru, 221, 224–5
Kallinikos, 98
Kalojan, Tsar, 221

Kantakouzenos, Dimitrios, 252
Karbonopsina, Zoe, 143–7
Kardam, 116
Kastriotes, George (Skanderbeg), 247
Kavadh of Persia, 63–4
Kavadh-Siroes of Persia, 87
Kedrenos, George, 183
Kekaumenos, Katakalon, 180, 184
Keroularios, Michael, Patriarch, 185
Khalid ibn-al-Walid, 90–2
Khosru I of Persia, 71, 75, 77
Khosru (Parvez) of Persia, 64, 77, 79–80, 82–7
Kilij Arslan II, 211–13
Komnene, Anna, 199–200, 203
Komnenos, Michael Angelos Doukas, 225
Kontostephanos, Andronikos, 212–14
Kontostephanos, John, 211
Kontostephanos, Stephanos, 209–10
Kormisosh, 112
Kourtikos, Basileios, 199
Krum, 120–6, 128–9, 136, 170
Kurkuas, John, 149–50, 152
Kurkuas, Romanos, 155
Kyrillos (Cyril), 136

Lactantius, 2, 9–10, 12–13
Ladislas of Hungary and Poland, 247
Lecky, W.E.H., vii
Leo I, Emperor, 54–5, 57, 59, 62–3
Leo I, Pope, 54
Leo II, 55, 57, 60
Leo III the Isaurian (Konon), 107–11
Leo IV, 114–15
Leo V the Armenian, 124–8
Leo VI the Wise, 140–4, 151
Leonard of Chios, 252
Leonidas I of Sparta, 47
Leon of Tripolis, 142, 144
Leontios, Emperor, 100–103
Leontios, Philosopher, 50
Leo of Lesser Armenia, 205
Licario, 231
Licinianus, 14
Licinius, Flavius, 10, 12–14
Liutprand of Cremona, Bishop, 141, 151–2, 156–8
Longinus, 60–1
Lothair III, Holy Roman Emperor, 205
Louis I (the Pious), Holy Roman Emperor, 133
Louis I of Hungary, 239
Louis II (the German), Holy Roman Emperor, 138–9
Louis VII of France, 208–209
Louis IX of France, 223, 229–30
Louis XIV of France, 18
Luke the Stylite, Saint, 142
Lupicinus, 39

Magnentius, 26
Malikshah, 194, 196, 202
Maniakes, George, 175–7, 182
Manjutekin, 169
Manuel I, 206–13
Manuel II Paleologos, 240–6
Maraptika, 215
Marcellinus, 26
Marcian, 53–4
Marcianus, 58
Maria, wife of John I Tzimiskes, 159
Maria, wife of Theodore I Laskaris, 222
Marie, wife of Manuel I, 211–12
Marlowe, Christopher, 244
Martel, Charles, 109
Martin I, Pope, 96
Martina, 83, 85, 95
Marwan II, 112
Mary Magdalene, 19
Maslamah, 105–108
Matthaios, son of John VI, 238
Maurikios, 76–80, 93
Maurus, 104
Maxentius, 1, 6, 9–12
Maximian, 5, 7–10
Maximinus Daia, 9, 12–13
Maximus, Magnus Clemens, 40–1
Mehmet I, 244
Mehmet II, 249–58
Mélisende, 211
Melissenos, George, 199
Mesonyktes, Theodosios, 162
Methodios, 136
Michael I Rhangabe, 123–5, 127
Michael II the Amorian ('the Stammerer'), 125–30

Michael III, 133–7, 140–1
Michael IV the Paphlagonian (Orphanotrophos), 176–8
Michael V Kalaphates, 178–81
Michael VI the Soldier, 183–4
Michael VII Doukas, 193–5, 197
Michael VIII Paleologos, 225–32
Michael IX, 233
Michiel, Domenico, 204
Michiel, Vitale, 212
Miltiades, Athenian general, 11, 85, 109
Miltiades, Bishop of Rome, 12
Minervina, 8
Minotto, Girolamo, 251–2
Mohammed, Tribal Leader, 206
Muawiyah, 95–9
Muhammad the Prophet, 23, 90, 96, 112, 241, 249
Mundus, 67
Murad I, 240
Murad II, 245–9
Musa, 244
Mustafa, 246
Muzalon, George, 226
Mystakon, John, 77

Narses, General in Italy, 67, 73
Narses, General on the Persian front, 77, 80
Nasr, 139
Nazianzen, Gregory, 29
Nero, 4
Nicholas I, Pope, 136
Nicholas III, Pope, 231
Nicholas V, Pope, 249–50
Nicholas of Crotone, Bishop, 230
Nicholas, Patriarch, 145–7
Nikephoros I, 118–19, 121–4, 162
Nikephoros II Phokas, 152–9, 165
Nikephoros III Botaneiates, 195–6
Nikephoros, Monk, 116
Niketas, 81
Noah, 19
Norwich, John Julius, vii, 23, 55, 65, 98, 111, 118, 145, 179, 207, 259
Notaras, Loukas, 252
Nur-ed-Din, 211

Odoacer, 56–9
Olga, 150
Omortag, 129
Oöryphas, Niketas, 135, 138–9
Orestes, 56–7
Orkhan, Emir, 234, 236
Orkhan, Prince, 249, 252
Orphanotrophos, John, 177–9
Orseolo, Pietro, 170
Osman, 232
Otto I (the Saxon), Holy Roman Emperor, 152, 157, 161
Otto II, Holy Roman Emperor, 161
Otto III, Holy Roman Emperor, 170, 174
Ouranos, Nikephoros, 171

Paleologos, Ferdinand, 259
Paleologos, George, 197, 226
Paleologos, Godscall, 259
Paleologos, Michael, General, 210
Paleologos, Nikephoros, 252
Paleologos, Theodore, 259
Paleologos, Theodoros, son of Ferdinand, 259
Paleologos, Theophilos, 257
Paschal II, Pope, 201
Patsilas, 154
Paul, Apostle, 17, 23
Pepin (the Short), 115
Péré Julia, 252
Peter, Apostle, 3, 17, 23
Peter of Courtenay, 221, 225
Petronas, 134–5
Petros, 78–80
Philip I of France, 201
Philip II Augustus of France, 217
Philippikos (Bardanes), 104–105
Phlatanelas, 253
Phokas, Bardas, brother of Leon Phokas (10th century), 152, 160
Phokas, Bardas, father of Leon Phokas (10th century), 150, 152, 156
Phokas, Bardas, son of Leon Phokas, 166–8, 174
Phokas, Emperor, 79–82, 104
Phokas, Leon, brother of Nikephoros II Phokas, 154

Phokas, Leon, General under Constantine VII, 146–7, 150
Phokas, Leon, son of Leon Phokas, 160
Phokas, Nikephoros, General (9th century), 139, 142
Phokas, Petros, 160
Photios, Patriarch, 135
Phrantzes, George, 255–6
Piriska, 204
Plato, 29
Polyeuktos, Patriarch, 159
Poplius, 11–12
Priscus, 53
Priscus Attalusz, 49
Priskos, 78
Probus, 11
Procopius, cousin of Julian, 38
Procopius, Historian, 38, 55, 66–7, 69–70
Prokopia, 123–5
Psellos, Michael, 174–80, 182–6, 188, 194
Pulcheria, 50–4

Raymond of Poitiers, 205–208
Razates, 87
Reynald of Châtillon, 210–11, 217
Richard I of England, 217
Richard II of England, 242
Richard of Acerra, 214, 216
Robert of Courtenay, 222
Robert of Loritello, 210
Roger IV of Sicily, 209–10
Romanos I Lekapenos, 146–51, 156
Romanos II, 153–4, 160, 165, 183
Romanos III Argyros, 175–7
Romanos IV Diogenes, 187–95, 206
Romulus (Augustulus), 56–8
Romulus, Legendary Founder of Rome, 57
Rua, 51–2
Rufinus, 41, 46–7
Runciman, Steven, vii, 255

Saad ibn-abi-Waqqas, 92
Saladin (Salah ad-Din), 216–17
Sallustius Secundus, 36
Samuel, Tsar, 166–7, 170–2, 178
Sanudo, Marco, 220
Sasan, 28
Sayf al-Dawlah, 154, 157
Sebastian, 39
Seljuk, 187
Sergios, Patriarch, 82, 86–8
Sergius I, Pope, 100
Sergius III, Pope, 144
Sesuald, 97
Shahrbaraz, 83–5, 87–8
Shapur I of Persia, 28
Shapur II of Persia, 25, 28, 31, 34, 36–8
Shirin, 87
Sichelgaita, 198
Simocatta, Theophylact, 79
Sklerina, 182–3
Skleros, Bardas, 160, 165–8, 182
Skylitzes, John, 162, 172
Sophia, wife of Justin II, 74–6
Sophocles, 219
Sophronius, Patriarch, 92
Sozomen, 35
Staurakios, Associate of Irene, 116
Staurakios, Emperor, 121–3
Stephanos, brother-in-law of John Orphanotrophos, 177–8
Stephanos, Official, 122
Stephanos, Torturer, 100–101
Stephen II of Hungary, 204
Stephen II, Pope, 115
Stephen III of Hungary, 212
Stephen Dushan of Serbia, 236–9
Stephenson, Paul, 23
Stephen Urosh II of Serbia, 232
Stilicho, 42, 45–9
Strategopoulos, Alexios, 223, 226
Suleyman, Arab General, 107–108
Süleyman, cousin of Alp Arslan, 196
Süleyman Pasha, 238
Süleyman, Sultan, 244
Svyatoslav of Kiev, 157, 160–2
Sylvester I, Pope, 16–17
Symeon of Bulgaria, 141, 145–8

Taragi, 191–2
Tarchaniotes, Joseph, 189–90
Tatikios, 201
Teia, 73
Telerig, 114–15
Teletz, 113
Tervel, 102–103, 105

Theodora, daughter of John VI, 237
Theodora, Empress, 175, 180–3
Theodora, second wife of John I Tzimiskes, 160
Theodora, stepdaughter of Maximian, 7, 9
Theodora, wife of Justinian I, 66–7, 70–4, 76, 83, 124
Theodora, wife of Justinian II, 102–104
Theodora, wife of Michael VIII, 226
Theodora, wife of Theophilos, 133–4
Theodore I Laskaris, 220–2, 224–5
Theodore II Laskaris, 225–6
Theodore, tutor to Constantine VII, 147
Theodore Stratelates, Saint, 162
Theodoric, 59
Theodoric (the Cross-eyed), 59, 63
Theodoros, brother of Heraclius, 91
Theodosius I, 39–46, 49, 76
Theodosius II, 49–54, 115
Theodosius III, 105–107
Theodosius, General, 38–9
Theodosius, son of Tiberius II, 78–80
Theoktistos, 133–4
Theophanes, Historian 85, 100, 108, 114, 117, 119
Theophanes, Official of Romanos I, 149–50
Theophano, mistress of Romanos II, 153–9, 165
Theophano, wife of Leo VI, 143
Theophano, wife of Otto II, 161, 170
Theophilos, 127–8, 130–3, 141, 152
Thomas the Slav, 127–9
Tiberius II Constantine, 74–8
Tiberius III (Apsimar), 101–103
Tiberius, son of Justinian II, 104
Tiberius, son of Tiberius II, 78
Timur of Kesh (Timurlane), 243
Tornikes, Leo, 182–3
Totila, 72–3
Trevisano, Gabriele, 251–2
Tughrul Bey, 186–7
Tzath, 64

Ubaydullah al-Mahdi, 148
Uldin, 48, 50
Umar, 91–2, 95
Umar ibn-Abdullah, 135
Umur, 236
Urban II, Pope, 200, 208
Urban IV, Pope, 229–30
Urban V, Pope, 239
Urban, Cannon-maker, 251–2, 256
Uthman, 92, 95–6

Valens, 37–9, 44–5
Valentinian I, 37–8
Valentinian II, 39–42
Valentinian III, 51, 56
Valerian, 28
Varronianus, 37
Verina, 59
Vetranio, 26
Victoria of England, 18
Vigilantia, 74
Vitalian, 62–3
Vladimir of Bulgaria, 141
Vladimir of Kiev, 167–9

Walter of Brienne, 233
William I of England (the Conqueror), 207, 248
William II of Sicily, 210, 214
William of Malmesbury, 16
William of Villehardouin, 226, 229
William, Prince, vii
Witigis, 71

Xerxes, 21
Xiphias, Nikephoros, 171

Yazdagird III of Persia, 92
Yazid, 97–8
Yazid ibn-abu-Sufyan, 91
Yolanda, 221

Zautsaina, Zoe, 143
Zautses, Stylianos, 140–2
Zayd ibn-Harithah, 91
Zengi, 206, 208, 221
Zeno (Tarasis of Rusumblada), 55, 57–61, 77
Zoe, 174–83
Zosimus, 14, 26, 46–47